AUSTRIAN CATHOLICS AND THE FIRST REPUBLIC

AUSTRIAN
CATHOLICS
AND THE FIRST
REPUBLIC

DEMOCRACY, CAPITALISM,

AND THE SOCIAL ORDER, 1918-1934

 BY ALFRED DIAMANT

PRINCETON, NEW JERSEY

PRINCETON UNIVERSITY PRESS

1960

TO THE MEMORY OF
CECIL H. DRIVER

PREFACE

As THIS IS WRITTEN, there are reports from Vienna that the two-party coalition which has governed Austria since 1945 has broken up. General elections have been scheduled and the expectations are that after the elections Austrian politics will return to the pattern familiar to the First Republic. The two-party coalition, the *Proporz* arrangement, has tended to obscure the fact that the distribution of political affiliations in Austria has remained practically unchanged since the first free elections were held in 1918: the existence of two large movements, Social Democrats and a Catholic-oriented political organization, with one or two small nationalist parties holding the balance of power. These three groupings were not political parties in the Western sense, but social movements claiming the entire life and loyalty of their followers. They were divided not only over questions of public policy within an agreed consensus concerning rules of the game, but faced each other over questions of *Weltanschauung* and the basic political framework of the country. This failure to reach agreement on fundamentals between 1918 and 1934 led to civil war and the establishment of an authoritarian regime. *Anschluss*, war, and foreign occupation all combined to produce *Proporz*, an attempt by the two political giants to heal the wounds caused by internal strife and so create an inter-party consensus on the issues which had divided Austria into hostile camps. Any attempt to understand the coming pattern of politics in Austria requires us to look to the ideas and movements which shaped the two major participants, the Socialist and the Catholic-oriented camp.

But the significance of Catholic social ideas and the Catholic social movement are not limited to Austria. In Europe, in Latin America, and increasingly in the United States, in Australia, and in Canada, the Roman Catholic Church and the laity who accept the guidance of the church in public affairs play a more important role in the conduct of these affairs than ever before, chiefly because today the church and its laymen make their influence felt on a mass basis through political parties and interest groups in all walks of life. The nature of Catholic social thought is poorly understood, especially in the United States, where the Roman Catholic Church and its laity are viewed as a monolith, acting in unison in some mysterious way with the help of a secret telephone line from the Vatican. It is imperative that scholars and practicing politicians get a better understanding of how the pastoral needs of the hierarchy, Catholic dogma and theology, reason and natural law, and the position of Catholics in actual societies interact to produce a social doctrine which, in turn, becomes the foundation of political action by Catholic-oriented political parties and interest groups.

My interest in the Catholic social movement goes back more than ten years to work I did at Indiana University under the direction and with the encouragement of Francis D. Wormuth, now at the University of Utah. I continued this work at Yale University, where an earlier version of this study was presented as a dissertation for the degree of Doctor of Philosophy. At Yale I was fortunate in receiving support, guidance, and inspiration from Cecil H. Driver, and I deeply regret that he will not see this work in its published form. Hajo Holborn and Frederick M. Watkins of Yale have helped in many ways during the various stages through which this work has gone.

Various institutions have provided financial assistance along the way. The Danforth Foundation of St. Louis, Missouri, awarded me one of its Teacher Study Grants which made possible a one-year leave of absence from teaching. The Yale University Graduate School has contributed to the support of publication of this study in its present form.

A special place in these acknowledgments must be reserved for Manning J. Dauer, chairman of the department of political science at the University of Florida at Gainesville, whose administrative talents and sympathetic understanding over many years contributed immeasurably to the completion of this work.

Portions of this study have previously appeared in the *Western Political Quarterly* and the *Journal of Central European Affairs* whose publishers have granted permission to use these materials in the present volume. Permission has also been granted by the Board of Commissioners of State Institutions of

Florida to use in Chapters v and vi findings reported in an earlier version as *Austrian Catholics and the Social Question, 1918-1933*, University of Florida Monographs, Social Science No. 2, published by the University of Florida Press (1959). I am also indebted to the following: the Paulist Press of New York, for permission to quote from the encyclical *Quadragesimo anno* contained in *Five Great Encyclicals*; Dr. Rafael Spann, of Vienna, for permission to quote in translation from his father's work *Der wahre Staat*; and Wilhelm Braumüller, Universitätsverlagsbuchhandlung Ges. m. b. H. of Vienna for permission to quote in translation from Ignaz Seipel, *Der Kampf um die österreichische Verfassung*. I acknowledge gratefully the help given me in all these instances.

ALFRED DIAMANT

New Haven, Connecticut
April 1959

CONTENTS

PREFACE   vii

I. INTRODUCTION: CATHOLICS AND EUROPEAN SOCIETY IN
   TRANSITION   3
   1. Catholics, the Modern State, and the Modern Economy   5
   2. Political Catholicism and the Modern State   6
   3. Social Catholicism and the Social Question   14
   4. Unity and Diversity in Catholic Thought   25

II. THE FOUNDATION OF AUSTRIAN POLITICAL AND SOCIAL
    CATHOLICISM   29
    1. Austrian Catholics and the Modern State   31
    2. Austrian Catholics and the Social Question   51
    3. Critique and Conspectus of Austrian Catholic Thought   64

III. THE CRITICISM OF DEMOCRACY: POLITICAL AND SOCIAL
     BASES   70
     1. Austrian Catholics and the Criticism of Democracy   70
     2. Austrian Society and the Three *Lager*   73
     3. Austrian Catholics and the Constitution of 1920   80
     4. Catholics and the Social Conflicts of the Republic   87

IV. THE CRITICISM OF DEMOCRACY: THE SPECTRUM OF
    CRITICISM, 1918-1934   99
    1. The Development of the Spectrum   101
    2. Ignaz Seipel and the Criticism of Democracy   106
    3. The Hierarchy and Austrian Democracy   116
    4. Catholic Trade Unions and the *Linzer Programm*   121
    5. Conservatism and Democracy: *Österreichische Aktion*   124
    6. The *Heimwehr*   130
    7. Müller and Hegel: The Romantic Doctrines of
       Othmar Spann   131
    8. The Vogelsang School and Austrian Democracy   140
    9. Criticism of Democracy: An Evaluation   148

· xi ·

CONTENTS

V. THE CRITICISM OF CAPITALISM: FROM *SOZIALPOLITIK*
TO *QUADRAGESIMO ANNO*   153

1. The Pattern of Criticism   153
2. The Austrian Hierarchy and the Social Question
   before 1931   159
3. *Quadragesimo anno, Sozialpolitik*, and *Sozialreform*   170
4. The Hierarchy and *Quadragesimo anno*   182
5. *Sozialpolitik* Theorists, 1918-1934   189

VI. THE CRITICISM OF CAPITALISM: RELIGIOUS SOCIALISM
AND THE ROMANTIC TRADITION   208

1. The Unity of the *Sozialreform* Critique   208
2. The Religious Socialists   210
3. The *Linzer Programm*   214
4. Vogelsang, Kant, and Marx: The Synthesis of
   Ernst Karl Winter   220
5. Othmar Spann: The Apogee of the Neo-Romantic
   Tradition   229
6. The Vogelsang School   240
7. The Critique of Capitalism: An Evaluation   250

VII. THE CULMINATION OF CRITICISM: THE CORPORATIVE
CONSTITUTION OF 1934   256

1. Constitutional Reform and the Failure of Consensus,
   1918-1934   257
2. The Structure of the Corporative Constitution   264
3. The Principles of the Constitution   271
4. The Constitution in Relation to the Traditions of
   Austrian Catholic Thought   279

EPILOGUE   286

BIBLIOGRAPHY   293

INDEX   313

AUSTRIAN CATHOLICS AND
THE FIRST REPUBLIC

CHAPTER I

INTRODUCTION: CATHOLICS AND EUROPEAN
SOCIETY IN TRANSITION

THE rapid transition that is now taking place in many parts of Asia and Africa from a traditional, agricultural, and often autocratic society to a modern, industrial, and democratic society increasingly occupies the attention of social scientists. In his recent study of the Middle East, Daniel Lerner pointed out that in order to comprehend the yearning of the Middle Eastern people to trade in their old lives for new, we must first understand "what historically happened in the West." Not even the rapid rate of change in the Middle East can obscure the fact that the sequence of events is based on a Western model, though often a deliberately distorted one. Urbanization, increased literacy, exposure to mass media, persistent demands for economic improvements and for political participation (voting) are all part of what Lerner considered to be the basic model of change common to all the modernizing societies. "The point is," he concluded, "that the secular process of social change, which brought modernization to the Western world, has more than antiquarian relevance to today's problems of the Middle East transition. Indeed, the lesson is that Middle Eastern modernizers will do well to study the historical sequence of Western growth."[1]

One important source for a critical, if not hostile, evaluation of this transition from a traditional to a modern society is found in the social doctrines of the Roman Catholic Church and of Catholic laymen, scholars, as well as practicing politicians. The causes as well as the consequences of this process of change were first recognized by the Catholic Church in Europe in the nineteenth century because it suffered severely from this metamorphosis of European society and of the European polity. The French Revolution and the Industrial Revolution had created

[1] Daniel Lerner, *The Passing of Traditional Society; Modernizing the Middle East* (Glencoe: The Free Press, 1958), pp. 46-47.

· 3 ·

polites and societies in which the Roman Church and its faith
ful came to play only peripheral roles. Attempting to reverse this
catastrophic loss of influence in state and society, members of
the hierarchy, as well as many laymen faithful to the church,
developed an elaborate literature in which they not only subjected these new societies and political regimes to a scathing
critique but also sought to prescribe methods for reestablishing
the traditional order—prescriptions which were singularly un-
successful chiefly because they failed to realize that urbanization,
industrialization, and democratization could not be reversed and
that European society could not be returned to some "ideal"
state which had existed before 1789, or before Adam Smith and
Karl Marx, or before the invention of the steam engine and the
power loom.

The social critique to which Catholics subjected this process
of modernization and the social movements they formed to combat the influence of "modernism" in state, society, and economy
have indeed, as Lerner points out, "more than antiquarian
relevance."[2] They help us to understand the dynamics of social
change from "traditional" to "modern" now taking place in
Asia and Africa. The dangers which result from the democratization of a political society lacking consensus on the fundamental
rules of the game, the agonies of an industrial society in which
the urban masses have been wrenched from their traditional
moorings and are groping for a new set of standards—these we
encounter again and again in the social doctrines of the Roman
hierarchy, the studies of Catholic social scientists, and the campaign speeches of Catholic politicians. The volume of writings
by these very people is enormous, and the literature about them
is growing. For this reason, it is most illuminating to examine
the literature and the social movements of a clearly recognizable
group, the Austrian Catholics between 1918 and 1934, but always against the background of the major pronouncements of
the Roman Church as a whole.

[2] *Ibid.*, p. 46. I have explored further this relevance of Western transition patterns to the non-Western experience in "Is There a Non-Western Political Process?" *The Journal of Politics* XXI (February 1959), pp. 123-127; see also Lucian
W. Pye, "The Non-Western Political Process," *The Journal of Politics* XX (August 1958), pp. 468-486.

1. Catholics, the Modern State, and the Modern Economy

In the course of the nineteenth century, Catholics in almost all parts of Europe were compelled to deal with the unprecedented political and social consequences of the French Revolution, the Industrial Revolution, and expanding capitalism. *Political Catholicism* dealt with these new political problems by finding ways for Catholics to participate effectively in the affairs of the neutral, republican state created by the French Revolution.[3] In this Catholics faced a double task. They had first to decide whether the republican form of government was compatible with Catholic social teachings; then they needed to develop new methods to influence public policy in the modern state, which lacked the unity characteristic of earlier periods. *Social Catholicism,* on the other hand, dealt with the "social question," i.e., the problems of the Industrial Revolution, and the new problems of capitalism.[4] The development of the market economy in which economic considerations had been divorced from ethical standards, and the wretched condition of the industrial workers which had resulted from this divorce, convinced Catholics that it was impossible to apply Scholastic social theory directly to the social conditions created by industrialism and capitalism. Consequently, social Catholicism sought to reformulate the social theories of the church in order to aid Catholics in solving these new issues.

For well nigh a century after 1789 the Catholic Church refused to admit that the old order in state and society was passing rapidly. This resistance reached its apogee in the pontificate of

---

[3] For the use of the term, see Ludwig Bergsträsser (ed.), *Der politische Katholizismus in Deutschland. Dokumente seiner Entwicklung.* Vol. II: *1871-1914* (Munich: Drei Masken Verlag, 1923), p. 5; see also Wilhelm Schwer, *Catholic Social Theory* (St. Louis: B. Herder Book Co., 1940), pp. 272-279. Heinrich Rommen found the growth of political Catholicism ". . . necessary wherever the political groups that controlled the 'neutral' state showed an outspoken enmity against the Church. . . ." *The State in Catholic Thought; A Treatise in Political Philosophy* (St. Louis: B. Herder Book Co., 1950), p. 608.

[4] Schwer, *op.cit.,* pp. 308-310; see also Johannes Messner, "Soziale Frage," *Staatslexikon im Auftrag der Görresgesellschaft* (fifth edition; Freiburg i.B.: Herder, 1926-1931), IV, 1659-1664. This is the last pre-1933 edition of the Catholic encyclopedia published in Germany, written by a group of German and Austrian Catholics. Hereafter cited as *Staatslexikon*; all references are to the fifth edition.

Pius IX and it remained for Leo XIII who acceded to the papacy in 1878 to come to grips with the problems of European society in transition. He made it possible for Catholics to participate in the public affairs of a republican government (as in France), and he simultaneously offered solutions for the "social question." In writing his encyclical letters on political and social questions, Leo XIII drew on a large body of ideas and reform proposals developed during the nineteenth century. These came from Catholics in many countries, from clergy as well as laity, and from international Catholic study groups, such as the *Union de Fribourg*.[5] By the end of the century, and certainly by 1918, the Roman Church had begun to make a serious attack on the problems of a society in the process of modernization and had developed an elaborate set of reform proposals to mitigate those conditions it considered pernicious—pernicious because they had undermined the position of the church as a major institution and because they had produced a social pattern which violated the very theological and moral concepts the church judged essential for a healthy society.

2. Political Catholicism and the Modern State

Catholics everywhere opposed the modern state created by the French Revolution because they believed it was based on a set of false assumptions about the scope of state activity, about the nature of political obligations and individual rights, and about the relations of church and state.[6]

[5] For the discussion of the various currents which influenced and shaped *Rerum novarum* see Wilhelm Schwer, "Zeitbedingte Elemente im Rundschreiben 'Rerum Novarum,'" *Die soziale Frage und der Katholizismus. Festschrift zum 40jährigen Jubiläum der Enzyklika "Rerum Novarum,"* Jakob Strieder & Johannes Messner, editors (published for the *Sektion für Sozial- und Wirtschaftswissenschaft der Görresgesellschaft*; Paderborn: Ferdinand Schöningh, 1931), pp. 403-415. This is a collection of essays on the social question by leading Austrian and German Catholics. It is indispensable for a study of Central European Catholic social thought. Hereafter cited as *Die soziale Frage*. Schwer warns that the encyclical could be understood only "against this background of specific crises and tensions."

[6] In this and the subsequent section of this chapter I have tried to present in a general way the "Catholic" position on the major secular forces of democracy and capitalism. For two excellent statements by German Catholics, see Goetz Briefs, "Wirtschaft, Staat und Gesellschaft im System des Kapitalismus," *Die soziale Frage*, pp. 243-264, and Theodor Brauer, "Der deutsche Katholizismus und die soziale Entwicklung des kapitalistischen Zeitalters," *Archiv für Rechts- und Wirtschaftsphilosophie* XXIX (1930-1931), pp. 209-254.

Catholics found equally unacceptable the Girondist and Jacobin strands of the French Revolutionary tradition, for both set improper limits to state activity.[7] They rejected Girondist theory because they believed that the state should be more than a policeman, that enforcement of laws and external defense did not exhaust the proper scope of state action. Such a definition of state power had brought about the exploitation of the majority of the people by a small group of capitalists, and had prevented the state from taking the necessary actions to protect the exploited majority. But Catholic opposition to the omnicompetent state of the Jacobins was even more violent than their condemnation of the Girondist *Nachtwächterstaat*. By giving all power to the state, the Jacobins had totally destroyed the autonomy of other social organs and had eliminated such areas of voluntary social action as charity and education. Enmity to religion was another reason why both the Girondist and Jacobin states aroused Catholic ire. While the former hid his enmity behind a mask of religious toleration, the latter openly suppressed religion. Finally, Catholics believed that the bourgeois liberal state of the Girondists would inevitably turn into the totalitarian state of the Jacobins, and for this reason they warned against an easy acceptance of the Girondist state as the lesser of two evils.

Catholics rejected the Revolutionary definition of political obligations and individual rights they professed to find in the writings of Rousseau. To make a social contract the foundation of the state and of political obligation would open the way to never-ending claims of "rights" and would make impossible a meaningful answer to the question of why one man should obey another. They claimed that this system of individual rights based on a social contract had been chiefly responsible for destroying the natural hierarchies that had once existed in society. Through *Loi le Chapelier* the followers of Rousseau had wrecked the natural social order of the *ancien régime* and had

[7] This analysis of the Revolutionary tradition in France follows David Thomson, *Democracy in France; The Third Republic* (London: Oxford University Press, 1946), pp. 9-38. In subsequent editions Thomson extended his analysis to cover the Fourth Republic as well, but his basic treatment has remained unchanged. See also Phillip Williams, *Politics in Post-War France; Parties and the Constitution in the Fourth Republic* (London: Longmans, Green & Co., 1954).

obliterated the distinction between state and society which Catholics considered an essential element of a healthy social order.

Finally, Catholics condemned the separation of church and state, the hallmark of the neutral republic created by the French Revolution. Eventually, Catholics admitted the damage done to the church during the period of absolute monarchy by Febronianism, Gallicanism, and Josephinism, but for over a century after 1789 they were able to see only the evil effects of the Revolutionary tradition on the relations of church and state. The attempts to destroy the church in France and the difficulties of the papacy with liberal Piedmont proved to Catholics how difficult it was to create satisfactory church-state relationships in the neutral, secular state.

Catholics outside France resisted the spread to other countries of institutions based on these false premises. This opposition was especially strong where the armies of Revolutionary France and of Napoleon, whom Catholics considered a natural child of the Revolution, had not only defeated the armies of the old order, but also helped destroy the political and social institutions of that order. Individual Catholics, as well as Catholic regimes like that of Metternich in Austria, were determined to eradicate the internal and international effects of the Revolutionary tradition. This Catholic resistance to the modern state lasted throughout most of the nineteenth century. During its early part, when Jacobin totalitarianism was not a serious threat in Europe, the church considered Girondist republicanism its principal enemy, and even those Catholics who supported radical social and economic reforms remained constitutionally conservative.

The most important effort to create a liberal Catholic movement took place in France, but the attempt of French Catholics to "relate Catholicism to the Constitutional state" was ultimately rejected by Pope Gregory XV.[8] In the encyclical *Mirari vos* of

[8] Joseph N. Moody, "The Papacy: The Church and the New Forces in Western Europe and Italy," in Joseph N. Moody (ed.), *Church and Society: Catholic Social and Political Thought and Movements 1789-1950* (New York: Arts, Inc., 1953), p. 66. Moody calls the period until the death of Pius IX the "time of resistance." This is an important symposium on Catholic social thought and movements in the principal countries of the world, but the quality of the contributions is rather uneven. Hereafter the volume will be cited as *Church and Society*.

1832 he condemned liberalism for condoning popular revolt and for espousing freedom of the press and of education. The Pontiff also criticized French Catholic liberals for making alliances with other liberals, even though these alliances would have meant more freedom of action for Catholics.

Catholic resistance to modernism in all forms reached its height during the pontificate of Pius IX. In the encyclical *Quanta cura* and the appended *Syllabus of Errors* Pio Nono rejected any compromise with the forces which were already changing the political and social physiognomy of Europe.[9] The severity of his condemnation of modernism must, however, be seen against the background of the difficulties with the temporal power in Italy during the last years of his pontificate. Though Leo XIII never openly disavowed the record of his predecessors—the "errors" of the *Syllabus* have remained errors to this day—a considerable shift in emphasis took place after Pio Nono's death. Where Pius IX had assailed liberalism in scathing terms, Leo XIII spoke only about the abuses of liberty.[10]

While a segment of Catholic liberalism had been condemned in *Mirari vos*, other Catholic liberals in France as well as the Low Countries managed to keep their political views within the limits set by the church.[11] But outside western Europe, Catholic political liberalism made little headway, and no Lammenais appeared among German Catholics. On the other hand, French Catholics did not contribute to the solution of the social question as did W. E. von Ketteler, Franz von Baader, and Franz Josef Ritter von Buss in Germany.[12]

[9] Ernesto Vercesi, *Pio IX* (Milan: Edizione Corbaccio, 1930), pp. 195-210; see also Frederick Nielsen, *The History of the Papacy in the XIX Century* (New York: E. P. Dutton, 1906), p. 258.

[10] *Immortale dei*, sections 37-38; for a convenient edition of Leo's major encyclicals refer to Étienne Gilson (ed.), *The Church Speaks to the Modern World; The Social Teachings of Leo XIII.* (New York: Doubleday & Co., Inc., 1954); see also Peter Tischleder, "Leo XIII.," *Staatslexikon*, III, 926-960 for an excellent summary of the Leonine contribution to the development of Catholic ideas on the modern state and the social question; and Eduardo Soderini, *The Pontificate of Leo XIII*, transl. Barbara Barclay Carter (London: Burns Oates & Washbourne, Ltd., 1934), pp. 150-158.

[11] Henri Haag, *Les origines du Catholicisme libéral en Belgique, 1789-1839* (Louvain: E. Nauwelaerts, 1950), pp. 132-138, 163-180. For developments after 1839 see Haag, "The Political Ideas of Belgian Catholics (1789-1914)," *Church and Society*, pp. 285-298.

[12] Johannes Messner, "Liberalismus," *Staatslexikon*, III, 968-989. For the best

The impact of Leo XIII on the modern Catholic Church has been called "profound enough to be considered revolutionary."[13] The Leonine genius had a specially marked impact on the relationships of Catholics to the modern state. Leo XIII redefined the position of the church on the nature of civil authority and the form of government, on rights and duties, on the proper scope of state activity, and on the relations of church and state. As a result, Catholics were able to participate in and could influence the affairs of the modern state. To be sure, the new encyclicals did not give instructions about the details of constitution-making, but they became a source of inspiration for those trying to come to terms with that new state.

Leo XIII reaffirmed the divine origin of civil authority, but conceded that the method of selecting those exercising that authority was not ordained by God.[14] He denied that it was ". . . of itself wrong to prefer a democratic form of government. Of the various forms of government, the Church does not reject any that are fitted to procure the welfare of the subjects. . . . Nor does she blame those who wish to assign to the State the power of self-government, and to its citizens the greatest possible measure of prosperity."[15] But any modern state, to be acceptable, would

---

summary statement of the development of German Catholic social ideas and movement, see Edgar Alexander, "Church and Society in Germany: Social and Political Movements and Ideas in German and Austrian Catholicism," *Church and Society*, pp. 363-583. Alexander's section on German Catholicism is the most significant contribution to this volume. The author was a member of the Center party in Germany before 1933 and uses this essay as a platform for attacking the Romantic conservative tradition in Catholic social theory, as well as the leadership of the Center party in the *Reichstag*. With these reservations Alexander's essay can be highly recommended. Hereafter it will be cited as "Church and Society in Germany."

[13] Moody, "The Papacy," *Church and Society*, p. 41.

[14] *Immortale dei*, 4; *Diuturnum illud*, 6-7. A violent controversy raged in the German-speaking Catholic community over the interpretation of these passages in the Leonine encyclicals. Drawing on these and other passages as well which dealt with the origin and nature of public authority, Peter Tischleder developed the strongest case for popular sovereignty put forth by European Catholics up to that time. In this Tischleder and a group of German Jesuits acknowledged their indebtedness to the Suarez-Molina tradition. Their opposition came chiefly from the ranks of the Austrian Romanticists, whose social ideas are developed in detail in the following chapter. See Tischleder, *Ursprung und Träger der Staatsgewalt nach der Lehre des hl. Thomas und seiner Schule* (M. Gladbach: Volksvereinsverlag, 1923), pp. 215-224. Heinrich Rommen, *op.cit.*, belongs to the same school.

[15] *Libertas praestantissimum*, 44, 45.

have to meet two conditions: it must recognize the divine origin of civil authority, and it must insure the welfare of its subjects. On both counts therefore, the Pontiff found much to criticize in the liberal state. Its proponents had refused to accept the divine basis of civil authority and had sought the state's origin in conquest, power, or a social contract. They had also rejected the welfare concept of state responsibility and embraced instead a system of *laissez faire* under which the rich exploited the poor. However, any state meeting the two conditions fixed by the Pope would be acceptable to the church, irrespective of its form of government. This declaration of "neutrality" concerning forms of government enabled Austrian Catholics in 1918 to accept a republican form of government. Not all Catholics did so, however. Many of them claimed that the First Austrian Republic had not met the two fundamental conditions fixed in Leonine doctrines, and they managed to postpone their acceptance of the Republic *ad calendas Graecas*.

The Pontiff also condemned the "liberties of 1789" because they were a manifestation of what has been called "the fundamental error," the refusal to recognize the existence of a supernatural order.[16] He considered them philosophically wrong because they constituted a denial of the divine origin of civil authority; he also rejected them because in implementing these liberties states tended to deny important claims advanced by Catholics, especially in the area of the family, school, and education. There could be no compromise in this matter, Leo asserted: "From what has been said it follows that it is quite unlawful to demand, to defend, or to grant unconditional freedom of thought, of writing, or of worship, as if these were so many rights given by nature to man."[17] Nevertheless, Leo XIII conceded that under certain conditions the church might well acquiesce in these modern liberties, "not because she prefers them in themselves, but because she judges it expedient to permit them."[18] No other statement illustrates better the shift from

[16] *Ibid.*, 15; Gilson points out that this error appears on many levels: it is called naturalism or rationalism on the level of philosophy, and liberalism on the level of ethics and politics; see his introduction to the collection of the Leonine social encyclicals *The Church Speaks to the Modern World*, p. 7.

[17] *Libertas praestantissimum*, 42.

[18] *Ibid.*, 34.

Mirari vos and *Quanta cura* to *Libertas praestantissimum* and *Diuturnum illud.*

In spite of such statements indicating willingness to accept expediential solutions, Leo considered a system of rights and duties based on a pluralistic social theory the only true alternative to the rights of 1789. The rights, duties, and functions of social organs, such as families, vocational groups, and local communities, were determined by the place they occupied in the hierarchical social order. These rights and duties were not "natural" in the Revolutionary meaning of the term, but social rights and duties which were derived from the position and function of the group in society. They were not created by the state, nor could they be abridged by it.

Pluralistic social theory also provided the basis for the Leonine definition of the proper scope of state activity.[19] According to this theory, the various social organs had a well-defined scope of action which was to be free from interference by superior social organs, and especially by the state. In like manner, there were certain duties and functions which belonged within the sphere of the state and could never be assumed by any other social organ. As a result of this attempt to strike a balance between state action and action by other social organs, it became necessary to defend Catholic social theory against the two-front attack by liberalism and socialism. Leo XIII considered the liberal who demanded the establishment of a secular state with an exclusive system of state schools as truly a proponent of absolutism as the socialist. He concluded that the liberal who adhered to rationalism on the level of philosophy and to indi-

19 For the manner in which Austrian and German Catholics developed and applied this pluralistic doctrine, see especially Otto Schilling, *Die christlichen Soziallehren* (vol. XVI of *Der katholische Gedanke*; Cologne: Oratoriumsverlag, 1926), pp. 155-156; Jakob Strieder, "W. E. Ketteler und die soziale Frage im deutschen Katholizismus," *Die soziale Frage*, pp. 52-56; and Paul Jostock, *Der deutsche Katholizismus und die Überwindung des Kapitalismus. Eine ideengeschichtliche Skizze* (Regensburg: Friedrich Pustet, 1932), pp. 56-61. Jostock attempted to develop a moderate Catholic position on the social question: that is to say, he was critical of the excessive accommodation to capitalism and the Wilheminian state on the part of leading German Catholic politicians. At the same time he was not prepared to join the social Romanticists in their demand for a radical reconstruction of the existing social order.

vidual rights and the limited state on the level of politics had thereby irretrievably opened the way for the totalitarian claims of the socialist.

Finally, Leo XIII distinguished between proper and improper forms of church-state separation. He admitted that the church might accept the separation of church and state, but warned that this could never be an ideal solution. He cited the United States as virtually the only example of an acceptable form of separation.[20] We see, then, that the difference in outlook between Pius IX and Leo XIII, together with certain developments affecting the temporal power, as well as the declaration of papal infallibility, combined to produce a considerable shift of emphasis in papal pronouncements on church-state relations.

In the later years of his pontificate Leo XIII was forced to return to the problem of the modern state. The reason was the birth of a new political phenomenon, the Christian Democratic movements in France and Italy. These became involved in controversies over organization for social reform in Italy, and over regime in France. In the encyclical *Graves de communi* published in 1901,[21] Leo XIII warned Italian Catholics against excessive reliance on state action for social reform, while in France where the Dreyfus affair had intensified the controversy over regime, Leo's successors were forced to consider the status within the church of the extreme anti-Dreyfusards. Certain writings of Charles Maurras were placed on the Index in 1914, but the decree was not published until 1927, when Pius XI extended it to cover all issues of *Action Française*; at the same time he also forbade Catholics to support the movement.

This brief review indicates clearly the roots of diversity in Catholic social thought. There are factors which tend to unify Catholic social thought, such as its direct relation to Catholic theology and the common problems of the modern state. But the wide variety of views held by Catholics on political matters can be traced to the social and economic diversities among Catholic groups within the same country as well as to the differences in outlook between Catholics in the various nation states.

[20] *Libertas praestantissimum*, 37-41.
[21] Text in Gilson, *op.cit.*, pp. 313-328.

3. Social Catholicism and the Social Question

Catholics traced the new problems of expanding capitalism to the operation of the market economy and the rise of a powerful finance capitalism. During the Middle Ages, Scholastic social theory had firmly established the ethical basis of the just wage and the just price, and had condemned unearned income in the form of interest. But the rise of a money economy and the development of trade had forced a modification of this ban on interest even before the growth of modern finance capitalism. This modification was followed by the elimination of the just wage and the just price. Like political liberalism, which had destroyed the system of political rights and duties which characterized the organic society of an earlier period, so economic liberalism, Catholics claimed, had put an end to the system of economic rights and duties which had imposed ethical standards on economic activity. They blamed the economic theory of liberalism, called *Smithianismus* in central Europe, for making materialism and egotism respectable and giving them the appearance of scientific laws.[22] The feverish quest for selfish personal gain had completely undermined the social character of property by eliminating all social and moral restraints on its use. While Catholics thus concentrated on the evil effects of *laissez faire*, they said little about the injustices which had resulted from the decay of the guild system and of the trading and other commercial privileges of mercantilism.

The Industrial Revolution intensified the problems created by the growth of the market economy. The workers forced into the cities by the reduced labor needs of agriculture and the destruction of the handicrafts soon found themselves at the mercy of the factory owners who controlled their only source of a livelihood. When the rationalization of production led to unemployment and reduction of wages, all members of a proletarian family were forced to go to work to support a single household. Catholics feared that this destruction of the family resulting

[22] For one of the earliest attacks on *Smithianismus*, see Adam Müller, "Welches sind die Erfordernisse eines zureichenden staatswirtschaftlichen Systems," and "Adam Smith," in *Adam Müller Ausgewählte Abhandlungen*, Jakob Baxa, editor (second enl. & rev. ed.; Jena: Gustav Fischer, 1931), pp. 32-40 and 76-81; for a later Catholic statement consult Oswald v. Nell-Breuning, S.J., "Die Eigentumslehre," *Die soziale Frage*, pp. 140-160.

from the full-time work of mothers and young children, as well as the deplorable living conditions in the cities of the nineteenth century, would lead workers to follow godless, totalitarian agitators. For this state of affairs they blamed the liberal bourgeoisie who had replaced the old organic order with a system based on individual rights, and had thereby opened the way for the proletariat to claim these very rights for itself, whether by peaceful means or by revolution. The more wretched their lot, the more likely that they would resort to revolution, Catholics warned. There was no hope for a solution of the "social question" unless workers were paid a wage based on their social needs—such as maintenance of the family, education of the children, savings for old age—instead of one based merely on the law of supply and demand.[23] So Catholics renewed their demand for a "just wage" but failed to realize that the complexity of modern industrial production had made it extremely difficult to fix the worker's "just" share in the result of his labor. This excessive reliance on the Scholastic formulation of wage, price, and interest inclined Catholics to propose medieval solutions for the "social question" that were quite unworkable in an industrial economy based on the market.

Just as Catholics in dealing with the modern state had attempted to steer a middle course between the unacceptable extremes of political individualism and totalitarianism, so in dealing with the "social question" they spoke about a two-front war against Adam Smith and Karl Marx, against *laissez faire* and socialism. Because they agreed on the necessity to avoid the extremes, but differed over the nature of the "middle course," they held a variety of views on the social question, ranging from those of Catholic liberals to Catholic (religious) socialists and corporativists.

[23] The Australian Court of Conciliation and Arbitration held that a "fair and reasonable" wage must meet "the normal needs of an average employee regarded as a human being in a civilized country." These normal needs included food, shelter, clothing, frugal comfort, provision for evil days, a reasonable amount of leisure, security to marry and to rear a family of about three children. W. K. Hancock, *Australia*, a volume in *The Modern World; a Survey of Historical Forces*, ed. H. A. L. Fisher (London: Ernest Benn Ltd., 1930), pp. 84-85. Hancock pointed out that in the Australian conception of a fair and reasonable wage "the medieval idea of a concrete externalized justice . . . joins hands with modern optimism, which insists that man is in control of nature and that he can make life tolerable if he chooses to do so." *Ibid.*, p. 85.

Catholics developed two types of solutions for the social question. Restoration of the old organic social order (*Sozialreform*) was one, gradual reforms within the existing social framework (*Sozialpolitik*) the other.[24] Their choice of solution and the methods proposed for implementing it were influenced by the degree and rate of industrialization of their country, political developments, such as the *Kulturkampf*, pastoral considerations, e.g., the position and needs of the hierarchy, and the nature of the "ideal" social order they had in mind.

Because the march of industrialization across Europe began in the west, and from there moved east, not all countries became industrialized at the same time, nor did their industrialization proceed at the same rate. The industrialization of France preceded that of central Europe, while the industrialization of Germany and Austria, though it began simultaneously, proceeded more rapidly in the former than in the latter country. The destruction of the old economic order in Germany, including the apprentice system and small-scale artisan enterprises, quickly forced German Catholics to come to terms with the new system. This need for accommodation gave rise to the Solidarist school of social theorists, led by the German Jesuits, Heinrich Pesch, Gustav Gundlach, and Oswald von Nell-Breuning. In Austria, on the other hand, where industrialization proceeded more slowly, where small-scale enterprises managed to survive in large numbers, and where corporative vocational organizations retained legal powers to control the economic activities of their members, Catholics remained strongly attached to Romantic social theory.

In spite of these differences in the rate and growth of industrialization in various countries, the treatment of the social question by most European Catholics evolved in four clearly discernible stages. (1) Before 1850 industrial production continued on a small scale, especially in the countries of the Metternich system, and was severely restricted by legislation which favored

24 Jostock, *op.cit.*, pp. 138-144; Karl Huemmer, *Der ständische Gedanke in der katholisch-sozialen Literatur des 19. Jahrhunderts* (doctoral dissertation, University of Würzburg, 1927) traced the development of *Sozialreform* in Germany. Heinz Herberg, *Eine wirtschaftssoziologische Ideengeschichte der neueren katholischen Soziallehren in Deutschland* (doctoral dissertation, University of Bern, 1933) presented a discussion of the distinction between these two tendencies.

the old methods of production. Catholic social theorists, preoccupied with the problems of pauperism and of the artisan, believed that Christian charity would suffice for the effective treatment of the economic dislocations caused by the Napoleonic Wars. (2) Between 1850 and 1870 the increasing tempo of industrialization hastened the end of the old economic order. The industrial proletariat emerged as a distinct socio-economic class which had little in common with the pre-industrial artisan. In Germany, Bishop W. E. von Ketteler was the first high-ranking member of the hierarchy to realize that the solutions appropriate for an artisan economy were totally inadequate for the industrial proletariat. (3) Between 1870 and 1880 the new industrialism suffered its first crisis—the boom and depression of 1873. (4) The increasing difficulties of the industrial proletariat and other lower middle class groups forced Catholics to give increased attention to the social question and led directly to the promulgation by Leo XIII in 1891 of the encyclical *Rerum novarum* which put an end to decades of discussion and controversy over that issue. Leo XIII gave official sanction to a body of ideas common to Catholics in many countries, and for years to come Catholic social thought was dominated by the classic formulation of the social question contained in that encyclical.

Catholic consideration of the social question was also influenced by national political developments.[25] In France and Italy, where Catholics faced difficult problems of church-state relationships, their social theorists paid less attention to the social question than did their co-religionists in Austria, where the question of regime did not arise until after 1918. Social thought was also shaped by the political position of the social groups which supported the church. For example, in imperial Germany, governed by a Protestant dynasty, Catholic social thought opposed the centralizing and *étatiste* tendencies of the Hohenzollerns. In Austria, on the other hand, Catholics relying on a benevolent dynasty looked favorably on state intervention in economic and social affairs.

Pastoral considerations have always influenced Catholic social thought. The concern of the church with the fate of the indus-

[25] Clemens Bauer, "Wandlungen der sozialpolitischen Ideenwelt im deutschen Katholizismus des 19. Jahrhunderts," *Die soziale Frage*, pp. 11-46.

trial proletariat stemmed in part from the disastrous decline of church influence over the urban masses. As urban churches emptied and urban parishes decayed, the church was obliged to consider the causes of this mass apostasy and devise counter-measures.

Finally, the ideal of a "right" social order formed the foundation of all Catholic social thought. Natural law, as interpreted by Catholics, as well as theology and revealed truth, shaped this "right" social order toward which Catholic social reform tried to work.

Among the proponents of *Sozialreform* who believed that the restoration of the old social order was the only solution to the social question, the most prominent were the Traditionalist Theocrats and the Romanticists.[26] The program of the Traditionalist Theocrats in France has been well summarized by Kothen: "We must exorcise the Revolutionary evil and return to the normal tradition."[27] The "normal tradition" was that of the *ancien régime* which, they claimed, had been destroyed by the rationalists, the individualists, and the partisans of the social contract. The Traditionalist Theocrats sought to counter the individualism of the Revolutionary tradition by stressing the collectivity and the authority of the state. Eventually, their emphasis on tradition and order led them to elevate the state over all other social organs, and caused the *Action Française*, whose roots were in traditionalist theocratic thought, to come into conflict with the church, because it sought to subordinate the church to the state.[28]

The German and Austrian Romanticists also opposed industrialization, criticized classical economic theory, and preached a return to the social order of the Middle Ages. Austrian Catholics

[26] Robert Kothen, *La Pensée et l'Action Social des Catholiques 1789-1944* (Louvain: Em. Warny, 1945), pp. 41-61. The sections dealing with France and Belgium are the best. See also Charlotte Muret, *French Royalist Doctrines since the Revolution* (New York: Columbia University Press, 1933), pp. 10-34.

[27] Kothen, *op.cit.*, p. 42. Rommen pointed out that from the point of view of Catholic theology ". . . a specific political theory cannot be held. St. Thomas bases political philosophy on natural reason and natural law, not on revelation and supernatural theology. . . . The attempts to exalt one form of government over another, e.g., monarchy over democracy, by an appeal to ecclesiastical and theological doctrine were blamed [sic] by Leo XIII as inadmissible . . . ;" *op.cit.*, pp. 111, 113.

[28] Rommen, *op.cit.*, p. 113.

who were strongly influenced by social Romanticism attempted to combine Romantic and Catholic elements in their social theorizing. Some critics of this tradition have charged that "Romantic" and "Catholic" are incompatible terms and that the Catholic Romantic movement was "incapable of building the foundations for a genuinely Catholic doctrine of state and society."[29]

The Romantic movement began as a revolt against rationalism in philosophy and absolutism in government. In Germany the Romanticists sought to revive the medieval German folk culture which, they charged, had been submerged by political absolutism and the spread of rationalist philosophy from France. The French Revolution stirred the Romanticists deeply, and they enthusiastically echoed its attacks on rationalism and absolutism. But they were soon disillusioned, both philosophically and politically. They condemned Jacobinism as the triumph of the rationalist strand of the Revolutionary tradition, and resented the nationalist expansion of France at the expense of Germany. The Romanticists now joined the German nationalistic revival and identified themselves with the political forces that opposed the expansion of France. Their demand for individual self-expression and their fight against absolutism abruptly changed into a defense of constituted authority against revolutionary forces. They no longer praised the Middle Ages for its Germanic folk traditions, but for its spiritual unity and the organic order of its social system. Consequently, the Catholic faith and a corporative social order became the chief Romantic attributes of the Middle Ages. Such an idealized picture of the Middle Ages had always been part of the Romantic utopia; the Romanticists simply returned to it after their short-lived flirtation with the Revolutionary tradition.

The critics of the Romantic movement have centered their attacks on two points. Carl Schmitt, for example, attacked the personal conduct of political Romanticists like Adam Heinrich Müller and Friedrich von Schlegel who exploited their conversion to Catholicism and absolutism for personal gain.[30] Others

---

[29] Alexander, "Church and Society in Germany," *Church and Society*, p. 369.
[30] The best study of the social Romantic movement is still Carl Schmitt, *Die politische Romantik* (second ed.; Munich: Duncker & Humblot, 1925). For a

have focused on the incompatibility of Romantic ideas and Catholic theology and social thought. Neither of these criticisms ought to detract one's attention from the long-range importance of Romanic thought for the development of Catholic social theories, especially in Austria. Throughout the nineteenth and early twentieth centuries while Catholics gradually abandoned *Sozialreform* and sought to work within the existing social system, Romantic social theorists clung to corporative ideas. When criticism of capitalism and democracy gained ground among Catholics after the First World War Romantic social thought again became a major source of inspiration for Catholics.

Neither the Traditionalist Theocrats nor the Romanticists wrote during periods of industrialization. Their view of the social question was therefore essentially pre-industrial, e.g., they were concerned with the problems of the artisan and small trader classes. Only Franz von Baader in Germany showed some understanding for the problems of the new industrial proletariat,[31] while all the other Romantic thinkers applauded the efforts of the Metternich regime to prevent industrialization and sought to wish away the problems of industrialism by grandiose projects for the strengthening of guilds and estates.

The proponents of *Sozialpolitik*, usually called Social Catholics, sought to solve the social question within the existing social and economic framework. They believed that Catholics could hasten its solution by participating in the affairs of the state and by pressing for legislation which embodied the demands of Catholic social theory. Because the proponents of *Sozialpolitik* pursued their objectives in an empirical manner, only a review of

---

briefer treatment, especially of the German Romanticists, see Karl Zimmermann, "Romantik," *Staatslexikon*, IV, 1011-1020. Some of the standard works are Reinhold Aris, *History of Political Thought in Germany from 1789 to 1815* (London: George Allen & Unwin, Ltd., 1936); Friedrich Meinecke, *Weltbürgertum und Nationalstaat. Studien zur Genesis des deutschen Nationalstaates* (sixth rev. ed.; Munich: R. Oldenbourg, 1922); and Paul Kluckhohn, *Persönlichkeit und Gemeinschaft. Studien zur Staatsauffassung der deutschen Romantik* (Halle: Max Niemeyer, 1925). A translation of selected essays and a good introduction in English are now available in H. S. Reiss (ed.), *Political Thought of the German Romantics* (New York: Macmillan, 1955).

31 Ludwig Baur, "Baader," *Staatslexikon*, I, 539-545; there is an excellent discussion of Baader in Alexander, "Church and Society in Germany," *Church and Society*, pp. 393-406.

events in some countries like France and Germany can illustrate the progress of *Sozialpolitik*.

In France the struggles over church and state absorbed the energies of Catholics throughout the nineteenth century. These controversies were not yet settled when social and economic questions began to demand attention. The small group of Social Catholics who might have supported *Sozialpolitik* was engaged in a bitter fight with the Catholic majority who refused to accept the Third Republic. But because of their minority position they could have done little to make *Sozialpolitik* prevail, even if their attention had not been centered on the intra-Catholic fight over the question of regime. As a result, French Catholic social theory was the work of adherents of *Sozialreform* from the anti-republican camp. But both the principal corporativist theorists, Albert de Mun and René la Tour de Pin, were monarchists. Their monarchist and paternalistic outlook gave a cast to their social reform proposals that made them quite unattractive to French workers then under the spell of syndicalism.[32]

While Social Catholicism remained an insignificant movement in France until after the Second World War, it became the dominant school in Germany long before the end of the nineteenth century, chiefly because of the efforts of one man, Wilhelm Emmanuel von Ketteler.[33] At first social Catholics tried to arrest the deteriorating conditions of the artisans, and Adolf Kolping, who founded the Catholic *Gesellenvereine*, journeymen's clubs, had only limited success in raising the social and economic conditions of journeymen.[34] Ketteler, on the other hand, took a new approach to the social question altogether, by concentrating his attention on the conditions of the urban prole-

[32] Georges Jarlot, S.J., *Le Régime Corporatif et les Catholiques Sociaux. Histoire d'une doctrine* (Paris: Flammarion, 1938), esp. ch. III, "Les chretiens sociaux, Vienne et Frohnsdorf," pp. 59-80. The failure of corporative doctrine in France is analyzed by Matthew Elbow, *French Corporative Theory 1789-1948* (New York: Columbia University Press, 1953); see also Parker T. Moon, *The Labor Problem and the Social Catholic Movement in France* (New York: Macmillan, 1921).

[33] The best study of Ketteler is Fritz Vigener, *Ketteler. Ein deutsches Bischofsleben aus dem 19. Jahrhundert* (Munich: R. Oldenbourg, 1924); a good short treatment is Hugo Graf Lerchenfeld, "Ketteler," *Staatslexikon*, III, 92-103; for Ketteler and the social question see Strieder, *op.cit.*, pp. 47-63.

[34] Harwig Bopp, O.Fr.M., "Adolf Kolping und die Gesellenbewegung," *Die soziale Frage*, pp. 99-114; see also Johanna Nattermann, "Kolping," *Staatslexikon*, III, 471-477.

tariat. He urged Catholic social thinkers to shake off their obsession with details of guilds, corporative organs, and artisan production and search instead for the truly permanent element of Scholastic thought—natural law. Thomist natural law would provide the general rules of economic and social organization and would become "an effective weapon in the conquest of a social-reactionary medievalism which had made impossible an unbiased understanding of actual social conditions."[35] In his early writings Ketteler still showed some corporativist inclinations. Even his *Die Arbeiterfrage und das Christentum*, published in 1864, which already showed the influence of Ferdinand Lassalle still contained corporative reform proposals. But a few years later, in 1869, he took the last step, by accepting trade unions as the appropriate form of workers' organization in the industrial economy.

Ketteler's influence, the rapid industrialization of Germany, and the rising prosperity during the decades following the Franco-Prussian War turned German Catholics permanently away from social Romantic theories and toward *Sozialpolitik*. Furthermore, the concentration of Catholic strength in industrial areas of western Germany compelled the Catholic social movement to compete with socialism for the loyalty of the workers. It could not fall back on a Catholic middle class in city and on the farm, as it could in Austria, if it should fail to win the workers. This decision of German Catholics to accept capitalism and the modern state is reflected in the ideas and policies of Georg von Hertling, one of their outstanding leaders. Hertling rejected the social Romantic view that corporativism was the only correct form of Catholic social organization and flatly denied the Romantic notion that the "present-day money and credit economy is the work of evil forces and machine production an invention of the devil."

Under the impact of industrialization after 1870 representatives of the various schools of Catholic social thought met in international congresses to draw up reform proposals. There was also a series of meetings during 1883-1884 sponsored by the Austrian social Romanticists led by Karl von Vogelsang. The "theses" which resulted from these meetings were generally anti-

[35] Quoted in Bauer, *op.cit.*, p. 21.

capitalist and anti-liberal. They called for a complete reconstruction of society, but actually devoted most of their efforts to
prescribing methods for compulsory corporative organization
of peasants and artisans. These meetings were continued after
1884 under the sponsorship of the *Union de Fribourg* and of
Cardinal Mermillod. Under this new sponsorship the reform
proposals became considerably less doctrinaire Romantic. The
framers of the Fribourg program still considered corporative
reorganization of society their long-range goal, but concentrated
their attention on current needs for social legislation on behalf
of the industrial workers. They demanded the establishment of
a wage sufficient for the worker's normal needs, that is to say,
one which would enable him to save and acquire property. They
also proposed restricting the work of women and children, setting maximum hours of work, and regulating international commerce.[36] The work of the *Union de Fribourg* was submitted to
Rome, where it became an important part of the background
material for a new encyclical letter on the social question.

In the encyclical *Rerum novarum* Leo XIII sought a solution
of the social question within the framework of the modern state.
He hoped that the encyclical would give Catholic social theory
direction and unity, and that it would quiet, if not settle, the
controversies which had been raging among European Catholics.
However, *Rerum novarum* was not entirely successful in this
endeavor. Because it treated social questions in a very general
way, it enabled both sides of these various disputes, partisans of
Sozialpolitik as well as *Sozialreform*, to claim victory and a papal
blessing for their argument. For example, in the controversy
over the proper form of industrial worker organization,[37] the
proponents of trade union organization and those who defend
workingmen's associations both alleged that the Holy Father
had decided the dispute in their favor.

Because he considered the social question to be a moral as
well as an economic problem, the Pontiff prescribed moral as
well as institutional reforms. Only a reconstruction of morals
could heal the ravages of that excessive individualism which had
brought on capitalism and industrialism. But moral reform

---

[36] Kothen, *op.cit.*, pp. 247-253.
[37] *Rerum novarum*, 40, 62.

alone would not be enough; several institutional reforms were needed as well for dealing with the economic consequences of capitalism and industrialism.

1. The workers must have the right to organize. Only if they were free to organize could they hope to improve their conditions and reap the benefits from such a cooperative effort. The Pontiff strongly defended this right and warned that the state could interfere with it only under exceptional circumstances.[38]

2. The worker must have a chance to own property to provide for his economic security. Leo XIII conceded that wages would have to be fixed after bargaining between employer and employee, but insisted that they should never be permitted to fall below a level sufficient "to enable him [the worker] comfortably to support himself, his wife, and his children. . . ."[39] If workers were assured such a wage they would be able to acquire property and thus be able to withstand the vicissitudes of the market. This special emphasis on the welfare of the worker was the result of the Pontiff's belief that the production of wealth depended to a large degree on the efforts of labor: "Indeed, their co-operation is in this respect so important that it may be truly said that it is only by the labor of workingmen that States grow rich."[40] Leo's desire to refute liberal economic theories which had disparaged the role of labor in the productive process seemed to have led him toward a labor theory of value. The above passage has been cited repeatedly by the extreme anti-capitalist Romanticists to support their contention that *Rerum novarum* had not rejected Romantic social theory. Actually, Leo firmly opposed the labor theory of value and insisted that both labor *and* capital were required for the creation of wealth. This treatment of wages and property reveals the influence of Ketteler, whom Leo XIII called his "great predecessor." Like Ketteler, he applied Thomist social theory, the concept of the "just wage" and of the dual character of property, to modern conditions but rejected the medieval social institutions the Romanticists proposed to revive.[41]

38 *Ibid.*, 48-52.
39 *Ibid.*, 46.
40 *Ibid.*, 34.
41 *Ibid.*, 43-45 on wages, and 7-10 on property.

3. Finally, Leo XIII advocated state intervention to control private property in the common interest, and to protect the worker in industrial disputes and against various hazards. He concluded that ". . . where there is a question of defending the rights of individuals, the poor and badly off have a claim to special consideration."[42]

Rerum novarum has been called a child of the nineteenth century, a description which fits the encyclical well. Though there were many references to the need for state action in social matters, Leo XIII relied primarily on voluntary organization supported by only a minimum of social legislation. *Sozialreform* could find little comfort in the encyclical which marked the victory of *Sozialpolitik*—of the moderates who were prepared to work for reforms within the existing social and economic framework.

The reception given the encyclical varied from country to country. In France the Dreyfus affair diverted the attention of Catholics to other questions. In Germany the controversy over the social question had been settled in favor of *Sozialpolitik* even before the publication of the encyclical. In Italy the struggle over church-state relations overshadowed all other controversies among Catholics. Finally, in Austria *Rerum novarum* hastened the decline of *Sozialreform* groups but did not put an end to their activities. In all these countries it stimulated the growth of Catholic trade unions and new political movements which pursued the Catholic social program with such zeal that they soon ran head on into other Catholic groups, less eager to promote social reforms.

4. Unity and Diversity in Catholic Thought

The profound changes in Catholic social thought in the course of the nineteenth century, the differences in outlook between national Catholic communities, as well as within a single national community, give rise to two queries: (1) What is it that sets off this body of ideas from that of other social thinkers, critics, and reformers? (2) What are the causes of diversity within the Catholic social tradition?

[42] *Ibid.,* 37.

The common features of Catholic social thought have been the result of a twofold influence: a common theology and a rich historical tradition shared by all Catholics. But in any discussion of "Catholic" political and social theory it is important first to establish clearly the meaning of the adjective "Catholic." Heinrich Rommen's answer to the question "What is Catholic political philosophy?" will help define the meaning of that adjective: "The adjective 'Catholic' here means, so to speak, the place where this philosophy grew and found its home. It does not imply that this political philosophy is based on theology or revelation. It is based on natural reason and rational principles. Political philosophy is a branch of social philosophy and of moral philosophy, not of dogmatic theology or moral theology."[43] In the same manner one can say that *Catholic* social theory indicates the home of that body of ideas. Catholic social theory is, therefore, based on natural reason, and not on dogmatic theology. The distinction between "natural reason and rational principles" on one hand and "dogmatic theology or moral theology" on the other is fundamental to the understanding of the adjective Catholic in Catholic social theory: ". . . the attribute Catholic means that theology is recognized as influencing, even directing, the division of tasks between philosophy and theology. Philosophizing is done . . . with continuous respect for theology. . . . And finally, in principle it accepts teaching and assistance from theology, does not seclude itself from it, and acknowledges that there is no twofold truth, so that what is philosophically true may be theologically false and vice versa."[44] Rommen concluded that from the confluence of theistic philosophy developed in the Christian tradition and Catholic ideas originating in theology had come a specific concept of man's nature and destiny, and ultimately a specific view about the structure of social organization. A social theory which accepted these truths would be entitled to the adjective "Catholic."

The second common influence in Catholic social theory was that of a historical tradition shared by all Catholics. One of the most important elements of this tradition was that of the Scholastics, which deeply influenced the social theorizing of Catholics

[43] Rommen, *op.cit.*, p. v.
[44] *Ibid.*, p. 13.

during the nineteenth and twentieth centuries. Under this Scholastic influence European Catholics studied industrialism and capitalism in the same manner in which the Scholastics had studied the social problems of their own day. As a result, Catholics found it difficult to separate the general social theory of the Scholastics from their prescriptions based on medieval conditions and institutions.[45]

In spite of such strong unifying tendencies, Catholic social theory showed much diversity. This diversity of Catholic schools has led some observers ". . . to find in it [Catholic social theory] an uncritical eclecticism or an opportunist syncretism of unrelated parts, artificially put together and polished in accordance with the interests of the Church as a political instrument for the power of 'popery' or of the 'clergy.' "[46] There are several reasons for this diversity. First, official church statements on political and social questions are usually very "general" and can be interpreted in a number of ways. The church has always recognized an obligation to deal with the affairs of this world and a duty to teach and admonish. These teachings on political and social questions are contained in encyclicals, pastoral letters, etc., that are addressed to the faithful in many countries. Only rarely does a papal encyclical approve or condemn specific institutions in one country, for the church refuses to be identified with transient human institutions. Furthermore, when the Pope speaks on social and political questions he does not proclaim dogma but deals with a subject based on reason and natural law. His statements on such questions enjoy the "highest authority" but are not binding in the same manner as dogma. For these reasons papal pronouncements on social questions have been interpreted by Catholics in different ways. Next, the historical experience of Catholics in the various nation states has influenced their political and social thought. The difficulties of German Catholics during *Kulturkampf*, the experiences of French Catholics with Gallicanism and with the Civil Constitution, the close tie between throne and altar in Austria—all these have profoundly affected the thoughts of Catholics in these coun-

[45] *Ibid.*, pp. 16-18; see also Bauer, *op.cit.*, pp. 20-21; and Schilling, *op.cit.*, pp. 170-174.
[46] Rommen, *op.cit.*, p. 19.

tries about the proper limit of state activity and the nature of church-state relationships. The more rapid industrialization of Germany compared with that of Austria accounts for much of the difference between German and Austrian Catholic social thought. While in Germany Catholics were prepared to participate in public affairs immediately after the end of the *Kulturkampf*, Italian Catholics were unable to do so because of the papal ban on such activities.

Finally, there are differences in Catholic social thought within one country, such as the division between proponents of *Sozialpolitik* and *Sozialreform*. These differences can be traced to the varieties of political and social theories held by non-Catholics, the difference in economic and social status of various Catholic groups, and the political and economic changes which occur over a period of time.

This survey of political and social Catholicism during the nineteenth century has identified the features in Catholic social thought common to European Catholics. These provided the elements of unity in Austrian Catholic thought—the specifically *Catholic* element. The next chapter will present the elements of diversity in that thought, i.e., the *Austrian* materials that went into the creation of Austrian Catholic social theory. In turn, Catholic thought during this earlier period provided the foundation for the social criticism of the years after 1918.

CHAPTER II

THE FOUNDATION OF AUSTRIAN POLITICAL
AND SOCIAL CATHOLICISM

DURING the century preceding the end of the First World War, Austrian Catholics were compelled to deal with the same political and social problems which held the attention of their co-religionists elsewhere. The foundations of this social theorizing, the papal encyclicals, a Catholic theology, and a common historical tradition—all these they shared with other Catholics. What distinguished this body of ideas and the movements which were based on it from those of other Catholics were (1) the social doctrines of the Romantic movement, and (2) a number of peculiarly Austrian institutions.

The chief element of this Romantic doctrine was defense of a strong monarchy and a set of essentially utopian demands for the corporative reconstruction of society. Though this corporativism was repeatedly pushed into the background of Austrian Catholic social doctrines, it was never abandoned altogether. When Austrian Catholics abolished the democratic constitution of 1920 they replaced it with institutions inspired chiefly by the corporative theory of the Romantic movement.

Three peculiarly Austrian institutions comprised the second distinctive characteristic of Austrian Catholic social theory before 1918: a close tie between throne and altar; a peasantry and petty bourgeoisie as principal supporters of Catholic political action; and well-developed corporative organizations in the professions, agriculture, and the trades (*Gewerbe*).[1] The close alliance between throne and altar that characterized the Austrian state until 1918 enabled Catholics to influence public policy to a greater degree than in other countries; this held true even after the rise of Austrian liberalism late in the nineteenth century.

[1] Geoffrey Drage, *Austria-Hungary* (London: John Murray, 1909), pp. 54-94. The chapter on agriculture in the western half of the Empire is still a good survey. Heinrich Waentig, *Gewerbliche Mittelstandspolitik. Eine rechtshistorisch-wirtschaftspolitische Studie auf Grund österreichischer Quellen* (Leipzig: Duncker & Humblot, 1898), pp. 136-220.

The Catholics of the German-speaking crownlands remained loyal to the Hapsburg Dynasty long after all the other national or political groups had deserted it.[2] Next, Catholic social theory reflected the economic and social needs of the peasants and the urban petty bourgeoisie, the principal supporters of the church, but paid scant attention to the needs of the industrial workers. No wonder that Catholic social theory, preoccupied as it was with the effects on peasant and artisan, of industrialism and expanding capitalism, failed to rouse the worker and to attract him to Catholic trade unions which struggled vainly to stem the triumphant rise of the free trade unions loyal to the Social Democratic party. Finally, Catholic social theory was influenced by the corporative traditions of the Austrian middle class. These groups were accustomed to rely on occupational "chambers" in agriculture, trades, and professions to protect their socio-economic position. The repeal of corporativist and mercantilist restrictions on the economy were taken as a direct threat to this elaborate system of corporative representation and occupational controls over economic activity. Consequently, demands for the reestablishment of powerful corporative chambers became an indispensable ingredient of Austrian Catholic social theory.

The admixture of these Austrian elements gave the social doctrines of Austrian Catholics a persistent conservative, corporativist, and *étatiste* bias which lasted throughout the period 1918-1934. In fact, Catholic criticism of democracy and capitalism during this later period was largely an elaboration of ideas developed during the preceding century. Though the establishment of a republican regime in 1918 and the publication of the encyclical *Quadragesimo anno* in 1931 led to some modifications of this theory, fundamental Austrian Catholic doctrine about the modern state and the social question changed little from the traditions established earlier. It now becomes incumbent upon us to examine the specific attitudes of Austrian Catholics to the modern state, in the first place, and then to the social question.

2 Oszkar Jaszi, *The Dissolution of the Hapsburg Monarchy* (Chicago: Chicago University Press, 1929), pp. 158-160; Rudolf Sieghart, *Die letzten Jahrzehnte einer Grossmacht. Menschen, Völker, Probleme des Habsburger-Reichs* (Berlin: Ullstein Verlag, 1932), pp. 316-317, 319. As a high-ranking civil servant and later as a banker Sieghart was one of the most powerful figures behind the scenes in the Christian Social party both before and after 1918. His bias is obvious, but his capacity as an observer of the political scene is of a high order.

1. Austrian Catholics and the Modern State

There is no description of the Austrian state prior to 1918 that does not in some way stress the "Catholic" nature of that state, and the deep attachment of the Hapsburg Dynasty to the Catholic Church. Taras von Borodajkewycz, a nationalist historian fundamentally unfriendly to church and dynasty, wrote: "One hundred years ago when Leopold von Ranke, our greatest historian, attempted to discover the decisive characteristics of Austria, he found two: Austria was not only a 'German' empire, it was a 'Catholic' empire as well. And when the Hapsburg realm disintegrated at the end of the World War the belief was widespread that the Catholic Church had been deprived of its most powerful support in state and politics."[3] It was the devotion of the dynasty to the church which helped preserve the Catholic character of Austria long after the laws of the country had turned it into a neutral state.

The protection of the church by the dynasty reduced the violence of the social and political struggles associated with the rise of the modern state, but did not eliminate them altogether. As a result, Catholics became involved in a bitter struggle with the Austrian liberal bourgeoisie who were determined to make Austria a neutral state and finally succeeded in forcing church-state separation on Francis Joseph I after the defeat at Sadowa. The efforts of Catholics to reverse this action through legislation was only partially successful. Eventually Catholics realized that the position of the church in Austria was secured not by legislation and constitutional provisions but by the social position of the dynasty and the power of the Emperor and his ministers to modify laws and constitutions by administrative subterfuge.[4] While this controversy over the Catholic character of the

---

[3] Taras von Borodajkewycz, "Die Kirche in Österreich," in Josef Nadler & Heinrich von Srbik (eds.), *Österreich: Erbe und Sendung im deutschen Raum* (Salzburg: Anton Pustet, 1937), p. 263. See also Jaszi, *op.cit.*, pp. 152-162; C. A. Macartney, *The Social Revolution in Austria* (Cambridge: Cambridge University Press, 1926), pp. 10-12; and for one of the best and most balanced views on Austria and its Catholic character, Franz Borkenau, *Austria and After* (London: Faber and Faber, 1938), pp. 118-123.

[4] Max Freiherr Hussarek von Heinlein, "Die kirchenpolitische Gesetzgebung der Republik Österreich," in Alois Hudal (ed.), *Der Katholizismus in Österreich. Sein Wirken, Kämpfen und Hoffen* (Innsbruck: Verlagsanstalt Tyrolia, 1931), pp. 28, 30. This volume, which contains several important essays, including one

Austrian state was still in full swing, Catholics were confronted with the social consequences of industrialization—with the "social question." In turn these political and social struggles were complicated by national rivalries which pitted the German-speaking Catholics of the western half of the Empire, the area of the future Austrian Republic, against socialists in disputes over the social question, against other nationalities over the German character of the Empire, and against German nationalists in their own midst over questions of clericalism and Pan-German nationalism.[5]

Church-state relationships in Austria bore the imprint of two events: the success of the counter-reformation, and of the Josephinist reforms: "Austria remained Catholic and maintained intact that great treasure—confessional unity. But the claim of the state to control the Church reached its apogee under Joseph II and what started as a reform of the relations between state and church, nearly became a revolt of throne against altar."[6] The victory of the counter-reformation with the military support of the Hapsburg state not only placed the Austrian church deeply in the debt of the dynasty, it also assured the domination of the state over the church. The Josephinist reforms strengthened this dominance and at the same time weakened the religious influence on Austrian life by fostering the ideas of the Enlightenment.[7] The efforts at church reorganization, toleration, administrative centralization, and Germanization of the Empire, though they failed to gain many of their short-range objectives, had two profound long-range effects: intelligentsia and middle class were lost to Catholicism, and the church became dependent on the state: "At that time the intelligentsia abandoned the church and embraced the Enlightenment; soon the middle class followed suit. The bourgeoisie and the middle classes have pre-

by the editor, will hereafter be cited as *Katholizismus in Österreich*. See also Jaszi, *op.cit.*, pp. 135-140.

5 Robert Kann, *The Multinational Empire; Nationalism and National Reform in the Habsburg Monarchy 1848-1918* (New York: Columbia University Press, 1950), I, 97-101; Sieghart, *op.cit.*, pp. 302-310.

6 Borodajkewycz, *op.cit.*, pp. 290, 303.

7 Paul von Mitrofanov, *Josef II. Seine politische und kulturelle Tätigkeit* (Vienna: C. W. Stern, 1910), II, 666-801; Hussarek, *op.cit.*, pp. 30-31; and Alois Hudal, "Der Katholizismus in Österreich. Sein Wirken, Kämpfen und Hoffen," *Katholizismus in Österreich*, pp. 13-14.

served this lack of an active Catholicism till today, without being fully aware of the origins of this attitude. . . . But the worst consequences of Josephinism can be seen elsewhere: in the loosening of Austrian Catholic ties with Rome and in the blind confidence of the clergy in the state. As a result, the clergy expected the state to furnish financial support for the Church and to provide police assistance for pastoral functions."[8]

After the death of Joseph II ideas of toleration and of the Enlightenment were ruthlessly suppressed. Austria became a center of reaction against the Revolutionary tradition, and Vienna the home of political and social Romantic doctrines. But all these counter-measures were to little avail, and the influence of these reformist ideas on the church and on other sectors of Austrian life continued into the twentieth century. Nevertheless, the Romantic revival sponsored by the highest authorities of the Austrian state had lasting effects on Catholic social thought. Romantic social ideas penetrated so deeply into that corpus of doctrine that it became impossible to conceive of it stripped of its Romantic elements.

(a) The Romantic Movement and Austrian Catholicism. The ideas of the political Romanticists, opposition to the Enlightenment, and defense of absolute monarchy were congenial to Austrian Catholics. Adam Heinrich Müller, Friedrich von Schlegel, and many others were attracted to Vienna, and in the Hofbauer Circle Catholicism and Romanticism combined to produce a Romantic Catholicism quite different from Catholic and Romantic thought elsewhere.[9]

The Romantic movement in the German *Kulturkreis* can best be defined in terms of a contrast: ". . . [the Romantic movement] represented the sharpest contrast to the Enlightenment of the eighteenth century. It demanded a religious foundation for the entire culture, and attempted to replace rationalism with a traditional and historical consciousness, and sociological atomism with the organic principle. This placed it in opposition to the political and economic tendencies of its day, to the ideas

---

[8] Hudal, *loc.cit.*

[9] M. Baptista Schweizer, "Kirchliche Romantik. Die Einwirkung des hl. Clemens Maria Hofbauer auf das Geistesleben Wiens," *Historisches Jahrbuch*, 48 (1928), pp. 389-460; Ernst Karl Winter "Hofbauer," *Staatslexikon*, II, 1266-1268; and the general literature cited in Ch. I, note 30, above.

of 1789 and those of classical economics."[10] In their revolt against rationalism the Romantic thinkers embraced what Carl Schmitt has called "occasionalist" individualism, that is to say, they treated everything merely as an "occasion" for their individual Romantic experiences.[11] This individualism led the Romanticists into a short-lived flirtation with the French Revolution. When they became disillusioned they quickly abandoned the individualistic elements of their thought and stressed the traditional, historical, and organic ideas of the Christian Middle Ages which had been part of Romantic doctrine all along. Because Romantic thought contained some elements which were compatible with Catholic social thought and some which were not, it becomes necessary to examine the relationship of Romantic doctrine to Catholic thought.

Romantic and Catholic thought appear incompatible first because Romantic individualism denies the fundamental Catholic concept of man as part of a higher order: ". . . while the Catholic believer seeks the world in order to dwell and act in it, fortified by his theological certitude, the Romantic makes use of his encounter with the world mostly in order to pass through its realities in his flight into the pseudo-theological incertitudes and perplexities of his occasionalist world concept."[12] There is still another conflict between Romantic and Catholic thought. While both stress the need for a religious foundation of all human cultural activity, the Romanticist, in his eagerness to insure the influence of religion, tends to exalt the transcendent element of Catholicism, the element of faith, at the expense of natural reason and rational principles. Austrian Catholics who found the Romantic defense of monarchy a useful part of their political theory tended to play down these incompatibilities. The revival of Thomist social theory by Leo XIII later in the nineteenth century intensified the clash between the Romantic emphasis on faith and the Thomist reliance on reason and nat-

10 Paul Jostock, *Der deutsche Katholizismus und die Überwindung des Kapitalismus. Eine ideengeschichtliche Skizze* (Regensburg: Friedrich Pustet 1932), p. 21.
11 Carl Schmitt, *Die politische Romantik* (second ed.; Munich: Duncker & Humblot, 1925), ch. II, "Die occasionalistische Struktur der Romantik," pp. 115-152; Heinrich Rommen, *The State in Catholic Thought; A Treatise in Political Philosophy* (St. Louis: B. Herder Book Co., 1950), pp. 110-116.
12 Alexander, "Church and Society in Germany," *Church and Society*, p. 370.

ural law which came to dominate Catholic social doctrine. Austrian Catholics considered the Romantic elements of their social thought a natural result of Austrian historical traditions and social developments, and therefore simply one of the many variations possible in Catholic social thought.

The most influential writer of political Romanticism was Adam Heinrich Müller, whose defense of corporative monarchy has occupied a central place in Austrian Catholic political thought. Friedrich Meinecke has identified three principal sources of Müller's political thought: Burke, Fichte, and the *Frühromantik*.[13] Müller accepted Burke's love of the past, his pluralism, and his emphasis on the non-rational factors of life: traditions, morals, and instincts.[14] He believed that these non-rational factors created a web of relations which grew naturally and drew together the life of the individual, the group, and the community. But in Müller, Burke's love of the past becomes blind veneration of the Middle Ages, and Burke's pluralism a corporative order controlled by the state: "When Burke praised the age of chivalry he was using a historical flourish to strengthen his position, but he would have been horrified at the idea that someone would use his arguments in order to revive feudalism. He had, as Lord Morley remarks, 'no puny sentimentalism, and none of the more romantic literary conservatism of men like Chateaubriand. He lived in a real world. . . .' Müller's conservatism, though it was strongly influenced by Burke, had more in common with de Maistre's mysticism and Chateaubriand's poetic vision."[15]

[13] Friedrich Meinecke, *Weltbürgertum und Nationalstaat. Studien zur Genesis des deutschen Nationalstaates* (sixth rev. ed.; Munich: R. Oldenbourg, 1922), p. 133.

[14] For Burke's influence on Müller, see Jakob Baxa, *Einführung in die romantische Staatswissenschaft* (second ed.; Jena: Gustav Fischer, 1931), p. 46. For a good illustration of this Burkian influence on the Central European Romanticists, see Frederick Gentz, *The French and American Revolutions Compared*, transl. John Quincy Adams (Chicago: Henry Regnery, Gateway Editions, 1955). Adams copied this essay from the *Historisches Journal* and translated it while he was United States minister in Berlin in 1800. It is interesting to note that the current revival of "conservatism" in America has now resurrected Gentz to bolster its own case. Gentz compared the two revolutions ". . . with regard to lawfulness of the origin, character of the conduct, quality of the object, and compass of resistance . . ." and came to conclusions much like Burke's.

[15] Reinhold Aris, *History of Political Thought in Germany from 1789 to 1815* (London: George Allen & Unwin, Ltd., 1936), p. 309.

Next, Fichte's philosophy helped Müller overcome the formalism of rationalist philosophy.[16] Fichte's accomplishment, Meinecke argued, was to have introduced dynamic elements into rationalism, and to have brought to bear on the state "the dynamics of reason and free will." Fichte could not conquer the state, but he could infuse it with a new spirit (*Lebendigkeit*). Though Müller's concept of the dynamics of state and society differed from that of Fichte, it showed a marked Fichtean influence. Finally, from the *Frühromantik* Müller received a concern for the individual and need for self-expression. However, Müller assigned individuality and self-expression to groups and whole states rather than to individuals. As a result, he reduced the individual to an inferior position and gave the needs of the collectivity a central place in his doctrine.

Müller's defense of corporative monarchy was actually a perversion of the ideas he had drawn from these three sources. The political system he proposed was not pluralistic but monistic. All power rested in a monarch while the multitude of corporative organs were in fact powerless against the central government. Some features of this political system were compatible with Catholic social thought; some were not. Catholics during Müller's time shared his veneration of the Middle Ages and his glorification of monarchy as the only correct form of political organization. They also supported Müller's contention that the individual was unthinkable outside the state.[17] Like Müller they considered states "natural" human organizations, not merely "accidental agencies for insuring human needs whose costs of operations nobody wants to assume."[18] Only in the state could the individual find freedom and a chance to follow his individual destiny "to be and to have the unlimited possibility to become that which is appropriate to his nature and to his individual developmental pattern."[19] Therefore Müller and Cath-

[16] Meinecke, *op.cit.*, pp. 141-157.

[17] Adam Heinrich Müller, *Elemente der Staatskunst*, ed. Jakob Baxa (Jena: Gustav Fischer, 1922), I, 29, 31; see also Paul Kluckhohn, *Persönlichkeit und Gemeinschaft. Studien zur Staatsauffassung der deutschen Romantik* (Halle: Max Niemeyer, 1925), pp. 69-70.

[18] Cited by Kluckhohn, *loc.cit.*; see also Müller, "Von der Idee des Staates," reprinted in Jakob Baxa (ed.), *Adam Müller Ausgewählte Abhandlungen* (second rev. & enl. ed.; Jena: Gustav Fischer, 1931), p. 4.

[19] Cited in Kluckhohn, *op.cit.*, p. 75.

olics alike rejected the definition of freedom and equality of 1789 and sought to replace it with a system of social rights and duties.

Catholics also accepted Müller's proposed corporative organization of the state. They agreed with his view that the state was not simply a "collection of egotists" but composed of "Estates, corporations, communes, families, cities, in short those small, varied and intimate communities to which the individual must belong in order to be in touch with the larger community."[20] There should not be merely isolated individuals and the state, but a host of intermediate organs whose members would share common attitudes and a common outlook. Only on the strength of these shared ideals could they claim representation in the state. Müller considered territorial constituencies poor substitutes for the estates of the Middle Ages, and believed that only through corporative representation would it be possible to give voice to the living generations, the *Zeitgenossen*, as well as to the past generations who had occupied the same area, the *Raumgenossen*.[21]

However, on the crucial question of the relations between the state and other social organs Müller's political doctrine came into conflict with Catholic social theory which claimed autonomy for a variety of social organs, especially for the church. Müller's definition of the state should have made impossible a compromise between his ideas and Catholic social doctrine: "The state is not simply a factory, farm, insurance company, or mercantilist enterprise. Rather, it is a seamless web of the total physical and spiritual needs, the total physical and spiritual wealth, and the total outward and inner life of a nation, fashioned into a great, energetic, endlessly moving, and active whole."[22] The first part of this definition was merely a poor paraphrase of Burke. The second part proves not only that Müller had completely misunderstood Burke, but also that Müller's

20 Müller, "Von der Idee des Staates," pp. 10-11; Kluckhohn, *op.cit.*, p. 72. For a definition of the "organic" state, see Müller, *Von der Notwendigkeit einer theologischen Grundlage der gesamten Staatswissenschaft* (new ed.; Vienna: Österreichische Leogesellschaft, 1897), p. 18.

21 Louis Sauzain, *Adam Heinrich Mueller (1779-1829). Sa Vie et son Oeuvre* (Paris: Librairie Nizet et Bastard, 1927), pp. 445-446, 454; see also Baxa, *Einführung in die romantische Staatswissenschaft*, p. 166.

22 Müller, "Von der Idee des Staates," p. 13; see also Kluckhohn, *op.cit.*, p. 71.

view of the state contradicted Catholic social theory. Catholics should have rejected a political doctrine based on a state which would not recognize the autonomy of the individual, the family, the occupational group, or the church, but nevertheless they found this Romantic, and later neo-Romantic, *étatisme* an attractive and useful ideology.

Friedrich von Schlegel was another important member of the Vienna Romantic group sponsored by Klemens Maria Hofbauer. Like Müller he was a convert to Catholicism, had been attracted to Vienna by the Romantic revival, and like Müller had been rewarded for his anti-Revolutionary and anti-Napoleonic activities with a position in the Austrian civil service. Schlegel shared with other Romanticists an early enthusiasm for the French Revolution. At that stage of his development he favored republican institutions based on a social contract, and rejected monarchy as incapable of representing correctly the will of the people. However, under the influence of the Romantic reaction against the Revolution he proposed a corporative monarchy which rested on the personal qualities of the monarch and on the support of the warrior and landowner estates who would actually govern the state. Schlegel agreed with Hofbauer that too close a tie with the state would not be beneficial to the church, but most of the Catholic Romanticists disagreed and were willing to place the church under the state's tutelage.[23] Apparently Josephinist influences had penetrated even into the Romantic revival.

(b) The Rise of Liberalism. The successes of the Austrian liberal bourgeoisie in 1848 were short-lived. The defeat of the revolution was followed by a reactionary regime which reinstituted absolutism and concluded the Concordat of 1855 whose terms were extremely favorable to the church: "This was a treaty the likes of which the Church had not been able to obtain for a long time. Though actual practice did not always conform to the letter of the agreement, the treaty constituted an irrevocable renunciation of the Josephinist 'state church' and insured legal equality of church and state. . . . The treaty freed the bishops from state control and assured the Church a voice in all areas

---

[23] See Aris, *op.cit.*, pp. 281-285, and Borodajkewycz, *op.cit.*, p. 45.

where it claimed a right of co-determination."[24] It had been the intention of the framers that the Concordat should end the church's position as a Josephinist "state church." They failed, chiefly because the Concordat retained the financial dependence of the church on the state and confirmed the role of the church as a government department, and of the clergy as civil servants and government pensioners.

One result of this attempt to assure the church an independent position in Austrian life was the growth of a popular literature in which Catholic writers, usually members of the clergy, dealt with current social and political questions. Another reason for the growth of this literature was the rise of liberal ideas in politics and economics which forced Catholics to deal with the demands for reform in society and economy which not even the counter-revolutionary regime had been able to silence.

The outstanding publicist of this period was a priest, Sebastian Brunner, whose *Wiener Kirchenzeitung* appeared regularly until 1874. Brunner was the first Catholic publicist to fight liberal ideas in magazine articles and pamphlets written in a popular style. He admitted that the Catholic faith had suffered from the close alliance between church and dynasty, but nevertheless condemned those who criticized the established order as "blasphemers of constituted authority and of the Church whose revolutionary fervor would stop at nothing."[25] The chief culprits in this revolt against church and dynasty were the Jews—an accusation which henceforth became a permanent feature of Catholic social thought. Catholics identified political and economic liberalism with the Jewish bourgeoisie who seemed to control all of Vienna's large banks, industries, and newspapers. Later on when Jewish intellectuals rose to positions of leadership in the socialist movement the task of Catholic pamphleteers became even simpler. They could blame Jews either for capitalist machinations or socialist conspiracies, or both. Was anti-Semitism the *raison d'être* of Catholic social thought, and the criticism of liberalism and capitalism merely window dressing, as some have

24 Borodajkewycz, *op.cit.*, p. 311; Robert Höslinger, *Rechtsgeschichte des katholischen Volksschulwesens in Österreich* (Vienna: Bundesverlag für Unterricht, Wissenschaft und Kunst, 1937), pp. 102ff.

25 Friedrich Funder, "Die katholische Presse," *Katholizismus in Österreich*, p. 191; Josef Brzobohaty, "Sebastian Brunner," *Die Kultur* IX (1908), pp. 293-301.

charged, or would Austrian Catholic social thought have followed substantially the same path during the nineteenth century even without the presence of large Jewish communities in Austrian cities? The extremely conservative and corporativist tendencies of this body of ideas were not merely an anti-Semitic reaction. They can be explained only as the result of specific Catholic and Romantic doctrines and of a number of historical conditions, of which the presence of a large number of Jews was only one, not necessarily the most important.

The *Ausgleich* and the Basic Laws of 1867-1869 which marked the zenith of liberal influence in the nineteenth century were a direct consequence of the Austrian defeat at Sadowa: "That was perhaps the greatest crisis and most fatal turning point of the monarchy. Now locked out from their imperial German connection and having lost its Italian properties, the traditional *fata morgana* of the Holy Roman Empire was dissolved and the road open to the historic mission of Austria which would have consisted of giving shelter, home, and defense, the possibilities of a national development for all those smaller nations which lived in Central Europe either in complete isolation or divided from their co-nationals."[26] Austria never fulfilled that "historic mission." The *Ausgleich*, instead of quieting nationalist demands, insured permanent warfare among the nationalities of the Empire.[27] The Hapsburg realm was now divided into two parts of which the Germans were to control the western half while the people of the eastern half were placed under Magyar dominance. Control of the western half by the Germans was secure as long as high property qualifications and the operations of a curial system of representation disfranchised the Slavs in Bohemia, Moravia, and Galicia. But when the conservative Taaffe government broadened the franchise to give the vote to the petty bourgeoisie who, it was hoped, would be less affected by the liberal virus than the middle and upper bourgeoisie, it seriously weakened the influence of the German liberal middle class. The Em-

[26] Jaszi, *op.cit.*, p. 106; see also Josef Redlich, *Emperor Francis Joseph of Austria; A Biography* (London: Macmillan, 1929), pp. 310-311, 348-349.

[27] Otto Bauer, *Die Nationalitätenfrage und die Sozialdemokratie* (Vienna: Wiener Volksbuchhandlung, 1907), p. 338. In spite of the obvious bias of the author, this has remained an indispensable book for an understanding of the national struggles in the Empire.

peror and his ministers now ruled with the support of the Iron Ring, a heterogeneous coalition which contained feudalist as well as petty bourgeois elements, Germans as well as Slavs.

The cancellation of the Concordat of 1855, following the action of the Vatican council on papal infallibility, the Basic Laws of 1867, together with the school legislation of 1868, and the laws concerning civil marriage, separated church and state, created a system of non-sectarian schools, and established a system of civil rights meeting liberal demands, including freedom of speech, press, and religion, security of domicile, etc. Though the Austrian hierarchy violently attacked that legislation, Bishop Rudigier of Linz drew a one-week jail sentence for denouncing the liberal measures in an inflammatory public address, the legal reforms of 1867-1869 remained in effect until 1934.[28] For an adequate understanding of the ideological and constitutional situation in post-1918 Austria it is important to emphasize this fact. When Catholics and socialists were unable to agree on the school, marriage, and civil rights sections during the constitutional debates of 1919-1920, they simply incorporated these basic laws into the 1920 document.[29] A Catholic author discussing the legal position of the Church after the First World War noted that the *legal* position of the church had remained unchanged under the Republic, but that its *social* position had changed radically.[30] Church and state had been legally separated in 1867, but the Catholic sectarian spirit of the public schools was maintained so effectively that anti-clericals complained that church influence over school affairs was as powerful as ever.[31]

(c) Karl von Vogelsang and the Attack on the Modern State. Increased industrialization and the stock market crash of 1873 created serious economic and social problems among the Austrian lower classes. The collapse of 1873 had not only exposed the weaknesses of Austria's infant industry, but had also affected agriculture and the handicraft economy. Catholics now renewed their search for a social theory which would help them to cope with these social and economic problems. They also sought to

---

[28] Borodajkewycz, *op.cit.*, pp. 309-310, 312; Höslinger, *op.cit.*, pp. 105-110.
[29] Brita Skottsberg, *Der österreichische Parlamentarismus* (Goeteborg: Elanders Boktrycheri Aktiebolag, 1940), pp. 213-214.
[30] Hussarek, *op.cit.*, p. 30.
[31] Höslinger, *op.cit.*, p. 112.

create a political movement based on this social program. In this search for program and movement, Karl von Vogelsang came to play the principal role.

Vogelsang was born in 1818 into a family of the Protestant landed nobility of Mecklenburg.[32] He served in the Prussian civil service but resigned in 1848 as a protest against what he considered the outrageous flirtation of Frederick William IV with the revolution of 1848. In Berlin he had made the acquaintance of Ketteler, who encouraged his pro-Catholic inclinations. Vogelsang then joined a group of Catholic intellectuals in Munich for further study and was baptized in Innsbruck in 1850. He returned to Mecklenburg to manage the family estate but was forced to leave six years later because of the prevailing anti-Catholic sentiment. Eventually he established contact with members of the Austrian nobility interested in social reform and was invited by this group in 1875 to come to Vienna as editor of *Vaterland* a newspaper they had sponsored.[33] In 1879 Vogelsang also assumed the editorship of a periodical devoted to social problems, later called *Monatsschrift für Sozialreform*, a position he held until his death in 1890. Vogelsang became the intellectual leader of this reform movement and left an indelible imprint on Austrian Catholic social thought. He has been praised as the "father of *Sozialreform*" and condemned because he gave Austrian Catholic social thought an extremely reactionary and medieval bias.

Müller and Ketteler were the principal sources of Vogelsang's social theory, in which he tried to combine the corporative, monarchist, and conservative views of Müller with Ketteler's

[32] What one might call an authorized biography of Vogelsang is Wiard von Klopp, *Leben und Wirken des Sozialpolitikers K. Frh. v. Vogelsang* (Vienna: Typographische Anstalt, 1930). Klopp, the son of the historian Onno von Klopp, was Vogelsang's son-in-law. The most recent biography is Johann Allmayer-Beck, *Vogelsang. Vom Feudalismus zur Volksbewegung* (Vienna: Herold, 1952). There is a short sketch of his life by one of his daughters who served as his personal secretary, Marie Freiin von Vogelsang, "Aus dem Leben des Sozialpolitikers Karl von Vogelsang," *Das neue Reich* VII (1924), pp. 43-46, 64-66. An analysis of Vogelsang's work by Anton Orel also contains a biographical sketch, *Vogelsangs Leben und Lehren* (second ed.; Vienna: Vogelsang Verlag, Ges. m. b. H., 1922).

[33] Ludwig Brügel, *Soziale Gesetzgebung in Österreich von 1848 bis 1918. Eine geschichtliche Darstellung* (Vienna: F. Deuticke, 1919), passim; Richard Kralik, *Karl Lueger und der christliche Sozialismus*, vol. I: *Vom Beginn bis 1900* (Vienna: Vogelsang Verlag Ges. m. b. H., 1923), pp. 141, 245.

concern for the social question, i.e., the condition of the industrial proletariat and the evils of capitalism.[34] In this manner the corporative, conservative, and *étatiste* bias of Austrian Catholic social thought fused with the Romantic and social elements in Vogelsang's ideas to produce an ideal social system called "social monarchy," a combination which henceforth characterized Austrian *Sozialreform* doctrines.

Vogelsang deduced the organization of the state and the nature of politics from the organic, corporative organization of society: "Politics does not exist in a vacuum, it is part of a higher totality of social functions—it is only a part, only one facet of society. Politics by itself floats in mid-air, and receives a firm foundation only in a concrete society. Now if politics is simply one of several activities carried on by society, it will be impossible to prescribe a political organization for a people which does not reflect its general social organization. Because this is so, the structure of society provides the model for the structure of the state."[35] It followed that the political organization of society, the state, was part of the natural organization of man: "Everybody must declare for the state, for it is innate in man, it coexists with him, it is a determinant of his existence. . . . It would be a confusion of ideas with the most far-reaching, pernicious, and practical consequences if one were to declare against the state, to reject it, and to portray it, even though it has truly

[34] Vogelsang's efforts were absorbed by his journalistic activities. As a result, he did not leave a systematic statement of his social theories and his program of action. August M. Knoll's doctoral dissertation at Vienna *Vogelsang als Nachfahre der Romantik* (1924) was not available, but his essay "Karl von Vogelsang und der Ständegedanke" in *Die soziale Frage*, pp. 64-85, was very helpful. The present study has relied on Wiard von Klopp (ed.), *Die sozialen Lehren des Freiherrn Karl von Vogelsang. Grundzüge einer katholischen Gesellschafts- und Volkswirtschaftslehre nach Vogelsangs Schriften* (second rev. ed.; Vienna: Reinhold Verlag, 1938). The first edition was published in 1894. From Vogelsang's journalistic output, from essays which appeared in various places, Klopp has created in this volume a useful and workable instrument for the analysis of Vogelsang's writings. The scholarship of those who have worked directly from the sources, such as Knoll, *op.cit.*, and Joseph Schwalber, *Vogelsang und die moderne christlich-soziale Politik* (doctoral dissertation, University of Munich, 1927), confirms the analysis made from Klopp's edition. See also Jostock, *op.cit.*, pp. 109-118. Further references to the literature by and about Vogelsang can be found in Knoll, *op.cit.*, footnotes to pp. 64-66. The Klopp volume will be cited hereafter as Vogelsang, *Lehren*.

[35] Vogelsang, *Lehren*, pp. 127-128.

natural functions, as an un-Christian revolutionary institution, as the antithesis of conservatism."[36]

The rules governing the conduct of the state were part of natural law, and could not be divorced from the moral and ethical standards of that law. Unfortunately, this unity had been destroyed by rationalism and liberalism: "The first step necessary for the establishment of the bourgeois regime was the separation of society and politics; the last step must now be the reunification of the two."[37]

The reforms which Vogelsang considered necessary to restore the moral basis of the state could be carried out only with the help of the state whose duty it was ". . . to exercise a decisive influence over the social and economic conditions of its members. It must keep a special watch over social and economic justice which is expressed, among others, through the principle of the just price."[38] The only correct political organization of the state to bring about these reforms would be ". . . the Christian social state, in other words, social monarchy."[39] This social monarchy would be the antithesis of the liberal state, whose "private" sector had been continuously increased at the expense of the "public sector." In this manner the liberal capitalist prevented the state from enforcing ethical standards on the conduct of social and economic affairs. What was needed, Vogelsang argued, was an expansion of the "public sector," though not necessarily of the state machinery. For in the social monarchy, as in the organic order of the Middle Ages, a variety of corporative social organs would exercise public powers alongside the state: "The state can be found even in the most primitive societies, in the patriarchal family, in the nomadic tribe. . . . Part of the state are also those secular social organs, from the family, the occupational corporation, and the municipality, to the largest territorial units, without which the purposes of the state could not be attained. All this is the 'state,' in contradistinction to those private interests which concern only individuals and

---

[36] *Ibid.*, p. 236. For the influence of Müller on Vogelsang's heavy reliance on state intervention see especially *Elemente der Staatskunst*, I, 48, 36, 35; and "Von der Idee des Staates," p. 23.

[37] Vogelsang, *Lehren*, p. 240.

[38] *Ibid.*, p. 251.

[39] *Ibid.*, p. 242.

have not been claimed as comprising the solidarity of the larger community."[40]

The constitution and laws of the proposed social monarchy would rest on the moral foundations provided by natural law: "Law [Recht] is inherent in objects and relations, and is judged by the standards of natural and revealed moral norms. A statute is, or rather ought to be, a reflection of these moral norms as perceived by proper legislative authority and promulgated in prescribed forms. Statutes which lack this normative substance have no moral, and often not even formal, binding force."[41]

But this constitution was not an artificial construct on the order of the positivist legal system which could be created, changed, and abolished at will: ". . . the constitution of a country is like the spiritual and physical constitution of the human body; only death can put an end to it. There is a constitution just as there is life, both can be brought to the level of consciousness through an act of reflection, but they exist even without that."[42] In the right political order, social monarchy, the corporative organization of society, determined not only the general outlines of state organization, but also the system of representation which Vogelsang considered the heart of the political system. He rejected the territorial method of representation because it was not based on an organic relationship between the representative and his constituents: "The basic fault is that there is no inner relationship between the representative and those he represents, no tie except the casual and superficial act of voting. This is a totally untenable situation. The representative must stand in a continuous and active relationship to his constituents; he must be thoroughly familiar with their affairs and with their needs. Only by virtue of such an organic relationship can he be a true representative."[43] Only a system of corporative representation at all levels would insure local and occupational autonomy and strengthen the organic fabric of society: "There is no doubt that a people that has lost its corporative institutions can only be governed and administered in the Byzantine manner, by a centralized and bureaucratized state apparatus."[44]

[40] *Ibid.*, p. 254.   [41] *Ibid.*, p. 257.   [42] *Ibid.*, p. 243.
[43] *Ibid.*, p. 245.   [44] *Ibid.*, p. 248.

Vogelsang rejected the separation of church and state and proposed a return to earlier conditions when close ties had existed between the two: "If one takes an overview of the history of Christianity one can only thank God for the many benefits and miracles which have accrued to mankind from this reciprocal relationship between church and state. . . . Therefore, Christians ought not to destroy lightly the traditional institutions and conditions, even if matters do not always proceed smoothly. . . ."[45] He insisted that there could be no grounds for friction if church and state would be satisfied to carry out their proper tasks, but warned that Catholics would never submit to the orders of a state which denied the divine basis of human institutions: "Our religious convictions command us to reject with horror the liberal theory of the omnicompetent state."[46]

The manner in which Vogelsang defined the state and the scope of state activity clearly harked back to Müller. Like him, he considered the state to be the totality of all material and spiritual activities and institutions. Even a Vogelsang disciple like Anton Orel had to concede that a state which controlled all aspects of life would ultimately destroy the autonomy of the very corporative order Vogelsang was trying to create: "He [Vogelsang] goes too far when he extends the definition of the state to cover all secular and social relations between men."[47] It is difficult to see how the *étatiste* tendencies of social Romanticists like Vogelsang can be squared with the social pluralism which should be the foundation of any social theory claiming the adjective "Catholic." Western European Catholics have called Vogelsang "the most resolute proponent of state socialism," and have complained that under his leadership Austrian Catholics seemed ". . . to believe that the only road to salvation was to entrust the entire socio-economic order to the Hapsburg Dynasty."[48]

Vogelsang's importance for Austrian Catholicism was twofold: he exercised great influence over subsequent Catholic social thought with his critique of liberalism, and he played a prominent role in the creation of a unified Catholic political move-

[45] *Ibid.*, p. 277.   [46] *Ibid.*, p. 274.   [47] Orel, *op.cit.*, p. 52, note 1.
[48] Knoll, "Karl von Vogelsang und der Ständegedanke," p. 71; see also Johannes Messner, "Zum Begriff der sozialen Gerechtigkeit," *Die soziale Frage*, p. 423; Schwalber, *op.cit.*, pp. 39-50; and Jostock, *op.cit.*, pp. 131-143.

ment. He condemned liberal legal theory because it denied the existence of a higher law and thereby entrusted vast powers to the font of positive law—the state. He also criticized liberal political theory for defining the sphere of public law so narrowly that the state had become powerless to regulate social and economic affairs. As a result, industrialists and capitalists were free to exploit economically weak groups without fear of state intervention. In short, the liberal state created by the bourgeoisie was being used for the benefit of those who had created it.[49] This analysis of the liberal state as both omnicompetent and powerless remained a key concept in Catholic criticism of democracy and capitalism.

Vogelsang was not only the father of *Sozialreform*; he also participated in the formation of the Catholic political movement. Though the quarrels of the two Catholic factions he tried to unite continued for some years after his death, his initial efforts at unification bore fruit before long: "He was 'Catholic-conservative,' the spokesman of feudalism, a representative of tradition, and a successor of the Romanticists. But he was also 'Christian-social,' tutor and educator of the Lueger movement which, beginning in the 1880's, wrested control of Austria from the Catholic Conservatives after many a hard-fought battle."[50] When Vogelsang first came to Vienna, the political leadership of the state was divided between a liberal *Grossbourgeoisie* (industrialists, bankers, and some intellectuals) and the Catholic Conservatives (feudal nobility, higher clergy, big landowners, and some members of the upper bourgeoisie). However, during the 1880's the middle class revolted against the industrialists and feudal landlords, and the leadership of the insurgents fell into the hands of lower middle-class demagogues like Karl Lueger, who also received the support of the lower clergy in his fight. The lines of opposition drawn as the result of this rebellion were complicated by the nationality question. The Catholic Conservatives who controlled the government and had the support of the Emperor could maintain a majority in the *Reichsrat* only with the help of Slav representatives. As a result, the lower middle class came to be torn between loyalty to the Catholic dynasty

49 Vogelsang, *Lehren*, pp. 256, 265.
50 Knoll, "Karl von Vogelsang und der Ständegedanke," p. 67.

and hierarchy and commitment to German nationalist sentiments. The controversy between the Catholic Conservatives and
the Christian Socials, as the new petty bourgeois movement was
called, became so bitter that the former charged the new movement before the Holy See with inciting class hatred and causing
the lower clergy to rebel against their bishops.[51] But Leo XIII
refused to discipline the new movement because he was impressed with the record of the Christian Socials in Vienna, especially their success in bringing the lower middle class back to
the church.

Late in the 1880's the antagonism between these two Catholic
factions began to subside, chiefly because the Catholic Conservatives were unable to stop the triumphant march of the
Christian Socials. Under the superb leadership of Karl Lueger
they first gained control of Vienna and ultimately of the countryside as well; they also sent a strong delegation into the *Reichsrat*. The responsibility of holding office soon softened the radicalism of the master carpenters, cabinet makers, and green
grocers. They rediscovered their devotion to monarchy and
dynasty, and became the most loyal supporters of the Empire.

Though the creation of a unified Catholic political movement
did not take place until 1905-1907, many years after Vogelsang's
death, the first efforts in that direction occurred during the last
three years of his life. Vogelsang not only recognized the leadership qualities of Karl Lueger and convinced the Conservatives
that the Catholic political cause could succeed only if it had a
popular base; he also persuaded the Christian Socials to adopt
his corporative social monarchy as their chief ideological instrument.[52] However, not even the adoption of this doctrinaire program seriously altered the essentially empirical approach to
politics of Lueger and his disciples. In later years the Christian
Socials moved easily from the monarchy to the republic, from
the republic to the corporative state, and, after an interval of
foreign occupation, back to the republic.

[51] See Friedrich Funder, *Vom Gestern ins Heute* (Vienna: Herold Verlag,
1950), pp. 82-154, for the details of this struggle between the entrenched Catholic
Conservatives and the rapidly rising Lueger movement. Funder was for many
years editor-in-chief of the *Reichspost*, the official daily paper of the Christian
Social party. See also Aemilian Schöpfer, "Katholizismus und Politik," *Katholizismus in Österreich*, pp. 444-448.

[52] Rudolf Kuppe, *Dr. Karl Lueger. Persönlichkeit und Wirken* (Vienna: Brüder Hollinek, 1947).

Austrian Catholics encountered many more difficulties in creating a unified political movement than did their co-religionists in Germany, where the *Kulturkampf* had forced Catholics to band together against the Bismarckian attacks. No such centripetal force existed in Austria. Some responsibility for the divisive tendencies in Austrian Catholicism probably rests with the curial electoral system of the Empire, which did not yield to universal, equal suffrage until 1905. Rudolf Sieghart, who played a prominent role in the Christian Social movement before 1918, remarked: "In the curial parliament of Austria, the peasant was separated from the city dweller, the large land holder from the small holder, and later on when a fifth curia was added, the workers were isolated from all the other strata of society. From the single ideology which inspired the German Center party, there sprang in Austria three parties, often at cross purposes, and one not knowing what the other was doing. The Christian Social program took on three distinct forms: the urban petty bourgeoisie turned it into a radical and often un-Christian anti-Semitism, while the peasants made it into a narrow agrarianism. Catholic workers fashioned it into a democratic socialism, but were unable to compete successfully with the Social Democrats, chiefly because they did not occupy the same secure position within the Austrian Catholic social movement, as did the German Catholic labor movement within the Center party."[53]

The diversity of doctrines which existed during the period 1918-1934, long after the political movement had been unified, can probably be traced to the fragmentation of Catholic political and social movements during the earlier period.

(d) The Beginnings of Liberal Catholicism. At the beginning of the twentieth century more liberal Catholic political ideas than those of Vogelsang became prominent among Austrian Catholics, though this shift did not weaken their loyalty to the dynasty. Ignaz Seipel was the first important Catholic thinker to

---

[53] Sieghart, *op.cit.*, p. 300. For a fair and perceptive examination of the differences between the German Center party and the Austrian Christian Socials, see Karl Renner, "Die Christlichsozialen in Österreich und das Zentrum im Reich," *Die Gesellschaft* vi (2) (1929), pp. 137-148, and "Die christlichsoziale Partei und ihr veränderter Charakter," *Der Kampf* xvi (September-October 1923), pp. 293-303. Renner, who held high government and Social Democratic party posts in both Austrian republics, represented the conservative wing of the Socialist movement.

abandon the extreme political conservatism of Vogelsang and his school. In his book *Nation und Staat*, published in 1916, he carefully stressed the distinction between state and society established in Thomist social theory.[54] Vogelsang, who merely gave lip-service to social pluralism, had been more interested in establishing the claims of the state over all sectors of society. Seipel, on the other hand, denied that the state could make unlimited demands on the peoples living within its boundaries: "Seipel simply carried Catholic social theory to its logical conclusion and illustrated his point by using Austrian examples. It took courage to do no more than that, given the intimate relations between political Catholicism and the ruling powers. . . . Seipel's first political treatise amounted to proof that the state was not an absolute value and, therefore, could not make absolute demands on its citizens."[55]

Seipel's political theory as developed in this treatise differed from that of the Vogelsang school in two ways. First, Seipel emphasized the distinction between state and society which Vogelsang tended to disregard. Secondly, by stressing the state-society dichotomy Seipel had restricted the scope of state activity and thereby repudiated the extreme state socialist tendencies of the Vogelsang doctrine. It is not unreasonable to argue that the ideas expressed in *Nation und Staat* would have required a far-reaching reorganization of the Empire into a federal state.[56] Actually, no federation would have been possible without the consent of the Magyars any time after 1867, unless the Magyars would have been willing to relinquish the concessions they had extorted in that year. By 1916 only victory of the Central Powers could have insured the continued existence of the Empire. *Nation und Staat* was significant because it demonstrated the development of a moderate non-Romantic tendency in Catholic political thought, not because it seemed to imply the federal reorganization of the Empire.

[54] (Vienna: W. Braumüller, 1916); see especially p. 57: "*Volk*, nation, and state are neither superordinated, nor subordinated in relation to each other, but are coordinate entities. They are different forms of human organization because they have grown from different roots, though following the same laws of growth."

[55] Werner Thormann, *Ignaz Seipel. Der europäische Staatsmann* (Frankfurt a.M.: Carolus Druckerei, 1932), pp. 23, 25; see also Kann, *op.cit.*, I, 212-219.

[56] See on this Seipel's "Gedanken zur Reform der österreichischen Verfassung," *Der Kampf um die österreichische Verfassung* (Vienna: Wilhelm Braumüller, 1930), pp. 3-29.

The appearance of this moderate school did not weaken Catholics in their rejection of the modern state and in their loyalty to the monarchy. They abandoned the extreme interventionist implications of the Vogelsang doctrine, but remained more tolerant of state interference in economic and social matters than most Catholics in Germany and western Europe.

2. Austrian Catholics and the Social Question

Austrian Catholics during the nineteenth century sought to formulate a social theory which would help them relieve the social consequences of industrialism and expanding capitalism. Because they conceived capitalism and industrialism to be the manifestations of liberalism in the sphere of economics, we must first determine their definition of liberalism. Vogelsang, who had such a profound influence on the Catholics of his adopted homeland, expressed well the prevailing Catholic view: "Liberalism as the principle of the autonomous individual is the very antithesis of the homogenous society which is dependent on God, obeys Him, and accepts the organic principle. . . . Excessive emphasis on selfish considerations in man's action and a ruthless struggle for existence are the inevitable consequences of a liberalism which makes subjectivism the foundation of thought, of law, and of human freedom. . . . In this liberal system social relations are based on a so-called general freedom which makes every individual completely independent and absolves him from all duties toward the community or his neighbors."[57]

In Vogelsang's view the economic system based on this autonomous individualism came to be characterized by an all-pervasive spirit of materialism. Though only a few individuals actually succeeded in amassing wealth, the pursuit of wealth came to dominate the entire society.[58]

Austrian Catholic prescriptions for the solution of the social question reflected the *Sozialpolitik-Sozialreform* dichotomy then prevalent in Catholic social thought. During most of the century the proponents of *Sozialreform* dominated the stage; but the publication of *Rerum novarum* in 1891 served to mute, if

[57] Vogelsang, *Lehren*, pp. 143-144.
[58] Jostock, *op.cit.*, p. 14.

not silence, the corporativist theorists, and make *Sozialpolitik* the principal school of social theorizing.

(a) The Social Doctrines of Adam Heinrich Müller. Austrian Catholic *Sozialreform* doctrines drew heavily on the social theories of Adam Heinrich Müller, especially his theory of corporative organization for economic activity, and his theories of productivity, of property, and of labor relations. Because this body of ideas reflected Müller's failure to grasp the new problems of industrialism and capitalism, Austrian social theory, influenced by him, showed a similar lack of understanding.

Two basic assumptions in Müller's social doctrine supported and strengthened his preference for corporative institutions: (1) his conception of society as an organism, and (2) his definition of the dialectical process as creating a web of interrelationships. Müller described society as an organism in which there existed a multitude of autonomous organs, each fulfilling a particular function but completely subordinated to a common purpose. He likened the state to such an organism and the corporative organs within the state to the members of a living body. In this manner his view of society as an organism confirmed his preference for a state whose economic activity was organized in a corporative manner: "Müller does not tire of describing the state as an organic entity. When he talked of feudalism he had a system in view in which there was no strife between Crown and the estates, in which the noblemen honored the arts and merchants followed the example set by the Hansa. When he objected to the concept of absolute private property he vaguely anticipated the complete social disruption which was to be the consequence of the mechanisation of labour."[59]

Müller's dialectic, his *Lehre vom Gegensatz*, emphasized inrelations of "things and persons" rather than their separate itity. In the dialectical process each *Satz* creates a *Gegensatz*, he two are then synthesized into the *Antigegensatz*. There-*Sachen* (material objects) and *Personen* (individuals as e entities) do not exist in isolation, but only as part of relationship with other persons or objects. Müller asality not to the isolated object or person, but only to

cit., pp. 312, 315-316.

the intricate web of relations that tied them all together.[60] Thus his dialectics as well as his corporativism placed the interrelationships of groups, and of individuals within groups, above their claims for separate identity.

With his theory of productivity, Müller attempted to measure the wealth of a nation by other than the material standards devised by Adam Smith. He argued that such items as the products of the human intellect should also be included in measuring the wealth of a nation: "If one were to accept Adam Smith's method of determining the economic wealth of a nation one would have to omit the products of the spirit, the products of the noblest minds which represent a nation's finest and loftiest gains. In estimating the total wealth of a nation he [Adam Smith] refuses to take into account the most glorious seeds, the most profitable manufactures—the thoughts of its statesmen and the words of its preachers and artists."[61]

Müller concluded that the rejection of spiritual values would encourage individuals to pursue only narrowly selfish and material objectives: "Thus Müller led the first attack against capitalism before it was fully developed and forty years before Marx and Engels initiated the other great anti-capitalist movement with the *Communist Manifesto*. The Romantic and Marxian criticism have one point in common. According to both, capitalism is nothing but disguised anarchy with the ruthless search for profit as its chief driving force."[62] Müller opposed his concept of "limited property" to the liberal theory of absolute property rights. He believed that without restraints on the use of property, its acquisition would become the center of all activities and would thereby contribute to the growing social anarchy: "But it is not money which is at the center of the economy, but autonomous capital. It is this capital which incites man to a boundless search for gain and to a continuous striving to transcend his natural environment. He loses the sense of peace and frugality, the love for his work—work for its own sake, and finally loses the organic connection between his place of work

---

[60] Müller, "Die Lehre vom Gegensatz," reprinted in Baxa, *Ausgewählte Schriften*, pp. 213-280; see also Kluckhohn, *op.cit.*, p. 73.

[61] Jakob Baxa, *Die Geschichte der Produktivitätstheorie* (Jena: Gustav Fischer, 1926), pp. 52-53.

[62] Aris, *op.cit.*, p. 316.

and his place of residence."[63] According to Müller's theory of limited property individuals would have the use of such property, under conditions prescribed and enforced by society, but could never own it outright. This was obviously modeled on the medieval institution of *Lehen*, but neither Müller nor any subsequent Romantic theorist had any clear notion how *Lehen* could be applied realistically to any form of property in the modern economy.

Finally, Müller proposed that relations between employers and employees should not be governed by purely material standards of production and wages. Instead these should be replaced by considerations of "honor" and "service."[64]

(b) Vogelsang and the Social Question. Until 1848 the Metternich regime attempted to enforce a public policy based on a social theory much like Müller's. It maintained strict controls over all economic activities, and tried to preserve the corporative organization in the professions, agriculture, and *Gewerbe*. The trade and artisan guilds were confirmed in their power to regulate internal affairs, including access to an occupation, standards of proficiency, etc. An anecdote involving Metternich himself well illustrates the power of the occupational corporations. The Chancellor once told a *nouveau riche* Jewish banker that he could appoint him to any office at court, that he could decorate him with any imperial award he would choose, but he could not make him a master cabinet maker in Brünn (a small provincial city in Moravia).

Industrialization made rapid strides in Central Europe during the second half of the nineteenth century. In Germany Bishop Ketteler's influence turned Catholic social thought definitely toward *Sozialpolitik*. In Austria, on the other hand, the social question received quite different treatment. As late as 1868 the Austrian minister of the interior, Giskra, the German Liberal, told a deputation of industrial workers: "There is no social question in Austria; as far as we are concerned the social question stops at Bodenbach [Austria's westernmost city]."[65] This sentiment was shared by the Catholic Conservatives as well. The col-

[63] Jostock, *op.cit.*, pp. 22-23.
[64] Kluckhohn, *op.cit.*, p. 74.
[65] Brügel, *op.cit.*, p. 58.

lapse of Austria's first boom in 1873 produced the first demands for social reforms. Two years after that collapse Vogelsang accepted the editorship of *Vaterland* and his writings on the social question only served to confirm Austrian Catholics in their *Sozialreform* bias.

Vogelsang considered the social question to be ". . . not merely a problem of income distribution, but [one which] affects all sectors of life, the religious-moral, the political, the economic, and the cooperative aspects of our existence."[66] He argued that the evil consequences of liberal policies had been so widespread that only radical reforms, corporative reorganization of economic activity, and strict state control would provide effective relief. This pronounced *étatisme* brought Vogelsang into conflict with liberal Catholics who wanted to limit the powers of the state in social and economic affairs. He condemned this liberal view and reaffirmed Müller's definition of the state as embracing all fields of human endeavor: "Many want to deny the state, or rather the secular authority, the right to deal with the most pressing problem of our day. They expect the free will of individuals to be a sufficient force. . . . For the rest, they are satisfied to let the free play of economic forces regulate matters . . . which means in reality that those who are economically strong can impose their will on all others. The antithesis of this liberal Catholic view is the one which, like Müller, defines the state as '. . . a seamless web of the total physical and spiritual needs . . . fashioned into a great, energetic, endlessly moving, and active whole.' The state in this view, is not only the community of the living generations . . . but also includes those who resided in the same area in the past and will reside there in the future."[67] He noted that liberal Catholicism was strongest in France and Belgium, the very countries where the spirit of 1789 had penetrated further than anywhere else in Europe.

It would be utter hypocrisy, it seemed to Vogelsang, to console the victims of social decay with promises of help through prayer and voluntary charity: "It would truly be a mockery to turn a deaf ear to the distress call of humanity sinking into the morass of capitalism; to repulse those willing to help by raising

---

[66] Vogelsang, *Lehren*, p. 180; see also *ibid.*, p. 208.
[67] *Ibid.*, pp. 211, 212.

the question of jurisdictional lines [between church and state], and to keep referring the drowning masses until kingdom come, exclusively to salvation by the spiritual powers of the Church."[68] This ferocious attack serves to remind us how difficult it is to distinguish socialist and Romantic attacks on the liberal state and the liberal economy, especially in the writings of Vogelsang, who was profoundly influenced by the German *Kathedersozialisten*, Rodbertus, Wagner, and Schäffle. But Vogelsang's critique of liberalism and capitalism served more than purely intellectual purposes. He also wanted to convince the industrial proletariat that socialism was not the only effective opponent of capitalism, that is to say, he hoped to win back the industrial workers who had left the church because they identified it with the established economic and social order.

Vogelsang held liberal concepts of equality and freedom responsible for the social evils of industrialism and capitalism: "It is the fundamental error of liberalism to base itself on the equality of all men, while closing its eyes arbitrarily to the natural inequalities that exist."[69] In the pursuit of this equalitarian chimera liberalism had destroyed the only true form of freedom: "The causes of this world-shaking revolt must be sought in the process of decay, in the souls of men, of the great principle of objectivity, of natural law, and of Christianity. The Declaration of the Rights of Man which raised the principle of subjectivity to be the dominant principle of modern society was followed by the law which dissolved all guilds, trade associations, etc., and proclaimed freedom of labor. This was the shallow, subjectivist freedom of labor which brought about separation of ownership and labor, which subjugated labor to the power of capital, and which, by degrading, demoralizing and proletarianizing labor, made it ripe for revolution. We know, however, that *true freedom* consists in the right and the possibility to make our lives conform to the divine moral law."[70]

In a state governed properly by "divine moral law" there could be no unlimited freedom, no conflict between the freedom of the individual and the needs of the state: "The state which

[68] *Ibid.*, p. 266.
[69] *Ibid.*, p. 69.
[70] *Ibid.*, p. 81 (italics added).

is ordered according to the rules of natural and revealed law, is the very postulate of freedom."[71]

There were at least three evil consequences which Vogelsang perceived to be flowing from these false concepts of equality and freedom. First, women and children were now working at the same tasks as men. This tended to destroy not only the unity of the family, a basic social organism, but also the differentiation of functions which is an essential element of any healthy social order: "The Christian Middle Ages were able to realize in an eminently ingenious manner the social principle of differentiation of national functions. It is this principle to which we owe, in a considerable measure, the great cultural flowering in the West."[72] Next, the destruction of the intermediate social organs had led to the elimination of socially binding rules governing wages, working conditions, hours of work, etc. The occupational corporations simply were no longer able to protect the interests of their members. Finally, the capitalists and entrepreneurs who had amassed economic power were freed from all restrictions on their economic activity—and used this freedom against economically weak groups, chiefly workers.

By disparaging religion and the established social order, liberalism had contributed to the rise of materialism, class warfare, and the destruction of the organic social order: ". . . this is not really a society, but a herd, a crowd, and, if we look at the matter properly, a mob [Pöbelhaufe]. . . . This disintegration of the natural, historic human organization is what characterizes the mob. . . . To the extent that most modern peoples have dissolved their traditional organizations, instead of assuring their continued development, they have been transformed into mobs."[73] No wonder that people came to believe that the established political, economic, and social order was directed against them: "The ruling capitalist system has reduced to a proletarian level the vast majority of our people, from the day laborer to the middle-level civil servant. This proletariat has only utter contempt for the isolated, timid, and sporadic attempts at social reform. The legal order of our states and the achievements of liberalism, once greatly admired, appear to be the mortal enemy of the proletariat . . . which is equally contemptuous of the whole re-

71 *Ibid.*, p. 79.   72 *Ibid.*, p. 71.   73 *Ibid.*, pp. 167-168.

ligious and moral tradition and world view."[74] Urban living conditions contributed to this feeling of utter despair, and cheap liquor and the Jewish press completed the process of degradation: "Gin and the Jew press, that is to say drunken stupor and obscenities, manage to kill the remaining memories of a Christian past in these unfortunate victims."[75]

Vogelsang also directed his attacks against the system of Roman law, which, he claimed, had intensified the evil effects of liberalism on social and economic organization: "It is essentially the legal system of a slave state and has no conception of the honorable place work should occupy in society. It is the perfect expression of a bare and shallow materialism."[76] This legal system had favored money at the expense of real property and at the expense of those earning their keep by honest toil. In this way Roman law exposed the owner of land and the manual worker to the evils of "free competition" and of a money economy, and fostered the growth of finance capitalism.

To overcome the evils of liberalism Vogelsang proposed a complete reorganization along corporative lines not only of economic activity, but of all segments of life: "Certain Catholic quarters have taken the position that the social question is entirely an economic problem [Magenfrage]. We reject this view emphatically because we are convinced that there is no better way to go astray in regard to this grave problem than to consider it a purely economic one."[77] The institutions which would serve as models for this reconstruction he found in the social order of the Middle Ages: "The basic principle of the feudal order is the full solidarity of all citizens, the congruence of economic, social, and political positions, the clear definition of national tasks, and a corresponding differentiation of political and social positions. Obligation to work is strictly enforced on all those who want to share in a social product which is distributed to each according to his contribution. There is no unrestricted private ownership of the means of production (as in Roman law), but merely use of the property for productive purposes. Finally, social protection is afforded all estates and individuals

74 *Ibid.*, p. 152.
75 *Ibid.*, p. 153.
76 *Ibid.*, p. 108.
77 *Ibid.*, p. 180.

against the danger of degradation to the level of a fourth estate, the proletariat, which works but does not own."[78] Vogelsang obviously was not concerned with the historical accuracy of this analysis of feudalism; to him feudalism became a utopian scheme which he hoped would prove attractive to peasants and the petty bourgeoisie, the groups closest to the hearts of Catholic social reformers.

The organization of society into *Stände* (estates or corporations) and the institution of *Lehen* (feudal tenure, fief) were the chief elements in Vogelsang's scheme of corporative reconstruction. Accordingly, individuals could never own property outright, but would be entitled to its use and would be obliged to render services to society in return. The organization of society into *Stände* would aid in carrying out state functions: "Bureaucratic routine services will become superfluous if all the estates will repay the state and the society for the use of the national means of production by assisting free of charge in the autonomous administration of the reconstituted territorial and social organs."[79] It is difficult to square this predicted "withering away" of the centralized bureaucracy with Vogelsang's preference for state intervention to curb and eventually eliminate the evils of unrestricted economic activity. By proposing that the state control internal, as well as international economic activity, Vogelsang returned in effect to the closed state of the Romanticists: "Some might call this an insufferable form of state socialism. One can take this position only if one considers normal and permanent what is really a pathological relationship between state and society. At present the omnicompetent bureaucratic state has managed to destroy society and to usurp its legal powers and functions. But conditions will be quite different when a reorganized society assumes again these legal powers and functions and thereby makes it possible for the state to take on, at least in part, new legal duties."[80] Though he denied that the state could ever be a substitute for the autonomous self-governing community operating through a multitude of corporative organs, he immediately proposed to turn these very corporative organs into obedient tools of an all-powerful state.

[78] *Ibid.*   [79] *Ibid.*, p. 189.   [80] *Ibid.*, p. 201.

Society would be organized into nine *Berufsstände* (occupational estates) which, in spite of their name, were not really occupational groups, but a combination of political, social, and economic organs which lacked any common characteristics.[81] These nine were: the royal estate, peasant estate, artisan estate, the estate of those engaged in large-scale industry, commercial estate, warrior estate, nobility, clerical estate, and estate of civil servants. He was extremely vague about details of this comprehensive scheme of social reconstruction, but centered his attention on three of these groups: peasants, artisans, and those in industrial production because these three had suffered most severely from the depredations of liberalism and capitalism.

Vogelsang was concerned with the conditions of the peasantry because of the destructive effects on them of the money economy and of international trade. It was imperative to isolate agriculture from the operations of the market, to reduce, if not altogether eliminate, the mobility of landed property. This could be best achieved by limiting the amounts of mortgages on agricultural property, by making entail inviolable, by banning foreclosure of peasant property, and by fixing low legal interest rates for loans and mortgages on peasant holdings. In addition, there should be created a peasant chamber which would exercise far-reaching controls over money and credit affecting agriculture.

The program for the reconstruction of the artisan estate was formulated by Vogelsang at a series of international conferences of Catholic social theorists held at Haid in Bohemia, and was part of the so-called *Haider Thesen*.[82] The reconstruction of the artisan estate, weakened decisively by the invention of the steam engine and the passage of *Loi le Chapelier*, he considered an essential stage in social reform, not because of the direct advantages it might bring to artisans, but because it would put an end to the separation of labor and capital which already had so gravely affected society as a whole. The first step in this reform would be restricting the economic area of the state, that is to say, reducing the size of the market supplied by the nation's econ-

---

[81] *Ibid.*, p. 119.

[82] *Ibid.*, pp. 294-299; see also Kralik, *op.cit.*, pp. 12-14. Most of the "theses" of these conferences are reprinted in August M. Knoll, *Der soziale Gedanke im modernen Katholizismus*, vol. I: *Von der Romantik bis Rerum Novarum* (Vienna: Reinhold Verlag, 1932), pp. 112-114, 120ff.

omy. As the market began to shrink, factory methods would become unprofitable, and handicraft methods would gain ground. Next, Vogelsang urged the creation of compulsory guilds, composed of masters, journeymen, and apprentices, who would control the economic and social conditions of their craft. In addition, the state would create favorable economic conditions for the guilds, by exercising strict controls over patents, trade marks, and copyright, by eliminating unauthorized traders and producers, and, above all, by granting the guild a legal monopoly for the sale of its products.

Finally, Vogelsang dealt with the condition of the industrial workers. He rejected the idea of placing all industrial workers into an *Arbeiterstand*: "What is often called a workers' estate is not an estate at all, but a proletarian precipitate which is the result of the decomposition of all the other estates."[83] This "social precipitate" at the bottom of society could not be removed by mechanical methods; it could be reabsorbed into society only if the workers became members of an estate which was an integral part of society, such as Vogelsang's proposed "estate of those engaged in large-scale industry." There would be at least three types of workers in this *Stand*: (1) highly qualified permanent members of an industrial enterprise; (2) qualified workers who would eventually move up into category one; and (3) casual employees without special qualifications.[84] This corporative organization of industry would also aid in solving the wage problem, by assuring the worker not only a "family wage," which Vogelsang considered a fraud, but the full share of the value created by the worker in the productive process.

This defense of the labor theory of value not only reveals deep-seated inconsistencies in the Vogelsang corpus of reform proposals, but points to an unavoidable clash between it and papal social theories, especially those developed in the major encyclicals by Leo XIII and Pius XI. There are some passages in which Vogelsang rejected the modern system of finance, especially the role of interest in that system, and condemned any form of income not derived from labor. But there are other passages in which he recognized that capital had at least an

[83] Vogelsang, *Lehren*, p. 314, note 2.
[84] *Ibid.*, p. 324.

equal claim with labor on the economic product. It must be understood that most of Vogelsang's writings were scattered in newspapers, magazines, and pamphlets. His son-in-law, Wiard von Klopp, who has attempted to systematize Vogelsang's ideas, has most certainly done violence to his father-in-law's position on the question of interest and the labor theory of value, though he is recognized as having been fair and accurate about the remainder of his father-in-law's ideas.[85] In the revised second edition of *Die sozialen Lehren*, published in 1938, Klopp tried to prove that Vogelsang's social theories did not conflict with papal doctrine as expressed in *Quadragesimo anno*. Actually, it was Vogelsang and his disciples whom the Pontiff had in mind when he attacked "intellectuals" who claimed that "all products and profits, excepting those required to repair and replace invested capital, belong by every right to the workman," and rejected the theory that "seeks to abolish all forms of ownership and all profits not obtained by labor."[86] Klopp tried to meet this difficulty by asserting that Vogelsang had made some statements which could be interpreted as an acceptance of the labor theory of value, but that it would be a misinterpretation of Vogelsang's general position on wages and interest to classify him as one of the extremist theorists condemned in the encyclical.[87] Klopp's contention is untenable. The whole tenor of Vogelsang's critique is anti-capitalist in the extreme and doubtful passages must be interpreted to favor more radical formulas, like the labor theory of value, rather than less radical ones.

Vogelsang's social and economic doctrines which exercised as profound an influence over Austrian Catholics as did his political ideas had a dual effect: they confirmed Austrian Catholics in their preference for *Sozialreform* solutions; they also produced immediate results in legislation under the Taaffe government in the 1880's. Prince Alois von Lichtenstein provided the legislative leadership for this program, which included

[85] *Ibid.*, pp. 345-429. The last section of the book, devoted to Vogelsang's economic theories, is the most unsatisfactory part of the work. It consists of a few snippets of Vogelsang and long interpolations by Klopp.

[86] *Quadragesimo anno*, sections 55 and 57, p. 141, as found in *Five Great Encyclicals* (New York: The Paulist Press, 1939). A full analysis of this important papal document can be found in Ch. v, below.

[87] See Vogelsang, *Lehren*, pp. 382ff.

accident and sickness insurance for workers, and a *Gewerbeord-nung* which sought to protect the artisans and small shopkeepers from the effects of price cutting, unfair competition, and mass production.[88] Most of these measures aided the artisan rather than the worker, and thereby offer additional evidence that the *Sozialreform* proponents who professed such great concern for the industrial worker produced neither the social program nor practical results in legislation which would have been attractive to the workers. When Austrian Catholics turned again to *Sozial-reform* ideas in the 1930's they behaved exactly like their prede-cessors fifty years earlier: they proclaimed as their goal the re-construction of society and the uplifting of the proletariat, but merely created a petty authoritarian state which oppressed the very workers it pretended to raise up.[89]

(c) *The Rise of Sozialpolitik.* The death of Vogelsang in 1890, and the publication of *Rerum novarum* in the following year, brought about a pronounced decline of *Sozialreform* in Austria. The intellectual leadership of Catholic social theorists passed to Franz M. Schindler, who was the mentor of Ignaz Seipel and his predecessor in the post of professor of moral theology at the University of Vienna. In 1905, while Schindler still considered the radical reconstruction of society the primary concern of Catholic social theory, he was compelled to admit that the greater freedom enjoyed under the social and economic system of his own day was clearly preferable to the restrictive institu-tions of past eras: "The precision with which he defines this ulti-mate goal does not prevent him from taking a realistic position on current questions of economic and social policy. His views, though moderate, are stated clearly and firmly. . . . With admir-able clarity Schindler defines the general welfare [*Gemeinwohl*] as the supreme goal of social science and social policy. He is never satisfied merely to spin intriguing utopian schemes, but goes resolutely to the heart of current problems."[90] Others like him, such as Josef Biederlack and Aemilian Schöpfer, also clung

[88] Brügel, *op.cit.*, pp. 110-111, 143, 151, 224, and passim; Jostock, *op.cit.*, pp. 210-221.

[89] Knoll, "Karl von Vogelsang und der Ständegedanke," pp. 67-69.

[90] Jostock, *op.cit.*, p. 43. A recent work on Schindler's role in the development of the social question is Friedrich Funder, *Aufbruch zur Sozialreform* (Vienna: Herold, 1953). See also Josef M. Schindler, "Das Kapitalzinsproblem," *Die Kultur* V (1902-1903), pp. 594-610.

to these Romantic goals; but like him they emphasized the need for making gradual changes to achieve immediate results, and rejected the grandiose reform plans of a Vogelsang.

Part of the credit for the Austrian turn toward *Sozialpolitik* must go to German Catholics and their wholehearted acceptance of that tendency. The *Volksverein*, founded in München-Gladbach in the year of Vogelsang's death, and its moving spirit Franz Hitze worked ceaselessly to fit German Catholics into the social and economic system of Wilhelminian Germany. München-Gladbach became synonymous with Catholic accommodation to capitalism and the modern state. The skill of political leaders like Georg von Hertling and Matthias Erzberger facilitated that accommodation by creating an effective political party which could speak for Catholicism in the political arena. These, then, were the models that inspired *Sozialpolitik* proponents in Austria.

Though *Sozialreform* declined sharply after 1890, the successors of Vogelsang continued the Romantic doctrines of their master. As a result, by 1918 Austrian Catholics subscribed to a variety of social theories ranging from the extreme social Romanticism of Vogelsang and his successors to the *Sozialpolitik* tendencies represented by Schindler.

3. Critique and Conspectus of Austrian Catholic Thought

By 1918, the essential elements of Austrian Catholic social thought had been fully developed, and the foundation laid for Catholic criticism of democracy and capitalism during the ensuing period. It now becomes appropriate, therefore, to examine some of the assumptions underlying that body of ideas and to determine to what extent Austrian Catholics clearly perceived the implications of their reform proposals for the modern state and the modern economy. This examination will make it possible to criticize Catholic doctrines formulated during the nineteenth century and to establish some guides for the understanding of their development in the twentieth. Subsequent chapters will show that the strength of Austrian Catholic thought during this latter period, its incisive criticism of liberalism and capitalism, as well as its weakness, the reactionary and impractical nature of its reform proposals, resulted from the influence of the ideas of the earlier era.

In spite of the considerable differences among Austrian Catholic thinkers, the critique and conspectus which follow deal with Austrian Catholic thought as a whole. Both critique and conspectus probably reflect more accurately *Sozialreform* rather than *Sozialpolitik* tendencies. This can be justified on the ground that during the nineteenth century the former was definitely the predominant doctrine, and that during the republican period Romantic ideas, after a temporary eclipse, returned triumphantly to form the basis for the Corporative Constitution of 1934.

The substance of Austrian Catholic thought during the nineteenth century can be expressed in four propositions. (1) Austrian Catholic theorists were deeply concerned with the individual and his physical and spiritual well-being. Catholic theology commanded them to place the individual and his immortal soul at the center of their attention, so that they could aid him in fulfilling his earthly, and ultimately his transcendent, mission. (2) Catholic social theory based on the natural-law tradition of the Scholastics called for a rich group life so that society could express itself through a multitude of social organs. (3) Austrian Catholics considered the state an important, but not the only, social organ which corresponded to man's natural needs on earth. Therefore, they wanted to reduce the bureaucratization and centralization of the modern state and return many of the functions it had usurped, during the period of absolutism, to the proper social organs, such as vocational groups, families, local communities. (4) They desired to create political and social institutions which would recognize the rich variety of individual and group experiences and would respect the important distinction between domestic society and civil society, the state. Much of Austrian Catholic thought after 1918 followed this broad outline, for the main tendencies of Catholic doctrine continued without interruption into the republican era.

The examination of nineteenth-century Catholic thought in the present chapter leads to the conclusion, which will receive additional support from the analysis of the subsequent period, that Austrian Catholics failed to devise political and social institutions which correctly expressed their basic propositions. Instead of providing for the undisturbed development of a multitude of social organs and for a reasonably clear distinction between state and society, Austrian Catholics continuously exalted the state at the expense of other social organs. This can be traced primarily to their concept of state and law as instruments for the enforcement of moral and ethical standards. A state which claims the right to enforce such standards inevitably will destroy, if not seriously weaken, the area of society, the area of the voluntary.[91] Austrian Catholics might have recognized theoretically the right of a variety of social organs to apply these moral and ethical standards, derived from theology and natural law, but they drew on a long *étatiste* tradition which predisposed them to appeal to the state and use the state for the enforcement of such standards.

Their concept of law and state as agencies for the enforcement of moral and ethical principles had important consequences for state, society, and economy. At this point it is possible to indicate only a few. The most important of these is the subjection of the economic sector of life to state control on the ground that the state must enforce the observance of moral standards in economic activity. But if the state in this manner claims control over the economic as well as all other aspects of social activity there will be a great amount of "congestion" at the center, that is to say, the state will need a huge bureaucratic machinery to supervise all these activities. As a result, the area of genuine voluntary activity will be minute. Furthermore Austrian Catholics who praise the state for taking unto itself all these concerns for the welfare of the individual and castigate the *laissez-faire* state for abandoning the poor and the weak, find it difficult to admit that on balance the individual might be worse off in their system simply because the state cannot fulfill all the tasks assigned it. There is still another reason why the individual is worse off under the political and social arrangements devised

[91] Sir Ernest Barker points out that it is not the business of law or any legal authority to control the inner life. Their business is merely to secure the external conditions of a process which is independent of law or legal authority. He notes the paradox that the only true way to connect law and ethics is to distinguish clearly their province; *Principles of Social and Political Theory* (London: Oxford University Press, 1951), pp. 121-122.

by Austrian Catholics. Devotion to a strong monarchy had predisposed Austrian Catholics to grant all powers of the state to the Emperor; yet they had never established any institutional safeguards to insure that such authority should be exercised in the interest of those individuals and groups on whose behalf the very grant had primarily been made.

Austrian Catholics also made the state supreme by their failure to distinguish clearly between voluntary social organizations and social groups acting as agents of the state. They could hardly conceive of a voluntary social organization which would act without any direction or grant of compulsory power from the state.[92] As a result, what they chose to call social organs were actually state instrumentalities, clothed with compulsory power by the state and made subject to state supervision. Finally, they exalted the state because they failed to provide for a genuine expression of the wide variety of talents, functions, and purposes of individuals and groups. They protested repeatedly that the guiding principle of their social theory was *suum cuique*—full possibility for the individual to achieve his purpose in society. It might be fruitful to compare their social theory and that of the British democratic tradition as Ernest Barker analyzed it. Both profess to base their system on that same principle— *suum cuique*. Barker contends that the only way to assure the individual such freedom of development is through a set of rules of general applicability ". . . a mode of treating things in general, things of all sorts and descriptions."[93] Austrian Catholics, on the other hand, insisted that such a system of law and individual rights would destroy all individual differences and create a society of isolated and uniform "atoms." In its place they proposed to put a highly developed hierarchical order which would supposedly provide an appropriate niche for the qualities, desires, wishes, etc. of every individual or group. They refused to see that such a system would quickly lead to anarchy unless held together by a strong central power. In this manner,

---

[92] Barker warns that the distinction between the method of the state—compulsion—and the method of society—voluntary action—"if true in the main is not always true." At times the state has voluntary aspects and social organs may assume coercive power. But this is a far cry from the attitudes of most Austrian Catholic social thinkers, who seemed to be unable to conceive of a truly voluntary social organ. Barker, *op.cit.*, pp. 43-44.

[93] *Ibid.*, p. 45.

they again strengthened the state at the expense of individuals and social groups.

Even a cursory examination of either an actual society organized on the basis of their social theories, or of the historical situation whose idealized image they used for their social theorizing, proves that their ideas worked out in the manner sketched above. Austrian Catholics saw the Middle Ages only as an era of group life; they rarely alluded to the social and political anarchy which was an inevitable result of this group system. Central European society never grew around the state in the manner familiar to Barker.[94] There was no body like the British Parliament which could speak for society and resist encroachments of the state. Central Europe for a long time also lacked the social leadership of the city dwellers. The continental cities were not really a part of a homogeneous society, for they were often independent city-states which had no ties to the people of the region in which they were located. Collaboration between the representatives of the cities and those of the landed gentry, the hallmark of the British Parliament from its inception, was not established until late in the nineteenth century. Finally, Central Europe lacked the leaven of non-conformity, the leaven of free religion and free trade. As a result, Austrian Catholics consistently deprecated economic activity and, in modern times, created a social theory which was fundamentally anti-capitalist and anti-industrialist.[95]

This critique of nineteenth-century Austrian Catholic thought, and conspectus of twentieth, suggests four conclusions: (1) Austrian Catholics lacked a genuine understanding of the distinction between the state as the area of compulsory and society as the area of voluntary action. As a result of this they were unable to foresee clearly the dangerous consequences for individual and group autonomy which would result from this lack. (2) This failure led them to erect a monistic system in place of the Thom-

[94] "The general process . . . was a process by which Society grew around the State—surrounded it, indeed, with growth—and yet left it as the hard core and legal substance of organization, affecting all the growths and affected by all the growths, in a constant interaction." Barker, *op.cit.*, p. 29.

[95] Everyone commenting today on the contrast between Protestant and Catholic views on capitalism and industrialization is, of course, indebted to R. H. Tawney, *Religion and the Rise of Capitalism; a Historical Study* (London: J. Murray, 1926).

ist pluralist scheme which they professed to have accepted. They elevated the state to a supreme position and subordinated all other social bodies to it.[96] (3) They were, therefore, caught in a dilemma. They had to profess a preference for a limited state which would recognize the autonomy of the church and of other social organs while their own social theory and their historical experience inclined them toward a strongly authoritarian, if not totalitarian, state. (4) Finally, their inability to conceive of a genuine state-society dichotomy explains their failure to understand the nature of democratic government and the role of political parties. In a nation in which state and society are one, there is no need for political parties which are primarily channels through which ideas and programs flow from society to the state. In such a nation there is also little chance for democratic government whose basis is discussion. For if there is no separate sphere of society in which a multitude of ideas can be developed, discussed, and then channeled into the state, there can be no democratic government. Where the state serves to enforce moral and ethical standards, the one *true* set of standards, there can be no discussion of possible alternatives.

It might be well to point out that the last of these conclusions will be particularly helpful in illuminating the Catholic criticism of democracy analyzed in Chapter iv. The other three should be kept in mind for the criticism of capitalism in Chapters v and vi. All of them will aid in understanding, in Chapter vii, the Corporative Constitution of 1934, the culmination of Catholic social criticism and theorizing.

[96] J. D. Mabbott suggested that there are four possible views of the relations between the state and other associations: Abstract Monism, Concrete Monism, Pluralism, and a fourth theory which can find no special functions for the state. Abstract Monism regards the existence of associations within the state as a sign that the state is lacking in unity and proposes to suppress all these associations. Concrete Monism admits the value of functional associations, but regards them as part of the state; as a result there will be complete state control in such a system. This scheme makes it possible to classify Austrian Catholic social thought as pluralistic in theory, but a "concrete monism" in practice. *The State and the Citizen; an Introduction to Political Philosophy* (London: Hutchinson's University Library, 1947), pp. 112-113, 119-123.

CHAPTER III

THE CRITICISM OF DEMOCRACY: POLITICAL
AND SOCIAL BASES

BEFORE 1918, Austrian Catholics were deeply divided over the social question. Many subscribed to Vogelsang's Romantic doctrine of social monarchy, while others like Ignaz Seipel and Franz M. Schindler advanced more liberal political and social reform proposals. But in spite of these differences they displayed a remarkable unity on the question of regime: they remained loyal defenders of monarchical government and supporters of the Hapsburg Dynasty.

The violent upheavals in Central Europe which resulted from the First World War had opened the way for what Catholics called the modern state of 1789 which had developed in the Western world during the nineteenth century. Austrian Catholics, helpless in this democratic flood, felt compelled to accept the political institutions created during this period of extreme radicalism. But they were critical of postwar democracy from the beginning. They agitated, at first, for its modification; later on they openly urged that it be abolished and replaced with political institutions inspired by Catholic social theory.

Austrian Catholic criticism of democracy during the period 1918-1934 was characterized by a great diversity of views which was the result of a variety of historical factors which have been discussed previously.[1] It is proposed to examine in the present chapter those Austrian political and social developments after 1918 which influenced that body of criticism. The next chapter will then be devoted to an analysis of the spectrum of criticism.

1. Austrian Catholics and the Criticism
of Democracy

At the end of the First World War Austrian Catholics were seriously concerned with two sets of problems: those raised by

[1] See above, Ch. I, section 4, for a discussion of the elements of diversity in Catholic thought.

the establishment of a republican regime, and those raised by the collapse of social and economic institutions. Catholics feared that the establishment of a republic would threaten the preferred and protected position the church had enjoyed during the monarchy and would accelerate the infiltration of liberal and socialist ideas into Austrian life. They were further disturbed by the demands for far-reaching social and economic reforms which had been generated by defeat in war, economic collapse, and the Wilsonian program of democracy and self-determination of nations.

Before 1918, Catholics had never been faced with a question of regime. They had been unable to resist the establishment of a neutral state in 1867, but after the tide of liberalism had begun to recede, Catholic Conservative governments, backed by the Emperor and the nobility, had nullified many of the liberal reforms by administrative action.[2] Francis Joseph I had consented to the cancellation of the Concordat of 1855, but continued to act as a loyal son of the church. Ministers and civil servants were given to understand that the dynasty considered its functions as the foremost patron of the church not a task to be carried out perfunctorily, but a duty of the highest order. In a social sense, therefore, Austria remained a Catholic state until 1918.[3] It is not surprising that faithful Catholics feared the establishment of a republic would deprive the church of its strongest protection.

Catholics also opposed the creation of a republic because they were afraid it would hasten the infiltration of liberal and socialist ideas. Even before 1918 large parts of the bourgeoisie had accepted liberal ideas, and an overwhelming majority of the workers had espoused socialism, which Catholics considered an inevitable consequence of liberal domination. Under a republic the influence of this bourgeois liberalism and proletarian socialism would increase and Austrian life would become completely secularized. As a result of this, the importance of the church and of religious ideas would decline even more rapidly than it had before 1918.

[2] Alois Hudal, "Der Katholizismus in Österreich. Sein Wirken, Kämpfen und Hoffen," *Katholizismus in Österreich*, pp. 18-20.

[3] Max Freiherr Hussarek von Heinlein, "Die kirchenpolitische Gesetzgebung der Republik Österreich," *Katholizismus in Österreich*, p. 28.

Catholics were further disturbed by the demands for far-reaching changes, generated by defeat in war, economic collapse, and the Wilsonian program, which threatened to destroy existing institutions. The demands for internal political changes within existing states and the clamor of the suppressed nationalities for the creation of new states merged with a social and economic revolution against established privileged groups. There was a tendency to justify all these reform demands in the name of democracy and to call undemocratic those who defended the *status quo*. The demands for democratic changes came chiefly from the opponents of political and social Catholicism. Consequently, where these changes were carried out they were the work of anti-Catholic forces and were influenced by liberal and socialist ideas. Catholics, therefore, opposed "democracy"—political, social, or economic—because they associated it with these attacks on existing institutions and proposals for change.

The economic collapse following the end of the war hurt most severely those social groups which had supported the church and accepted the Catholic social program, that is to say, the peasants and the middle class, artisans and shopkeepers, white-collar workers, and professional men. The discontent of these social groups was intensified by the improvement in the economic position of the workers. Finally, Catholics opposed the demand for self-determination of the non-German nationalities because it threatened the unity of the Empire. Catholics opposed all these demands as long as possible, but they were finally forced to accept most of them. As a result, they became extremely critical of the new institutions created by these political, social, and national revolutions. They condemned them as inspired by an evil set of ideas about state and society.

Catholic opposition to the new political forces and to the demands for republican institutions gave rise to a body of literature devoted to the criticism of democracy. This criticism was developed from Catholic social theory, whose general Catholic and specifically Austrian sources have been examined in Chapters I and II respectively. It was also influenced by political and economic developments in the Austrian Republic. The first of these was the division of the country into three major social groups and the position of these groups on the question of regime and social organization. Then there was the political struggle over the form and content of the 1920 constitution. Finally, the perennial rivalry between the three major groups as well as controversies within the Catholic camp itself also helped shape the Catholic attitude towards democracy and democratic institutions.

2. Austrian Society and the Three *Lager*

The political and social development of the Austrian Republic was dominated by the existence of three major groups which the Austrian historian, Adam Wandruszka, has called *Lager*.[4] Each *Lager* drew its support from specific social groups and each had a political organization which acted as the political representative of its interests. Each *Lager* also attempted to develop a *Weltanschauung*, and to foster social and ideological homogeneity among its followers. Thus it hoped to establish "totalitarian" control over its members and shape their entire lives. These three *Lager* were the Socialist, the Nationalist, and the Christian-social conservative (*christlichsozial-konservativ*).[5] Their origin can be traced to the national, social, and religious struggles of the Empire during the nineteenth century. The development of Austrian politics since 1945 gives proof of the persistence of the three-*Lager* pattern. The growth of National Socialism and the question of *Anschluss* upset the "normal" pattern in the early 1930's, but when Austrian politics returned to normal in 1945 the three *Lager* reemerged. The Socialist and Christian-social conservative camps again dominate the scene while a small Nationalist movement attempts to play the role of a balancer. However, the determination of the two large camps to avoid the mistakes of the First Republic has so far prevented the Nationalists from exercising a decisive influence over the distribution of political power as they had done between 1918 and 1934.

(a) The Socialist Lager. Of the three, the Socialist *Lager*, the camp of the industrial workers, most nearly attained homogene-

---

[4] Adam Wandruszka, "Österreichs politische Struktur. Die Entwicklung der Parteien und der politischen Bewegungen," *Geschichte der Republik Österreich*, Heinrich Benedikt, editor (Vienna: Verlag für Geschichte und Politik, 1954), pp. 289-485.

[5] *Ibid.*, pp. 291-292.

ity. Its political representative was the Social Democratic party. In addition, the so-called Free Trade Unions were so closely allied with the Social Democratic party organization that they were considered an integral part of the Socialist *Lager*. Through the Social Democratic party, the trade unions, and a host of other organizations the Socialist *Lager* had created a separate sphere of life for its members,[6] a separate universe in which the workers lived among fellow Socialists in municipal public housing units, read Socialist newspapers, and joined Socialist stamp collecting or pigeon fancying clubs. They enrolled their children in the Socialist youth organization, hiked through the Vienna woods with comrades from the Socialist *Naturfreunde*, and stayed overnight in mountain lodges maintained by Socialist Alpine Clubs. At work they belonged to a trade union whose principal leaders sat in parliament as Social Democrats. After their death they were cremated in a municipal crematorium operated by a Socialist city administration. This last act of their earthly career was also their ultimate gesture of defiance against a clerical bourgeois world. The Christian Social Government, urged by the church, had tried to stop the construction and operation of the crematorium ostensibly on technical, legal grounds. Actually, the Christian-social conservative camp opposed cremation on religious grounds and attempted in this way to enforce its *Weltanschauung* on a resisting proletariat.

The Austrian worker considered active membership in the Socialist *Lager* his way of protesting against the privileged position of the old nobility, the clergy, and the industrialists. This protest also found expression in an extremely militant ideology,

[6] "After 1918 the party had not only grown to be a mass organization of unique size and vigor but a spiritual power whose effects were lasting and profound. . . . Far beyond the realm of politics it shaped the lives and thoughts of its active members. . . . Its broad organizational structure had room for all trades and professions. It enabled all ages to organize their entertainment requirements, their educational plans, their purposes in life, their cultural desires, their hobbies, even their follies, and to fuse them 'ideologically' with the aims of the party in serious and ridiculous fashion. In this mass of hundreds of thousands, anyone capable of rising above the merely personal, found in the party a new meaning to his life. This fulfillment was as strong and as enduring as a religious tie." Joseph Buttinger, *In the Twilight of Socialism. A History of the Revolutionary Socialists of Austria* (New York: Frederick A. Praeger, 1953), pp. 20-22. Buttinger was one of the principal figures in the illegal Socialist movement between 1934 and 1938.

Austro-Marxismus,[7] a term which became synonymous in Europe with extreme left-wing Marxism. This ideology was given an especially radical formulation in the Social Democratic party's *Linz* program of 1926. The emphasis on a violent class struggle and the determination to seize power by force contained in the *Linz* program greatly exaggerated the doctrinaire Marxist tendencies of the Socialist *Lager.* Austrian Socialists never applied this doctrinaire Marxism,[8] but pursued instead a gradualist policy and were committed to change by peaceful means. Nevertheless, Austrian Catholics came to identify the Republic of 1918 with the Socialist *Lager* and considered Social Democracy its principal enemy.

The Socialist *Lager* drew its principal strength from the industrial workers in Vienna and the industrial centers in the provinces.[9] It also had a large following of intellectuals, especially Jewish intellectuals who found in it career opportunities as organizers, educators, and party theorists not open to Jewish intellectuals elsewhere.[10]

[7] In spite of his pro-Socialist bias, Gulick's chapter on Austro-Marxism is an excellent summary and critique. Charles A. Gulick, *Austria from Habsburg to Hitler,* vol. II: *Fascism's Subversion of Democracy* (Berkeley: University of California Press, 1948), ch. XXVII, "Theory and Practice of Austro-Marxism," pp. 1363-1400. Gulick showed that in spite of an appearance of violent Marxism the theories of Austrian Socialism were "dictated by their steadfast adherence to the principles of democracy and of intellectual and spiritual freedom . . . and by their deep sympathy with those who suffer and need help" (p. 1400).

[8] Anton Rintelen for many years *Land* governor of Styria and one of the more sinister figures in republican Austria admitted: "It was a miracle that Marxism did not sweep away all conservative obstacles in its march to total power. . . . Communism radicalized Social Democracy but was unable to carry it along all the way. In fact, on crucial issues Social Democracy resisted, and even opposed Communism actively." Rintelen, *Erinnerungen an Österreichs Weg. Versailles-Berchtesgaden-Grossdeutschland* (Munich: Verlag F. Bruckmann, 1941), p. 98. Rintelen was slated to be chancellor in the government to be installed after the assassination of Dollfuss in July 1934. The book is largely anti-Christian Social and anti-clerical and, therefore, more favorably disposed to anyone else who also might have been anti-clerical. Rintelen recalled that in 1919 at the height of what he called Communist riots in Graz only the support given to the regular police forces by the Socialist *Arbeiterhilfskorps* saved the day and broke the fury of the riots. *Ibid.,* p. 104.

[9] Rudolf Schlesinger, *Central European Democracy and its Background; Economic and Political Group Organization* (London: Routledge & Kegan Paul, Limited, 1953), pp. 178-179.

[10] Buttinger estimated that eighty percent of the intellectuals who joined the Socialist movement were Jewish and that there were secret arrangements by the party executive to insure an "Aryan" majority in the party's top echelons: "The Austrian worker's awe of mental achievement gave to many intellectual

(b) The Nationalist Lager. During the first decade of the Republic the Nationalist *Lager* was the weakest of the three. It was composed of anti-clerical middle-class groups in urban as well as rural areas. Under the influence of the social question and of the nationality struggles the German middle class of the Empire had split in two. Those who emphasized social and economic problems followed Lueger into the Christian-social conservative *Lager.* Those who were more concerned with threats to the national position of the Germans within the Empire followed Georg von Schönerer and his anti-clerical, Pan-German program. These anti-clerical nationalist groups formed the nucleus of the Nationalist *Lager* in 1918.

Two political parties represented the Nationalist *Lager* between 1918 and 1934. The *Grossdeutsche Volkspartei* drew its strength from urban middle-class groups, especially civil servants. In fact, defense of the civil servants and lobbying for civil service legislation consumed most of the energies of that party.[11] The *Landbund* represented a group of well-to-do anti-clerical peasants in Carinthia and Styria. In Carinthia the *Landbund* gained the support of East Prussian Protestant peasants who had fled from the East Prussian territories ceded to Poland after the war, and had taken over land vacated by Carinthian Slovenes who had been forced to return to Yugoslavia in 1918.[12] Both parties collaborated with the Christian Socials until 1934. In fact, their votes in Parliament were indispensable for an anti-socialist majority. The rise of the Nazi movement deprived

Jews the first and deepest happiness of their lives. This was their real escape from the loathsome Ghetto . . ." *op.cit.,* pp. 80-81. Even though Jewish intellectuals joined the Social Democratic party in large numbers, the Jewish members of high finance, big business, and industry did not share this radicalism and supported the *Heimwehr,* in spite of its open anti-Semitism, because it "protected" business and industry. Franz Borkenau, *Austria and After* (London: Faber and Faber, 1938), pp. 106-107.

[11] George Maria von Alexich, *A Study of the Political Parties in Austria, 1918-1938* (Georgetown University Ph.D. dissertation, 1948), pp. 218-226. Alexich was a member of the Austrian diplomatic service until 1938. The dissertation has an outspoken pro-Christian Social bias.

[12] *Ibid.,* pp. 227-229. In Styria the Landbund was fairly strong and Rintelen, who led the Christian Socials in that *Land,* complained that his party could fight the *Landbund* only with difficulty. The Christian Socials could not entirely neglect either rural-agricultural or urban-industrial interests while the *Landbund,* a purely agricultural interest group, could appeal to the peasants strictly on their own terms. Rintelen, *op.cit.,* p. 57.

these two parties of all their followers. Ultimately the Nazis drew a large number of middle and lower middle-class supporters into the Nationalist *Lager*.

(c) *The Christian-Social Conservative Lager.* The Christian-social conservative *Lager* centered around the church and those groups which accepted Catholic social theory: peasants and the urban petty bourgeoisie. It also received the support of financial and industrial leaders who sought to fashion a political instrument with which to destroy the powerful position of the workers. In this manner the Christian-social conservative *Lager* became the focal point of an anti-socialist alliance.

The lower middle class in the cities and on the farm comprised the principal support of the Christian-social conservative *Lager*. Artisans, shopkeepers, some white-collar workers, and above all the peasants constituted the social base of that *Lager*. The Christian Social party and a multitude of Catholic organizations, most of them closely supervised by the clergy, were the principal organizational weapons of the Christian-social conservative *Lager*.[13] Catholics considered this network of organizations indispensable in their struggle against bourgeois-liberal as well as socialist influences in Austrian life. They feared that the Socialists would be able to win over a majority of Austrians and establish a dictatorship of the proletariat on the Russian model —a fear which seemed well-founded in view of the extreme doctrinaire Marxian program proclaimed repeatedly by the Socialists. The Christian-social camp realized that it was engaged in a grim struggle: "The fight must be conducted along two fronts: in parliament among deputies, and outside parliament among the Austrian people. Therefore Catholicism must be prepared to do combat on both fronts. . . . Because Socialists have focused their energies on the task of obtaining a majority in the legislature, Catholic Action must do everything to create the sort of electorate which will choose a parliament where the Socialists' strength will be reduced and the enemies of religion will not have a majority.[14] Aemilian Schöpfer, a prelate of the Catholic

13 Aemilian Schöpfer, "Katholizismus und Politik," *Katholizismus in Österreich*, pp. 448-449. However, Alexich was of the opinion that the youth groups, for example, which had a highly complex organizational structure in parishes and dioceses, did not amount to very much, *op.cit.*, pp. 86-87.

14 Schöpfer, *op.cit.*, pp. 442-443.

Church and a leader of the Christian Social party in the Tyrol, reflected in that statement the commonly accepted assumption during the interwar period that a political movement which would gain a clear majority in the legislature would immediately proceed with a complete reshaping of the country's social, economic, and political institutions, in line with that party's *Weltanschauung*.

To counter the Socialist network of trade unions, youth organizations, hiking clubs, weight lifting and pigeon fancying societies, Catholics attempted to create a similar network of organizations in which the faithful would follow a Catholic pattern of life and a Catholic *Weltanschauung*, just as the Socialist *Lager* tried to create a Socialist world for its own people.

The Catholic camp could not match the homogeneity of its Socialist rival. Under the influence of industrialists and large land holders who traditionally play a prominent role in Austrian life, Christian Social governments pursued policies which did not always favor the small holders and the artisans, the Christian Social rank-and-file. Some of the provincial politicians, like Anton Rintelen, and Catholic trade union leaders like Leopold Kunschak, castigated their own party chieftains for their pro-big business bias.[15]

(d) The Three Lager and the Failure of Consensus. The failure of the major Austrian social groups to establish a consensus on fundamentals of political and social organization perpetuated the division of the country into three *Lager*. The major opponents in this struggle were the Socialist and the Catholic camps, with the Nationalists joining the Catholics in a bourgeois anti-Socialist alliance. In spite of this parliamentary alliance between two of the *Lager*, the three were divided on fundamen-

[15] Rintelen seems to be very bitter about the policies which favored industry at the expense of the peasants. One must remember, though, that Rintelen, in writing his memoirs, would tend to overemphasize the differences between him and the less nationalist and more strongly clerical views of those in Christian Social party headquarters in Vienna, *op.cit.*, pp. 48-51. Rintelen pointed out that before the First World War there had been no contact at all between the peasants, safely rooted in the Catholic conservative fold, and the nationalist bourgeoisie of the small and medium-sized towns of Austria. Men like Rintelen were largely responsible for assuming the leadership of part of the peasantry and also for alienating the peasants from the clerical leadership. They thereby prepared the way for the sweeping victories of National Socialism especially in Styria and Carinthia.

tal issues involving the social question, church-state relationships, and German nationalism. Austria, therefore, lacked what P. T. Lux, a Swiss, long-time resident of Austria, has called a "vital, unified, national idea."[16] Consequently, each *Lager* tried to become the center of all loyalties of its followers, and the struggle for the votes of the people turned into a struggle for their souls. Aemilian Schöpfer was correct when he insisted that ". . . the Socialist youth organizations and the freethinker societies were non-political means to a political end and had, therefore, tremendous political significance."[17] They were part of the network of organizations with which the Socialists tried to spread their theology to win new followers and maintain the loyalty of the faithful. Otto Bauer, the Socialist, on the other hand, considered the Catholic Church not simply a religious institution but the propaganda arm of the Socialists' principal opponent: "The clergy fanned the flame of peasant resentment against the workers. . . . They organized and strengthened the peasant movement as the most effective counterforce to the proletarian revolution. Newspapers and sermons reminded the peasants . . . that the revolution would socialize their property and destroy the Church."[18] C. A. Macartney, whose *The Social Revolution in Austria* is critical of the Social Democrats, wrote: "The Catholic Church of Austria is the real enemy of Socialism. She is the living representative of the old order. . . . She is the upholder of conservatism, loyalty, piety, respect and obedience. . . . Until her hold over the spirits of the people has been weakened, Socialism, the very reverse of all this, cannot move. The Catholic Church, too, was and is an active political force. . . . Therefore we find that even to this day the real battle of Austrian Socialism is directed against the Church. . . . For under these circumstances the Socialist maxim that 'religion is every man's private affair' is already a direct challenge, since Catholicism admits no neutrality."[19]

Ever since the days of the Josephinist reforms and of Schö-

[16] P. T. Lux, *Österreich 1918-1938. Eine Demokratie?* (Graz: Leykam Verlag, G.m.b.H., 1946), p. 76.

[17] Schöpfer, *op.cit.*, p. 441.

[18] Otto Bauer, *Die österreichische Revolution* (Vienna: Wiener Volksbuchhandlung, 1923), p. 124.

[19] C. A. Macartney, *The Social Revolution in Austria* (Cambridge: University Press, 1926), p. 54.

nerer's *Los von Rom* campaign, political struggles in Austria
have been religious rivalries, and religious rivalries have been
turned into political controversies. Under such conditions political parties become armed camps of religious crusaders, determined to drive the infidels from the field: "Parties which serve
as a shield for powerful private interests have a tendency to become totalitarian and to suppress all those who disagree with
them. This was especially true in Austria whose parties were
extremely doctrinaire and committed to definite ideologies. This
gave them the character of secular religions—and distinguished
them sharply from most Western parties which were held together not by an ideology but by common traditions or interests.
As a result, all parties in Austria, tended to identify their own
interest with that of the entire country."[20]

3. Austrian Catholics and the Constitution of 1920

(a) Catholic Loyalty to Monarchy and Dynasty. During the last
years of the Empire German-speaking Catholics and the Christian Social party were the only groups still loyal to the dynasty.
When the Christian Socials gained control of the Vienna city
administration and created an Empire-wide organization with
a strong delegation in the *Reichsrat*, the radicalism of its petty
bourgeois leaders and followers subsided. They were one of the
few groups in the *Reichsrat*, when it was recalled in 1917 after
a three-year recess, willing to support a government which had
the confidence of Charles I.[21] However no majority could be
found for a cabinet which the Emperor was willing to accept.
Early in 1918 the government resigned when it failed to get
Reichsrat approval for the budget.[22] Charles I refused to accept
the resignation and the *Reichspost*, the official Christian Social
newspaper, supported the Emperor against the majority in the
legislature. The editorial in the *Reichspost* seemed to indicate
that the Christian Socials as late as 1918 had little interest in
parliamentary government and could see no reason why a gov-

[20] Lux, *op.cit.*, p. 3.
[21] Viktor Bibl, *Der Zerfall Österreichs*, vol. II, *Von Revolution zu Revolution 1848-1918* (Vienna: Rikola Verlag, 1922-1924), pp. 520, 529.
[22] *Neue Freie Presse*, February 8, 1918.

ernment which had the support of the Emperor should have to yield to a legislative majority.[23]

Because of Christian Social loyalty to the dynasty, Charles I relied heavily on Christian Social politicians and faithful Catholics outside the party organization for his last governments. Among the last prime ministers of the Empire were two Catholic university professors with close ties to the church, Max Hussarek von Heinlein, professor of canon law, and Heinrich Lammasch, professor of international law, and a member of the extreme conservative wing of the nobility, Count Clam-Martinitz.[24] In the Lammasch cabinet, Ignaz Seipel held his first government position as minister of social welfare.[25] These intimate connections with the government of the Empire deeply influenced the position of the Christian Social party, and of Catholics in general, on the question of regime.

When the Empire disintegrated and all parties and groups demanded the establishment of a republic and the democratization of all segments of public life, Catholics were not prepared to go beyond a change to a constitutional monarchy. After Charles I had published the federation manifesto in October 1918, the Christian Social group in the *Reichsrat* issued this declaration: "While *maintaining their fundamental loyalty to the monarchical form of government*, the Christian Social deputies will work for the *democratization of Deutschösterreich. They propose that this democratization take the form of popular participation in legislation and administration."[26] The left wing of the Catholic camp, the Catholic workers' organizations, also affirmed their continued support of the monarchy during these last days of October 1918: "The Catholic workers demand for *Deutschösterreich* a monarchy resting on a broad popular basis."[27] Even after 1918 Catholics and the Christian Social party

[23] *Reichspost*, February 8, 1918; see also Brita Skottsberg, *Der österreichische Parlamentarismus* (Goeteborg: Elanders Boktrycheri Aktiebolaget, 1940), pp. 132-133.

[24] Skottsberg, *op.cit.*, p. 127.

[25] Rudolf Blüml, *Prälat Dr. Ignaz Seipel. Ein grosses Leben in kleinen Bildern* (Klagenfurt: Im Verlag der St. Josefs-Bücherbrüderschaft, 1933), pp. 132-133.

[26] Provisorische Nationalversammlung Deutschösterreichs, *Stenographische Protokolle*, 1918-19, p. 8, cited in Skottsberg, *op.cit.*, p. 147.

[27] Leopold Kunschak, *Österreich 1918-1934* (Vienna: Typographische Anstalt, 1934), p. 41. Leopold Kunschak, who was a saddler journeyman, joined the

continued to support the legitimist claims of the Hapsburg family and to agitate for the repeal of punitive legislation which had stripped the Hapsburg family of its possession in Austria. The Monarchist movement, which was created soon after 1918, drew its principal support from members of the hierarchy, Christian Social party members, and from those social groups which had served the Empire until the end, officers, judges, and civil servants.

Austrian Catholics continued to defend monarchical government as the only form appropriate for their country. They admitted that there might be need for gradual reforms within the framework existing in 1918, but rejected any radical changes in political or economic organization, such as republican government or the nationalization of the means of production. In 1920 Bishop Sigismund Waitz of the Austrian hierarchy asked, in the course of an article in a Catholic weekly, whether Leo XIII would have advised Austrian Catholics to accept the republic, and answered his own question in the negative.[28] He denied any similarity between conditions in Austria in 1920 and those in France during the 1880's. He argued that Leo's decision concerning the Third French Republic had been motivated entirely by expediency, and condemned the Pontiff for sacrificing the French royalists in order to gain some advantages for the papacy. Waitz rejected the new Austrian political institutions because they were ". . . simply the work of Freemasons who sponsored republican institutions not primarily from anti-monarchist motives, but because they expected to use these institutions in their fight against Christianity."[29] In short, Waitz considered the postwar republic the work of anti-Christ in alliance with Freemasonry. He concluded that acceptance of the republic would weaken the Catholic faith and reminded his readers that the major Catholic social theorists from Aquinas to Cortes and Ketteler had considered monarchy "relatively speaking the most ideal form of the state."[30]

Catholic trade union movement at its inception. This book is part memoir, part defense of the trade unions against *Heimwehr* and other attacks from within the Christian-social conservative *Lager*.

[28] Bischof Dr. Sigismund Waitz, "Papst Leo XIII. und die französische Republik," *Das Neue Reich*, IV (1920), pp. 5-7, 27-31, 39-41, 59-61, 71-74.

[29] *Ibid.*, p. 72.   [30] *Ibid.*, p. 73.

Catholics feared that the establishment of a republic would open the country to all the liberal influences which the monarchy had at least kept in check. They believed that under the influence of the two principal enemies of Catholicism—the liberal bourgeoisie and the socialist proletariat—the republic would become anti-clerical. They also feared that a politically powerful proletariat would make the republic hostile to the rights of private property. Catholics concluded that the greatest danger came from the proletariat, and therefore entered into an anti-Socialist alliance with the anti-clerical bourgeoisie.[31] This alliance lasted for over a decade because both partners refrained from reopening the clerical question. The Nationalists abstained from forming an anti-clerical majority with the Socialists, and the Christian Socials did not press decisions on religious education, church marriages, and like issues. The rise of Nazism forced the Christian-social conservative camp into a two-front war against Socialists as well as Nationalists. The Austrian Republic was too weak to withstand such a three-cornered civil war. Constitutional government was suspended in 1933; a year later the republic was destroyed by gunfire.

(b) The Compromises of the Constitution. The Constitution of 1920[32] was written by an all-party coalition, but reflected the balance of political power during the first postwar years, namely,

[31] The two parties which formed the majority coalition with the Christian Socials throughout most of this period were the *Landbund* and the *Grossdeutsche Volkspartei.*

[32] The literature on the Austrian Constitution of 1920 is fairly extensive and of good quality. The discussion of the constitutional period in Skottsberg, *op.cit.*, is excellent because the author is concerned not so much with the legal details but with presenting an analysis of the political forces which produced the constitution; see especially Ch. VI, "Das Werden der Bundesverfassung," pp. 189-218. A good, short account in English is Mary Macdonald, *The Republic of Austria 1918-1934. A Study in the Failure of Democratic Government* (London: Oxford University Press, 1946), pp. 23-45. See especially her chapter on the influence of the party system on the development of democratic government, pp. 63-81. The standard collections of Austrian constitutions and constitutional laws for the period of the First Republic were edited by Hans Kelsen and Ludwig Adamovich. These two also wrote treatises on Austrian public law. Hans Kelsen, *Österreichisches Staatsrecht* (Tübingen, J. C. B. Mohr, 1923) and Ludwig Adamovich, *Grundriss des österreichischen Staatsrechtes* (2nd edition; Vienna: Julius Springer Verlag, 1923.) A violent condemnation of the constitution-making period, 1918-1920, can be found in Erich Voegelin, *Der autoritäre Staat. Ein Versuch über das österreichische Staatsproblem* (Vienna: Julius Springer Verlag, 1936), pp. 89-101.

the predominant position of the Socialist *Lager*.[33] Democracy, federalism, and legislative supremacy were the three basic principles of the 1920 Constitution. Catholics proposed a federal distribution of power in order to preserve the position of the historic *Länder*, most of whom were controlled by lop-sided Christian Social majorities. Catholics made this their principal demand. As a result, they had compromised some of their other constitutional proposals, especially their proposal for a strong president and cabinet. On these points the Christian Socials had to bow to the radical-democratic *Zeitgeist* of the postwar period. The Socialists, who were considered the principal proponents of democracy, believed that a constitution which deserved to be called democratic must insure that the voice of the people be fully heard in the decisions of the state. Two institutions they considered necessary to carry out that democratic mandate: proportional representation and legislative supremacy. Proportional representation would assure that all groups in the country were represented according to their strength among the electorate. The legislators chosen on the basis of this most democratic system would then form an assembly which would rule supreme over all other organs of government. The Socialists were also determined to create a legislature which would not be at the mercy of ministers responsible only to the head of the state, a legislature where ministers governed by playing off parties against each other.

Federalism, democracy, and legislative supremacy were the key principles of the new constitution. Catholics *demanded* the first; they were *forced* to accept the others.[34] As postwar radical-

[33] Hans Kelsen, "Der Drang zur Verfassungsreform—Eine Folge der politischen Machtverschiebung," *Neue Freie Presse*, October 6, 1929. Kelsen considered the 1920 Constitution a constitutional and legislative success "with which both parties, in spite of divergent ideologies, could be satisfied, and *at that time actually had been satisfied*." (Italics added.)

[34] The process of compromise and adjustment which led to the agreement on the Constitution of 1920 is an excellent example of the protracted and painful efforts needed to reach agreement between two great political camps which start all discussion from totally divergent positions. The Social Democrats presented constitutional drafts demanding a unicameral, omnicompetent legislature and a unitary state. The anti-Socialist groups presented drafts which were strongly federal, if not confederate, and had provisions for a balance of powers between legislature and executive. In successive stages of the haggling between the two major groups, each side modified its own position, until in 1920 the constitutional committee could announce that the two major parties had reached sub-

ism diminished, Catholic criticisms of democracy and democratic government became louder. Much of that criticism was directed against the two institutions which Catholics considered the epitome of postwar extremism: proportional representation and assembly rule.[35]

Another feature of the constitution which was affected by the clash between Socialist and Catholic *Weltanschauungen* was the bill of rights.[36] During the constitutional debate the two *Lager* quickly realized that they would be unable to effect a compromise on the question of individual rights. That conviction was so strong that the subject was not even opened for discussion in the constitutional committee of the Constituent Assembly. Catholics avoided the subject because they feared that in any discussion of individual rights, Socialists and the liberal bourgeoisie might make common cause and force through a radical separation of church and state. In her book, *Der Parlamentarismus in Österreich*, Brita Skottsberg reports Kelsen's observations on the civil rights issue: "According to a memorandum sent me by Kelsen the Christian Socials did not want any codification of basic individual rights. They preferred to

stantial agreement on a constitutional document into which each had been able to incorporate some of its proposals. In general, Social Democrats achieved more of their demands, while the anti-Socialist groups had to wait until later to modify the constitution in a manner more acceptable to them. For example, the first Christian Social draft constitution presented to the Constituent Assembly was strongly federal, provided for a bicameral legislature with coequal chambers and for dissolution of the legislature under certain conditions. The last Christian Social constitutional draft to be submitted to the Constituent Assembly before final agreement was reached had departed considerably from the earlier version and had moved toward the position of the Social Democratic proposals. For the two drafts, see Konstituierende Nationalversammlung Deutschösterreichs, *Stenographische Protokolle*, Beilagen nos. 231 and 888, dated May 14, 1919 and June 25, 1920 respectively; see also Skottsberg, *op.cit.*, pp. 189-190, 204.

35 The constitutional reform of 1929 weakened assembly rule. But because constitutional change was possible only with the consent of the Social Democratic party, the changes made in 1929 did not go far enough to satisfy the more extreme element in the anti-Socialist camp. On the other hand, Social Democracy could not block all efforts at constitutional revision, and finally agreed to a compromise; see Skottsberg, *op.cit.*, Ch. IX, "Die Verfassungsreform von 1929," pp. 351-404.

36 In his report to the Constituent Assembly, Seipel stated frankly that there was no hope for agreement on this topic: "Here we are confronted not merely with differences of opinion on matters of constitutional law or party programs, but with a fundamental cleavage of world views and ideologies." Ignaz Seipel, *Der Kampf um die österreichische Verfassung* (Vienna: Wilhelm Braumüller, 1930), p. 96. Seipel's report is reprinted there in full, pp. 90-106.

continue in force the old Basic Law of 1867 which had been liberal in its own day, but was rather backward when compared with the Weimar constitution. The Christian Socials feared that Socialists and Nationalists would use any attempt at codifying individual rights as a means for imposing on them separation of church and state. They feared a weakening of the Catholic Church in Austria. However, the Socialists gave way on that point—an event which Seipel considered a great success for the Catholics."[37]

As a result, the only modification in civil rights matters was made in obedience to the minority provisions of the Treaty of St. Germain,[38] and the position of the church under the republic remained largely what it had been before 1918.[39] When Christian Social governments controlled the republic they gave the church substantially the same protection and assistance it had received under the dynasty.[40] For example, membership in Catholic fraternities continued to be a *sine qua non* for government service. On the other hand, the nationalistic fraternities whose *alte Herren* (alumni) held most of the university chairs seemed to have more influence over academic careers.[41] Church-state relationships in Austria were not changed radically until 1934 when a new Concordat was incorporated in the Corporative Constitution of May 1, 1934.[42]

Hans Kelsen has pointed out that a constitution is ". . . the expression of the political forces at work in a people. . . . It certifies to the existence of an equilibrium between the groups contending for power. The demand for constitutional change

[37] Skottsberg, *op.cit.*, p. 214; see also Bauer, *op.cit.*, p. 224.
[38] Hussarek, *op.cit.*, pp. 28-29.
[39] *Ibid.*, p. 28.   [40] *Ibid.*, p. 40.
[41] The Catholic fraternities were organized through the *Cartell Verband* (C.V.) and the individual members were called by these initials "*Cefauer.*" Alexich points out that "certain government departments, such as the Department of Cult and Education, were considered the private hunting grounds of the C. V. . . . This accusation is partly true, although it was natural for the government to recruit its future officers from associations whose members were known to be reliable." Alexich, *op.cit.*, pp. 87-88. But even the *Heimwehr*, a close ally of the Christian Socials, sometimes complained about the favoritism shown the C. V. alumni. See Ernst Rüdiger Prince Starhemberg, *Between Hitler and Mussolini* (New York: Harper & Brothers, 1942), p. 267.
[42] The standard legal commentary on the Concordat of 1934 is Johann Häring (ed.), *Kommentar zum neuen österreichischen Konkordat. Text des Vertrages mit Erklärungen* (Innsbruck: Tyrolia Verlag, 1934).

which becomes so insistent that it can no longer be disregarded constitutes a sign that a shift of power has taken place which demands recognition in the constitution."[43] The provisions of the 1920 Constitution reflected that balance of political power during the first postwar years, that is to say, the predominant position of the Socialist *Lager*. However, after 1922 an anti-Socialist coalition controlled the executive and administrative branches of government but was continuously frustrated by an omnicompetent assembly in which the Socialists held enough seats to prevent constitutional change without their consent. The anti-Socialist *Lager* became increasingly dissatisfied with assembly rule and pressed for constitutional reforms which would give expression to the changes in the position of the three *Lager*. Brita Skottsberg pointed out that the 1920 document established a constitutional monism, a rigid concentration of political power which made impossible any adjustment of power between the branches of government: "In the Austrian Constitution monism was elevated to be the governing principle, and henceforth all political power gravitated toward one point: the popular assembly. This monism not only deprived the parliamentary system of its flexibility, it also sealed executive subservience to the legislature. The rigidity of this Austrian parliamentarism prevented any and all power adjustments between the branches of the state machinery."[44] As a result of this rigid constitutional framework Catholics were forced to work in a political system which had been fashioned largely by their opponents. They had submitted to the radical *Zeitgeist* of the postwar years because they had not felt strong enough to resist it. But when they saw the radical postwar flood recede their demands for constitutional reform became ever more insistent.

4. Catholics and the Social Conflicts of the Republic

(a) The Social Classes, Postwar Collapse and Recovery. The rump Austria created by the Treaty of St. Germain was an economic anomaly. It retained the old Empire's center of finance and commerce, the city of Vienna, as well as some of the prin-

---

[43] Kelsen in *Neue Freie Presse*, see above, n. 33.
[44] Skottsberg, *op.cit.*, p. 239.

cipal industrial areas, but was cut off from the Empire's sources of food stuffs and raw materials. As a result, its unbalanced economic system could not hope to achieve a healthy level of economic activity in an era of excessive economic nationalism.[45] This weakness of the Austrian economy affected all social groups, and intensified the political and social tensions in the young republic.

The working class suffered badly after 1918, but its relative position in the Austrian economy improved considerably compared with pre-1918 conditions. The Socialist *Lager* proposed a number of major economic reform measures which, it hoped, would improve the economic position of the working class. Of these, only one, nationalization of key industries, was not enacted.[46] Among those adopted the most important were the fiscal and social welfare program of the city of Vienna, and the social legislation forced through the national parliament by the Socialists in the first postwar years.[47] However, the total economic picture for the interwar periods was less favorable for the industrial worker, and after the collapse of 1929 permanent mass unemployment became a principal feature of working class conditions.[48]

[45] Schlesinger, *op.cit.*, pp. 206ff., makes a convincing argument that Austria's economic condition between the two World Wars was not as desperate as was usually assumed. It appeared worse, especially to foreigners, because (1) Austrian governments painted as gloomy a picture as possible to get foreign aid and then force on the country an economic policy they could not have put across otherwise, and (2) the Austrian middle-class intellectuals, who were the chief contacts for foreign students, observers, etc., had been hit hardest by the turn of economic events after the First World War. However, even Schlesinger finally had to admit that Austria's basic industries, steel and iron, remained in a state of depression throughout the period.

[46] Bauer, *op.cit.*, section 11, "Die Revolution in den Betrieben," pp. 161-182; see also Gulick, *op.cit.*, vol. 1: *Labor's Workshop of Democracy*, pp. 134-143.

[47] The best and most sympathetic analysis of the record of the Viennese Social Democrats can be found in Gulick, *op.cit.*, vol. 1, in the chapters on cooperatives, municipal housing and tenant protection, welfare work, education, child and youth and workers' cultural activities, pp. 309-643.

[48] *Österreich. Die soziale und wirtschaftliche Struktur* (Berlin: Arbeitswissenschaftliches Amt der Deutschen Arbeitsfront, 1938), appendix E: *Löhne, Preise und Arbeitslosigkeit*. Unemployment fluctuated from a high of 478,000 in 1933 to a low of 407,000 in 1937. This represented approximately fifteen per cent of the persons occupied in Austria. See Emanuel Januschka, *The Social Stratification of the Austrian Population*, transl. Robert Lorenz (U.S. Works Progress Administration Foreign Social Science Monographs No. 21. New York: Columbia University, 1939), p. 6; Friedrich Thalmann, "Die Wirtschaft in Österreich," *Geschichte der Republik Österreich, op.cit.*, pp. 495-500.

The social groups which supported the church and subscribed to Catholic social theory were hit hardest by the postwar economic collapse. The urban middle class of professional people, small property owners, and artisans suffered severely because of the disappearance of the Empire and the currency inflation of the early 1920's. Vienna had been the capital of a mighty Empire which required the services of many types of experts, civil and military servants, lawyers, doctors, fiscal specialists, etc. Now they were no longer needed because the small state created by the peace treaties simply had no use for such a large number of white-collar specialists. The general lowering of the level of economic activity caused by the disappearance of the Empire also affected other middle-class groups, such as artisans and shop-keepers.

The position of these middle-class groups deteriorated after 1918 while that of the two competing groups improved. The currency inflation had destroyed or severely damaged many of the "old" bourgeoisie while fostering the rise to prominence of a group of war and postwar profiteers.[49] The currency inflation also helped to improve the relative position of the industrial workers whose weekly wages and strong bargaining position afforded them better protection against the effects of the dizzily declining *Krone* than the fixed salaries or incomes from savings and investments of the middle class. The four bourgeois groups most severely affected by the postwar economic chaos were certain parts of the established entrepreneur group, the *rentiers*, the *Hausbesitzer*, and the free professions and civil servants. The established entrepreneur group had suffered from the disappearance of war production, but it was confident that it could re-establish its position, if it were only freed from troublesome government controls and the financial burden of welfare legislation forced on the country by the Socialists.[50] The *rentiers* were almost wiped out when the new Austrian government repaid imperial war bonds in worthless paper currency. The *Hausbesitzer*, an important and fairly large urban middle-class element whose property consisted entirely of rental housing, suf-

[49] See Macartney, *op.cit.*, pp. 217ff., for a dramatic description of these profiteers and their "deals."

[50] Ernst Ritter von Streeruwitz, *Springflut über Österreich. Erinnerungen, Erlebnisse und Gedanken aus bewegter Zeit* (Vienna: Bernina Verlag, 1937), p. 218.

fered severely because government controls kept rents at pre-war levels of paper currency and thereby effectively expropriated the owners of rental housing. The position of the free professions and civil servants declined sharply when government pay scales failed to keep pace with the rising currency inflation and an impoverished population had little need for the services of its professional people. These were the members of what one might call the *Altwiener Patriziat*, the elite of intellectuals, artists, and civil servants who have been called the "real" rulers of the old Empire, an Empire which, lacking the popular political base for a constitutional monarchy, was governed by a professional class. As Otto Bauer has pointed out, these were "the real losers of the World War."[51] They hated both the rising working class below them and the newly-risen speculators and profiteers, the *Schieber* (those who push) above them.

The difference in outlook between the entrepreneur group and the other three was reflected in the social and economic theories which appealed to them: "Books like Othmar Spann's *Der Wahre Staat* and Ludwig Mises' economic treatises represent the two types. The former wants to return to Adam Müller and Romantic political thought, the latter to Bentham and the liberal Manchester school. Spann represents the flight into the Romantic ideal of a corporative state of a bourgeois intelligentsia ruined by currency devaluation. Mises, on the other hand, personifies the rediscovered self-consciousness of an entrepreneurial group carried upward by the boom resulting from the collapse of the currency and demanding the abolition of all restrictions imposed by the state and by the bargaining power of trade unions."[52]

The economic position of the peasants did not deteriorate as sharply as that of the urban middle class. The peasants profited from the scarcity of food following the end of the war; later on Christian Social governments influenced by their agricultural constituents shielded the Austrian peasant from the effects of fluctuating world prices of agricultural commodities by protective tariffs and import quotas.

By 1924 Austria's postwar economic and fiscal troubles had been solved, largely with foreign aid administered through the

[51] Bauer, *op.cit.*, p. 207.   [52] *Ibid.*, p. 211.

League of Nations. But the postwar economic recovery which began in 1924 was short-lived. The collapse of the Vienna *Creditanstalt* in 1931 led to a general depression from which Austria did not fully recover before 1938.[53]

(b) The Effects of Postwar Radicalism on the Christian-Social Conservative Lager. The extreme political radicalism of the immediate postwar period abated quickly, but had three important long-range effects on the Christian-social conservative camp. First, under the impact of this extreme radicalism Catholics had accepted the Republic, but had tried to stem the democratic tide by offering a program of "democratic monarchy." However, in 1918 such a concession proved insufficient, and Catholics submitted to what they considered irresistible demands for "democratization." Their opponents charged that Catholic acceptance of the republic had been grudging and hedged with many reservations: "The Republic was a fact of life which they realized they could not escape, at least for the time being."[54] On the other hand Catholics claimed that they had been sincere in their acceptance of a republican regime:

"The Christian Social program also contained the dominant slogan of the post-war years, democracy, by which was meant that the people were to be the only source of public power."[55]

"It is significant for [an understanding of] this position . . . that it was backed by the full power of Seipel's personal influence. It was he who told the Constituent Assembly on September 29, 1920, during the debate on the draft constitution: 'We all share the conviction that our constitution must for all times be based on democratic principles.' "[56]

When Seipel discovered less than ten years later that the *Heimwehr*, a Fascist armed formation, was the one hope for "true democracy" in Austria, one wonders what sort of defini-

[53] Thalmann points out that both those who affirmed and those who denied the economic *Lebensfähigkeit* of a separate Austria during the period of 1918-1938 could make a convincing case. Fundamentally Austria's chances for economic survival depended on her ability to accommodate herself to a specific set of conditions. This the Austrian economy managed to do with some success. Today the presumption seems to be in favor of Austria's *Lebensfähigkeit* as a separate entity. Thalmann, *op.cit.*, pp. 510-512.

[54] Bauer, *op.cit.*, p. 277.

[55] Skottsberg, *op.cit.*, p. 166.

[56] Adolf Merkl, *Die ständisch-autoritäre Verfassung Österreichs. Ein kritisch-systematischer Grundriss* (Vienna: Julius Springer, 1935), pp. 1-2.

tion for the term "democracy" Seipel had in mind when he spoke in 1920.

Next, the leadership in the struggle against this radicalism fell into the hands of Viennese industrialists who also provided the funds to carry on the fight. As a result, the industrialists gained control of the Christian Social party, and forced on the party an economic and social program favorable to big business and industry but not necessarily to the "small man" on the farm and in the city. Ernst von Streeruwitz, who was federal chancellor for a short time in 1929, described in his memoirs how the *Hauptverband für Industrie* established a fund for the creation and continued operation of an armed formation which would be able to check the Socialists.[57] Streeruwitz who was a prominent industrialist and active in the *Hauptverband* took it for granted that industrialists would have to respond to what he considered the continuous provocation and arrogance of the workers and their trade union organization by gaining a voice in the affairs of state: "It was only appropriate that they should have gained positions as advisers to, and even as policy makers in, Austrian governments. During these days of bourgeois spinelessness, only the leadership of peasants and industrialists prevented the worst from happening. . . ."[58]

In his memoirs Streeruwitz chided the Christian Social politicians, like Seipel and Fink, for failing to grasp the importance of economic affairs and economic policy. Streeruwitz believed that this shortsightedness forced industrialists to seek seats in parliaments and posts in the cabinet. He complained about the difficulties he had in convincing the peasant politicians who ran the Christian Social party organization of the need for assigning industrialists good positions on the party ticket, an important consideration in a rigid list system.[59] Ultimately, in-

[57] The proposal to create and subsidize an armed force was greeted with sneers, and the man who made the proposal was asked whether he had ambitions to become a general. Streeruwitz concluded that the motion was passed even though a large number of those present seemed to be ready "to capitulate before the [red] terror"; Streeruwitz, *op.cit.*, p. 216.

[58] *Ibid.*, p. 218.

[59] *Ibid.*, pp. 380-383. Contrast the complaints of Streeruwitz, that the "peasant politicians" ran the party in the interest of agriculture and were reluctant to recognize the interest of industry, with those of Rintelen that the Viennese industrialists arranged affairs to suit their own interests only. See above, n. 15.

dustry gained a controlling voice in the Christian-social conservative camp which was never successfully challenged. Conditions in Austria today reflect similar arrangements. The present Austrian Chancellor, Raab, who had represented industry in the *Heimwehr* before the Second World War, now leads the *Volkspartei*, the successors of the Christian Socials.

The peasants often differed with this Viennese industrialist leadership in Christian Social affairs. Immediately after the end of the war the peasants wanted their sons and husbands back from the army to till the soil; they wanted to be freed from government food regulations and to curb the rights of the nobility to maintain wild game which destroyed the peasants' crops.[60] As a result, the provincial peasants under the leadership of Jodok Fink became the radical wing of the Christian Social Party. Otto Bauer has described the tensions between the peasants and the urban middle-class elements: "The peasant representatives were under extremely severe pressure from their followers . . . who wanted to make common cause with the proletariat in establishing a radical, republican, anti-militaristic, and anti-plutocratic regime. . . . The representatives of the urban bourgeoisie, especially those from Vienna, did not share these sentiments at all. . . . Rural and urban Christian Social deputies disagreed openly during the debates over bills which dealt with the expulsion of the Hapsburg family from Austria and the confiscation of their property, and the abolition of titles of nobility. This threatened split within the Christian Social party was averted only by the influence and power of the Church. . . ."[61]

Bauer has undoubtedly exaggerated the intensity of this intra-Catholic dispute, because an open split in the Christian-social conservative camp would have been to the advantage of Social Democracy. Though this radicalization of the peasants was short-lived, it left a deep imprint on Catholic political attitudes.[62] Austria is usually pictured as split between a red Vienna—liberal, if not socialist, and progressive—and a black countryside, conservative, if not reactionary, and dominated by the village clergy. Actually, the peasants and their leaders who did not have

[60] Wandruszka, *op.cit.*, p. 320.
[61] Bauer, *op.cit.*, p. 129.
[62] Skottsberg, *op.cit.*, p. 179.

to contend with powerful Socialist political machines in their districts were often less militantly anti-Socialist than their colleagues from Vienna.[63] However, the split between the provinces and Vienna was not as clear-cut as it might seem at first glance,[64] because the Vienna wing of the Christian Social organization was itself divided. The Catholic trade union group led by Leopold Kunschak and Franz Hemala was often at odds with the militantly anti-labor industrialist leadership.[65]

The rise of armed formations, like the *Heimwehr*, was a third long-range effect of postwar radicalism. These armed formations were founded for a dual purpose: to help repel external aggression against Austrian territory at a time when Austria had no regular armed forces, and to oppose the armed formations of the Socialist *Lager*. The *Heimwehr* originated in Carinthia and Styria to defend the region against the attempts of the newly-created Kingdom of the Serbs, Croats, and Slovenes to occupy the Klagenfurt basin and present the peace conference with a *fait accompli*.[66] Though similar groups developed in the other provinces there were few attempts to unify these scattered elements. All of these armed groups fell into one of two categories: (1) a nationalist wing, primarily in Carinthia and Styria, which was completely absorbed by the Nazis before 1934, and (2) a clerical wing, primarily in Upper and Lower Austria, led by Rüdiger von Starhemberg, which supported the corporative state and became part of the *Vaterländische Front* organization

[63] Though they might be more conservative and more closely controlled by their village priests, they did not have the same kind of fear of organized Social Democracy as the Christian Socials in Vienna.

[64] Pro-Socialist writers had a tendency to attach too much importance to the disagreements between the Viennese and the provincial Christian Socials. They took their cue from Bauer, whose *Die österreichische Revolution* influenced not only avowed Marxists like Schlesinger but also such non-Marxists as Skottsberg. The cleavage existed for a short period immediately after the First World War. But when the peasants found that the new republican government continued to requisition agricultural products and that the workers' councils insisted on collecting food for the starving cities by force, if necessary, the radicalism of the peasants disappeared rapidly. Nevertheless, men like Jodok Fink continued to play important roles in republican politics and managed to soften somewhat the anti-democratic tendencies in the Christian Social camp.

[65] Schlesinger, *op.cit.*, pp. 318-319.

[66] The history of the *Heimwehr* had to be collected from many sources. Books like Starhemberg's and Rintelen's, together with the memoirs of Schuschnigg, provide the major sources. Rintelen, *op.cit.*, "Evolutionäre Kräfte: Der Heimatschutz," pp. 124-155. See also Wandruszka, *op.cit.*, "Die Heimwehrbewegung," pp. 359-368.

after 1934. At first the *Heimwehr* was financed almost entirely from domestic sources, but later on Mussolini supplied both funds and ideological inspiration. These funds paid for arms, ammunition, and uniforms, as well as five *Schillinge* per man for every day of "active duty."[67]

During the last years of the Republic the *Heimwehr* came into conflict with the moderate and urban trade union elements of the Christian-social conservative *Lager*. In this controversy the *Heimwehr* represented the new demands for an authoritarian government while the trade union group were the last remnant of "democratic" sentiment and advocates of compromise with the Socialists. The controversy became intensified when the management of the *Alpine Montangesellschaft*, Austria's largest steel maker, used a *Heimwehr* union to destroy not only the Socialist Free Trade Unions, but the Catholic trade unions as well.[68] The *Heimwehr* bitterly attacked what they considered the democratic tendencies of the Catholic trade union leadership: "Kunschak belongs to the genus of bourgeois politicians who are convinced that the Austrian state had been created only to provide them with a living wage and a position of influence."[69] *Heimwehr* leaders referred to those in the Catholic camp who were willing to attempt an inter-party compromise with the Socialists as "being unable to wait to go to bed with the red wh - - -."[70] Starhemberg in his memoirs, published in 1942, described the situation with more restraint: "Dollfuss felt particularly cramped by the narrow mindedness of certain Christian Social Party politicians. . . . The real cause of dissension was the struggle and maneuvering for posts at the disposal of the various parties."[71]

These squabbles were inevitable, because the need for a united anti-Socialist front had brought many social groups into the Christian-social conservative *Lager*: ". . . [it] included nearly all the non-Socialist forces, from near Fascists and open representatives of the vested interests . . . to advanced social reformers and to the working class element in the Christian trade

[67] Rintelen, *op.cit.*, pp. 127, 134-135; Wandruszka, *op.cit.*, pp. 360-361.
[68] Kunschak, *op.cit.*, pp. 93-94.
[69] *Ibid.*, p. 101.
[70] *Ibid.*, pp. 100-101.
[71] Starhemberg, *op.cit.*, pp. 169-170.

unions.''[72] Streeruwitz noted that these divergent groups were held together chiefly by the skill of Seipel's leadership. As an industrialist and conservative he viewed these leftist elements with suspicion: ''. . . a number of persons whose genuine social concerns incline them to seek identification, more than is advisable, with the working class movement and with the leading radical worker representatives.''[73] This diversity of social groups contributed to the great variety of social theories advanced in the Christian-social conservative *Lager*.

(c) Collapse of the Balance of Power. The period of political peace during the 1920's was even shorter than the period of economic stability. The fundamental struggle between the Socialist and anti-Socialist camps grew more bitter after the burning of the Ministry of Justice building in 1927: ''In Austria with a well-developed two-party system, the transition from a parliamentary democracy to a regime operating under extra-parliamentary pressure began to rise early. . . . The interlude between the establishment of some degree of political equilibrium after the stabilization crisis and its shattering by a new right-wing offensive did not last longer than two years—from the autumn of 1924 to the autumn of 1926.''[74] The rise of the Nazis in the early 1930's isolated the Christian-social conservative camp completely. The Nazis absorbed the followers of *Landbund* and *Grossdeutsche* leaving the parties' ministers in the cabinet without a following. Catholics were now forced into a two-front war against Socialists as well as Nazis. This isolation and the lack of a majority in parliament forced Catholics to suspend the constitution in 1933, and led to civil war and abolition of the republic in 1934.

For almost a decade the struggle between the three *Lager* was carried on under the rules of the Constitution of 1920. The demands for constitutional change which rose in the late 1920's were, as Kelsen has pointed out,[75] an expression of the changed power relationships. For over a decade the anti-Socialist camps had controlled the executive and as a result had been able to

[72] Schlesinger, *op.cit.*, p. 254.
[73] Streeruwitz, *op.cit.*, p. 405.
[74] Schlesinger, *op.cit.*, p. 312.
[75] Kelsen, article in *Neue Freie Presse*, see above, n. 33.

eliminate Socialist influences in army, police, and civil service. But as long as Austria was governed by a strong assembly, whose power had been diminished only slightly by the constitutional amendments of 1929 which sought to strengthen the executive, Social Democracy was assured a voice in public affairs. Such an even balance between two camps which face each other suspiciously and fully armed cannot be maintained indefinitely. Such a stalemate encourages the extremists in both camps to silence the moderates and to demand a change of the rules, by force of arms if that cannot be done by constitutional processes. As Schlesinger observed: "The power of the opposition Social Democrats created conditions in Austria in which latent civil war between Social Democracy and the right wing of the bourgeois camp coexisted with hardly veiled coalition with the more moderate elements in the same camp; any shift in the relations of strength within the two main camps . . . might bring about the breakdown of the artificial equilibrium."[76]

When Austrian parties took on the "character of religion," as P. T. Lux put it, they destroyed Austrian democracy and threatened the existence of the Austrian state. A party which considers opposition to its ideas and program "heresy" destroys what Ernest Barker has called the essence of democratic government—discussion.[77] Ultimately, a party which claims the entire loyalty of its followers subverts the common political institutions by becoming totalitarian; that is to say, it first turns into a state within a state, and then attempts to take over the state. Thus Austrian Catholics destroyed the Republic. They had condemned the Republic almost from the beginning because it was based on a wrong set of principles about the nature of political organization. They continued to condemn it because it opened the country to liberal and socialist ideas. Finally, many of the social groups loyal to the church associated the Republic with a disastrous decline in their social and economic status. Drawing

[76] Schlesinger, op.cit., p. 272.

[77] Ernest Barker, Principles of Social and Political Theory (London: Oxford University Press, 1951), p. 207. Democracy, he says "is not a solution, but a way of seeking solutions. . . . The core of democracy is choice, and not something chosen." Democracy, he concluded, "was incompatible with any form of one-idea state."

inspiration from Catholic and Romantic social theory and influenced by these political, social, and economic conditions Austrian Catholics developed a body of anti-democratic criticism. Catholic social theorists proposed to replace the Republic with political institutions drawn from Romantic and Catholic social theory. These reform proposals were given increasing prominence in the Catholic camp during the last years of the republic, and were finally realized in the Corporative Constitution of 1934.

CHAPTER IV

THE CRITICISM OF DEMOCRACY:
THE SPECTRUM OF CRITICISM, 1918-1934

AUSTRIAN CATHOLICS had defended monarchy and dynasty against all attacks and had fought for the continued existence of these institutions until the last possible moment. They had hoped to save monarchy and dynasty by reforms within the existing framework, such as the establishment of a "democratic monarchy." However, none of these efforts was successful. Monarchical institutions and the personal rule of the Hapsburg Dynasty were swept away by a wave of "democratic" reforms. In some instances, support for these reforms was the result of temporary conditions. For example, the radical views of the Austrian peasants can be traced to a specific set of war and postwar conditions. When these disappeared the peasants returned to more traditional political and economic views. But what proved to be the permanent disappearance of monarchy and dynasty was not the result merely of passing emotions intensified by four years of hardships suffered in war. It was the result of a long historical process which was often obscured by the religious homogeneity of the Austrian people and the close tie between throne and altar; that is to say, it was tempting to conclude from the Catholic character of the monarchy and the loyalty of the dynasty to the church that Austrians, who were overwhelmingly Catholic, were unanimous in their support of monarchy and dynasty. Actually, during the century preceding the end of the First World War, group after group had become disaffected until in 1918 the loyalty of a small segment of the German middle class in the Alpine regions was not enough to stem the anti-monarchic and anti-Hapsburg tide.

The first groups to become disaffected were the non-German nationalities within the Empire. Some went into opposition earlier than others. For example, Poles remained loyal longer than

Czechs. But by 1918, under the impact of the Wilsonian program, all non-German groups in the Empire demanded self-
determination and independence. It might have been possible
to preserve dynastic rule in rump-Austria if the people of that
part of the Empire had been united on this fundamental issue.
But the process of disaffection which had destroyed dynastic
support among non-Germans had also been at work among Germans. Furthermore, the uncompromising anti-Hapsburg attitude of the succession states would have made impossible either
the continuation of Hapsburg rule or the return of the dynasty
any time after 1918, even if the people of rump-Austria had
been united in their pro-dynastic sentiments. By 1918 the overwhelming majority of the Austrian industrial workers had become definitely anti-monarchic and anti-Hapsburg. In the first
election held after 1918, their votes cast, with only minor exceptions, for the Social Democratic party, amounted to almost
forty percent of the electorate. To this large bloc must be added
a considerable segment of the middle class, especially the urban
middle class, who had deserted the monarchy under the influence of liberal or anti-clerical ideas which had originated in the
Enlightenment and the Josephinist reforms, or in the nationalist,
Pan-German propaganda of Schönerer. If one adds to these two
groups the Austrian peasants, eager for peace and freedom from
excessive government restrictions, one is forced to conclude that
the support for the dynasty rested on a narrow base indeed. The
examination of the hierarchy's position on the new Austrian
state (which follows later in this chapter) leaves no doubt that
the Catholic Church remained a steadfast supporter of the dynasty till the very end. Nevertheless, anti-Catholics critics of
the hierarchy have suggested that in *Nation und Staat*, written
in 1916, Ignaz Seipel was preparing a position to which the
church could retreat in case of an overwhelming attack on the
dynasty. In that study Seipel had argued that "nation," "state,"
and *"Volk,"* were not always identical, that a *Volk* had a life
of its own, and that the state could not make unlimited demands
on it.[1]

Though monarchy and dynasty disappeared in 1918, Catholic

[1] See above, Ch. II, section 1 d.

social theory in Austria was not prepared to accept a neutral, democratic state in their stead. The formation of such a state, therefore, created a novel situation for which the ideas and attitudes developed during a period of harmonious church-state relationships were no longer adequate. Consequently, Austrian Catholics had to consider the problem of working in a neutral, democratic state and fitting their views about democracy into the total pattern of political and social theories within the country. The present chapter will first examine the place of Catholic views about democracy in Austrian political thought and then present the spectrum of Catholic criticism of democracy during the period of the First Austrian Republic, 1918-1934.

1. The Development of the Spectrum

Catholic views about democracy were part of the "liberal-conservative" and the "left-right" dichotomies which existed in Austrian political thought. In previous chapters Austrian Catholic social thought has been characterized as having a strong, conservative, corporativist, and *étatiste* bias; that is to say, it has been described as favoring a strong monarchy and the corporative organization of society.[2] On the other hand, few Austrian Catholics were liberals, that is to say, were prepared to come to terms with the modern state and accept the theories of the classical economists.[3] This is not surprising, for there were not many

[2] The successors of Adam Müller and Karl von Vogelsang during the period 1918-1934 defined their conservative position as follows: "True conservatism is based on specific dogmatic and philosophical assumptions, and therefore seeks out those cultural, political, and economic phenomena which harmonize with these preconceptions. From this starting point it tries to build bridges into the present and the future." Alfred Missong, "Europa," *Die österreichische Aktion. Programmatische Studien*, August M. Knoll, editor (Vienna: Im Selbstverlag der Verfasser, 1927), pp. 37-38. This conservatism claimed to venerate not simply what happened to have existed in the past, but only those features of the past which conformed to the dogmatic and philosophical norms of conservatism. Austrian Romanticists always contrasted their own conservatism with Prussian conservatism, which they accused of accepting whatever institutions and ideas had existed in the past. In practice the ideas and institutions which Austrian Romantic conservatives found "dogmatically and philosophically" correct could hardly be distinguished from those of Prussian conservatism.

[3] Liberal Catholics wanted to use the popular liberties of the nineteenth century to insure the spiritual and material well-being of the people. They had no fixed prescriptions for the evils created by the modern state and the modern economy, but relied strongly on the traditional means of charity and on private initiative and cooperation. They wanted to limit the state to "negative" measures

supporters of liberal doctrines among Austrians as a whole. Because the terms "liberal" and "conservative" were used in Austrian Catholic thought in the manner described here, this usage will be followed throughout this study. The reader must keep this usage clearly in mind and not confuse it with the use of these two terms in current American political thought and political debate. A conservative Catholic theorist, therefore, is not one who favors a public policy friendly to business and who wants to keep government intervention at a minimum. He is, rather, a supporter of the social theory of Catholic thinkers like Vogelsang. Also, a liberal Catholic thinker is not one who supports a program of state intervention in economic affairs usually associated with the American "New Deal." He is a Catholic who is prepared to come to terms with the modern state and with the established capitalist system, and who wants to keep government intervention at a minimum.

The terms "left" and "right" were used in Austria after 1918 to identify positions on the question of the neutral democratic state, as well as on the question of capitalism. Austrians used the term "left" to identify the position of the Socialist *Lager* and of the industrial proletariat who supported the neutral democratic state and opposed capitalism.[4] Though the Austrian Socialist program was thoroughly Marxist and envisaged the forcible overthrow of the existing bourgeois capitalist order, Austrian Socialists were committed to gradualism and to the democratic institutions which they had helped establish in 1918-1920.[5]

---

in protecting the weak and eliminating the worst abuses, leaving everything else to private initiative. Robert Kothen, *La Pensée et l'Action Sociale des Catholiques, 1789-1944* (Louvain: Em. Warny, 1945), pp. 156-157; see also Paul Jostock, *Der deutsche Katholizismus und die Überwindung des Kapitalismus. Eine ideengeschichtliche Skizze* (Regensburg: Friedrich Pustet, 1932), pp. 56-61.

[4] Wandruszka points out that in all three camps there were large groups who demanded *Anschluss* and denied the capacity of an independent Austria to continue in existence for any period of time. But of the three only the Socialists "were committed unconditionally to the republican form of government." Adam Wandruszka, "Österreichs politische Struktur. Die Entwicklung der Parteien und der politischen Bewegungen," *Geschichte der Republik Österreich*, Heinrich Benedikt, editor (Vienna: Verlag für Geschichte und Politik, 1954), pp. 422, 447.

[5] Social Democracy handed its opponents a powerful weapon in the manner in which it defined the use of force in its program of 1926. The 1926 program stated that the working class would have to use "Mittel der Diktatur" if the bourgeoisie should resort to conspiracy, counter-revolutionary measures, or outside help to prevent the working class from carrying out its task—social revolu-

Because the Socialist *Lager* developed into a steadfast supporter of the Austrian Republic, anti-socialism soon became associated with anti-republicanism. As a result, the opponents of socialism believed that they could defeat their enemies only if they abolished the political institutions which had given socialism a decisive voice in Austrian affairs.

The "right" in Austria was composed of two groups, the Nationalist and the Christian-social conservative *Lager*. The Nationalists were socially on the "right" but shared with the "left" a long tradition of anti-clericalism and anti-Hapsburg sentiments, and gave at least some support to Austria's democratic institutions during the early years of the Republic.[6] The Christian-social conservative *Lager*, on the other hand, was on the "right" both socially and politically. The "right" also held a variety of views on the question of capitalism. The Nationalist *Lager*, which did not have a well-developed economic theory, opposed both socialism and *laissez-faire* capitalism, and supported a vague program of corporativism. As a result, Nationalists did not join forces with the left on economic questions, as they tended to do occasionally on clerical issues. It is not possible, therefore, to compare the anti-clerical bourgeoisie of Austria with the Radical Socialists of the Third French Republic.[7] The German Nationalist in Austria might have found congenial the republicanism and anti-clericalism of the Radicals, but not their economic *laissez-faire* views. In the Christian-social conservative *Lager* the supporters of capitalism got along well with the Nationalists because the latter held no well-defined views on economic issues. However, the opponents of capitalism did not combine opposition to capitalism with preference for democracy, as did the *Popolari* in Italy. With the exception of a

---

tion. Catholics cited the 1926 program as proof that Austrian socialism was committed to the use of force to establish the dictatorship of the proletariat. Actually, the history of Austrian socialism until 1934 shows that the movement used force very reluctantly, and that the doctrinaire formulas of Otto Bauer did not go unchallenged within the party. The principal weakness of the movement was its inability to make a clear choice between revolution and cooperation with the other camps in the state, between revolution and evolution. Wandruszka, *op.cit.*, pp. 447-452.

6 *Ibid.*, pp. 296, 373.

7 Philip Williams, *Politics in Post-War France. Parties and the Constitution in the Fourth Republic* (London: Longmans, Green & Co., 1954), p. 15.

small group of Religious Socialists, the opponents of capitalism demanded the establishment of an authoritarian state on a corporative basis. Consequently, it is impossible to apply to Austria the analysis of political opinion which distinguishes between socially progressive and socially conservative elements on the "right," because there was in Austria during the period 1918-1934 no significant socially progressive group of Catholics corresponding to the *Popolari*. This pattern has persisted into the Second Republic. Though the *Österreichische Volkspartei* finally abandoned the Romantic conservatism of the prewar period, its social program since 1945 has remained closer to that of the Christian Socials before 1934, than to that of the M.R.P. or *Democrazia Cristiana* in Italy since 1945.

Austrian Catholic criticism of democracy between 1918 and 1934 mounted as the tide of postwar radicalism receded. There were two principal reasons for Catholic criticism and ultimate abandonment of democracy. Catholics came to identify the Republic with their principal opponents, the Socialists; they also grew dissatisfied with the working of Austria's constitutional system, which perpetuated the dominant position the Socialist *Lager* had been able to secure during the first years of the Republic. This chorus of anti-democratic criticism confirmed the opponents of Catholicism in their opinion that Catholics had never been sincere in their acceptance of democracy in 1918; that they were not really interested in reforming democracy, but only in abolishing it. Catholic criticism of democracy became especially intense after 1927, and by 1934 the Christian-social conservative *Lager* strongly supported the abandonment of democratic institutions in favor of an authoritarian, corporative state. They thereby returned to a Catholic tradition which had been dormant during most of the postwar period, namely, the social Romantic tradition of Vogelsang. Actually, the Vogelsang disciples and other Romantic theorists had not remained silent during the postwar years. As a result, Austrian Catholic criticism of democracy was characterized by a wide variety of views which can be explained in part by the multiplicity of social theories which have always existed within the Catholic social tradition, and in part by the social position in Austria of the various groups advancing these theories.

The following chart attempts to diagram the distribution along a spectrum of Catholic social theories and the changes that took place between 1918 and 1934. The two extreme positions in this spectrum were: pro-democratic, pro-capitalist, and anti-democratic, anti-capitalist.

First Years of the Republic		*Last Years of the Republic*
Hierarchy Seipel	Pro-democratic Pro-capitalist	
Trade unions *(Linzer Programm)*	Pro-democratic Anti-capitalist	Trade unions *(Linzer Programm)*
Monarchists *Heimwehr*	Anti-democratic Pro-capitalist	Hierarchy Seipel Monarchists *Heimwehr*
Spann Vogelsang school	Anti-democratic Anti-capitalist	Spann Vogelsang school

An analysis of the spectrum suggests three observations about the distribution of social theories during the First Republic. The most significant fact about the period 1918-1934 was the abandonment by Austrian Catholics of their initial pro-democratic position. In his writings and political activities Ignaz Seipel, federal chancellor of Austria longer than any other man, not only laid the foundation for Catholic acceptance of the Republic; he also guided Catholics in their initial critique and ultimate rejection of democracy. The official statements and actions of the Austrian hierarchy performed a similar function. Next, it is interesting to note that some of the groups had definite political but poorly developed socio-economic programs. This was the case of the *Heimwehr* and the monarchists. The former was financed by Austrian industrial interests and simply defended the existing economic system. The social thought of the monarchist movement was concerned almost entirely with the problem of Hapsburg restoration. Finally, the followers of

Karl von Vogelsang and Othmar Spann and his school were the two consistently anti-capitalist, anti-democratic groups of the Christian-social conservative *Lager*. During most of the republican period Spann and the followers of Vogelsang were a minor group within the Catholic camp. But when Catholics attempted to find a social theory which would aid them in reconstructing state and society, the writings of Vogelsang and his successors became prominent again, as did the Romantic doctrines of Othmar Spann. Spann considered himself a nationalist and some of his students were from the beginning openly in the Nazi camp and pursued anti-clerical policies. Nevertheless, the Romantic doctrines of the Spann school reinforced the Romantic tendencies of Austrian Catholic thought first introduced by Müller and Vogelsang. The revival of corporative doctrines spurred by the publication of *Quadragesimo anno* served to establish Spann and the Vogelsang school as the principal corporativist theorists in Austria. Their writings played an important role in the shaping of the Corporative Constitution of 1934.

2. Ignaz Seipel and the Criticism of Democracy

The writings of Ignaz Seipel expressed most succinctly Austrian Catholic criticism of democracy and the Catholic position on the modern state.[8] In 1918 Seipel had urged Catholics to accept democracy. Subsequently he severely criticized democracy and advocated changes which, if carried into effect, would have

[8] The literature about Ignaz Seipel is divided between those who want to rescue him from his enemies and those who want to save him from his friends. Into the first category fall Rudolf Blüml, *Prälat Dr. Ignaz Seipel; ein grosses Leben in kleinen Bildern* (Klagenfurt: Im Verlag der St. Josefs-Bücherbrüderschaft, 1933) and Bernhard Birk, *Dr. Ignaz Seipel. Ein österreichisches und europäisches Schicksal* (Regensburg: Verlagsanstalt vorm. G. J. Manz A.G., 1932). In the latter category falls Werner Thormann, *Ignaz Seipel. Der europäische Staatsmann* (Frankfurt a.M.: Carolus Druckerei, 1932). Of his own writings the most useful work is the collection of articles, speeches, etc., which Seipel edited in 1930, *Der Kampf um die österreichische Verfassung* (Vienna: Wilhelm Braumüller, 1930). Hereafter cited as Seipel, *Kampf*. His *Nation und Staat* (Vienna: Wilhelm Braumüller, 1916) has already been discussed. Two books which date from the last years of his life and the collection of addresses edited by Josef Gessl contain little on the problem of the modern state which is not expressed much better in his addresses and papers dating from the periods of his intensive involvement in the conduct of the Austrian Republic: *Der christliche Staatsmann* (Augsburg: Haas und Grabherr, 1930); *Wesen und Aufgaben der Politik* (Vienna: Tyrolia Verlag, 1930); and *Seipels Reden in Österreich und anderwärts. Eine Auswahl zu seinem 50. Geburtstag*, Josef Gessl, editor (Vienna: Heros-Verlag, 1926).

destroyed it. Because an overwhelming majority of Austrian Catholics followed Seipel's leadership, this change in his position was one of the most significant developments in Austrian Catholic social thought during the period 1918-1934.

Seipel's career spanned almost the entire life of the Republic. In 1917 he succeeded his teacher, Franz M. Schindler, in the post of professor of moral theology at the University of Vienna, and in the following year he assumed his first public office as a member of the last imperial cabinet headed by Heinrich Lammasch, a devoted pacifist and former professor of international law. Seipel had become an influential adviser of Charles I and had drafted the Emperor's last official act, an abdication statement which omitted the word abdication. This opened the way for the subsequent contention of the monarchists that Charles I had never abdicated and that, therefore, the dynasty had never forfeited its claims to the Austrian throne.[9] Seipel became the undisputed leader of the Christian Social party, not because he was a popular "vote-getter," but because there was no one to challenge his grasp of political problems and the strength of his intellectual leadership. It has been suggested that he had little understanding for, or sympathy with, the petty bourgeois and rural priest rank and file of the party.[10] If this was indeed the case, it did not prevent him from rising rapidly in the party and becoming federal chancellor from 1922 to 1924, and again from 1926 to 1929. He died in 1932.

In 1918 Seipel persuaded a majority of Austrian Catholics to accept the Republic. In his report on the draft constitution to the Constituent Assembly he urged the adoption of that document in the strongest terms. But it was his work in the Constitutional Committee which had made the constitution acceptable to Catholics by softening the extreme "democratic" proposals

[9] According to Wandruszka the Empress Zita and the legitimists accused Seipel of bringing about Charles' abdication and criticized the Christian Socials for having pursued an "opportunistic" policy in 1918; *op.cit.*, p. 322. Writing the Seipel entry in the post-World War II volume of the *Neue österreichische Biographie*, August Knoll recounts the following incident reported to him by Zita in 1932. When Seipel called on Charles in Switzerland he told him: "I will not tolerate any restoration attempts at the present time; but in ten years I will call on the Emperor [to return]." *Neue österreichische Biographie ab 1815* (Zurich, Leipzig, Vienna: Amalthea Verlag, 1956), first section, vol. IX, pp. 113-129, at 120.

[10] Thormann, *op.cit.*, p. 15.

of the Socialists and by retaining the civil rights legislation of 1867.[11] How did Seipel define democracy and the democratic constitution whose adoption he urged in 1920? He set down these definitions within a week after the proclamation of the Republic on November 11, 1918 in a series of articles in the official Christian Social daily *Reichspost*.[12]

(a) *Democracy and Catholic Social Theory*. Seipel attempted to show that democracy as he defined it was compatible with Catholic social thought. According to his view, a state in which all people participated in public affairs met the requirements of democracy. It also met the requirements of Catholic social theory; that is to say, it was a natural organ in which man could live: "Each [of the forms of government] is acceptable if it meets two conditions: first, piety and authority, the foundations of every [form of government] must be present . . . and secondly, it must not violate the principle that those things which ought to be in common are indeed held in common and are administered in the common interest."[13] He concluded that there was no conflict between democratic demands for popular sovereignty and free elections, and the statement in the encyclicals that all power came from God: "There can be no contradiction between a *correctly conceived democracy* and the conviction, shared by all religious people, that all power comes from God."[14] It was this reservation about a "correctly conceived" democracy, later often termed "true democracy," with which Seipel attempted to explain his hostility to the republic. He claimed that Austrian democracy had departed from the true path he had prescribed for it, and needed to be redirected into the proper channels.

(b) *The Bases of Democracy*. According to Seipel, self-determination of the people, self-government by the people, and universal participation in decision-making were the bases of democ-

[11] See above, Ch. III, section 3 b.

[12] The four articles entitled "Das Recht des Volkes," "Das Wesen des demokratischen Staates," "Die demokratische Verfassung," and "Das Volk und die zukünftige Staatsform" appeared in the *Reichspost* on November 19, 20, 21, and 23, 1918. They are reprinted in Seipel, *Kampf*, pp. 49-66.

[13] *Ibid.*, p. 179.

[14] "Kirchliches und staatliches Organisationsprinzip," paper delivered before the Vereinigung katholischer Akademiker "Logos," March 26, 1925, reprinted in Gessl, *op.cit.*, p. 199.

racy. A constitution which contained these features was demo
cratic, and therefore the appropriate basis for a democratic form
of government. First, democracy required that a people determine its own fate. He warned the Austrian people that if
they did not speak out for themselves they would remain ". . .
an unfree people, one not yet of age, without control over its
own destiny."[15]

What was the basis for a people's claim to determine its own
fate? Seipel answered thus: "The people want this simply because they *must*, and that is really the *most compelling legal
claim* a people can make who want to determine their own
fate."[16] He noted that the people had waited patiently to gain
a voice in public affairs, but that the militaristic, bureaucratic,
absolutist, and capitalist character of the old regime had denied
them this right.[17] As a result, people had begun to hate that
regime: "The people do not understand why they are consulted
in minor matters, but in major affairs must bow to the higher
wisdom, not of the supreme ruler, but of some obscure imperial
counsellor."[18] Seipel concluded that those demanding sweeping
reforms would not be satisfied with alteration in the outward
forms of the state, but would insist on fundamental changes in
its method of operation.[19]

Next, democracy required that people be governed by rulers
of their own choosing. Therefore a free democratic state was the
opposite of the autocratic state (*Herrschaftsstaat*).[20] Such a democracy ". . . must guarantee all segments of the population,
first of all a free life in the new state, and the possibility to
achieve on their own their physical and cultural well-being.
It must also enable them to share in the direction of the state,
proportionately to their strength and position."[21] Seipel insisted
that in a democratic state those who lost an election must never
fear that "a brutal victor will trample their ideals underfoot."
They must have a chance to present their minority views and
to persuade others to join them, hoping eventually to become
a majority.[22]

Finally, democracy also required that all areas of state activity

[15] Seipel, "Das Recht des Volkes," *Kampf*, p. 50.   [16] *Ibid.*, p. 51.
[17] *Ibid.*, p. 53.   [18] *Ibid.*   [19] *Ibid.*, p. 54.
[20] Seipel, "Das Wesen des demokratischen Staates," *Kampf*, p. 54.
[21] *Ibid.*, p. 57.   [22] *Ibid.*, p. 58.

and the actions of all state officials be subject to decisions based on universal suffrage. This form of democratic control must extend to the administrative branch, especially the foreign service, which must not remain the preserve of an aristocratic minority. However, Seipel saw two dangers to such an enlargement of the area subject to democratic decision-making. A state which was based only on a territorial system of representation and universal suffrage would soon become a mere collection of atomistic individuals, voicing selfish preferences. Furthermore, under such a system all questions of public policy would be decided on purely political grounds: "The state organized on a territorial basis consists simply of isolated individuals who enjoy full equality in theory but who are in reality very unequal. We consider a state which does not follow these principles as healthier and better ordered. . . . For in parliamentary negotiations political considerations have long ago pushed all other considerations, including economic ones, into the background."[23] Actually, there would be many questions which would have to be decided by experts on the basis of economic or other criteria: "Still, there are many questions of public policy which need to be considered by a different forum than the political one, and which must be decided by another method of voting than that used in the political arena."[24]

Only after a constitution had been written which embodied these three principles would it be necessary to choose a form of government, that is to say, choose between a democratic monarchy or a democratic republic. Seipel insisted that Catholics preferred the former, but would be satisfied with the latter if a majority of the people desired it.[25] Thus, Seipel and Austrian Catholics accepted the neutral democratic state in 1918. There is no doubt that they considered such a state preferable to Communist regimes like that of Bela Kun in Hungary and Kurt Eisner in Munich. But acceptance of a republic as a lesser of two evils is not the same as sincere commitment to the principles of democratic government. Nevertheless, Austrian Catholics tried to obey the "rules of the game" during the early years of the

23 *Ibid.*, p. 60.
24 *Ibid.*, p. 63.
25 Seipel, "Das Volk und die künftige Staatsform," *Kampf*, pp. 63-66.

Republic.[26] Later on when Catholics became increasingly critical of democracy their opponents accused them of subverting the very institutions they had helped shape in 1918-1920. Their spokesmen like Seipel replied that Catholics had agreed to support only a "correctly conceived" democracy.[27] When Socialists charged Seipel with undermining the position of parliament he pointed out that he had warned against an omnicompetent assembly all along. He did not want to destroy parliament, he declared, but simply to implement his earlier suggestion that additional representative bodies were needed for the expression of other than purely "political" interests.

(c) Early Criticism of Democracy. Seipel's early criticism of democracy concentrated on four features. He repeated these criticisms often and elaborated on them continuously during the first decade of the Republic. First, he complained that parliament in a democracy decided all questions of public policy on the basis of political considerations, to the exclusion of all others. This was a traditional criticism of Catholic theorists who demanded that the state and its legislature be freed from the burden of making other than political decisions. However, these same theorists failed to see the anarchical implications of their proposal, to vest decision-making powers not in one but several parliaments. Seipel, as we will see, was aware of these objections to a multi-chamber corporative parliament, but continued to complain about the concentration of power in the "political" legislature. Next, Seipel condemned strict party controls over the democratic legislature because they fostered a spirit of narrow and selfish party interest. He apparently refused to admit that the "narrowness" of the Austrian party spirit was the result of a lack of consensus in Austrian society rather than the fault of parliamentary institutions. Third, control by one party over a key position in government could block effectively the will of the majority. This was chiefly an attack on the Social Democrats, whose strength in parliament was sufficient to block constitutional amendments. Finally, Seipel traced the fear of leaders

[26] Ernst Karl Winter, "Die Staatskrise in Österreich," *Wiener Politische Blätter*, I (April 16, 1933), pp. 23-38.
[27] Seipel, *Kampf*, p. viii. Seipel denied that he had accepted the constitution without reservations and referred his opponents to his report to the Constituent Assembly in 1920.

to take responsibility and to defend the general interest against selfish party pressures to the predominance of that party spirit mentioned above: "In my book democracy does not mean that at every step of the way as many people as possible are heard, including those who do not want to assume any responsibility. Rather it means that the individual who acts in the name of the people must assume responsibility, especially when the decisions are difficult."[28] He blamed the proponents of the majority principle for assuming that "the majority is the more intelligent part of society and must therefore be right."[29] What was needed, he argued, was not talk, but leaders willing to take responsibility: ". . . in place of the democracy of mere voting we need the democracy of *true* responsibility."[30]

Seipel believed that the operation of Austrian political institutions after 1918 had stifled the voice of important segments of the people and had violated the democratic character of the Austrian Republic. He therefore urged a reform of Austrian democracy in order to give a voice in public affairs to the new social forces not heretofore properly represented. He suggested that this could best be done by providing other methods of representation in addition to the system of representation based on territorial constituencies. However, not until 1928 did Seipel make unmistakably clear whom he considered to be among the social forces not properly represented in the Austrian state. He came out openly in support of the *Heimwehr*: "Nothing is further from the truth than the assertion that the *Heimwehr* movement . . . constitutes a threat to democracy. On the contrary, desire for true democracy is one of the strongest motivating forces of that movement. This is why I have full confidence in it and why I am prepared to identify myself with it."[31] He insisted that only a reform of existing institutions which would accommodate the *Heimwehr* would be a move in the direction of "true" democracy.

[28] Speech before the *Industriellen Klub*, November 9, 1922, reprinted in Gessl, *op.cit.*, pp. 49-50.

[29] "Die grossen Linien der geistigen Entwicklung unserer Zeit," paper delivered before the *Sozialer Winterkurs des Volksbundes der Katholiken Österreichs*, January 5, 1924, reprinted in Gessl, *op.cit.*, p. 89.

[30] *Ibid.*, pp. 92-93.

[31] "Der Ruf nach der echten Demokratie," address before the Graz Christian Social party organization, December 18, 1928, reprinted in *Kampf*, p. 133.

(d) *Criticism of Democracy at its Height.* During the years 1928-1929 Seipel advanced his most comprehensive criticism of Austrian democracy; though, like other members of the Catholic camp, he had become dissatisfied with what he called "sham democracy" long before 1928.[32] As Kelsen has pointed out, by 1928 the 1920 Constitution no longer reflected correctly the balance of power between the major political forces in the country.[33] Catholics were especially displeased with the weakness of the executive which they had controlled without interruption from the beginning of the Republic. Seipel therefore joined other Austrian Catholics in their demand for constitutional reforms which would strengthen the cabinet and provide for the popular election of the federal president.[34] However, he was less enthusiastic about Catholic proposals to establish corporative assemblies.

During all these attacks on democracy Seipel continued to affirm his adherence to a "correctly conceived" democracy as the best form of government: "I believe that there is no better form of organizing, leading, and administering political society than democracy, true, correctly conceived democracy."[35] As late as 1929 he admitted that the Austrian Republic, though shaky, was a sturdy edifice ". . . under whose protection we can still live together in peace."[36] He obviously clung to the democratic symbols because of the continued support for democracy among the Austrian people. At the same time he insisted that Catholics could not continue to support a form of political organization which did not meet the two conditions he had stated earlier, that is to say, which was not based on piety and authority, and which did not permit the administration of common affairs in the general interest.[37] Seipel insisted that the Austrian Republic

[32] Speech at election meeting, November 27, 1928, reprinted in *Kampf*, p. 123.
[33] See above Ch. III, n. 33.   [34] Seipel, *Kampf*, p. 132.
[35] "Die Münchener Kritik der Demokratie" paper delivered at the University of Munich, January 22, 1929, reprinted in *Kampf*, pp. 167-177, and "Die Tübinger Kritik der Demokratie," paper delivered at the University of Tübingen, July 16, 1929, reprinted in *Kampf*, pp. 177-188. These two addresses constituted Seipel's major critiques of Austrian democracy. Seipel wanted to give the impression that these two attacks on Austrian democracy were not political actions, politically motivated, but "theoretical" discussions before an academic audience.
[36] "Die wahre Republik," paper delivered at the University of Vienna, November 10, 1928, reprinted in *Kampf*, p. 154.
[37] See above, n. 13.

in 1929 no longer met these two conditions. The influence of godless socialism in Austria had undermined all respect for piety and authority, and the pervasiveness of the party spirit had thwarted the administration of public affairs in the interest of the common good: ". . . the root of this evil is our form of party government. He who cleanses democracy of this rule by party, will truly revive it."[38] Seipel therefore considered party government the principal malaise of democracy. Because parties controlled their representatives in the legislature, the representatives of the people obeyed not those who had chosen them but party bosses who had never received a popular mandate.[39]

Seipel especially criticized two features of Austrian political institutions: the existing suffrage qualifications and electoral laws, and the lack of representation for economic and other interests. It is significant that Seipel, who had many years of practical political experience, rejected most of the Romantic reform proposals on the grounds that they were impractical and would only intensify existing problems or create new ones which had not existed before. He rejected any proposals for tampering with universal, equal suffrage, such as preferential treatment of householders or intellectuals, because the lack of popular confidence in the assembly would not be offset by any gains such reforms could produce.[40] He was also skeptical about the possibilities of economic representation and economic chambers because he saw two dangers. If the territorial legislature were abolished, the economic chamber would become a political assembly, and economic groups would take on the character of political parties. If a corporative chamber were added to the territorial legislature, there would simply be several parliaments where there had been only one. He did not believe that one could solve the problems of parliamentary government by multiplying the number of parliaments.[41]

(e) The Abandonment of Democracy. Even critics of Seipel from within his own camp, such as Ernst Karl Winter, pointed out that by 1929 the leadership of the Christian-social conservative *Lager* had fallen into the hands of men no longer committed to democratic procedures. New men and ideas appeared ". . .

38 Seipel, *Kampf*, pp. 181-182.   39 *Ibid.*, p. 186.
40 *Ibid.*, p. 182.   41 *Ibid.*

who lacked commitment to the parliamentary-democratic rules of the game and whose entire experience inclined them to the corporativist-militaristic leadership principle."[42] Encouraged by Seipel, these new leaders with an authoritarian-militaristic background were not really interested in reforming democracy, but only in destroying it. Winter accused Seipel of trying to deceive the Austrian people about the nature of these new tendencies by his talk about "true democracy" when all he really meant by "true democracy" was a military dictatorship: "This is most transparent in the case of Seipel's famous slogan about 'true democracy.' . . . With one hand (the left one, of course) he swore to uphold the legal, democratic order while he freed his skilled right hand for the job of destroying it. . . . There was in Seipel's arsenal a whole rat's tail of concepts which he managed to turn into their exact opposites by adding the adjective 'true.' Thus he talked about 'true peace' when he referred to a set of conditions which could only lead to permanent warfare of all against all."[43]

This examination of Seipel's writings as well as his record as a leader of the Christian Socials reveals three principal reasons for his initial acceptance and ultimate abandonment of democracy.[44] There were, of course, pastoral reasons for this change. Seipel was, after all, a priest and must have considered the effect on the church of whatever political actions he took. It has been suggested above that his *Nation und Staat* could be interpreted as an attempt by the church to disengage itself from the dynasty. This view of Seipel's role is supported by his activities in 1918, namely, his decisive pro-Republic influence on his fellow Catholics. When the neutral democratic state seemed to endanger the church and the position of Catholics in Austria in subsequent years, his abandonment of democracy must have been influenced by such pastoral considerations. Next, reasons of political strategy also played a role. Seipel accepted democracy because such an acceptance seemed inevitable in 1918; in like manner he thought it best to assume leadership of the anti-democratic

[42] Winter, "Die Staatskrise in Österreich," *op.cit.*, p. 25.
[43] Ernst Karl Winter, "Österreich und der Nationalsozialismus," *Wiener Politische Blätter*, I (December 3, 1933), p. 198.
[44] See the discussion in Wandruszka, *op.cit.*, pp. 324-325.

forces which began to arise late in the 1920's. He gave an aura of respectability to these authoritarian tendencies, but he certainly cannot be blamed for having been solely responsible for their rise to prominence. He obviously thought he could use them for his own purposes—much like conservative politicians of many parties thought to use Hitler in Germany. Finally, there must have been a genuine disappointment with the working of the neutral state after 1918. Seipel had always subscribed to the Leonine view that forms of government were a matter of theological indifference as long as they met certain conditions. If as a Catholic he believed that the democratic institutions of Austria did not meet certain minimum conditions established in Leo's encyclicals he was bound to urge changes in these institutions.

3. The Hierarchy and Austrian Democracy

Josef Lehrl, surveying Catholicism as an educational force in Austria, wrote: "Nowhere else has the corpus of Catholic teaching become so deeply embedded in the historical consciousness of a people as in that country. . . . In Austria the relations between church and state differed radically from those in other countries. In Austria church and state were not simply parties to a legal contract, but two different expressions of the same idea, each moving in its own manner toward a common goal. . . . Church and state were not two independent powers, but members of a common Christian order."[45] Because of the close ties which continued to exist between the church and those who governed the Austrian state after 1918, the views of the hierarchy about the nature of democracy influenced the development of the Austrian Republic and Austrian Catholic thought.

(a) From Monarchy to Republic. As late as August 1918, Austrian bishops considered popular sovereignty, majority rule, and self-determination of nations incompatible with the Catholic theory of the state: "The gravest evil of our time is the feverish search for independence and free will. Modern man's desire to be fully independent is part of that false body of ideas, such as 'popular sovereignty, majority rule, self-determination of na-

---

[45] Josef Lehrl, "Der Katholizismus als Bildungsmacht in Österreich," *Bildungskräfte im Katholizismus der Welt,* Friedrich Schneider, editor (Freiburg im Breisgau: Herder & Co., 1936), pp. 65-66.

tions,' which threaten the foundations of the social order hereto-fore based on the legal wisdom of the Christian tradition."[46] The bishops especially condemned the attacks on the reigning monarch as diabolical machinations which constituted a revolution against the deity.[47] They insisted that ". . . not only the power to rule comes from God, but Divine Providence also designates those who are to exercise this power."[48] In short, Divine Providence had placed the Hapsburgs on the Austrian throne and revolt against them "is not permitted under any circumstances."[49]

However, in a letter to parish priests dated November 12, 1918, Friedrich Gustav Cardinal Piffl of Vienna informed the clergy about the changes in regime. He explained that there had not been a revolution but that Charles I had turned the state over to "his" people: "The faithful are to be properly informed about these *faits accomplis* and are to be exhorted to pledge unconditional loyalty to the state *Deutschösterreich* which was now a legitimate regime."[50] The Cardinal insisted that the church was prepared to accept these *faits accomplis* only because the Emperor had of his own will turned public power over to his people. But he warned that the church could express no preference for any form of government and referred Austrian Catholics to Leo XIII's encyclical *Immortale dei*.[51] But even after having accepted the political and constitutional framework of the Republic,[52] the hierarchy continued to criticize democracy and the spirit of liberalism which, it claimed, pervaded the life of the Austrian Republic. The hierarchy placed most of the blame for this on the Social Democrats and continuously exhorted the faithful to vote and work only for political parties loyal to the church.

[46] Pastoral letter of the archbishops and bishops of Austria, August 4, 1918, reprinted in *Kardinal Piffl und der österreichische Episkopat zu sozialen und kulturellen Fragen, 1913-1932*, August M. Knoll, editor (Vienna: Reinhold Verlag, 1932), pp. 26-27. The collection will be cited as *Episkopat*.

[47] *Ibid.*, p. 27.   [48] *Ibid.*, p. 29.   [49] *Ibid.*, p. 30.

[50] Letter to parish priests by Friedrich Gustav Cardinal Piffl of Vienna, November 12, 1918, reprinted in *Episkopat*, pp. 45-46.

[51] *Immortale dei*, section 4.

[52] Throughout the republican period, members of the clergy held a multitude of elected and appointed public offices. Not until 1933 did the Austrian hierarchy order members of the clergy to resign all elected public offices. Such an order would have been unthinkable before Seipel's death in 1932. Wandruszka, *op.cit.*, p. 327; see also Leopold Kunschak, *Österreich 1918-1934* (Vienna: Typographische Anstalt, 1934), p. 198.

(b) Democracy and its Abuses. Though the bishops recognized the right of the people to govern themselves, they warned against the abuses of democracy as early as January 1919: "The revolution has brought democracy into our land; therefore we want to say a word about democracy. This *foreign* word means rule of the people. . . . The supreme power comes from God, but the people can entrust it to one or to several persons. . . . But if democracy severs its ties with Christianity then we have no longer a people which rules itself, but the tyranny of a political party which has usurped all power."[53] The bishops first called attention to the fact that democracy had come to Austria as the result of revolution and that it was actually a "foreign" word; that is to say, they considered democracy foreign to the genius of the Austrian people and Austrian political institutions. They pointed out that Aquinas had urged the participation of the people in government, but that the jurists of the Enlightenment had rejected this prescription in favor of autocratic rule by a prince. As a result, the people revolted against this absolute rule, and demanded freedom and self-government. The hierarchy deplored the tendency to equate self-government with freedom from all religious and moral restraints, and warned that the abuses of democracy would result in the people being tyrannized by a single political party. Only a vote for political parties supporting the church would be a safeguard against such a tyranny: "Whoever casts his vote for agnostic or anti-church representatives shares in committing a public sin. Every Catholic has a public religious duty to cast his vote in a Catholic spirit."[54] With the exception of the 1930 election when the *Heimwehr* had entered separate lists, such an exhortation could have meant only a vote for the Christian Socials, for even their coalition partners, *Grossdeutsche Volkspartei* and *Landbund*, were openly anti-clerical. Repeatedly the hierarchy warned Catholics against casting their vote for a party or candidate "whose electoral programs contain un-Christian principles and tendencies."[55] It urged the faithful to ". . . close ranks behind the great Catholic organization whose

---

[53] Pastoral letter of the archbishops and bishops of Deutschösterreich, January 23, 1919, reprinted in *Episkopat*, pp. 54-55.

[54] *Ibid.*, pp. 57-58.

[55] Proclamation of the Austrian bishops concerning the national elections of November 9, 1930, October 26, 1930, reprinted in *Episkopat*, p. 174.

leaders will be able to advise you best. Listen to the exhortations and instructions of your priests. . . . The enemies of the clergy are also the enemies of the people . . . do not trust them."[56] The bishops identified liberalism as the principal enemy of Catholicism because it had undermined the place of religion in Austrian life, and had been the "pacemaker" for socialism and communism: "Just as liberalism is the pacemaker for socialism, so socialism logically ends in bolshevism with which it is ninety per cent identical. . . . Whoever demands socialism, indirectly opts for bolshevism. A faithful Catholic who takes his religion seriously can never be a friend or adherent of socialism."[57]

These pastoral letters of the Austrian hierarchy reflected the effectiveness of the Socialists' anti-religious campaigns.[58] The church again and again attacked Socialist youth organizations, like *Kinderfreunde* and *Rote Falken*, for subscribing to progressive methods of education which lacked a proper spiritual and religious basis.[59] The church also blamed the Socialists for intensifying the existing social tensions within Austria by fostering the class consciousness of the proletariat. Next, the bishops attacked the Socialist city and *Land* governments, for destroying Christian marriage by permitting the remarriage of persons previously married in the Catholic Church.[60] Finally, the church

[56] *Ibid.*, pp. 175, 176.

[57] Bischof Johannes Maria von Linz, "Hirtenbrief: Vom Bolschewismus," *Hirtenbriefe des deutschen und österreichischen Episkopats* (Paderborn: Junfermannsche Buchhandlung, 1930), pp. 253-254). These annual volumes of pastoral letters will be cited as *Hirtenbriefe*, together with the year.

[58] Withdrawals from the Catholic religion in Austria during the ten-year period between 1918 and 1928 totalled more than 135,000, Alois Hudal, "Die kirchliche Einteilung Österreichs mit der allgemeinen Statistik," *Katholizismus in Österreich*, p. 53; see also Erzbischof Friedrich Gustav Kardinal Piffl von Wien, "Hirtenbrief: Freidenkerkampf gegen die Kirche und seine Abwehr," *Hirtenbriefe 1930*, pp. 219-225.

[59] Bischof Johannes Maria von Linz, "Hirtenbrief: Autorität," *Hirtenbriefe 1927*, pp. 225-237.

[60] The Socialist city government of Vienna, which under the constitution was also the *Land* government, claimed the power to administer civil marriages involving persons whose previous church marriage had never been dissolved. The federal constitutional court upheld the Vienna *Land* government, saying the court could not inquire into the administrative discretion of the *Land* governor. Thousands of persons in Vienna took advantage of these rulings, obtained divorces, and remarried. Max Freiherr Hussarek von Heinlein, "Die kirchenpolitische Gesetzgebung der Republik Österreich," *Katholizismus in Österreich*, pp. 37-38; see also Fürstbischof Johannes von Bressanone, "Hirtenbrief: Vom Geiste der Katholischen Aktion," *Hirtenbriefe 1931*, p. 258; and *Hirtenbriefe 1926*, pp. 220-227; *Hirtenbriefe 1927*, pp. 197-210, 220-224; *Hirtenbriefe 1936*, pp. 222-226, 227-233, 234-239.

considered Socialist efforts to separate church and state and to make religion *Privatsache* the forerunners of attempts to establish a godless state.[61] As Macartney has pointed out, the church feared that Socialist efforts to make religion a "private affair" would lead to an elimination of religion and not merely a reduction of the public position of the church. Socialists replied that they were not concerned with eradicating religion, but simply with combatting clericalism.[62]

(c) The Church and the Regime. Thus the church became deeply involved in the struggle over regime. One might paraphrase de Tocqueville's observation that in America political problems become judicial questions to be settled in the law courts, and say that in Austria religious problems inevitably become political issues to be fought out by parties. The church tended to identify one party and one *Lager*, the Socialist, as their principal enemy. Because the Socialists strongly defended the institutions and ideas of 1918, the church came to equate democracy with socialism and ultimately with bolshevism. The Socialists, in turn, blamed all their political difficulties on clericalism and charged the church with being a front for the forces of reaction and privilege.[63] Both sides admitted that religion and politics could not be neatly separated. As one Austrian bishop remarked: "Religion and politics certainly occupy separate spheres, but they are not always independent of each other. There are many contacts between them, and church as well as state may be interested in the same affair or object."[64] In spite of this recognition of common interests, neither side made any serious efforts to find a *modus vivendi*.

These difficulties of the church serve to illustrate the three persistent features of Catholic social thought: (1) the importance of pastoral considerations; that is to say, the needs of the church at a given time will influence decisively the general tendencies of Catholic social thought; (2) the close connection between political and social problems, that is to say, the identification of

---

61 Fürstbischof Adam Hefter von Gurk, "Hirtenbrief: Religion ist Privatsache," *Hirtenbriefe 1927*, pp. 211-219.
62 See above Ch. III, section 2 d.
63 Wandruszka, *op.cit.*, p. 151.
64 *Hirtenbriefe 1931*, p. 259.

various social classes as political supporters or opponents of the church; and (3) the church's concept of the "ideal" social order which led it to criticize Austrian democracy and to accept willingly the Corporative Constitution of 1934.

4. Catholic Trade Unions and the
Linzer Programm

The Catholic trade unions, led by Leopold Kunschak, supported Austria's democratic institutions longer than any other group in the Christian-social conservative *Lager*. However, they were only a small minority in that *Lager* and exercised little influence.[65] The reasons for this weakness have been discussed earlier.[66] However, the most important of these was the unattractiveness for the industrial workers of the Austrian Catholic social program. The Romantic doctrines of Vogelsang appealed mostly to peasants and the petty bourgeoisie of artisans and shopkeepers. The Catholic trade union movement was weakened still further because ". . . most trade unions' executive committees consisted of master craftsmen and their sons, as well as priests. No wonder little attention was paid to the trade union struggle for better wages and working conditions."[67]

The social thought of the trade union movement was contained in the *Linzer Programm* adopted in 1923. Karl Lugmayer, a *Gymnasium* teacher and social theorist of the Vogelsang school, assisted in the formulation of that program and wrote the official commentary on it.[68] Its political section was part of a general analysis which began with the observation that the dissolution of society was proceeding at a rapid rate and could be arrested only by a corporative reorganization of state and society.[69] In this reorganization the future *Berufsstände* would receive far-reaching legislative powers.[70]

[65] For a comparison with the position of Catholic unions in Germany, see Alexander, "Church and Society in Germany," *Church and Society*, pp. 430-434.

[66] See above Ch. II, section 1 d.

[67] Fritz Klenner, *Die österreichischen Gewerkschaften. Vergangenheit und Gegenwartsprobleme* (Vienna: Verlag des österreichischen Gewerkschaftsbundes, 1953), II, 1044.

[68] Karl Lugmayer, *Das Linzer Programm der christlichen Arbeiter Österreichs* (Vienna: Verlag der Typographischen Anstalt, 1924). This volume contains both the text of the program and Lugmayer's commentary.

[69] *Ibid.*, p. 7.

[70] *Ibid.*, p. 8.

The political section of the *Linzer Programm* centered around these three propositions:

"The temporal welfare of the entire community is the principal purpose of the state. . . .

"We reject the concept of the omnicompetent state. The state is not the ultimate source of law. . . .

"We are democrats and demand for the worker full equality of political rights, freedom to organize, and extension of the principle of proportional representation to all elections."[71]

This endorsement of democracy in the *Linzer Programm* was one of the strongest pro-democratic statements to come from the Catholic camp. Catholic trade unionists realized that their socio-economic proposals would find a hearing among industrial workers only if they were associated with a democratic program which safeguarded the political rights of the workers. The political section of the *Programm* concluded with a plea that the leadership of the state be taken out of the hands of the Jews and be entrusted to native Christian leaders.

The *Linzer Programm* had little impact outside immediate Catholic trade union circles. The Catholic unions were not only a small group within the Catholic camp; they were also inferior to the Free Trade Unions. Though the membership in Catholic trade unions increased from 78,000 to 130,000 between 1921 and 1932 while the Free Trade Union membership dropped from 1,000,000 to 500,000 during the same period, the Catholic unions were weakest among industrial workers where their membership amounted to less than ten per cent of Free Trade Union strength.[72]

What influence the Catholic trade union wing managed to exercise in the Catholic *Lager* was chiefly the result of Leopold Kunschak's political leadership.[73] Kunschak had been a sad-

---

[71] *Ibid.*, p. 10.   [72] Klenner, *op.cit.*, pp. 1097, 1098.

[73] Unfortunately two recent books about Leopold Kunschak have not been available. One is a volume of memoirs, Leopold Kunschak, *Steinchen am Weg (Erinnerungen)* (Vienna: Typographische Anstalt, 1952). The other is Franz Stamprech, *Leopold Kunschak, Portrait eines christlichen Arbeiterführers* (Vienna: Verlag der "Freiheit," 1953). But enough has been collected from various sources, especially from Kunschak's own *Österreich 1918-1934*, to give a full picture of the man and his ideas. Wandruszka confirms the present judgment when he notes that Kunschak's "opposition to the authoritarian *Heimwehr* tendencies will always be remembered," *op.cit.*, p. 349.

dler journeyman before he joined the Catholic trade union movement at its inception in the 1890's. Because of his occupational background his outlook remained that of an artisan rather than of an industrial worker. But in spite of his nostalgia for the monarchy and his virulent anti-Semitism, he defended Austrian democracy after most of the Catholic camp had abandoned it. He repeatedly clashed with the *Heimwehr* who attacked him and other moderates in the Christian Social camp for wanting to save their positions by advocating compromises with the Socialists.[74] His sharpest clash with the *Heimwehr* was over the latter's *Korneuburg* program of May 1930, which will be discussed later in this chapter. In brief, the *Korneuburg* program rejected democracy and proposed the establishment of a fascist state: "We reject democracy and parliamentary government. We pledge allegiance to the principles of fascism."[75] Though the Christian Social party never stated unequivocally that such a program was incompatible with loyalty to the Republic,[76] Kunschak would have no part of it: "We reject the Korneuburg program because it contradicts in essential points the social and political principles of the Catholic workers and employees movement."[77]

Kunschak opposed much of the authoritarian and dictatorial program advanced by the right wing of the Catholic camp, because he feared for the continued existence under such a system of all trade unions, including Catholic trade unions. These fears were confirmed after 1934 when the corporative regime established a unified trade union movement, the *Einheitsgewerkschaft*.[78] Though some of the leaders of Catholic trade unions were active in the new organization,[79] they had less influence on

[74] See above Ch. III, section 4 b.

[75] Cited in Kunschak, *Österreich 1918-1934* (Vienna: Typographische Anstalt, 1934), p. 118; see also Anton Rintelen, *Erinnerungen an Österreichs Weg. Versailles-Berchtesgaden-Grossdeutschland* (Munich: F. Bruckmann, 1941), pp. 143-144.

[76] Charles A. Gulick, *Austria from Habsburg to Hitler*, vol. II: *Fascism's Subversion of Democracy* (Berkeley: University of California Press, 1948), pp. 894ff.

[77] Kunschak, *op.cit.*, p. 119.

[78] Max Stoffel, *Die österreichische Ständeordnung. Ihre ideellen und verfassungsmässigen Grundlagen und die Anfänge ihrer konkreten Verwirklichung* (Doctor of Laws dissertation, University of Zurich, 1938), pp. 153-167.

[79] Klenner, *op.cit.*, pp. 1147ff. Men like Staud and Lugmayer occupied top positions in the unified trade unions. A number of middle- and lower-level free trade

labor affairs than they had before 1934. As a result there were many complaints from the Catholic trade union group that the corporative state created in May 1934 did not meet the demands of the *Linzer Programm*.[80]

5. Conservatism and Democracy:
Österreichische Aktion

The abandonment of democracy by Seipel and the hierarchy several years before the end of the republic left Kunschak and the Catholic trade union group as the only defenders of democracy in 1934.[81] The other groups of the Catholic camp had never accepted democracy and the neutral Republic, and had proposed a variety of monarchical or authoritarian schemes instead. Of these four groups—monarchists, *Heimwehr*, Spann, and the Vogelsang school—the first two lacked a well-developed economic program while the last two subscribed to the anti-capitalist doctrines of Romantic social thought. The monarchists were preoccupied with the problems of Hapsburg restoration, and the *Heimwehr* obviously had no other economic program than the defense of those interests which provided the funds for their uniforms, arms, and daily allowances.[82] Rüdiger von Starhemberg reported that Mussolini had criticized the *Heimwehr* for this lack of a program and their tame brand of fascism: "It is, what I call a bourgeois burglary insurance, a kind of militia to defend the private property of the bourgeois and peasant classes against possible encroachments and Communist attacks."[83]

---

union officials were retained in the new union organization. See Joseph Buttinger, *In the Twilight of Socialism. A History of the Revolutionary Socialists of Austria* (New York: Frederick A. Praeger, 1953), pp. 179-181.

[80] Klenner, *op.cit.*, II, 1141-1142. Under the guise of a commentary on *Quadragesimo anno*, Rudolf Hausleithner, a priest, violently attacked the corporative system in Austria for its failure to aid the worker and the "small people." Rudolf Hausleithner, *Der Geist der neuen Ordnung* (Vienna: Typographische Anstalt, 1937). See below, Ch. v, section 1 c, for some comments on the disappointment of the Romantic social reformers with the corporative state.

[81] See chart on p. 105, above.

[82] Rintelen, *op.cit.*, p. 128; see also Wandruszka, *op.cit.*, pp. 359-368, and Ernst Ritter von Streeruwitz, *Springflut über Österreich. Erinnerungen, Erlebnisse und Gedanken aus bewegter Zeit 1914-1929.* (Vienna: Bernina Verlag, 1937), pp. 229-230.

[83] Ernst Rüdiger Prince Starhemberg, *Between Hitler and Mussolini* (New York: Harper & Bros. Publishers, 1942), p. 23.

The most significant intellectual effort of the monarchist movement was *Österreichische Aktion*, a collection of essays published in 1926 by Ernst Karl Winter, Alfred Missong, and others, including H. K. Zessner-Spitzenberg, a biographer of Charles I and prominent in monarchist movements.[84] These essays were first read in the *Leogesellschaft*, an official Catholic cultural and scientific society, and therefore constitute a recognized Catholic effort to define the problems of monarchism in the Austrian Republic.

(a) The Conservatism of the Österreichische Aktion. The movement[85] and the book of essays whose name it bore were inspired by *Action Française* and the principle of monarchic-dynastic legitimacy. The proponents of the *Aktion* argued that the church had condemned *Action Française* but not the principle of legitimacy.[86] From this basis *Österreichische Aktion* developed a comprehensive critique of democracy and condemned the impact of liberalism in Austria. It proposed the establishment of a "social monarchy" which would be an alliance of throne and nobility with the industrial proletariat directed against the evil effects of political and economic liberalism. Its slogan, first stated by Winter was ". . . 'to stand on the right and to think with the left,' i.e., to be rooted in tradition, but to recognize in the name of tradition the needs and demands of our day, no matter how leftist they may appear."[87]

Österreichische Aktion has not been classified as part of the extreme Romantic tradition because its program, though definitely based on Romantic doctrines, differed in several impor-

[84] August M. Knoll (editor), *Die österreichische Aktion. Programmatische Studien* (Vienna: Im Selbstverlag der Verfasser, 1927). The contents of the volume are as follows: August M. Knoll, "Kaisertum und Proletariat oder die soziale Monarchie," pp. 186-215; Alfred Missong, "Europa," pp. 37-59; "Österreichische Politik 1866/68. Eine politische Gewissensforschung," pp. 92-112; "Entproletarisierung," pp. 216-243; Wilhelm Schmidt, "Die österreichische Jugend," pp. 270-284; Ernst Karl Winter, "Der europäische und der österreichische Raum," pp. 11-25; "Die österreichische Idee in der Geschichte," pp. 26-36; "Das konservative und liberale Österreich," pp. 113-126; "Souveränität," pp. 143-162; "Die katholische und die österreichische Aktion," pp. 244-269; and H. K. Zessner-Spitzenberg, "Das Völkerreich des Hauses Habsburg," pp. 60-91; "Kaiser Karl," pp. 127-142; "Legimität und Legalität," pp. 163-185; "Die Zukunft des Hauses Habsburg," pp. 285-302. The collection will be cited as *Aktion*.
[85] Schmidt, "Die österreichische Jugend," *Aktion*, pp. 270-284.
[86] See the introduction to *Aktion*, p. 8.
[87] *Ibid.*, pp. 9-10.

tant respects from that of Spann and the Vogelsang school. *Österreichische Aktion* disagreed with the extreme Romanticists over economic and cultural policies. Though it proposed the "uplifting of the proletariat" (*Entproletarisierung*) as part of its socio-economic program, it was not as radically anti-capitalist as these other Romantic theorists; that is to say, *Österreichische Aktion* wanted to improve the conditions of the proletariat but was not overly concerned with economic reorganization.[88] It also disagreed with the Romantics over cultural policies. Vogelsang had been definitely anti-Prussian and had opposed the political and cultural predominance of Prussia in Germany and Austria. He had been repelled by the pronounced Protestantism and Old Germanic paganism which became associated with the rise of Prussia. However, his successors, men like Richard Kralik and Anton Orel, had fallen under the influence of Richard Wagner.[89] As a result of that influence there developed two distinct cultural tendencies among Austrian Catholics. One group, though continuing in the Catholic philosophical tradition, stressed cultural unity with Germany and the German character of Austria. Kralik and Orel were the outstanding representatives of this group. They helped spread in Austria the influence of Richard Wagner, especially that part of the Wagner tradition associated with the composer's turn toward religion, namely, *Parsifal* and the mythology of the Holy Grail. The other group of Catholics

[88] Seipel, for example, had considerable doubts about the possibilities for creating a workable corporative system and he pointed out at least two grave defects which a system of occupational representation would have: (1) if there were a single corporative chamber, the occupational groups within that chamber would simply replace political parties and the struggle would continue, probably in a more ruthless fashion; (2) if one attempted to replace the existing legislature with several corporative chambers, one would simply multiply the problems —one could not cure the ills of parliamentary government by creating several new parliaments, "Tübinger Kritik," *Kampf*, pp. 183-186. In another pamphlet from the Catholic camp, Raimund Günther attacked the Republic and the existing party system, but rejected corporative institutions as possible alternatives for the republican institutions of Austria. Günther argued that corporativism would destroy the distinction between state and society—an arrangement which Catholics could not accept. Though it might be possible to give interest groups an advisory voice, direct participation of interest groups in decision-making would lead to a splintering of state authority, to corporative anarchy. Raimund Günther, *Diktatur oder Untergang. Neue Wege für Staat und Wirtschaft* (Vienna: Verlag Carl Konegen, 1930), pp. 26-34.

[89] Wandruszka, *op.cit.*, p. 318. The influence of Wagner was particularly strong on Richard von Kralik. See Josef Eberle, "Richard von Kralik zum 70. Geburtstag," *Das Neue Reich* IV (1921-1922), pp. 1007-1013.

rejected as foreign to the true Austrian tradition the literary and cultural Germanizing tendencies of Kralik and his *Gralbund*. *Österreichische Aktion* was part of this latter group. Its members shared the anti-Prussian, anti-Protestant doctrines expressed in the writings of men like Friedrich Wilhelm Förster.[90]

(b) The Destruction of Familial Organization. The proponents of the *Österreichische Aktion* program rejected democracy because it was incompatible with the correct theory of sovereignty and legitimate authority. They believed that the only sociologically correct structure of sovereignty was one in which ". . . the individual personality and the family were the basic cells as well as the crown of the system, and therefore the effective organizing principle."[91] Democracy, which proclaimed the equality of all human beings, had thereby destroyed the multitude of organic sovereignties (individual personality and the family) which had existed in society. The destruction of these intermediate units which the *Österreichische Aktion* chose to call "organic sovereignties" had made the state omnicompetent, they argued. They considered this omnicompetence a caricature of God and of the church, and called this new theory of the omnicompetent state a secularized theology. However, they suspected that behind this façade of omnicompetence there was concealed a state of anarchy which was the result of the abolition of all these intermediate units: "At long last we see modern state sovereignty for what it really is: an absolutely anarchical principle which has gathered into its hands all the lesser sovereignties within the state."[92]

The destruction of these old centers of sovereign power, families, estates, etc., had made impossible the continuation of the only truly healthy social order. The condition of anarchy which the writers of the *Aktion* claimed to observe in the modern state was the very opposite of a healthy social order: individuals were no longer organized in a multitude of small social units. As a result, the perfect whole, created by membership in these partial units, with many and contrasting purposes, had disappeared.[93]

[90] Missong, "Europa," *Aktion*, pp. 37-38, developed the concept of a true Austrian conservatism which he opposed to a Prussian pseudo-conservatism ". . . which was only a handmaiden to liberalism and a Teutonic ideology" (p. 38).
[91] Winter, "Souveränität," *Aktion*, p. 148.
[92] *Ibid.*, pp. 155-156.
[93] Missong, "Europa," *Aktion*, pp. 42-43.

Finally, positivist legal theory, an element of democracy, completed the destruction of the healthy social order by denying the existence of any source of law outside the political order existing at any given moment.[94]

(c) The Destruction of Legitimate Authority. The *Aktion* contended that democracy had not only destroyed the multitude of so-called sovereignties in the organic order; it had also put an end to legitimate political authority. The revolt of the people, who demanded the right to govern themselves, had caused the destruction of legitimate authority and the creation of *de facto* regimes which pretended to govern in the interest of the common good. But these new regimes could never extinguish the claims of the legitimate rulers: "The *fait accompli* of revolution . . . can never extinguish existing claims and cannot elevate injustice to the level of justice."[95] No matter how long the legitimate authority had been deprived of its rightful position, no matter how small the number of those who still supported the claims of the legitimate authority ". . . the suppressed claims of the legitimate system never lapse, though they might become unenforceable in practice."[96] Not even the claims that the *de facto* regime governed public affairs in the common good could justify Catholics in recognizing such a regime.[97] The *Aktion* rejected the proposition advanced by many Austrian Catholics that the new Republic governed in the interest of the common good *(Gemeinwohl)* and that Catholics, therefore, should accept the Republic. They argued, instead, that the very demands of *Gemeinwohl* required the restoration of the legitimate Austrian authority: "Once we depart from the path that inexorable logic prescribes there is no stopping and we will succumb to the theory of naked power and the principle of the *fait accompli.*"[98]

(d) The Platonic-Augustinian Tradition. The theories of legitimacy of the *Aktion* were part of the Platonic-Augustinian tradition of Catholic political philosophy which considered the rule of the prince and the authority of the prince over the state an extension of the authority of the father over the family: "the sociology of the princes and fathers."[99] As the authority of the

---

[94] Zessner-Spitzenberg, "Legimität und Legalität," *Aktion*, p. 165.
[95] *Ibid.*, p. 174.   [96] *Ibid.*, p. 177.   [97] *Ibid.*, p. 176.   [98] *Ibid.*, p. 178.
[99] "Introduction," *Aktion*, p. 9.

father over the family never ceased, so the authority of the prince also could never be extinguished.[100] The writers of the *Aktion* argued that Catholics could never reject the claims of a legitimate prince, for they were part of Catholic dogma like those of the father over the family.[101] From this the *Aktion* concluded that the authority of the Hapsburgs over Austria was part of Catholic dogma, and Catholics could not accept the republic which had been established on the ruins of these Hapsburg claims. Such a theological theory of political authority suggests two observations: (1) It prevented the states created after 1918 from parts of the Hapsburg Empire from ever being recognized as legitimate authorities. (2) Even more important, it leads to the conclusion that forms of government were not an indifferent matter to Catholics, as Leo XIII had suggested. According to the theory of the *Aktion* there was only one form of government, monarchy. But not a constitutional monarchy as it had existed in Austria, especially after 1867, when ". . . the sovereign monarch signed his abdication decree by sharing the patrimony of his governing power with an irresponsible parliament composed of johnnies-come-lately demagogues."[102] Therefore, legitimate, social monarchy was the only correct form of political organization. It is obvious that this doctrine disregarded the Leonine teachings on the nature of the state and forms of government.

The *Aktion* also attacked the Christian Social party and the Catholic *Lager* for espousing what it considered wrong principles of social and political organization. The proponents of the *Aktion* accused their co-religionists of having become infected with current democratic and socialist ideas and of opposing conservative Catholics who advocated the only correct Catholic social theory.[103] Furthermore, *Aktion* argued that the preoccupation of Austrian Catholics with the activities of the modern state

[100] Zessner-Spitzenberg, "Legitimät und Legalität," *Aktion*, p. 163.

[101] The Catholic "sociologia perennis," according to the authors of the *Aktion*, is based on three theses: (1) monogamy stands at the beginning of human development; (2) the family is the social organization in whose image the state is formed; and (3) authority in the state is the culmination of marriage and the family. Paternal authority is the prototype of state authority; consequently, this state authority does not control a shapeless mass of individuals, but a "structure of individual personalities," Souveränität, *Aktion*, pp. 146-147.

[102] Missong, "Österreichs Politik 1866/68," *Aktion*, p. 97.

[103] Winter, "Das konservative und liberale Österreich," *Aktion*, p. 122.

had detracted the priest and the father from their proper functions and had dragged them into politics.[104] Therefore, the first step in social reorganization would have to be the return of priest and father to their proper tasks in parish and family. The *Aktion* denied that the withdrawal from the activities of political Catholicism would adversely affect the interest of the church. Political Catholicism had been so ineffective in protecting Catholic interests that matters could hardly be worse if all these activities were abandoned.[105]

The *Aktion* also disagreed with the majority of Austrian Catholics over questions of philosophy and theology. The *Aktion* considered itself part of a long tradition in Catholicism, the Platonic-Augustinian tradition of the Dominicans, and opposed the Aristotelian-Thomist tradition of the German Jesuits. It condemned the Solidarist social theories of these Jesuits because their attempt to achieve a *modus vivendi* with capitalism and the modern state was inspired by a reprehensible Thomist-Jesuit tendency to accept whatever institutions happened to exist without regard for the claims of legitimate authority. The foremost exponent of the Augustinian tradition was Ernst Karl Winter, who pleaded for a revival of Platonism in Catholic philosophy and sociology. In the years after the publication of the *Aktion* essays, Winter moved away from the monarchist movement. He became genuinely concerned with the fate of the Austrian worker under authoritarian rule and attempted to win the workers over to the Dollfuss-Schuschnigg regime by a program which consisted of socialist, democratic, Romantic, and monarchist elements. Fundamentally he was close to the Vogelsang tradition but quarreled with all the theorists of that tradition as well as with many other groups in the Christian-social conservative *Lager*.[106]

6. The *Heimwehr*

The *Heimwehr* was primarily an armed formation, little burdened with social theory. Its anti-liberal and anti-democratic program ran along familiar lines. In the *Korneuburg* program of 1930 the *Heimwehr* rejected democracy, parliamentary in-

104 *Ibid.*, p. 123.
105 Winter, "Die katholische und die österreichische Aktion," *Aktion*, p. 259.
106 See below, Ch. VI, for further discussion of Winter's social doctrines.

stitutions, and political parties.[107] Because the *Heimwehr* drew followers and support from both the Nationalist and Christian-social conservative *Lager* its official ideology contained references to the deity as well as to the unalterably German character of Austria: "Every comrade must acknowledge his responsibilities as a bearer of the new German concept of the state. He must be prepared to sacrifice himself and his worldly goods for this cause and he must be loyal to these three powers: belief in God, his own stern will, and the word of the leader."[108] Much of this language consciously imitates the "tough" language of blood and iron which characterized both the Italian and German Fascist ideologies. At the same time the *Heimwehr* was careful to have its flags and guidons blessed by the church and *Heimwehr* units began field exercises with a *Feldmesse*. This made them respectable in the eyes of the Catholic camp, which supported the *Heimwehr* as the principal counterweight to the *Schutzbund*, the armed formation of the Social Democratic party.[109] The units of the *Heimwehr* in Lower and Upper Austria, the former led by the present federal chancellor, Raab, the latter led by Starhemberg, became part of the unified political movement of the authoritarian state and abandoned most of their ideological controversies with other groups in the Catholic camp about the basis of political authority. They became concerned chiefly with obtaining lucrative posts in the government or in the *Vaterländische Front*.

7. Müller and Hegel: The Romantic Doctrines of Othmar Spann

We have now traversed the spectrum of Catholic criticism of democracy and have arrived at the extreme anti-democratic, anti-capitalist position of Othmar Spann and the Vogelsang

---

107 Rintelen, *op.cit.*, p. 144. Wandruszka traces much of the corporative ideology of the *Heimwehr* to Othmar Spann and one of Spann's pupils at Graz, Walter Heinrich; *op.cit.*, p. 364.

108 Rintelen, *op.cit.*, p. 144.

109 Wandruszka points out quite correctly that the long and acrimonious arguments about whether the *Schutzbund* was created because of the existence of the *Heimwehr*, or vice versa, were quite beside the point. A political party or movement which does not share a common consensus with its opponents but fears that the opposition may resort to force whenever the ballot box does not yield the desired result will not hesitate to create its armed formations to be ready for "the day," *op.cit.*, p. 360.

school. These two schools delivered the most persistent attacks on Austrian democracy and on the Republic throughout the entire postwar period. They never wavered in their opposition to democracy and always clung to their corporative, Romantic reform proposals. These proposals received increased attention from Austrian Catholics during the late 1920's and furnished the basis for the corporative reorganization of the Austrian state in 1934.

Othmar Spann's criticism of democracy and his proposals for the corporative reorganization of state and society exercised great influence over Austrian Catholics. In spite of controversies over the Hegelian elements of Spann's philosophy and sociology, Catholics approved his condemnation of liberalism and democracy, and drew heavily on his social theory. The personal and intellectual relations between Spann and the Catholic camp will be explored in more detail after a full examination of Spann's principal political theories.

(a) Individualism and Universalism. Spann's criticism of democracy was based on his theory of society and his social science methodology. He contended that human society could be organized only in one of two ways: individualistic or universalistic:

"1. In the first, society is like a pile of loose rock. It appears to be a true collectivity, but is really only the sum of isolated and independent atoms . . .

"2. In the second, society is a totality [*Ganzheit*] whose parts are not independent, but are members of this totality."[110]

The individualistic society was merely a conglomerate of isolated individuals, seeking autarky in the pursuit of their selfish ends. The universalistic society, on the other hand, was an organic whole where individuals and groups were organic parts of a greater entity, not merely isolated atoms. These two answers to the question "What is society?" were the "foundation of all theoretical and political understanding about the nature of society."[111]

These two theories of society were also the basis for opposing ideological systems or *Weltanschauungen*, Spann asserted:

[110] Othmar Spann, *Der wahre Staat. Vorlesungen über Abbruch und Neubau der Gesellschaft* (2nd revised edition; Leipzig: Quelle & Meyer, 1923), p. 11.
[111] *Ibid.*, p. 12.

"These theories of society can, yea they must, have ideological consequences in the area of morals and philosophy, even though the theories themselves have no relation to any specific value system."[112] But he denied that the elevation of universalism to the position of the only correct social theory and social science methodology was based on a preference for universalism as a *Weltanschauung*. He then proceeded to "prove" that individualism was an incorrect method for studying society, a "fundamental mistake,"[113] because it committed three errors. Individualism assumed the existence of an "absolute individual"[114] who considered himself intellectually and morally autonomous and denied any reality except that of his own individuality. Next, it proceeded in social research on the premise that the individual was the source of all "original truths" (*ursprüngliche Wahrheiten*)[115] in society when actually that "original truth" was not in the individual but in the supra-individual entity which created him. Finally, it flattered the individual by making him appear to be master of his fate at all times, when in reality it left him lonely and helpless.[116] Thus, by "proving" the validity of universalism—that is to say, that the "whole" was superior to the "part"[117]—as a social theory and methodology he attempted to disguise his ideological preferences with scientific trappings.

112 Spann thus neatly "proved" that individualism was a wrong methodology because individualism carried to its logical conclusion—anarchy—was not a workable form of human organization. However, he did not choose to follow universalism to its inexorable conclusion in the same manner. Having already established that there were only two possible forms of human organization, this left him with only one form—universalism. So he skips easily from individualism as a philosophical principle to individualism as a methodological concept to individualism as a method for organizing society, *op.cit.*, pp. 69-70.

113 *Ibid.*, p. 68.

114 *Ibid.*, p. 17.

115 *Ibid.*, pp. 44-45.

116 *Ibid.*, pp. 69-70.

117 The universalist "theory of categories" was the core of Spann's system and the basis for his corporative state and economy. It can be reduced to five principles: (1) the whole does not exist "as such"; (2) the whole exists only in its members, for it cannot exist as such; (3) the whole is prior to the members, not necessarily in time, but logically; (4) the whole is not merely the sum of the members; and (5) therefore the whole is the source of the members' existence. Because Spann dominated corporative thinking in Germany and Austria his corporativist system became "the theoretical equipment of the most diverse tendencies. It simply became *the* corporative science. . . ." Justus Beyer, *Die Ständeideologie der Systemzeit und ihre Überwindung* (Darmstadt: L. C. Wittich, 1941), p. 174.

Spann, who was a prolific writer, considered the whole field of *Gesellschaftswissenschaften* his domain and produced works on sociology, philosophy, history, politics, economics, and social science methodology. The result was a vast self-contained system in which the parts certainly were subordinated to the whole and where by a methodological sleight of hand he used data from his sociology to prove what he wanted to prove in economics.

Having disposed of individualism as an incorrect theory of social organization and false method of social research, Spann proceeded to show that individualism had caused a serious crisis of ideas during the early years of the twentieth century. He defined the two fundamental aspects of that crisis as the "spiritual, theoretical crisis of individualism whose two practical consequences are the political crisis of liberalism and democracy, and the economic crisis of capitalism."[118] Spann also noted a crisis in Marxism which he considered part of the same breakdown of individualism. Finally, he saw in the political crisis of the German people following the end of the war still another result of individualist influences.[119]

(b) The Three Forms of Political Individualism. Spann distinguished three forms in which individualism had appeared in history: Machiavellianism, anarchism, and natural law or contract theory. He admitted that Machiavellianism had some advantages over the other two because it produced order by establishing a hierarchy of ruler and ruled.[120] But he condemned the other two forms because they were unworkable and produced complete atomization. He suggested that natural law or contract theory could take two forms. In the first, the people transferred their power for all time to one individual who would protect the natural rights of the other parties to this contract. This was the system of enlightened monarchy. In the second, the people retained power but delegated authority to elected officials.[121] Such a state would be organized on three principles: individual freedom, minimum scope of state activity, and limitations on

118 Spann, *op.cit.*, p. 102.
119 Spann considered the revolution of his time not part of another stage in the victorious march of liberalism, but the first stage of a counter-revolution against liberalism; *op.cit.*, p. 4.
120 Spann, *op.cit.*, p. 23.
121 *Ibid.*, p. 22.

individual freedom only to the extent necessary to insure equal freedom for all.[122] Such a society, Spann insisted, would be atomistic because all members of it were deemed to be equal. It would also be highly centralized because the demand for rigid equality would require the destruction of all intermediate units on the ground that these would abridge the equal standing of the individual. Spann pointed out that the second of the natural law or contract theories had prevailed in the western world since the break-up of the Middle Ages, and was, therefore, responsible for the crisis of individualism in the western world during the twentieth century.

(c) Liberalism and Democracy. Spann identified liberalism and democracy as the two political ideologies appropriate to this second form of natural law or contract theory: "Liberalism which is the moderate form of this natural law theory was able to accommodate itself to constitutional government. Democracy, on the other hand, tried to bring about full political equality and government by the people, and thereby provided the purest expression of social contract theory and of popular sovereignty."[123] Liberalism he considered the more moderate of the two. Democracy, on the other hand, was the extreme form of popular sovereignty. The outstanding example of this extreme form was the United States, where there was a complete turn-over of civil servants after a presidential election.

Spann found a number of serious defects in democracy. First, in a democracy people were organized according to outward forms of common activity, but remained intellectually isolated and lonely.[124] Next, majority rule, the method for deciding issues in a democracy, robbed the individual of his intrinsic value by equating the value of his vote mechanically with that of every other individual.[125] As a result, the voice of the expert was stilled altogether: "Using the ballot box to decide questions of truth and justice is the most ridiculous suggestion I have heard. . . . Nobody can live by the majoritarian principle, but only on the basis of value and truth."[126] The third major fault of democracy was, according to Spann, that it assumed people made rational decisions based on independent knowledge. If this were true,

122 *Ibid.*, pp. 23-24.   123 *Ibid.*, p. 107.   124 *Ibid.*, pp. 108-109.
125 *Ibid.*, p. 111.   126 *Ibid.*, p. 112.

Spann felt that majority decisions would represent, if not "truth," at least a common consensus.[127] But he denied that this was the case, for people had no independent sources of information at all when they reached decisions. They simply listened to their so-called leaders and did what they were told to do: "Popular will as political will must be shaped by a leader before it can become articulate. This means that the will of the people is created by the very persons whose sole task it is, according to democratic theory, to carry out the orders given by that popular will."[128]

Spann concluded that pure democracy had never existed because it was "against the nature of things" but had always deteriorated immediately into a system where leaders, cliques, and political parties exercised the powers the people should have exercised themselves.[129] It might be well to point out that this caricature of "democracy," was widely accepted in Central Europe. It was a standard item in the arsenal of all anti-democratic demagogues. That it should be offered to university students as part of a series of lectures on the "true state" by a senior professor indicates how deeply Romantic anti-democratic ideas had penetrated certain groups of middle-class intellectuals.

However, Spann's denunciation of democracy was not yet exhausted. He also charged individualism, the creator of democracy, with having destroyed the organic unity of the Middle Ages and spawned the French Revolution: "First came the shattering of the corporative spirit, of the corporative harmony of the Middle Ages, as it found expression in guild, church, fief, cooperative and fraternal organs of all kinds. This was followed by the mighty eruption of the individualistic spirit during the French Revolution."[130] We meet here again the *fata morgana* of the Middle Ages and its "rich group life" which had been a part of Romantic theory since the days of Adam Heinrich Müller. Finally, Spann accused individualism of exalting the individual at the expense of the collectivity, denying any value to the state and thereby limiting the scope of state activity.[131] This limited state was, therefore, not in a position to cope with the evil effects of economic individualism, called capitalism.[132]

127 *Ibid.*, p. 114. 128 *Loc.cit.* 129 *Ibid.*, p. 115.
130 *Ibid.*, p. 83. 131 *Loc.cit.* 132 *Ibid.*, p. 85.

(d) The Ideenwelt of Individualism. Spann summarized the world of ideas of individualism in this manner:[133]

(1) *In the Area of Ideas*: anti-metaphysical, empiricist, relativist, subjective, inductive, causal-oriented, utilitarian.

(2) *In the Area of Political Institutions*: cosmopolitan in relations with other people, atomistic and centralist with regard to inner political structure.

(3) *In the Area of Economic Institutions*: capitalist, *laissez-faire.*

Spann rejected liberalism and democracy but detected congenial features in Marxism. He found evolutionary socialism unacceptable because he considered it hopelessly caught in liberal-democratic individualism. On the other hand he identified certain universalist and corporativist elements in Russian Bolshevism.[134] At the same time that the first edition of *Der wahre Staat* appeared, many Romantic theorists were inclined to see in the Russian system of soviets a twentieth-century realization of their Romantic corporative theories.[135] These same thinkers also applauded the creation of works councils in Central Europe immediately after the end of the war. These tendencies were, of course, part of the general concern for economic democracy during the postwar years. German demands for economic democracy found expression in the Weimar Constitution in the creation of a *Reichswirtschaftsrat*. In England the Guild Socialists advocated the addition of an economic parliament to the existing "political parliament."

(e) Spann's Relations with Catholics and Nationalists. Spann occupied an ideological and political position midway between the Nationalist and Christian-social conservative *Lager*. As a result, he was in turn claimed and attacked by both of these camps. The Nationalists, including the Nazis, attacked him because of what they considered his anti-*völkisch* bias: "The academic defender of this so-called corporative state was the Viennese professor O. Spann who denied the need for *völkisch* unity in order

---

[133] *Ibid.*, pp. 89-90.   [134] *Ibid.*, p. 189.

[135] Arnold Bergsträsser, "Neuere Literatur zum Gedanken des berufsständischen Staates," *Schmollers Jahrbuch für Gesetzgebung, Verwaltung und Volkswirtschaft* XLVII (1923), pp. 283-299: "They attempt . . . to assess the political potential of the economic organizations whose power position has enabled them to challenge the state."

to protect corporative interests and the honor of the supra-national Church."[136]

Justus Beyer, a German Nazi official writing in 1941, confirmed this judgment of Spann contained in an official document of the *Deutsche Arbeitsfront*, written in 1938. The Nationalists rejected Spann because they feared his corporative system would weaken the unity of Nazi state and *Volk*.[137] They also suspected that Spann's emphasis on medieval institutions was a result of fundamental pro-church and pro-Catholic sympathies. Beyer condemned Spann on both of these points. He insisted that Spann's corporative pluralism would negate the *Führerprinzip*.[138] He also devoted considerable effort to show that Spann's philosophy and methodology were based on a *"mittelalterlich-kirchliches Weltbild."*[139] Beyer claimed that in Spann the spiritual-metaphysical had precedence over the material and that this preference led Spann to consider theocracy the best form of political rule. Even in the second best form, the church, though formally subordinate to the state, would actually control it.[140] Beyer also objected to Spann's assigning the church a place as a separate *Stand* in a corporative system which Beyer considered to be a conscious imitation of the structure of the Catholic Church.[141] Finally, Beyer called attention to a doctoral dissertation approved at the Institute for Scholastic Philosophy at Innsbruck, which purported to prove the compatibility of Spann's universalistic system with Scholastic philosophy.[142]

The Catholic *Lager* found Spann to be a troublesome companion.[143] Catholics approved his critique of liberalism and capitalism, but found it difficult to reconcile the Hegelian elements in Spann, his glorification of the collectivity at the expense of the individual, with Catholic social pluralism. The sharpest controversies between Spann and the Catholic *Lager*

[136] *Österreich. Die soziale und wirtschaftliche Struktur* (Berlin: Arbeitswissenschaftliches Amt der deutschen Arbeitsfront, 1938), p. 60.

[137] Beyer realized that a movement making totalitarian claims could not tolerate a genuine corporative pluralism, not even in theory; *op.cit.*, p. 340.

[138] *Ibid.*, p. 330.   [139] *Ibid.*, p. 212.   [140] *Ibid.*, p. 214.   [141] *Ibid.*, p. 218.

[142] *Ibid.*, p. 219; Arnold, "Wiener Richtungen," *Staatslexikon*, IV, 1296.

[143] Spann participated in many Catholic congresses and study courses and usually became the center of acrimonious controversies and debates. See Othmar Spann, "In eigener Sache," *Ständisches Leben*, II (1932), pp. 330-333.

involved the German Solidarists, the school of Josef Pesch.[144] With the aid of the Solidarist principle, Pesch had attempted to achieve a balance between the claims of the individual and of the collectivity. As a Catholic, Pesch had to give primary consideration to the individual, his soul and his salvation. As an economist and sociologist concerned with the social question, Pesch wanted to use the state to protect the economically weak against the effects of *laissez-faire* capitalism and industrialism. Spann, on the other hand, insisted that there was no *tertium quid* between individualism or universalism, there was no social theory or social system which could successfully balance the claims of the individual and the collectivity. He attacked the Solidarists for having accommodated themselves to individualism and having concealed that accommodation by their Solidarist scheme. The Solidarists retorted that Spann's universalism was an un-Christian totalitarianism, unacceptable to Catholics.[145]

Franz Arnold treated Spann more kindly in the article on *Wiener Richtungen* in the *Staatslexikon*, the official Catholic encyclopedia written by a group of Austrian and German Catholics. He insisted that Spann's assigning priority to the whole over the part was an "analytical, sociological theory" which did not destroy the "Eigenwert des Individuums."[146] There is some support for this interpretation because Spann had insisted that universalism gave the individual ". . . what properly belongs to him, his uniqueness and his individuality. Reality can reside in the totality without constituting a destruction of the uniqueness of the individual."[147] However, the universalist theory of categories which, according to Spann, governed the relations between the whole and the parts had clearly established the priority of that whole. As a result, the presumption, in Spann's system, was always in favor of the collectivity.

Because of the influence of Romantic doctrines on their social thought, Austrian Catholics found Spann more congenial than did their German co-religionists. Spann was a regular contributor to Catholic magazines and maintained close contact with

---

144 See below, Ch. v, for a discussion of Solidarism.

145 Beyer noted that the universalist-solidarist controversy was the long-standing "ecclesiastical-philosophical dispute between Platonic and Aristotelian modes of thought"; *op.cit.*, p. 220.

146 Arnold, *op.cit.*, p. 1295.   147 Spann, *op.cit.*, p. 46.

the Catholic corporative theorists who considered him a mighty fighter against liberalism, positivism, and democracy: "This manifested itself most passionately in the *Ganzheit* philosophy of O. Spann. How long he stood isolated in his fight against atomistic and mechanistic social science. . . . With unmatched skill he linked together sociology and economics, to form a system of ideas which was borne along by the force of a religious world view. . . . It was necessity, not accident, which caused O. Spann to carry forward the religion-oriented concept of the *Reich* of Adam Müller, and which made him the herald of the universalistic 'true state.' "[148]

But Austrian Catholics were troubled by the Hegelian elements in Spann's thought, especially his concept of the *Kulturstaat*, which claimed jurisdiction over areas Catholics considered the exclusive domain of the church, the family, the school, or other social organs: "This *Kulturstaat* represents the highest form of spiritual and intellectual unity. It is not content to deal only with the purely mechanical problems of social life, but takes over the nurture of intellectual life and of all the spiritual and intellectual contacts between the members of the state."[149] Thus the state of Spann takes its place in a line that reaches back to Vogelsang and ultimately to Müller. However, Catholics who had failed to perceive clearly the incompatibilities with Catholic social theory of the writings of Müller and Vogelsang showed a similar lack of understanding in the case of Spann.

8. The Vogelsang School and Austrian Democracy

(a) The Decline of Sozialreform. During the first years of the republic, the Vogelsang school did not play an important part in the development of Austrian Catholic thought. Nevertheless, the successors of Vogelsang continued during that period the extreme anti-democratic and anti-capitalist tendencies of their teacher. There were five causes which contributed to the decline of social Romantic (*Sozialreform*) doctrine during that period. (1) The publication of *Rerum novarum* in 1891 was considered a victory of *Sozialpolitik* over *Sozialreform*.[150] As a result, the

---

148 Lehrl, *op.cit.*, p. 68.   149 Spann, *op.cit.*, p. 66.
150 Jostock, *op.cit.*, pp. 138-143; see also above Ch. I, pp. 23-25, for a discussion of *Rerum Novarum*.

opponents of the Romantic tradition now received support from the highest authority in the church for their program of economic and social improvements within the existing framework of the modern state and capitalism. Until 1891 the proponents of *Sozialreform* had relied on the strongly anti-modernist doctrines of *Pio Nono* and had claimed that they alone represented a truly Catholic social theory. (2) The death of Karl von Vogelsang in 1890 also contributed to the decline of *Sozialreform* in Austria. After his death there seemed to be no one to influence Catholic social thought in favor of Romantic doctrines as Vogelsang had been able to do. (3) The weakening of Romantic influences can also be traced to the rise of Karl Lueger as leader of the new political Catholicism. Lueger was a skilled politician but had a strong distaste for programs which, he said, would restrict his freedom of movement in politics.[151] *Sozialpolitik*, which approached social problems empirically, was better suited to the needs of the new leader of Austrian Catholics. (4) The decline of Austrian *Sozialreform* was hastened also by the developments in German Catholicism where *Sozialpolitik* had won the upper hand even before the publication of *Rerum novarum*.[152] These German developments had a profound influence on Austrian Catholic thought. (5) The creation of the Austrian Republic and the prominent role political Catholicism came to play in the government of the republic sealed the decline of Romantic doctrines. In the years after the war Austrian Catholics attempted to minimize their quarrels with the modern state. They devoted their energies to governing the Austrian Republic and attempted to accommodate themselves to the political and social institutions established in 1918. Social Romantic theory, which was profoundly critical of the modern state, simply was not an appropriate doctrine for Austrian Catholics during the early years of the Republic.[153]

Even during this period of *Sozialreform* decline the writers of the Vogelsang school carried on the Romantic tradition of

[151] Joseph Schwalber, *Vogelsang und die christlich-soziale Politik* (doctoral dissertation, University of Munich, 1927), pp. 37, 51. Schwalber quoted a remark of Lueger which illustrated this distaste for doctrinaire programs: "Please no programs, they only tie our hands."

[152] Schwalber, *op.cit.*, p. 51.

[153] August M. Knoll, "Vogelsang und der Ständegedanke," *Die soziale Frage*, p. 69.

their master. However, their criticism of democracy and capitalism showed little of the originality and fervor of Vogelsang. Compared with his their writings seem carping and petty. They also seemed out of date because they merely elaborated the anti-capitalist and anti-democratic doctrines of Vogelsang without taking into account the vast social and economic changes which had occurred since Vogelsang had first attacked the crudities of rising industrialism during the 1870's.

(b) Anton Orel and the Judenrepublik. Anton Orel was the leading writer in this school, and the recognized successor of Vogelsang: "Taken together his books, pamphlets, and articles form the logical continuation of the activity of Karl von Vogelsang, the father of Viennese *Sozialreform*."[154] Orel had been involved in a series of controversies with the hierarchy and the Christian Social party, extending over many years. For example, in 1909 the Christian Social party, as the "true" representatives of Vienna's artisans and shopkeepers, had supported the resumption of compulsory night and Sunday vocational schooling for apprentices. Under existing legislation apprentices had to be released from work once or twice during the week for attendance at continuation school. Orel broke with the party over that issue and founded a youth movement of his own to compete with the official Christian Social movement which he considered to have become corrupted by excessive Christian Social accommodation to capitalism.[155] Orel returned to the party fold in 1922, but in 1923 he ran a separate ticket in the Vienna municipal election and won two seats.[156]

The violence of Orel's attack on democracy was matched only by that of his teacher. In language reminiscent of Vogelsang he condemned democracy because he considered it the rule of a moneyed oligarchy aided by unscrupulous demagogues (he included most Christian Social politicians in that category): ". . . modern democracy is a cancerous growth which must be excised. We desperately need an authority whose ultimate source of power is God. All the democratic instruments like universal suffrage have turned out to be frauds. . . . There is not a trace

---

[154] Richard Kralik, "Martin Spahn und Anton Orel," *Das Neue Reich* IV (1921-1922), p. 371.
[155] Schwalber, *op.cit.*, p. 81.
[156] *Ibid.*, p. 82.

of true democracy anywhere, instead we have been saddled with an oligarchy of demagogues in cahoots with the plutocracy. True popular government, on the other hand, can exist only through the organic participation of all natural, healthy, and properly organized forces."[157]

Orel traced democracy to a "relativism of social institutions"[158] which considered all forms of government equally acceptable. He contended that even Catholics had become infected by this false doctrine. In support of this contention he quoted with horror a Catholic professor of moral theology to the effect that both feudalism and capitalism were compatible with Christian moral law, provided both systems recognized the force of that moral law.[159] Orel pointed out that modern relativism considered social institutions purely immanent affairs which followed their own laws of development. As a result, Christian morality became merely a framework within which this development took place. Orel condemned this as simply the most recent form of Manicheism which irretrievably divided matter from spirit, the immanent from the transcendent, and recognized separate principles for the two spheres.[160] Catholics, Orel claimed, could accept only a Christian universalism which was based on a fundamental unity of matter and spirit, not merely their equality.[161] The only form of social organization which could be derived from this fundamental unity of spirit and matter was the *Lehensordnung*, feudalism. Orel concluded that "Christianity is incompatible both with capitalism and communism which are respectively the individualistic and pseudo-socialistic manifestations of the materialistic-mammonistic spirit in society and economy. . . ."[162]

Orel urged Catholics to reject Austrian democracy and the Constitution of 1920 because they violated the organic principles of social organization and were the result of social relativism.

---

[157] Quoted in Kralik, *op.cit.*, p. 372.

[158] Anton Orel, *Das Verfassungsmachwerk der "Republik Österreich" von der Warte der immerwährenden Philosophie aus und im Lichte von der Idee, Natur und Geschichte Österreichs geprüft und verworfen* (2nd ed.; Vienna: Vogelsang-Verlag G.m.b.H., 1921), pp. 3-6.

[159] This could well be a reference to Seipel, who continued to hold the chair of moral theology at the University of Vienna until 1922, when he became chancellor.

[160] *Ibid.*, p. 4.   [161] *Ibid.*, p. 5.   [162] *Ibid.*

The Constitution of 1920 was unacceptable to Catholics because it was based on a false major premise, namely, that all *Recht* emanated from the people. To accept a state which in this manner denied the only true source of authority constituted an act of revolution against the "permanent legitimate authority."[163] Such attacks on the Constitution of 1920 by members of the Christian-social conservative *Lager* became commonplace during the last years of the Republic. But in 1921, when Orel thundered against the republican regime, the vast majority of his co-religionists were more concerned with legislative majorities and cabinet posts than with philosophical discussions about the nature of civil authority. They rediscovered the anti-democratic epithets of the Romantic doctrine later on when they began to search for suitable weapons with which to attack democracy.

Orel also examined the other articles of the 1920 Constitution and condemned the weak executive, the party system, and the electoral laws—the same points, incidentally, which Seipel attacked seven years later in his Munich and Tübingen critiques of Austrian democracy. Orel found the president to be a figurehead and the cabinet at the mercy of the legislature. The legislature, in its turn, was controlled by the party machines which had reduced the members of the legislature to mere puppets. The operation of a rigid list system reinforced party rule because it barred the people from any effective choice of representatives.

He came to the conclusion that the real rulers of Austria were the Jews, who controlled industry and the press, and were supported in this dominant position by none other than members of the clergy and Christian Social politicians. In violent and abusive terms Orel condemned the Austrian Republic and all those who had any part in its operation: "This is why the true ruler needs to mask his hideous visage marked as it is by mammon worship, the murder of the Messiah, and the eternal curse of the Almighty. . . . This is the mask called popular sovereignty and republican constitution, and behind it we will find the invisible, but real, ruler of our miserable Jew republic. . . . And to think that the representatives of Catholic groups, even prel-

[163] *Ibid.*, p. 10.

ates of the Catholic Church, from stupidity or from cowardice, or both, helped fashion this mask and fasten it to the face of the Jewish overlord."[164] Catholics had a duty, Orel argued, to carry out a counter-revolution against this revolutionary republican regime.

(c) Josef Eberle, Das Neue Reich, and Schönere Zukunft. Josef Eberle and the contributors to his periodicals *Das Neue Reich* and *Schönere Zukunft* adopted positions only slightly less extreme than those of Anton Orel. Eberle was editor of the first periodical from 1918 to 1925, when he took over *Schönere Zukunft* and continued as its editor until 1934.[165] These periodicals published articles which represented a variety of Catholic views on political and social questions, but the general editorial position was definitely in the Romantic tradition and strongly legitimist.[166] For example, *Das Neue Reich* repeatedly criticized the German *Zentrum* leadership for being too liberal, for co-operating with the Social Democrats, and for defending the Weimar Republic.[167] However, there was little criticism of the Austrian hierarchy and the Christian Social party. This is not surprising, for many Austrian Catholics after the war considered the *Zentrum* to be entirely too liberal or found many other faults in the Catholic movement in the *Reich*, while closing their eyes to conditions in the Catholic *Lager* at home.

[164] *Ibid.*, p. 30.

[165] See Ruth Werner, *Die Wiener Wochenschrift "Das Neue Reich" (1918-1925); ein Beitrag zur Geschichte des politischen Katholizismus* (Breslauer historische Forschungen Nr. 9; Breslau: Priebatsch, 1938); see also the section on Eberle in Arnold, *op.cit.*, pp. 1301-1303. Johanna Gierse followed the basic analysis of the Vienna tendencies in the *Staatslexikon* article, but examined the various groups in more detail. She was less impartial than Arnold and condemned the entire Romantic direction as "unrealistic." Johanna Gierse, "Sozialromantische Richtungen im Katholizismus der Gegenwart," *Soziale Revue*, XXXII (September and December 1932), pp. 129-176, 193-233.

[166] Eberle noted that the enemies of Hapsburg were the Jews, Freemasons, liberals, and Pan-Germans. This listing of the "enemies" of *Das Neue Reich* serves to define the editorial policy of that periodical: anti-Semitic, anti-Freemason, anti-liberal, and anti-German nationalist. Joseph Eberle, "Kaiser Karls zweite Ungarnfahrt," *Das Neue Reich*, IV (1921-1922), pp. 69-70; see also "Die dermalige Ausschaltung Habsburgs aus der Weltpolitik," *Das Neue Reich*, IV (1921-1922), pp. 129-135, where Eberle praised the dynasty thus: "There is no dynasty in the world whose services to Roman Catholic Christianity can measure up to those [of the Hapsburgs]."

[167] Martin Spahn, "Mein Wechsel der politischen Partei," "Parteifragen in Deutschland," "Zentrumspolitik," *Das Neue Reich*, IV (1921-1922), pp. 136-139, 255-259, and 289-290.

The criticism of democracy in *Das Neue Reich* was generally in the Romantic tradition. One writer identified legal positivism, which denied the existence of eternal and natural law, as the basis of democracy: "This doctrine of the origin of justice and public authority free from divine influence leads logically to the omnicompetent state. In turn, this doctrine of the omnicompetent state of purely human origin leads us to popular sovereignty, and thereby directly to bolshevism. . . ."[168] The writers of *Das Neue Reich* shared with many other Catholics the conviction that the slightest concession to any sort of liberal doctrine would set up a chain reaction which would unquestionably end in communism. Catholics were exhorted to oppose liberal institutions no matter how harmless they might appear because they carried within them the seed of a Bolshevik revolution. These dire threats prevented the development of any truly liberal tendencies in the Catholic camp and repelled the moderate liberals outside the camp. As a result moderates in both camps lost out to extremists who were determined to destroy the republic.

Another writer denied that the people really governed in a democracy: "Every intelligent person knows that this is not an idea but merely a slogan, for any attempt of the people to govern themselves can only end in chaos and anarchy. Therefore popular government is not rule by the people but the rule of demagogues and parties who constitute only a tiny minority and not the entire people."[169] Even if the rise of demagogues could be prevented, the division of the people in a democracy into parties, factions, and interest groups destroyed the moral unity of a Christian people, and the moral basis of the political order.[170] The contempt of Romantic writers for the process of politics in a democracy, for political parties, and for the representation of interests, indicates their failure to understand the workings of a democratic system. They talked grandly about the people as a "moral idea"; they expressed concern for the common good which they claimed was threatened by selfish interest. But

[168] Sigismund Waitz, "Das moderne Staatsrecht—ein Verhängnis für die Völker," *Das Neue Reich*, IV (1921-1922), p. 790.

[169] Joseph August Lux, "Demokratie—Demagogie," *Das Neue Reich*, IV (1921-1922), p. 736.

[170] *Ibid.*, p. 737.

in their eagerness to insure the rule of "das ganze Volk" they proposed to destroy those institutions and political processes which made possible an expression of the multitude of ideas, proposals, etc., which arise in a complex modern society. What they proposed to do in the interest of the "whole people" was to create an omnicompetent state, the very thing they had deplored, a state which supposedly would stimulate the growth of a "rich group life" but would actually govern autocratically in the name of the "whole." The anti-democratic tendencies of Eberle and his circle were best summed up by the writer in *Das Neue Reich*, who concluded that the world had only a choice between "theocracy and the rule of Satan, between the Christian spirit in government and the Masonic principles of Godlessness and hostility to religion."[171] Theocracy was not simply the rule of God over the state, the writer contended. It was the supremacy of the moral world order combined with the willingness of the public order of the state to subordinate itself to that moral rule.[172] The writer concluded that any other form of political organization was equivalent to the rule of Satan. He then gave examples of what he considered theocracy and the rule of Satan: "This great conflict between the rule of God and of Satan found a tragic expression in the heroic fate of Charles of Austria. Emperor Charles I had to make such a choice between Christian principles and Freemasonry in government. . . . Oh, Austrian people it is up to you to follow the heroic example of your Christian emperor. It is your turn now to choose the Christian state, theocracy, and to reject the rule of Satan."[173]

Thus, the republic was identified as the rule of Satan and the Hapsburg regime as theocracy. This left Catholics no choice but to oppose the very republican regime their representatives had approved in the Constituent Assembly. It is not surprising, therefore, that the opponents of the Catholic camp questioned Catholic loyalty to the Republic. They heard one member of that camp issue a call for true democracy and then identify a fascist armed formation, the *Heimwehr,* as the defenders of that true democracy. They heard another urge his co-religionists to engage in a counter-revolution against the Republic, and still

[171] Waitz, *op.cit.*, p. 818. [172] *Ibid.*, p. 789. [173] *Ibid.*, p. 818.

a third one identify the Republic as the rule of Satan. They concluded that Catholics were not really interested in "reforming" democracy but only in abolishing it altogether.

9. Criticism of Democracy: An Evaluation

Austrian Catholic criticisms of democracy can be summarized under two headings: those which deal primarily with the machinery of democratic government, and those which address themselves to the effects of democracy on society. There were four criticisms of the machinery of democracy most often advanced by Catholics during the First Republic. Catholics attacked the system of proportional representation because it prevented the creation of stable working majorities in the legislature and the executive. They condemned Austrian political parties because they claimed the entire life and allegiance of their followers and thereby threatened the common consensus necessary for the operation of democratic institutions. They complained that under the rules of the Austrian democracy the two major opposing parties each controlled one of the two principal branches of government. Deadlock resulted from such an arrangement; government was paralyzed and unable to deal with the great problems facing the Austrian state. Finally, Catholics were dissatisfied with the territorial system of representation. They argued that such a system left unrepresented important social and economic groups in society.

The Catholic critics of democracy in Austria also condemned what they considered the evil effects of democracy or, as they sometimes called it, "political individualism," on Austrian society. They blamed this "political individualism" for the destruction of the traditional value system of the Austrian people, the weakening of the moral and religious basis of public life, the elimination of small territorial and occupational groups through which the individual could express his wishes and his personality, and last, but not least, the application of material standards to all forms of human activity.

It was suggested in Chapter II that a review of nineteenth century Catholic thought led to four conclusions, one of which was particularly relevant for the present chapter. It was proposed there that the inability of Austrian Catholics to conceive of a genuine state-society dichotomy helped explain their failure to understand the nature of democratic government and the role of political parties. This suggestion should be taken together with the explanation for the abandonment of democracy by Austrian Catholics advanced at the beginning of this chapter, namely, that Catholics identified democracy and republican institutions with their principal enemy, the Socialist *Lager*, and that they became dissatisfied with the Constitution of 1920 because it perpetuated the dominant position that *Lager* had gained during the early years of the Republic. These two will enable the reader to judge the validity of the Catholic criticisms of Austrian democracy between 1918 and 1934.

The uncompromising hostility of the overwhelming majority of Austrian Catholics to the Socialist *Lager*, their unwillingness to seek a *modus vivendi* with that *Lager*, and their determination to destroy its political and social position reveals the first four criticisms advanced against Austrian democracy to be simply manifestations of impatience with a political system which prevented Catholics from silencing their enemies at will. All Catholics meant when they complained about the system of proportional representation was that their majority was not sufficiently large for them to proceed with social and economic legislation which would harm the Socialists. Actually, the distribution of political strength in Austria has been remarkably stable. Elections under the Second Republic revealed that a decade of *Grossdeutschland* and foreign occupation had not changed the strength of the major parties as first revealed in elections during 1918-1920. Catholics would probably have preferred single-member constituencies, not because of a devotion to democratic principles, but because they hoped that such an electoral system would increase their representation in the legislature.

In regard to their second criticism they bear at least equal blame with their major opponents for having converted political parties into quasi-religious orders who propagated a true faith, a *Weltanschauung*, and considered their opponents heretics and infidels, to be suppressed at all costs. It was the nature of the three *Lager* during the period of the First Republic which made impossible the growth of a consensus on fundamentals of political and social organization, not the actual form of party organization. The experience of the Second Republic so far seems to indicate that there is now at least a minimum degree of consensus among Socialists and Catholics on the continuation of democratic institutions. The same would have been possible under the First Republic if the two *Lager* had been willing to agree on maintaining that Republic rather than resorting to arms.

The complaints of Austrian Catholics about the paralysis of republican government can again be traced to their uncompromising hostility to the Socialists. It is true that the Christian Socials alone did not command a majority in parliament and had to govern with the aid of minor bourgeois parties whose fear of the Socialist economic program made them willing partners in an anti-Socialist alliance. What Catholic critics of democracy seemed to imply was that their majorities in the legislature were not large enough to push through constitutional amendments which did not have the support of the Social Democrats. On the other hand, Catholics were quite correct when they pointed out that the Constitution of 1920 had created an omnicompetent assembly which greatly overshadowed the cabinet executive. Just the same, Catholics and their allies had always sufficient votes to put through legislation requiring only normal pluralities or majorities, but they were continuously forced to modify their program to meet the demands and objections of the Socialists.

Finally, the dissatisfaction of Austrian Catholics with the system of territorial representation in the "political" parliament demonstrates most clearly the lack of their understanding of democratic government. Their opponents soon discovered that the forces which supposedly lacked adequate representation in the political legislature organized on a territorial basis were groups like the *Heimwehr*, a fascist armed formation without any sizeable popular following. The demands of Seipel and other Catholic critics for the representation of social groups amounted to an admission that they were casting about for some other method of representation which would increase their own strength and reduce that of their opponents. The industrial workers were especially suspicious of these Catholic corporative proposals because they feared that the occupational corporations would be controlled by the employers, and that in the total corporative structure the industrial workers would become an insignificant minority. They discovered in 1934 that their fears were not exaggerated.

Catholic critics of the modern state since Vogelsang have insisted that the principal benefit which society would derive from a system of corporative representation would be the relief of the state and the political parliament from the excessive burdens of welfare functions and centralized controls. The occupational organizations would take over these functions and would leave the state only with its proper "political" duties. The major fallacy in this argument has been clearly stated by Ernest Barker:

"The State, in the shape of the political parliament through which it acts, is the only organ and maker of law. The State . . . is only a legal association; but, by the same token, it is also the only legal association. Because it is that, the political parliament is the one adjustment centre. There cannot be a plurality of adjustment centres. If there were, they would themselves need to be adjusted. There must be one, single, final adjustment centre; and that adjustment centre is necessarily compelled by its nature not only to adjust finally all sovereign issues . . . , but also to take the initiative in formulating their adjustment. . . . Men will always seek to go straight to it, and the institution of other instances will not defeat or deflect the attraction. That attraction will be especially strong in the field of economics. Economic issues . . . are swept particularly, and swept directly to the final adjustment centre. . . ."[174]

In modern complex industrial society a corporative system either dissolves into anarchy or becomes dominated completely by a political authority—the experience of Austria after 1934 proved that only the second alternative was a realistic one in the twentieth century. It was suggested at the end of Chapter II that Austrian Catholics viewed the state as an agency for the enforcement of moral and ethical standards and that, therefore, they were unable to conceive of a genuine state-society dichotomy. One might add that the omnicompetence of such a state

[174] Ernest Barker, *Principles of Social and Political Theory* (London: Oxford University Press, 1951), pp. 82-83.

would be increased by the establishment of a corporative system which proposed to divide the powers of the political legislature among several corporative chambers. As a result, the government—that is to say, the executive—would be in full control, checked only by temporary coalitions of occupational corporations who combined to press some common objective but could easily be bought off by the central political authority.

Little need be added to what has been said at the end of Chapter II about the effects of democracy on Austrian society. Catholic critics of democracy after 1918 continued in the nineteenth-century tradition of expressing concern for the well-being of the individual, the need for a rich group life, and for a reduction of the powers and functions of the state. But their proposals for remedying these faults were based on the same mistaken assumptions as those of their co-religionists during the previous century. The Corporative Constitution of 1934, which will be examined in Chapter VII, will read like a catalogue of all these misconceptions about the nature of the modern state and the modern economy.

CHAPTER V

THE CRITICISM OF
CAPITALISM: FROM *SOZIALPOLITIK*
TO *QUADRAGESIMO ANNO*

AUSTRIAN CATHOLIC criticism of capitalism and industrialism during the period 1918-1934 was in the tradition of social thought developed during the nineteenth century when Austrians were first forced to deal with the social question. Consequently, Austrian Catholic social doctrines during the period of the First Austrian Republic closely followed the *Sozialreform-Sozialpolitik* pattern developed during that earlier period.[1] Though the publication of *Rerum novarum* contributed to the decline of *Sozialreform* proposals in Austria after 1891, the *Sozialpolitik* tradition did not remain unchallenged. As the analysis of the Catholic criticism of democracy in the previous chapter indicated, Romantic doctrines continued to exercise considerable influence in Austria, especially after Catholics had become dissatisfied with the democratic institutions they had helped to establish during the years 1918-1920.[2] The continuation of the basic *Sozialreform-Sozialpolitik* pattern makes it possible to divide the critics of capitalism and industrialism into two groups. We propose to examine the *Sozialpolitik* doctrines in the present chapter, and those of *Sozialreform* in Chapter VI.

1. The Pattern of Criticism

(a) The Influence of Political and Economic Developments. The development of Catholic social theory during the period 1918-1934 was influenced by political, social, and economic de-

[1] The proponents of *Sozialreform* demanded a radical reconstruction of society, inspired chiefly by medieval corporative institutions, while the advocates of *Sozialpolitik* proposed to work for gradual changes in the existing socio-economic framework. See Paul Jostock, *Der deutsche Katholizismus und die Überwindung des Kapitalismus. Eine ideengeschichtliche Skizze* (Regensburg: Friedrich Pustet, 1932), pp. 138-144, and the works cited in Ch. I, note 24, above.

[2] See the chart on p. 105 for the shift toward Romantic anti-democratic doctrines which took place during the last years of the Republic.

· 153 ·

velopments in the same manner that social doctrines during the nineteenth century bore the imprint of contemporary Austrian institutions, such as a close tie between throne and altar, a strong urban and rural middle class as principal supporters of the church, and a great variety of corporative organizations in agriculture and the trades (*Gewerbe*). It might be appropriate, therefore, at this point, to summarize briefly those political and social developments during the republican period which decisively influenced the tendencies of social theorizing in Austria during the period 1918-1934.

Austrian Catholic criticism of capitalism and industrialism was profoundly influenced by the powerful position of the industrial working class and the Social Democratic party. The strength of the Socialist *Lager* forced Catholics into an anti-Socialist alliance with fundamentally pro-capitalist bourgeois groups. As a result the influence of Catholic labor groups on the formulation of the Catholic social program, which had been slight anyway, was even further reduced.[3] That program continued to stress ideas favorable to the lower middle class in the cities and on the farms, the two groups which had remained the principal supporters of the church in Austria. However, the public policy of Catholic governments had become strongly influenced by big business and big agriculture. Consequently, Catholic governments found it difficult to pursue policies which reflected accurately and simultaneously the wishes of big business and the anti-capitalist tendencies of petty bourgeois and agrarian groups. This divergence between Catholic social theory and the public policy of Christian Social governments increased the difficulties of the Christian-social conservative *Lager*. The need for an all-inclusive anti-Socialist alliance brought into that *Lager* many social groups ranging all the way from Fascists to radical social reformers, who advanced a variety of social theories and engaged in bitter disputes such as that

[3] The Catholic labor movement must bear at least part of the blame for its weakness and its lack of influence on the Catholic social program. From its inception it had been under the influence of master craftsmen and of intellectuals from the Vogelsang school. As a result its social and economic program was based on Romantic social doctrines and was concerned primarily with the problems of the artisan. Karl Lugmayer (ed.), *Das Linzer Programm der christlichen Arbeiter Österreichs* (Vienna: Verlag der Typographischen Anstalt, 1924), p. 7, and Lugmayer's commentary, pp. 15-69, *passim*.

between the *Heimwehr* and the trade union group. Finally, the economic position of the groups which supported the church also influenced the social programs advanced by Austrian Catholics. The urban middle class of shopkeepers, artisans, and white-collar and professional people had been the principal victims of the currency inflation and the postwar economic collapse. Their own economic position deteriorated rapidly while at the same time that of competing groups, such as the industrial workers and a new upper class, improved. Their hostility to the Republic and to the capitalist system was reflected in their rediscovery of the corporativist and authoritarian doctrines of the political Romanticists. The depression of 1929 further weakened the position of these social groups. Austria, as a whole, never recovered from the effects of mass unemployment and deflation before the beginning of the Second World War.

(*b*) *Rerum novarum, Solidarism, and Quadragesimo anno.* The creation of a Republic in 1918 had placed Austrian Catholics in an entirely new political situation. Though they had been forced to cope with many of the problems of the modern state even during the monarchical period, the fundamental loyalty of the Hapsburg Dynasty to the church had served to soften the impact of these problems on the Austrian state. On the other hand, the postwar period did not confront Catholics with a radically different economic situation. Catholics, assisted by other bourgeois groups, had been able to withstand the nationalization demands of the Socialist *Lager* though they had been forced to permit the passage of an extensive welfare and social security program.[4] As a result, the postwar Austrian economy differed little from that of prewar days, and the social problems raised by that economy did not require any reformulation of Catholic doctrine on the social question as found in *Rerum novarum*. The publication of Leo XIII's encyclicals had encouraged the formulation of comprehensive social programs along *Sozialpolitik* lines. The most significant of these was the Solidarist social theory developed by a group of German Jesuits. This Solidarist theory, which was fundamentally pro-capitalist,

---

[4] Charles A. Gulick, *Austria From Habsburg to Hitler*, vol. I, *Labor's Workshop of Democracy* (Berkeley: University of California Press, 1948), pp. 134-143, 190-214; Otto Bauer, *Die österreichische Revolution* (Vienna: Wiener Volksbuchhandlung, 1923), pp. 161-182.

dominated the social thought of the Austrian hierarchy and of many lay theorists who closely followed church doctrines. Austrian Catholic treatment of the social question during the early years of the Republic was, therefore, profoundly influenced by the Solidarist theories of Heinrich Pesch and his school.

The vast economic and social changes since 1891, and especially the consequences of the depression of 1929, led Pius XI to make a number of important modifications in the Leonine corpus of social theory. These changes were incorporated in the encyclical *Quadragesimo anno*. As a result, the Austrian hierarchy and many Austrian lay theorists were forced to reconsider their social doctrines in the light of the changes announced in the encyclical. They attempted to follow the papal call for social reconstruction but maintained their pro-capitalist Solidarist position and their opposition to extensive government intervention in the economy.

In spite of the predominance of *Sozialpolitik* doctrines among Austrian Catholics during the early years of the Republic, a small group of social Romanticists continued to advocate the *Sozialreform* program. However, their influence on Austrian Catholic thought during these early years was negligible.[5] The overwhelming majority of their co-religionists were preoccupied with controlling the modern state and with satisfying the demands of big business and big agriculture; they had, therefore, little use for the wide variety of Romantic political and economic theories which existed during this period. Actually, the doctrinal differences between these Romantic "schools" were not great. They were united in their opposition to capitalism and industrialism, and agreed on the fundamentals of the social Romantic program.

Under the influence of the social encyclicals and German Solidarism on one hand, and the Romantic social tradition on the other, there developed in Austria two distinct tendencies of social theorizing. One group, under the leadership of the hierarchy, proposed to work within the existing social and economic framework of capitalism. The other group which con-

[5] August M. Knoll, "Karl von Vogelsang und der Ständegedanke," *Die soziale Frage*, pp. 67-69; Josef Schwalber, *Vogelsang und die moderne christlich-soziale Politik* (doctoral dissertation, University of Munich, 1927), pp. 52-53.

tinued the Romantic social theories of Müller and Vogelsang, demanded far-reaching social and economic changes. Because of the sharp differences between these two groups which continued the *Sozialpolitik* and *Sozialreform* traditions, respectively, developed during the nineteenth century, the metaphor of the spectrum, useful in describing the varieties of criticism of democracy, breaks down in the case of social and economic criticism. Nevertheless, the organization of the present chapter as well as the next is determined by the manner in which the various theorists can be arranged in a recognizable pattern which ranges from the initial pro-capitalist position of the Austrian hierarchy, as subsequently modified by *Quadragesimo anno*, to the extreme anti-capitalist Romanticists of the Vogelsang school. There is, therefore, some resemblance to the pattern of democratic criticism presented in the previous chapter. The fundamental division between *Sozialpolitik* and *Sozialreform* tendencies, however, makes it impossible to apply the device of the spectrum to the treatment of the social question in Chapters v and vi. An attempt has been made on p. 158 to present a chart showing the distribution of Austrian Catholic views on the social question during the period 1918-1934.

(c) The False Hopes of the Corporative Constitution. In 1934 the Christian-social conservative *Lager* seemed to be united in its determination to destroy the Republic and to establish a corporative constitution. Catholics were now agreed on abandoning democracy and also seemed to have settled their disputes over the social question. As a result, Catholics considered the Corporative Constitution of 1934 the culmination of their criticism of democracy and capitalism. However, many *Sozialreform* theorists soon became disillusioned with the realities of the corporative state. The majority of Austrian Catholics had been quite willing to use Romantic theories for attacking and destroying democracy, but they were not prepared to carry out the social and economic reforms contained in these Romantic doctrines. In this they proved to be the true successors of Lueger, who in 1889 had protested against the resolution of a Catholic social congress on the question of interest: "Gentlemen! We Catholics are generally poor people, even though we manage to hold on to a few stocks and bonds. It is my humble opinion

AUSTRIAN CATHOLICS AND THE SOCIAL QUESTION:
1918-1934

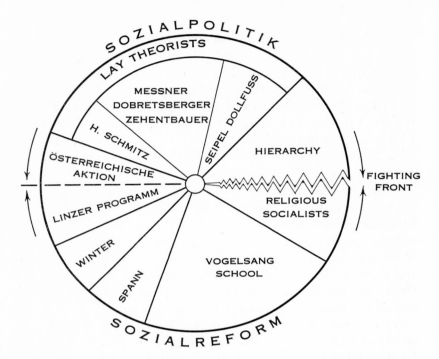

This chart reflects the fundamental division of social theories between *Sozialpolitik* and *Sozialreform*. Individuals and groups are arranged in the approximate order of their commitment to existing socio-economic institutions, beginning with the Hierarchy (strong commitment) and moving counterclockwise to the Religious Socialists (strong opposition). The chart also reflects the notion that the sharpest clash of ideas ("Fighting Front") occurs between the groups most strongly committed to *Sozialpolitik* and *Sozialreform*, respectively, while there is little difference on the social question between the *Österreichische Aktion* and the *Linzer Programm*.

that you will only upset our people and cause them to worry about their coupons if you pass this resolution."[6] This defense of the "small man" holding a few shares of stock reads like the

---

[6] Schwalber, *op.cit.*, p. 51. Lueger had only contempt for theories and programs, especially when they interfered with his pursuit of *Realpolitik*. Even his anti-Semitism was subject to reinterpretation. He is credited with the classically elastic definition of a Jew: "I'll say who is a Jew and who isn't."

plea on behalf of the widows and orphans who reputedly control the fate of American industry, and would suffer untold hardship if taxes were increased, or industry subjected to government regulation.

Corporative institutions became a mask for the continuation of existing capitalist practices and were used to protect the various interests from any outside interference. As a result, the radical social and economic reforms envisaged by the Romanticists were never carried out.[7] The Corporative Constitution of 1934 was a pyrrhic victory for the proponents of *Sozialreform*. Christian Social politicians erected a Romantic corporative façade behind which they perpetuated the capitalist system. The victory of the political and economic reaction in 1934 put an end to Catholic social reform programs. *Sozialreform*, as well as *Sozialpolitik*, were silenced in Austria.

2. The Austrian Hierarchy and the Social Question before 1931

(a) The Influence of Solidarism. Leonine social theory, especially *Rerum novarum* whose treatment of the social question was presented in Chapter I, continued to be the principal source of official Catholic social thought in Austria during the period 1918-1934. In addition, the hierarchy's critique of capitalism was profoundly influenced by the writings of the German Solidarists, especially Heinrich Pesch, whose social and economic doctrines were undoubtedly the most original contribution to Central European Catholic thought.

Pesch and his disciples devised a social theory which, they claimed, was a middle road between the extremes of economic

[7] This failure to carry out genuine corporative social and economic reforms has been documented abundantly. See especially Gulick, *op.cit.*, vol. II: *Fascism's Subversion of Democracy, passim.* But some of the strongest indictments of the corporative order came from members of the Catholic camp, such as Rudolf Hausleithner, *Der Geist der neuen Ordnung* (Vienna: Typographische Anstalt, 1937), pp. 75-83, 97-98, 104-105; and Josef Dobretsberger, *Katholische Sozialpolitik am Scheideweg* (Graz: U. Moser, 1947). Discussing the failure of the corporative experiment, Dobretsberger remarked caustically that the actions of the corporations never measured up to the standards of Christian ethics, but that every one always quoted the encyclicals. This included the barbers who demanded legislation against *Selbstrasieren* that would require all men to be shaved only by licensed barbers. *Ibid.*, p. 79.

individualism and collectivism.[8] Solidarism was a comprehensive synthesis based on specific concepts of man and society. This synthesis the Solidarists then applied to the analysis of social institutions and used as a basis for their critique of other social theories.

Pesch conceived of man as a rational and moral being whose personality was the true source and foundation of his social nature and social life: "Solidarism does not proceed from the idea of a completely self-sufficient and independent individual, as does Liberalism. . . . Pesch . . . called his system 'anthropo-centric-teleological,' but this in no way proves that he desired to see the individual *as such* become a center or considered a final end. . . . He is . . . concerned only with explaining clearly and definitely the inalienable nature of man as a 'person,' i.e., his relative autonomy and his central and dominant position in the cosmos. . . . Man's ential personality is the true source and foundation of his social nature and social life."[9]

[8] The principal work of Pesch was *Lehrbuch der Nationalökonomie* (3 vols., Freiburg i.B.: Herdersche Verlagsbuchhandlung, 1905-1913) which went through four editions before the author's death. Pesch was one of the first in a long succession of German Jesuits, including Josef Biederlack, Victor Cathrein, and others, who laid the foundation for the *Sozialpolitik* orientation of German and Austrian Catholic thought. This earlier generation was followed by another group of Jesuits, Otto Schilling, Gustav Gundlach, and Oswald von Nell-Breuning, who were active chiefly during the decades following the First World War. Their Solidarist social theories successfully aided German Catholics in reaching an accommodation with the modern state and the modern economy. In Austria, on the other hand, though Solidarist theories were officially accepted by the hierarchy, the Romantic tradition never disappeared completely. When dissatisfaction with democracy and with the capitalist economy increased, Austrian Catholics returned to the Romantic ideas of Müller and Vogelsang. For this reason, the development of Austrian Catholic social thought between 1918 and 1934 was a dialogue between Solidarist and Romantic ideas. This dialogue can best be observed in the columns of the Catholic "intellectual" periodicals. *Stimmen der Zeit* and *Hochland*, both published in Germany, represented chiefly the Solidarist side; *Schönere Zukunft* and *Das Neue Reich*, published in Vienna, the Romantic arguments.

The fundamental ideas of Solidarism can be traced to Ketteler; see Ch. I, above. Encouraged by the Thomist revival sponsored by Leo XIII, and especially by *Rerum novarum*, the Solidarists developed a body of ideas which has remained unchallenged as the principal tradition of Catholic social theorizing in Central Europe. Franz H. Mueller, *Heinrich Pesch and His Theory of Christian Solidarism* (St. Paul: College of St. Thomas, 1941), pp. 40-44. See also Richard Mulcahy, *The Economics of Heinrich Pesch* (New York: Henry Holt & Co., 1952). The German efforts to work out the implications of Thomist social thought paralleled those of Catholics in France and Belgium; see Robert Kothen, *La Pensée et l'Action Social des Catholiques 1789-1944* (Louvain: Em. Warny, 1945).

[9] Mueller, *op.cit.*, p. 14.

Thus Pesch placed man at the foundation of society. But this society was neither a mere sum of individuals, nor a substance independent of the individuals who composed it: "Society . . . is a permanent union of individuals. In such a society individuals are obliged to bend a common effort toward social goals and are directed by the society's legitimate authority toward its ultimate purposes."[10] In society, man was engaged in common activities for a common goal, but did not become completely subordinated to these common pursuits and goal. Pesch warned, therefore, against describing human society as a biological organism. Society was not a biological organism, he argued, but a moral organism with a moral personality. By stressing the moral character of society Pesch hoped to prevent the subordination of the individual to the collectivity which he considered the principal defect of Romantic doctrines: "For Solidarism does not regard society as a mere sum total of individuals as a union of men bound together only by contract, or, on the other hand, as a substance independent of the personal cooperation of the members, but holds that it is a *moral* collective person, with its own kind of subsistence and its own specific manner of existence."[11] He rejected these Romantic organic theories because they reduced man to the role of a cell when actually the individual in society retained his character as an "end" and full responsibility for his actions.[12]

From these definitions of man and society Pesch derived his concept of solidarity, that is to say, the concept of the ordered integration of efforts toward a moral common end: "Solidarism is the social system whose governing principle is . . . the solidary tie of the community to its members and of the members to their community."[13] But he insisted that solidarity was more than the mutual relations of men in society, that this social interdependence was more than an empirical fact: "The reciprocity and mutuality of human interests is based on the rational nature of the human personality and ultimately on God's will. Therefore the principle of solidarism correctly sees the moral

[10] Pesch, *op.cit.*, I, 137. This definition of society appears to be strongly collectivist. Furthermore, Pesch seemed unable to conceive of society without support of the legal order, *ibid.*, I, 138.

[11] Mueller, *op.cit.*, p. 17.

[12] Pesch, *op.cit.*, I, 141.

[13] Gustav Gundlach, "Solidarismus," *Staatslexikon*, IV, 1613.

character of human relations as a reflection of the divine world view."[14] That is to say, Pesch considered the sociability of man not simply an arrangement of convenience; he believed that it constituted a moral element of man's nature.

Because the "working of man in the midst of society" was the fundamental principle of Solidarism, Solidarist economic theory placed man at the center of economic activity, and of all solutions for the social question: ". . . according to God's will man stands at the center of and controls the material world. . . . He is never merely the object or tool of the economy, but its subject and ultimate purpose. . . . At the same time, the entire system is forever subject to the will of Him . . . who governs with sovereign power the world He has created. This anthropocentric-teleological conception controls our attitude to all practical questions of the social order."[15] Therefore, Pesch accepted the principle of wage labor, and of the separation of labor and capital.[16] He demanded, however, that the state interfere to prevent capitalist excesses which might threaten the economic status of individuals, especially their private property, which he considered essential to the "anthropocentric-teleological" nature of the Solidarist system; that is to say, he insisted that man must have private property to fulfill his function in society.[17]

The organization of economic activity, which Pesch called the "social system of industry," was based on three forms of solidarity: the solidarity of all men, the solidarity of fellow citizens, and the solidarity of those engaged in the same trade or occupation.[18] The national economy, according to Pesch, was

[14] Pesch, *op.cit.*, I, 31.

[15] *Ibid.*, I, 17-18.

[16] Pesch argued that man as a rational being, endowed with an immortal soul, was the ultimate measure of all endeavors and achievements. Just as political society, the state, presupposed the person and the family, so economic society presupposed the economically active individual and the private economy. See Mueller, *op.cit.*, pp. 20, 23.

[17] Private property, according to Pesch, was justified by the nature of man, the natural rights of man, and the needs of the family. *Op.cit.*, I, 188. At the same time Pesch recognized that there were certain limitations on private property: (1) private property must be used within the boundaries of the moral order; (2) *Eigentumsrecht* was not the highest form of *Recht* and must, therefore, give precedence to other requirements; and (3) property must not be considered an end in itself; *op.cit.*, I, 206-207.

[18] Pesch, *op.cit.*, I, 384; see also Mueller, *op.cit.*, pp. 24-26.

based on the solidarity of all citizens within a country. Pesch, who had been a student of Adolf Wagner and Gustav Schmoller, had come under the influence of the *Kathedersozialisten* and their economic theories. As a result, Pesch's concern for the individual in economic affairs was tempered by an inclination to accept a high degree of government ownership and intervention. This helps to explain the role Pesch assigned the "state authority" (*rechtliche Gewalt*) in his definition of society, namely, leading man in the correct path toward the achievement of common goals.[19] The political bonds which held together the national community were to be strengthened, according to Pesch, by the joint obligations arising out of economic activity: "The totality of the economic activities of the citizens as citizens—this is national economy."[20]

This solidarity of fellow citizens was supplemented by the solidarity of those engaged in the same trade or occupation. Pesch, therefore, denied that the state should control all economic activities or alone carry out all economic tasks. He argued that just as the state recognized the role of other political entities and groups in carrying out political functions, so the national economy, according to the principle of subsidiarity, was required to respect the occupational organizations of those engaged in a common economic activity.[21] Pesch believed that these voluntary occupational groups would eventually become the basis of economic activity, and would be able to remedy the evils of economic individualism. At the same time, he was determined to uphold the claims of private property against the collectivist proposals of the socialists as well as the social Romanticists.[22]

[19] Pesch, *op.cit.*, I, 137.

[20] "It is not therefore the external phase of economic activity and commerce which constitutes the essence of national economy . . . but the subordination according to social justice of all economic agents to the purpose of political society. In other words, because all individuals concerned are united through a political bond, through their joint obligation toward the common good, their economic activities, also, are comprised in this unity." Mueller, *op.cit.*, p. 23.

[21] Pesch stressed that autonomous association ". . . constitutes an absolutely justified and very effective form of spontaneous civil activity." Quoted in Mueller, *op.cit.*, p. 25. Originally Pesch did not have a clear concept of corporative organization but mentioned *Genossenschaften* and mutual aid societies as the outstanding examples of the organization of *Standesgenossen*, *op.cit.*, I, 386.

[22] "Therefore Solidarism continues to adhere to the private enterprise economy," *op.cit.*, I, 385.

The attempts of the Solidarists to fashion a "middle course" inevitably involved them in disputes with extremists on both sides. Ludwig von Mises, for example, classified Solidarism among the crypto-socialist theories.[23] A Frankfurt dissertation, *Solidarismus und Liberalismus*, came to the conclusion that ". . . full implementation of the Solidarist institutional prescription can only lead to socialism. . . . Consequently there can be no doubt about the crypto-socialist character of Solidarism, and liberalism must reject unequivocally Solidarism as well as its neighbor, Socialism."[24] On the other hand, the Romantic theorists attacked Solidarism as disguised individualism and condemned it for condoning the evils of capitalism and industrialism.[25] Actually, some of the strictures of both Romanticists and liberals were justified, for Solidarism in its eagerness to satisfy the claims of the individual as well as those of state and society tended to make its economic and social system self-contradictory and utopian. It relied for the adjustment of these conflicting claims on a natural harmony in society which simply did not exist in the twentieth-century industrial system.[26] The manner in which Pesch tried to outline his economic system illustrates the ambiguities of Solidarism:

[23] Ludwig von Mises, *Socialism. An Economic and Sociological Analysis*, J. Kahane, transl. (New York: The Macmillan Co., 1932), pp. 263-266. This is a translation of *Die Gemeinwirtschaft* originally published in 1922.

[24] Kurt Böhme, *Solidarismus und Liberalismus. Eine Kritik des Solidarismus von Heinrich Pesch S.J. vom liberalen Standpunkt* (doctoral dissertation, University of Frankfurt a.M., 1929), pp. 200, 226.

[25] One would have to cite almost the entire literature of Austrian Catholic social theorists on this point. The following articles attracted most of the attention and became the center of considerable controversy: Eugen Kogon, "Der Ständestaat des Solidarismus," *Hochland*, xxv, pt. 2 (1928), pp. 1-21, 178-200, 291-300; Ernst Karl Winter, "Die beiden Schulen des mitteleuropäischen Katholizismus (Karl von Vogelsang und P. Heinrich Pesch, S.J.), *Neue Ordnung*, iii (1927); and "P. Heinrich Pesch im Rahmen der katholischen Soziologie," *Schönere Zukunft*, i (1925), pp. 831-876.

[26] One should add, though, that the Solidarists were not the only ones among Catholic social thinkers to erect an elaborate edifice on assumptions about the actual working of social institutions which were totally invalid. It seemed that all Catholic theorists took for granted a much greater degree of harmony in the modern industrial system than they had any reason to assume. One is led to the conclusion that Catholic social thinkers, whenever they were faced with a dangerous social situation and with bitter social conflicts, retreated to the plane of love and charity and took the position that by exhorting employers and employees to follow the principles of social justice in wage negotiations they had been absolved from having to solve these difficult problems.

"Solidarism is the sociological-legal organizing principle of the national economy. It refuses to tolerate either an individualistic or a collectivist society. It demands the sort of community in which the objectives of social solidarity can be realized. It does not want a nation-wide system of economic cooperation, but a unified private economy . . . with the degree of autonomy compatible with the general welfare, in short, a system in which widely-shared sentiments produce a strong feeling of togetherness. The general welfare is not produced by an automatic mechanism but is a goal toward which all are obliged to work. . . ."[27]

Neither individualism, nor collectivism; neither a totally controlled economy, nor private property, freed from all restrictions. Such ambiguities invited the attacks of both liberal and Romantic theorists on Pesch and his Solidarist doctrines. But these very ambiguities also made Solidarism an attractive social program during periods when Catholics wanted to work within the existing political and social framework. It enabled Catholics to stress *laissez faire* or collectivist elements of their social thought as changing conditions required.

After the end of the war, the disciples and successors of Pesch, especially Gustav Gundlach and Oswald von Nell-Breuning, attempted to adapt Solidarism to the *Zeitgeist* of the postwar world which was becoming increasingly hostile to capitalism. But in spite of these modifications of their more pronounced pro-capitalist doctrines, Solidarists continued their attack on the social Romanticists whose theories they considered totalitarian and incompatible with Catholic social theory. For example, Solidarists and Romanticists disagreed violently over fundamentals of social organization. Romantic theorists insisted that a social organization based on *Stände* was the only correct social organization.[28] Gundlach was prepared to admit that in a stable economy, where the principles of public welfare were universally

---

[27] Pesch, *op.cit.*, I, 379.

[28] Most of the Romantic theorizing during the period of the Republic was based on the social theories developed by Karl von Vogelsang, see above, Ch. II. The theories of the Romantics during the years 1918-1934 are discussed in the subsequent chapter. The most elaborate corporative theory developed after 1918 was that of Othmar Spann, *Der wahre Staat, Vorlesungen über Abbruch und Neubau der Gesellschaft* (2nd rev. ed.; Leipzig: Quelle & Meyer, 1921), pp. 260-305.

accepted, society would be organized into *Stände* which he defined as ". . . groups made up of people pursuing the same or related occupations. These in turn combine with similar occupational groups of the same national society to determine and ultimately to realize the immediate end of the state, the 'general welfare.' "[29] But in an unstable economy, based on wrong principles and lacking the concept of a generally recognized "public welfare," groups would form for the purpose of protecting their own interests. Such groups, called classes, would attempt to stabilize the social order, realizing that only under conditions of stability could they hope to achieve their ends. Therefore, "sociologically correct" classes—that is to say, those trying to stabilize the social order—would actually tend in the direction of the *Stand*: "A class, based on the principle of self-help, is a corrective societal instrument. It attempts to achieve full solidarity within the national society, by transforming the unstable pattern of cooperation into a stable one."[30] It was possible, Gundlach argued, for Catholics to accept class organization of society. He denied Romantic accusations that his treatment of "class" was copied from Marx, and retorted that if his concept of class was inspired by Socialist doctrines at all, they were not those of Marx but of Lassalle, who had defined class as ". . . the ethical will to full citizenship in the democratic state."[31]

Gundlach also criticized the social Romanticists for having clothed medieval feudal institutions with absolute religious values: "It is the tragedy of the Catholic Christian-social movement that from religious motives it tried to assign absolute value to transient institutions. In the end, the vitality of the church in human society depends primarily on a genuine Catholic feeling for what is relative and transient. . . ."[32] He therefore denied that religious principles required Catholics to prefer a corporatively organized state over one organized on the basis of political par-

[29] Gustav Gundlach, S.J. "Stand und Klasse," *Stimmen der Zeit*, CXVII (1929), p. 292.
[30] *Ibid.*
[31] *Ibid.*, p. 293. The German social Catholics continued to be attracted by Lassalle, whose influence on Bishop Ketteler has been noted above; see Jacob Strieder, "W. E. von Ketteler und die soziale Frage im deutschen Katholizismus," *Die soziale Frage*, pp. 52-55.
[32] Gundlach, "Christlich-soziale Tragik," *Stimmen der Zeit*, CXVI (1929), p. 180.

ties and parliamentary representation.[33] He thought that Romantic theorists hampered the development of a true sociology by creating a social science in which transient forms were given absolute value. Finally, he rejected not only the Romantic claim to have developed the one true Catholic sociology, but also the notion that there was one "correct" Catholic sociology at all. If one examined a list of so-called Romantic theorists, such as De Maistre, Bonald, Donoso Cortes, Müller, Baader, Haller, and Görres, one would find many different sociological systems and very little agreement on the one correct social order.[34] However, in his desire to refute Romantic claims, Gundlach overstated his case. He was justified in stressing the differences between the doctrines of these various writers. But at the same time he let the great variety of Romantic theories obscure the essential unity underlying all *Sozialreform* doctrines.

(b) The Advent Pastoral Letter of 1925. The first important statement of the Austrian hierarchy on the social question appeared in 1925 when the bishops published an Advent Pastoral Letter on that subject and followed it up in 1926 with *Instructio pro clero in re sociale.*[35] Though the bishops severely criticized capitalism, they did not propose any fundamental changes in the existing system.

By 1925 the church had become concerned over the unpopularity of the pro-business policies of Christian Social governments and their anti-socialist bourgeois allies. The hierarchy, therefore, tried to defend the church and Catholic governments against the accusation that they sided with capitalists and employers against the workers: "We brand as false as well as malicious the accusation that the Catholic Church preached the workers' obedience and meek acceptance of capitalist arrogance, while it favored and protected entrepreneurs and plutocrats."[36] It pointed to the opposition of the church to all forms of usury and exploitation as proof that Catholics were sincerely concerned with the problem of the poor. However, the hierarchy did not condemn capitalism in toto, but only the excesses of

[33] *Ibid.,* p. 182.
[34] *Ibid.,* p. 179.
[35] "Rundschreiben der österreichischen Bischöfe Advent 1925," and *"Instructio pro clero in re sociale* April 1926," reprinted in *Episkopat*, pp. 77-127, 127-136.
[36] *Episkopat,* p. 80.

capitalism—"mammonistic" capitalism—which it considered the gravest evil of modern times.[37] Those who controlled wealth, the bishops explained, had set up a "rule of force" which assured them of profits at all times, whether in peace or war: "Finance capitalism rakes in huge profits by exploiting and robbing the people of this earth. It snatches away the savings of the thrifty, and by impoverishing ever larger groups forces the people to their knees and totally enslaves them."[38] These industrialists and financiers had destroyed not only the proletariat, but also the peasants, artisans, and small entrepreneurs.

The bishops did not reject big enterprise, the wage system, or the system of credit and interest as such. Rather, they condemned the evil consequences of these institutions, namely disregard for the laws of God, production beyond satisfaction of basic needs (*Deckung des Bedarfs*), destruction of the family and of the dignity of the worker.[39] The existence of these evils had led workers to combine for common action and to embrace socialism and communism, the bishops admitted: "The industrial workers simply did not want to be isolated and helplessly exposed to the power of capitalism. From this rose their desire to unite and help each other in breaking up, through their combined organizational strength, the slavery imposed by capitalism."[40] But they cautioned the workers against using this organized strength for the purpose of damaging other social groups: "The demand of the workers for co-determination in the economy . . . is quite justified, provided it remains within proper limits, and does not aim at infringing the rights of others, either of entrepreneurs or other groups in society."[41] They warned against socialism and communism—the bishops used these terms interchangeably—because these ideologies opposed the creation of a healthy social order based on *Stände*, threatened to destroy

[37] This distinction between "capitalism" as a form of economic organization and the excesses of capitalism was foreshadowed in Pesch, who condemned "the boundless mania for profits . . . which has completely perverted the natural relations between labor and capital." Pesch, *op.cit.*, I, 212. In turn, Pius XI developed this distinction between capitalism as an acceptable form of economic organization and the excesses of monopoly capitalism which Catholics were exhorted to combat.

[38] *Episkopat*, p. 86.

[39] *Ibid.*, pp. 83-85.

[40] *Ibid.*, p. 91.

[41] *Ibid.*, p. 97.

private property, and ultimately the state, the only protection against the "money powers."[42]

In spite of this bitter attack on capitalism and industrialism, the bishops were not really prepared to advocate radical changes in the existing social and economic system. They placed great emphasis on an equitable wage policy as an aid to industrial workers and suggested three specific reforms. Capitalists should use their wealth not for financial speculation, but for the common good, by creating useful employment and making credit available to artisans and peasants. Next, they should at all times be conscious of the social obligations imposed by the ownership of private property. Finally, the bishops urged that employers treat their workers as "men and Christians."[43]

This appeal to the Christian virtues of the employers was part of a long-standing tradition of the Catholic Church, especially in Austria. The church often avoided difficult social problems by appealing to spiritual remedies, charity, love, and justice. The Austrian hierarchy followed a similar course in 1925-1926. It realized the grave consequences for the church of social unrest among the workers because it followed the Advent Letter with an *Instructio pro clero in re sociale* in which it warned the clergy against two dangers in their dealing with social questions. The clergy must not appear to favor one social system over another, and it must maintain, at all times, a proper balance in its criticism of socialism and mammonistic capitalism.[44]

The hierarchy reiterated its Solidarist position in 1930, in the course of a dispute with the Religious Socialists and with Anton Orel, who had adopted an uncompromising Romantic opposition to capitalism. The hierarchy again denied that it favored capitalism and warned the anti-capitalists of the Vogelsang school that their anti-capitalism could lead only to socialism

---

42 *Ibid.*, p. 99.

43 *Ibid.*, pp. 88-90.

44 The letter of instruction on the social question gives the impression that the hierarchy had become concerned with the effectiveness of the Socialist appeal to the workers. There must have been some members of the clergy who had taken sides either by an excessively vigorous defense of capitalism and of the established order, or by accepting some of the anti-capitalist arguments of the Socialists. The hierarchy concluded with this warning: "We categorically condemn those who vote for Social Democratic representatives in municipality, *Land*, or nation, because the Social Democratic program contradicts Christianity." *Instructio*, p. 135.

and collectivism. It rejected the proposition advanced by some anti-capitalist Romanticists that bishops speaking on questions of wages, property, strikes, and other economic issues were not speaking as bishops but merely as social theorists. The bishops asserted that man's right to private property was based not merely on economic consideration. Man needed private property so that he could fulfill moral and social functions defined in natural law. Therefore a bishop was concerned with private property *qua* bishop, and not *qua* sociologist.[45] This exchange between the hierarchy and Orel was simply another stage in the long-standing dispute between the Vogelsang school and the Austrian hierarchy over social policy. The Vogelsang disciples had maintained all along that *Rerum novarum* represented the opinion of the man who happened to be the head of the church, but not social and economic doctrines Catholics were bound to accept. This opposition to *Rerum novarum* indicated that the Austrian theorists in the *Sozialreform* tradition had never become reconciled to the victory of *Sozialpolitik*. They continued to expound their social Romantic theories and to condemn the prevailing trend in Catholic social thought as a violation of Catholic social doctrines and as constituting an accommodation to capitalism and the modern state.

3. *Quadragesimo anno, Sozialpolitik* and *Sozialreform*

The publication of *Quadragesimo anno* had special significance for the development of Austrian Catholic social thought. The encyclical forced the hierarchy and a number of Austrian lay theorists to make certain adjustments in their social doctrine. Furthermore, the encyclical devoted considerable attention to the extreme Romantic social doctrines which had remained more prominent among Catholics in Austria than in any other country. In this respect, *Quadragesimo anno* provides an illuminating commentary on Austrian *Sozialreform* ideas both before and after the First World War.

(a) The Task of Quadragesimo anno. Pius XI set out to accomplish three tasks in *Quadragesimo anno*.[46] He planned ". . .

[45] Letter of the Austrian Bishops, reprinted in *Episkopat*, pp. 155-165.
[46] Pius XI, *Quadragesimo anno*. Encyclical Letter of His Holiness Pius XI on Reconstructing the Social Order and Perfecting it Conformably to the Precepts

to recall the great benefits which this encyclical *Rerum novarum* has brought to the Catholic Church and the World at large . . ."; to ". . . vindicate the social and economic doctrines of so great a master against certain doubts which have arisen, and to develop more fully some of its points . . ."; and finally, ". . . after arraigning modern economics and examining the nature of socialism, to expose the root of the present social disorder, and to point out the only salutary course. . . ."[47] Of these three the most significant is the second because Pius XI not merely "vindicated" but definitely reinterpreted some of the social teachings of Leo XIII and introduced two new elements into official Catholic social thought: the concept of social justice, which had been discussed by Catholic social theorists long before *Quadragesimo anno*, and the proposal for the reorganization of the social order along corporative lines.

(b) Catholic Organizational Efforts Reviewed. Pius XI opened the encyclical with a review of the impact of *Rerum novarum* on the activities of the church, the state, and the various social classes.[48] He particularly praised Leo XIII for overthrowing the "tottering tenets of liberalism"[49] which had hampered effective government intervention. He also commended the growth of associations of workingmen, but deplored the lack of such associations among employers. The Pope criticized those who had been suspicious of workingmen's efforts to organize and had condemned these efforts as the work of Socialist agitators.

This was clearly an attack on the Catholic Romanticists who had consistently opposed the *Sozialpolitik* tendencies of official Catholic thought since 1891. By praising the work of Catholic trade unions, *Quadragesimo anno* also settled a long standing argument over trade union versus Catholic workingmen's associations which had troubled German and Austrian Catholics.[50]

---

of the Gospel, in Commemoration of the Fortieth Anniversary of the Encyclical "Rerum Novarum," reprinted in *Five Great Encyclicals* (New York: The Paulist Press, 1939), pp. 125-168. All references are to this edition. Citations will give both section and page numbers.

[47] *Ibid.*, 16, p. 128.　　[48] *Ibid.*, 16-40, pp. 129-135.　　[49] *Ibid.*, 27, p. 131.

[50] *Ibid.*, 31-36, pp. 133-134; see Jostock, *op.cit.*, pp. 145-146, for a discussion of the bitter fight between those who supported the work of the trade unions, usually associated with the *Volksverein*, which had its headquarters in München-Gladbach, and those who opposed Catholic trade union organizations and their activities, the so-called Berlin tendency.

In effect, Pius XI supported the defenders of trade unions, but urged that Catholic workers should belong to trade unions as well as to Catholic workingmen's associations, because the first would look after the workers' economic, the latter after their cultural and spiritual needs. Pius XI closed this review of the impact of *Rerum novarum* with a defense of that encyclical against those who had belittled its importance. He noted that the continued disputes over social theory had made necessary an interpretation of *Rerum novarum* in the light of changing conditions. This passage, too, constituted a reprimand of those Romantic theorists who had insisted that the social theory of *Rerum novarum* was not really binding on Catholics.[51]

(c) The Social Doctrines of Pius XI: Property, Wages, and the Need for Corporative Reconstruction. The part of *Quadragesimo anno* which had the most profound influence on the development of Austrian Catholic thought, and especially on the course of the *Sozialreform-Sozialpolitik* disputes was the second section of the encyclical, where the Pope examined and restated some of the principal concepts of Leonine social theory, such as property, capital, uplifting of the proletariat, the just wage, and the need for the reconstruction of the social order.[52]

Before considering these concepts, Pius XI found it necessary to reassert the right of the church to deal with social and economic problems. He declared that economic science and moral discipline were each guided by their own principles. Consequently, the laws of economics determined what was feasible in economic affairs and the church could therefore offer no guidance in technical matters. But the moral ends of economic activity were determined by the principles of moral discipline: ". . . while reason itself clearly deduces from the nature of things and from the individual and social character of man, what is the end and object of the whole economic order assigned by God, the Creator."[53] It is important to keep in mind this definition by Pius XI of the relation of social science and moral discipline. Unlike Romantic theorists who claimed that social activity, including economic activity, was guided by principles derived from the revealed truths of the Catholic religion, Pius

[51] *Quadragesimo anno*, 40, p. 135.
[52] *Ibid.*, 41-98, pp. 135-152.
[53] *Ibid.*, 42, p. 136.

XI insisted that reason and the "nature of things" set the moral standards which guided economic activity.[54]

The Pope then defended Leo's concept of property and of wages against the Religious Socialists and the social Romanticists who had attacked Leo XIII and the hierarchy for defending capitalism and private property.[55] At the same time, however, Pius XI modified Leo's teachings on wages and property by introducing the concept of social justice. Pius began by reaffirming the dual character of property, individual and social. He considered the right to own property given by the Creator, but noted that man could enjoy the ownership and use of property only in a stable social order. He denied the accusation of social Romanticists, like Vogelsang and his school, that the church had embraced a pagan concept of private property, namely that of the Roman Law.[56] The right to own property could never be forfeited by non-use or mis-use, Pius insisted: ". . . it is even less true that the very mis-use or even non-use of ownership destroys or forfeits the right itself."[57] Such a theory of property would so weaken the individual character of property ". . . as actually to destroy it."[58] But the Pope then balanced the re-

---

[54] Pius XI seemed to be quite confident that "reason itself clearly deduces from the nature of things and from the individual and social character of man, what is the end and object of the whole economic order. . . ." He concluded that "if this law be faithfully obeyed, the result will be that particular economic aims, whether of society as a body or of individuals, will be intimately linked with the universal teleological order . . . ," *ibid.*, 43, p. 136. It is difficult to see how one could expect all reasonable men, including non-Catholics, to agree on such things. For Pius XI assumed that all men agreed on the standards of reasonable conduct and on the interpretation of natural law. One is continuously amazed at the confidence Catholics had in the easy and harmonious resolution of the social, economic, and political conflicts of a modern industrial society. This Catholic tendency is particularly surprising if one contrasts it with Catholic emphasis on the corrupting influence of original sin. Ernst Troeltsch put it this way: "In this respect the Church herself . . . was full of the most unpractical idealism. She seemed to think that if the spiritual government of the world were functioning properly, and if faith and love were strong and healthy, then all difficulties would solve themselves." *The Social Teaching of the Christian Churches*, Olive Wyon, trans. (3rd impr.; London: George Allen & Unwin, Ltd., 1950), I, 246.

[55] See Franz Arnold, "Wiener Richtungen," *Staatslexikon*, v, 1298-1304; Johanna Gierse, "Sozialromantische Richtungen im Katholizismus der Gegenwart," *Soziale Revue*, XXXII (1932), pp. 129-176, 193-233.

[56] Wiard von Klopp (ed.), *Die sozialen Lehren des Freiherrn Karl von Vogelsang. Grundzüge einer katholischen Gesellschafts- und Volkswirtschaftslehre nach Vogelsangs Schriften* (2nd rev. ed.; Vienna: Reinhold-Verlag, 1938), pp. 107-108.

[57] *Quadragesimo anno*, 47, p. 138.   [58] *Ibid.*, 48, p. 138.

quirements of the individual character of property against the needs of its social character. He recognized the right of the state to "adjust ownership to meet the needs of the public good,"[59] and thereby denied the charge of Liberal Catholics that such action would weaken property. On the contrary, such action would protect and strengthen it, the Pontiff asserted.[60]

Next, Pius XI attempted to strike a balance between the claims of labor and of capital for a share of the economic product, and developed the concept of social justice as a guide for a proper distribution of shares between the two claimants.[61] As the analysis of Austrian social thought in the last part of this chapter and in the next one will show, the problem of distribution was at the hub of the controversy between the Romantic and anti-Romantic schools of Austrian social thought. Though Pius XI condemned the excessive advantages which capital had been able to gain at the expense of labor, he denied that this condition had been as bad as one might have suspected from an examination of the *theories* of the Manchester school. This is evidently a reference to the tendencies of Romantic theorists to base their condemnation of economic and political liberalism not on an examination of actual liberal institutions, but on a logical examination of liberal theories. This method of Romantic social research has been exposed in the preceding chapter in the case of Othmar Spann.[62]

Perhaps the most significant passage of the second section of *Quadragesimo anno* was the condemnation of the labor theory of value, a fundamental concept of Romantic theory. Pius XI rejected the contention of those who claimed for labor "the whole product of their industry." He considered the labor theory of value a more subtle poison than the socialist demands for the nationalization of the means of production. He called the proponents of this theory ". . . intellectuals . . . who set up in opposition to this fictitious law [claiming all benefits for capital] another equally false moral principle: that all products and profits, excepting those required to repair and replace in-

59 *Ibid.*, 49, p. 139.
60 *Ibid.*
61 *Ibid.*, 53-58, pp. 139-142.
62 See above, Ch. IV, p. 133. See also the discussion of the social program of the *Österreichische Aktion* in the present chapter.

vested capital, belong by every right to the workingman. . . . It is an alluring poison, consumed with avidity by many not deceived by open Socialism."[63] On the basis of this authority the Austrian hierarchy refused the imprimatur to the writings of Anton Orel and several other of the extreme Romanticists in Austria. This same passage also caused Wiard von Klopp considerable trouble when he reissued the writings of Karl von Vogelsang in 1938, because much of Vogelsang's work on capital, interest, and usury stood condemned in the light of this passage in *Quadragesimo anno.*[64]

The Pope concluded the discussion of property by recognizing officially the principle of social justice as a basis for distributing the profits of economic production among the various claimants. Neither capitalist nor laborer could claim all the profits; rather a just distribution must seek to alleviate what Pius XI considered the gravest evil of modern times, the discrepancy between the wealth of a few and the poverty of the many. A just principle of distribution would enable the worker to acquire possessions which would ease his hand-to-mouth existence and enable him to provide for his family.

The discussion of property, therefore, led the Pope directly to the question of wages, for the worker could acquire property only if he received a "just wage."[65] Again Pius XI touched on a Romantic social doctrine held widely among Austrian theorists, that of the *Gesellschaftsvertrag.* He attacked the Romanticists

[63] *Quadragesimo anno,* 55, p. 141. Romantic Catholic theorists contended throughout the nineteenth century that the teachings of the church forbade any form of unearned income. They pointed to the long history of the church's uncompromising opposition to usury. Some of these theorists began to realize that in the modern industrial economy the profits of capitalists would become a more important source of unearned income than ownership of land. Karl von Vogelsang, principally under the influence of Rodbertus, developed an economic program which included a ban on the free movement of landed property, legal limits on indebtedness of such property, etc. Klopp, *op.cit.,* pp. 292-299. The successors of Vogelsang, especially Anton Orel, began to claim for the industrial worker the full *"Arbeitsertrag."* Though writers like Orel continued to refer to the Catholic sources of the ban on unearned income, they were influenced chiefly by the writings of Marx, Lassalle, and Rodbertus on the labor theory of value. There is no doubt that the economic doctrines of the Romantic theorists contained elements of the Catholic as well as the Marxist critique of capitalism. Anton Menger, *Das Recht auf den vollen Arbeitsertrag in geschichtlicher Darstellung* (Stuttgart: Verlag der J. G. Cottaschen Buchhandlung, 1886), pp. 129-138.

[64] Klopp, *op.cit.,* pp. 374-388.

[65] *Quadragesimo anno,* 63-75, pp. 143-146.

for rejecting the wage contract (*Arbeitsvertrag*) and wanting to replace it with such a *Gesellschaftsvertrag* which would be based on the workers sharing in ownership and profit.[66] But the Pontiff admitted that the wage contract needed to be supplemented by giving the workingman some share in ownership or in profits.[67] He concluded that the just wage, based on the dual character of labor, individual and social, must meet three requirements: it must support the worker and his family; it must permit business to continue in operation; it must meet the exigencies of the common good.[68] This section on the just wage is probably the best known of the encyclical. It has been discussed at great length by Catholics as well as non-Catholics. But the present analysis has been focused on those parts of the encyclical which are especially relevant for the development of Austrian Catholic thought. Therefore, no further discussion is needed here because the concept of the "just wage" did not raise any special problems in Austrian Catholic thought.

The most significant result of Pius XI's discussion of capital, wages, and property for Austrian Catholic thought was his rejection of the social theories held by the Austrian Romanticists. Nevertheless if *Quadragesimo anno* has usually been regarded as a revival of *Sozialreform* doctrines and a setback for those of *Sozialpolitik*, this contention was based chiefly on the remaining part of the second section in which Pius XI advocated the reconstruction of the social order along corporative lines. In that part of *Quadragesimo anno*, the Pope greatly encouraged the Austrian Romanticists and their corporative doctrines.

The proposal for the reconstruction of the social order along corporative lines was the most significant element of Pius XI's reinterpretation of Leonine social theory.[69] Like Leo XIII, Pius suggested two methods of social reconstruction: institutional reform and moral improvement.[70] But unlike his predecessor, who had relied primarily on voluntary associations as agents of in-

---

[66] *Ibid.*, 68, p. 144.
[67] *Ibid.*, 65, p. 144.
[68] *Ibid.*, 71-75, pp. 144-146.
[69] *Ibid.*, 76-98, pp. 146-152.
[70] Pius XI only stated the *need* for moral reform at this point, but postponed the discussion of moral reform methods until the last part of the encyclical. *Ibid.*, 127-148, pp. 160-168.

stitutional reform, Pius XI assigned the state the principal role in initiating and implementing institutional reforms: "When we speak of the reform of the social order it is principally the State we have in mind. Not indeed that all salvation is to be hoped for from its intervention, but because on account of the evil of Individualism, as We called it, things have come to such a pass that the highly developed social life which once flourished in a variety of prosperous institutions organically linked with each other, has been damaged and all but ruined, leaving thus virtually only individuals and the State."[71]

The Pope admitted that changing conditions had made it necessary for large units to carry out tasks once done by the smaller units. But he warned the superior unit against assuming any tasks a subordinate could carry out just as well. Rather, the superior unit should aid subordinate units and individuals in carrying out as many tasks as possible. Consequently, Pius XI assigned the state two principal duties in the reconstruction of the social order: helping to reestablish harmony between the ranks of society, and restoring the true guiding principles of economics.

Social harmony could best be restored by the reestablishment of vocational groups. These would replace the social classes which were based on the opposing groups in the labor market and were engaged in a struggle which threatened to destroy social harmony: "But there cannot be a question of any perfect cure, except this opposition be done away with, and well-ordered members of the social body come into being anew, vocational groups, namely, binding men together, not according to the position they occupy in the labor market, but according to the diverse functions which they exercise in society."[72] It is easy to understand the elation of the *Sozialreform* theorists with such a sweeping approval of the central ideas of their doctrine. They were also pleased with Pius XI's definition of the twofold purpose underlying these vocational groups: (1) employers and employees within a single vocational group should unite to give service and produce goods, and (2) all vocational groups should

[71] *Ibid.*, 78, p. 147. This passage of the encyclical gave considerable comfort to those Austrian Catholics who planned to use this papal call for a reconstruction of society as a device for destroying the Austrian Republic.

[72] *Ibid.*, 83, p. 148.

unite to produce, each within its own sphere, the common good.[73] They were less pleased with the Pope's warning that what Leo XIII had said about forms of government should be applied to vocational groups: "Here, too, men may choose whatever form they please. . . ."[74] Furthermore, Pius XI encouraged the formation of voluntary groups within the vocational organs, in the same manner as citizens of a geographic community formed voluntary organizations. The Romanticists preferred compulsory corporative organization along rigidly prescribed lines and controlled by the state.

The second task of the state, according to Pius XI, was the restoration of the true guiding principles of economics. The Pontiff held the "individualistic school" responsible for the evils of class warfare because it insisted that self-direction and the open market could produce better economic results than "any created intellect." But he went on to say that in recent years free competition had been replaced by an arrogant monopoly rule. The Pope concluded that if the vocational groups helped the state by taking over some of the burdensome tasks it now bore, they would thereby free the state for the task of protecting the correct principles of social justice and social charity.[75]

Pius XI then examined an existing system of corporativism, the Italian Fascist corporative state. Among its advantages, he noted the system of compulsory settlement of disputes between competing classes. On the other hand, he cited some observers who felt that, under Fascism, the state often "substituted itself in the place of private initiative," and that the whole corporative system seemed to serve narrow political ends and not the common good.[76] This part of the second section of *Quadragesimo anno* was also widely discussed in the years before the Second World War. Austrian Catholics who had been casting about for a political system to replace the Republic interpreted *Quadragesimo anno* as favoring the Italian corporative state. Consequently, they took the section on the reconstruction of the

[73] *Ibid.*, 84, p. 148.
[74] *Ibid.*, 86, p. 149.
[75] *Ibid.*, 88-89, pp. 149-150. Obviously the Pontiff shared the view of many of his faithful that it was necessary to purify the state by reducing its functions.
[76] *Ibid.*, 91-98, pp. 150-152.

social order and, encouraged by the earlier statement that the state should play an important role in this reconstruction, used it as a model for the Corporative Constitution of 1934. But because that Constitution became merely a convenient disguise for perpetuating the predominance of big business and of authoritarian political leaders, it will not be surprising to discover that in implementing the Corporative Constitution between 1934 and 1938, Austrian Catholics violated most of the principles set out by Pius XI, and actually never attempted the social reconstruction which was the declared goal of the encyclical.

(d) *The Evils of Capitalism and Socialism and Their Remedies.* In the concluding section of *Quadragesimo anno*, Pius XI examined certain economic and ideological changes since Leo's pontificate in order to underscore the need for moral reform.[77] He contended that the healthy social order which had existed in the past had perished not because it was incapable of institutional adaptation, but because of the wrongdoing of men. Before examining the changes in capitalism and socialism since the death of Leo, Pius XI reemphasized his predecessor's commitment to the economic system based on the separation of labor and capital. Leo had simply wanted to adjust this economic system to the standards of true justice, that is to say, he had wanted to prevent the capitalists from diverting the entire profit into their own pockets.[78]

The two most notable developments in capitalism, according to Pius XI, were its extension to almost all parts of the world, and the growth of monopoly power. Some economic activities, like farming, once free from the effects of capitalist evils, had become infected to an increasing degree. At the same time, countries once entirely untouched by the capitalist economic regime, especially in Asia, had recently been drawn into the capitalist orbit. Concurrently with this expansion of capitalism there had occurred an accumulation of wealth in the hands of a very few who then used this wealth to exercise despotic powers. This

---

[77] *Ibid.*, 99-148, pp. 152-168.

[78] In this section Pius XI took up the theme developed by the Austrian bishops in their letter of 1925, namely, that capitalism in itself was not bad, but merely the excesses of capitalism: "And surely it is not vicious of its very nature; but it violates right order whenever capital so employs the working or wage-earning classes as to divert business and economic activity entirely to its own arbitrary will. . . ." *Ibid.*, 101, p. 152.

concentration had led to a threefold struggle: for dictatorship in the economic sphere, for control of the state, so its authority could be used in the economic struggle, and for international supremacy, that is to say, clashes between states. As a result, economic life had become a continuous and cruel struggle for existence, and entire nations were now engaged in an economic competition which took the forms of economic nationalism and imperialism. Furthermore, those with economic power had managed to capture the state and were using it for their own evil purposes. Thus the state no longer ruled above all parties in a "kingly fashion" but was being used by capitalists to exploit other economic groups.

There were four remedies for these evils, according to the Pope: (1) The dual character of labor and property must be recognized in order to avoid the dangers of individualism as well as collectivism; (2) the mutual relations of labor and capital must be governed by commutative justice; (3) the civil authority must control competition and monopoly; (4) public institutions must conform to the standards of social justice.[79] Obviously, such a reform program, on balance, favored *Sozialreform* rather than *Sozialpolitik* doctrines. As a result, Catholic groups like the Austrian hierarchy and the lay theorists who accepted the leadership of the hierarchy in social questions were faced with the task of reformulating some of their social theories, especially their fundamental pro-capitalist ideas.

The Pontiff noted that socialism as well as capitalism had undergone important changes since 1891. The violent section of socialism, called communism, had degenerated in the same manner as capitalism; that is to say, power had become concentrated in the hands of a few, and was being exercised in a dictatorial manner.[80] The more moderate section, which had retained the name socialism, had considerably modified its position on the class struggle and private property.[81] The Pope noted that the extent to which it had done this made it appear that its economic views were little different from those of the church. In this passage, Pius XI acknowledged the problem posed by the existence of a small but intellectually powerful group of

[79] *Ibid.*, 110, p. 154.
[80] *Ibid.*, 112, p. 155.
[81] *Ibid.*, 113-126, pp. 155-160.

Religious Socialists in Germany and Austria who claimed that the Marxist social and economic program was identical with the social theories of the church. Pius XI insisted that no matter how far socialism had gone in modifying its social and economic doctrines, it would remain incompatible with Christianity because it was based on a view of society and man foreign to Christianity, namely a materialistic *Weltanschauung.* The Pope argued, in effect, that there was a fundamental difference between socialism and Christianity which should not be obscured by the similarities of their anti-capitalist critique.[82] He warned against "cultural socialism," that is to say, socialist efforts to propagate its materialistic ideology through education.[83] But he also urged Catholics to have understanding for those who had deserted to socialism, especially in view of the fact that many Christians had abused religion: ". . . worse still, that there are those who out of greed for gain are not ashamed to oppress the workingman. Indeed there are some who abuse religion itself, cloaking their unjust imposition under its name, that they may protect themselves against the clearly just demands of their employees."[84]

The final paragraphs of the encyclical were devoted to moral renovation, the second of the methods of social reconstruction. These passages are of less interest to the social scientist because they deal almost exclusively with the spiritual tasks of the church and of the faithful in bringing about a social reconstruc-

[82] ". . . whether Socialism be considered as a doctrine, or as a historical fact, or as a movement, if it really remains Socialism, it cannot be brought into harmony with the dogmas of the Catholic Church. . . . The reason being that it conceives human society in a way utterly alien to Christian truth." *Ibid.,* 117, p. 157. Pius XI apparently recognized the danger to Catholic social doctrines from the moderate or gradualist Socialist programs, because he stated unequivocally that ". . . 'Religious Socialism,' 'Christian Socialism,' are expressions implying a contradiction in terms. No one can be at the same time a sincere Catholic and a true Socialist." *Ibid.,* 119, p. 158.

[83] *Ibid.,* 121-122, p. 158. The section on "Cultural Socialism" was especially appropriate for Austria, where the Socialist *Lager* had developed an extremely ambitious and effective program to provide for its followers a way of life dominated entirely by a Socialist *Weltanschauung.*

[84] This passage reflected an earlier papal statement critical of capitalists. In an article in *Osservatore Romano* dated April 3, 1930, the Holy See attacked capitalists who "cloaked" their unjust actions with Christian phrases. See Oswald von Nell-Breuning, *Die soziale Enzyklika. Erläuterungen zum Weltrundschreiben Papst Pius XI. über die gesellschaftliche Ordnung* (Cologne: Katholische Tat-Verlag, 1932), p. 209.

tion. There was, however, one passage which reflected the influence of Romantic ideas on papal thought. Pius XI traced many of the evil effects of unchecked economic competition to the diffusion of accountability and responsibility which had resulted from the operation of the modern business corporation.[85] Romantic theorists in Austria had attacked what they called the anonymity of capital; they had attacked the modern business corporation because its organization divorced ownership from control and thereby from responsibility. Directors who were simply employees were concerned only with making profit for the stockholders, while the latter had no direct operating responsibility. The Romantic theorists believed that under a single entrepreneur, workers would be less subject to abuse than under a corporate board of directors. However, like much of Romantic criticism of the modern economy, this seems to have been based less on actual observation than on the kind of theoretical analysis Pius XI had condemned earlier in the encyclical.[86]

Quadragesimo anno concluded by exhorting Christians to inspire economic activity with a Christian spirit, and to supplement commutative justice with traditional Christian charity.

4. The Hierarchy and *Quadragesimo anno*

(a) The Solidarists Reconsider Sozialpolitik. The publication of *Quadragesimo anno* forced the Austrian hierarchy to reconsider the Solidarist elements of its social theories. Such a reconsideration was easier for the Austrian hierarchy than for the German Solidarist theorists who had inspired so much of Austrian Catholic thought after 1918: "It was questionable whether Solidarism, the dominant sociological and economic theory of social Catholicism . . . was able to make the switch to corporative principles as required by *Quadragesimo anno*. It could do no more than accept corporativism passively; it certainly was incapable of participating actively in corporative construction."[87]

The principal Solidarist theorists, Gundlach and Nell-Breun-

[85] *Quadragesimo anno*, 132, pp. 161-162.
[86] See for a similar analysis the *Österreichische Aktion* section of this chapter, 5 e, below.
[87] *Wiener Politische Blätter*, I (April 16, 1933), p. 51.

ing, repeatedly asserted that *Quadragesimo anno* could not be considered a victory for *Sozialreform*.[88] Gundlach, writing in 1933, expressed the fear that the corporativism of the Catholic Romanticists, based largely on medieval social institutions, would tend to falsify the reforms advocated in the encyclical. He denied that corporativism must necessarily be anti-Marxist, anti-capitalist, and anti-parliamentary: "In spite of all the current anti-parliamentary and anti-democratic tendencies, it is quite misleading to consider the corporative order to be the antithesis of parliamentary democracy."[89] He also suspected that the corporative proposals then under consideration would probably result in perpetuating capitalism and protecting primarily the employers. Most important, he feared that the corporativism of the Romanticists would permit the state to swallow up society: "They [the Romanticists] justify the absorption of society by the state with the need to transcend parliamentarism and the liberal bourgeois rule of law. . . . Though social philosophy and natural law both condemn as false these basic principles of liberalism, this should not lead us into the opposite error of defining society as part of the state and letting the state engulf society."[90] Gundlach condemned such an absorption as totalitarian; he considered the corporative state which swallowed society as objectionable as the capitalist society which had devoured the state.

The most cogent and most comprehensive defense of Solidarism against the attacks of the *Sozialreform* theorists who claimed that *Quadragesimo anno* had vindicated their doctrines, was Nell-Breuning's *Die soziale Enzyklika*.[91] In the guise of a commentary on *Quadragesimo anno*, Nell-Breuning actually turned the encyclical into a *Sozialpolitik* document. The work was translated into several languages, including English, and had considerable impact on international Catholic social thought. Unfortunately, most non-German readers considered the work

[88] Gustav Gundlach, "Fragen um die berufsständische Ordnung," *Stimmen der Zeit*, cxxv (1933), pp. 217-226; Oswald von Nell-Breuning, "Um den berufsständischen Gedanken. Zur Enzyklika 'Quadragesimo anno' vom 15. Mai 1931," *Stimmen der Zeit*, cxxii (1931), pp. 36-52. See also Constantin Noppel, S.J., "Rerum Novarum und Quadragesimo Anno," *Stimmen der Zeit*, cxxii (1931), pp. 156-169.
[89] Gundlach, "Fragen um die berufsständische Ordnung," p. 226.
[90] *Ibid.*, p. 225.
[91] See above, note 84.

simply an official commentary on *Quadragesimo anno* and were
unaware of the bitter disputes which raged among German and
Austrian Catholics over the interpretation Nell-Breuning had
placed on the complex edifice of social thought of the encyclical. It has been possible to select only a few points from Nell-
Breuning's detailed comments. The items chosen are those
which were discussed most widely among Austrian Catholics
and were the subject of controversy between Romantic and anti-
Romantic schools.

One might begin by citing Nell-Breuning's contention that
Quadragesimo anno and its author had not initiated a new
trend in Catholic social theory, but had simply continued the
Sozialpolitik doctrines of Leo XIII: ". . . it is of considerable
importance that the highest authority of the church had only
fulsome praise for the *Sozialpolitik* doctrines, so bitterly reviled
by many."[92] Nell-Breuning then pointed out that the Pope had
vindicated the position of the moderates in the German Catholic
disputes over trade unions by defending the workers against
those who would deny them the right to organize. He expressed
particular satisfaction with the manner in which Pius XI had
castigated those among Catholics ". . . who flirted with notions
of patriarchal rule and with socially reactionary ideas. . . ."[93]
He noted that similar treatment had been given those who
claimed that the economic system *must* produce whatever the
reformers demanded: "No harm will be done if well-meaning
reformers, including some in priestly habit, create beautiful
utopias and then simply demand that the economy perform the
necessary miracles. This is harmless, but doesn't help much
either."[94]

Nell-Breuning then devoted considerable effort to show that
the papal concept of property, central to the argument of *Quadragesimo anno*, gave little comfort to the Vogelsang school.
He cited Pius XI's condemnation of those theorists who had
accused the church of embracing a pagan law system, who continued to cling to the labor theory value, and who claimed that

[92] Nell-Breuning, *Die soziale Enzyklika*, p. 35.
[93] *Ibid.*, p. 39. Nell-Breuning characterized as reactionary those Catholics
who disliked political parties, parliamentary government, and democracy. He
predicted that they would use the encyclical as an excuse for destroying existing
institutions—certainly an accurate prediction for Austria.
[94] *Ibid.*, p. 61.

misuse of property destroyed title to it. For example: "Angrily, even indignantly, the Pontiff rejected the assertion that an un-Christian or even pagan property concept had found its way into the social theory of Catholic moral theologians, and that one needed to suppress these pagan principles and replace them with correct Christian ones."[95]

Nell-Breuning also felt it necessary to defend those passages of the encyclical which had pleased the Romanticists. For example, he denied that one could quote *Quadragesimo anno* in support of state intervention in economic and social affairs. Rather, Pius XI had approved the principle of subsidiarity, a central concept in Solidarist doctrine, when he said that the "true aim of all social activity should be to help individual members of the social body, but never to destroy or absorb them."[96] Nell-Breuning considered this statement an endorsement of "the oft-cited and famous subsidiarity principle in social action, indeed a basic notion of Christian sociology."[97]

Nell-Breuning's *Quadragesimo anno* commentary also expanded the *Stand-Klasse* argument of Gundlach,[98] but attempted to provide a more prominent place for corporative organization in society than Solidarist theory had been prepared to grant before the publication of the encyclical. He pointed out that the Pope had recognized both occupational and territorial organizations and, most important, had insisted on the voluntary character of the occupational groups.[99] While the Romanticists stressed the section of the encyclical favorable to Italian Fascist organizations, Nell-Breuning stressed those which were critical of that system, as well as those which emphasized the voluntary character of corporative organization.[100] Finally, he insisted that *Quadragesimo anno* had not invalidated anything in the 1925-1926 statements on social questions of the German and Austrian

[95] *Ibid.*, p. 65.   [96] *Ibid.*, p. 79.

[97] *Ibid.*, p. 145. Nell-Breuning insisted that it simply would not do to call Leo XIII an individualist and Pius XI an universalist, especially not in the sense of the universalist school of Spann: "The basic orientation of the Encyclical [*Quadragesimo anno*] is quite clear: it is neither individualistic, nor universalistic, but tries to hold to the golden mean—a position much maligned these days." *Ibid.*, p. 79.

[98] Gustav Gundlach, "Klasse," *Staatslexikon*, III, 386-387; see also Nell-Breuning, *Die soziale Enzyklika*, p. 153.

[99] Nell-Breuning, *Die soziale Enzyklika*, p. 158.

[100] *Ibid.*, pp. 104-105.

clergy. However, he provided little concrete proof for that assertion. Nell-Breuning's commentary and his controversies with the Romantic schools furnish additional proof for the suggestion advanced earlier that papal encyclicals on social questions usually reflect the views of a variety of Catholic social schools but cannot be taken as clear-cut victories for any one of them. As a result, official efforts to settle existing disputes actually give rise to new controversies over the interpretation of the papal statement concerning the nature of the original dispute. *Rerum novarum* and *Quadragesimo anno* settled some of the controversies over Catholic social theory; they left many others unsettled and, in their turn, provided food for future disputes.

(b) *The Hierarchy Adjusts to Quadragesimo anno.* The Austrian hierarchy had less difficulty adjusting to the changes in papal social theory than the German Solidarists. It found the emphasis of *Quadragesimo anno* on corporative organization congenial to Austrian social thought, and called on the faithful to direct their efforts to replacing the existing conflict between classes with ". . . the harmonious cooperation of the estates."[101] However, in a major pastoral letter on the encyclical the hierarchy selected only certain topics from *Quadragesimo anno* for discussion and placed great stress on the conformity of current official Austrian doctrine with the principles of the encyclical. The bishops supported Pius XI's defense of trade unions, but chose to emphasize the part of the encyclical that urged workers to join both trade unions and workingmen's associations. The Austrian bishops then devoted special attention to the need for Catholic organizations among peasants and the middle class. They complained about a new organization which had sprung up among peasants: "A movement has sprung up which poses as a class organization. It recognizes only agrarian interests and cares not an iota about the needs of other groups."[102] This was obviously an attack on the *Landbund*, which, as a purely agrarian party, could afford to make promises to peasants without having to consider the effect of these promises on urban-non-peasant voters.

[101] Address by Friedrich Gustav Cardinal Piffl before the *Volksbund der Katholiken Österreichs*, 22 October 1931, reprinted in *Episkopat*, p. 187.
[102] Pastoralschreiben der österreichischen Erzbischöfe und Bischöfe Februar 1932, reprinted *Episkopat*, p. 191.

Finally, the bishops reviewed the conditions of Catholic organizations among employers: ". . . they are formally and ideologically neutral, but their social ideals are really inspired by liberalism. Their concern for the preservation of private property sometimes forces them unto the side of conservative parties; now and then they even make a few obeisances in the direction of the church, the greatest conservative force. But all that does not alter the fact that their liberal ideals are incompatible with the Christian social reform program."[103] By devoting considerable attention to the details of organizations within the existing social framework the Austrian hierarchy attempted in a subtle manner to play down the demands for radical social reforms contained in the encyclical.

Repeatedly the bishops asserted that the encyclical had confirmed their earlier statements on the social question, and supported them in their controversy with the social Romanticists, especially on the question of private property: ". . . there are some writers even in Catholic periodicals who do not fully espouse the teachings of *Quadragesimo anno*. They try to falsify the meaning of the encyclical, and use it to defend the very errors they have always advocated. [*Quadragesimo anno*] reaffirms [our] original definition of private property and therefore rejects those views which would undermine that concept."[104] As a result, the hierarchy did not emphasize economic reform measures as much as the encyclical, but stressed instead charity, love, and abstinence. The bishops seemed to expect important results from their suggestion that the government withhold licenses from those planning lavish Mardi Gras (*Fasching*) festivals.[105] The tendency of the Austrian hierarchy to stress moral and spiritual methods in the case of difficult social problems, evident in the pastoral letter of 1925, reappeared in the discussion of *Quadragesimo anno*.

Nevertheless, the Austrian hierarchy and Austrian Catholics welcomed the publication of *Quadragesimo anno* because it provided them with a rallying cry against the Austrian Republic. Catholics could now demand the abolition of the neutral, un-Christian Republic and its replacement with a new

[103] *Ibid.*, p. 193.
[104] *Ibid.*, p. 216.
[105] *Ibid.*, pp. 221-222.

system inspired by papal social doctrines. However, Cardinal Piffl, who died before the establishment of the corporative state in 1934, cautioned against any rapid abandonment of existing economic and social institutions, especially those uncomfortable to employers.[106] He defended the role of trade unions against the vocal anti-labor element among his flock and deplored the lack of Catholic-inspired organizations among employers. Finally, he warned against those who supported corporative doctrines because they hoped to use them to deny the just claims of the workers: "There are influential elements who used to proclaim the virtues of the corporative social order long before the Holy Father—usually in the secret hope that they could thereby do away with the social benefits the workers had secured for themselves."[107] Unfortunately the warning of the leader of the Austrian Catholics went unheeded. The so-called corporative state had a shameful record of destroying worker organizations and depriving workers of social and economic benefits provided by law. Often workers' consent to these deprivations was enforced by blackmail, by threatening political and criminal prosecution for alleged participation in the 1934 uprising.

Despite its turn toward *Sozialreform*, the hierarchy persisted in its condemnation of the extreme social Romantic theorists. It reasserted the authority of the bishops in matters of social and economic theory, first stated in 1929, for it considered the social question a moral as well as an economic question: ". . . the social question is not a purely economic one, it is the problem of the very existence of human society itself. . . ."[108] The bishops insisted that Pius XI had not rejected capitalism as such, but, like the Austrian bishops in 1925, had condemned the excesses of the capitalist system. Separation of labor and capital and the defense of private property were the cornerstones of papal economic doctrine and even though Pius XI had advocated the reconstruction of the social order through occupational groups, he had maintained the separation of labor and

106 Piffl, " '*Quadragesimo Anno*' in Österreich," *Die soziale Botschaft des Papstes. Vorträge über Quadragesimo Anno* (Vienna: Volksbundverlag, 1931), pp. 91-100. The collection of essays will be cited as *Die soziale Botschaft*.

107 *Ibid.*, p. 98.

108 Statement by Bishop Sigismund Waitz of Innsbruck-Feldkirch, reprinted in *Episkopat*, p. 240.

capital, by recognizing these two as separate entities within the corporative system.[109]

5. *Sozialpolitik* Theorists, 1918-1934

The writings of the lay theorists who accepted the leadership of the hierarchy in social questions reflected the changes in the social doctrines of the church. Important statements on Catholic social theory came from leading Catholic statesmen such as Ignaz Seipel and Engelbert Dollfuss, as well as from a number of academic theorists such as Johannes Messner, Josef Dobretsberger, Hans Schmitz, and the writers of the *Österreichische Aktion*. Seipel has been included among the lay theorists because his writings on social and economic questions after 1918 always bore the stamp of the practicing statesman.

(*a*) *Ignaz Seipel.* Seipel's social thought, though based on Catholic theology and the social theories of the Scholastics, was definitely in the *Sozialpolitik* tradition of his teacher, F. M. Schindler.[110]

Because he rejected Romantic social doctrine, Seipel recognized that state and economy were separate spheres with well-defined boundaries and autonomous principles of action. This basic assumption, developed during the 1920's, foreshadowed the encyclical of 1931. There were cultural interests, Seipel asserted, which the state must foster, but never in a manner detrimental to the economy. For example, the state must not pursue a public policy favorable only to one class, nor must it threaten the moral basis of economic activity; that is to say, it must protect private property rights and other individual economic interests. On the other hand, economic activity should not be carried on in violation of the state's cultural activities. The economy must recognize its proper limits and cannot deny the claims of the state: "The economy is important, but not all of politics deals with economic problems. There are social and intellectual interests which, in a higher sense, serve the material interests of the people . . . but whose connection with economic interests and legislation cannot be easily established in each

[109] Waitz, "Quadragesimo Anno und Solidarismus," *Das Neue Reich* xiv (1932), p. 650.
[110] August M. Knoll, "Die ideengeschichtlichen Grundlagen der Sozialphilosophie Ignaz Seipels," *Neue Freie Presse*, November 14, 1934.

case. Cause and effect in human affairs cannot always be neatly isolated. . . . Therefore the economy may not reject politics, because it is influenced by politics, and in turn exercises influence over it."[111]

During the debate over constitutional reform during 1929, Seipel was very skeptical about the possibilities of corporative reforms, and especially about the feasibility of a corporative parliament. He pointed out that the *Stand* of pre-constitutional days was not a vocational group, but was based on land ownership, and that the projected *Berufsstände* of the twentieth century had nothing in common with these medieval forms of organization.[112] Seipel then examined the modern use of the term *Stand*, as in *geistlicher Stand* (priesthood), *Soldatenstand* (the military estate), and others, and suggested that though members of the same *Stand* might be engaged in a variety of pursuits, they retained certain ties which transcended these material interests: "Certainly there exists a corporation of scholars (*Gelehrtenstand*). Because of their concern for the discovery and the propagation of truth which dominates their entire lives and thoughts, scholars are members of a single community. It does not really matter that one might be a full professor at the university, and another a substitute teacher at a secondary school. . . ."[113] Consequently, a *Stand* could never be simply an economic interest organization, acting as a pressure group in politics.

Seipel's discussion of class and *Stand* was, therefore, a refutation of Gundlach's argument that both of these forms were social organizations acceptable to Catholics: "*Stand* is incompatible with class. One must choose one or the other: either the vertical or the horizontal organization of society. In the former, which embraces all those who are engaged in the same area of endeavor, everyone from the highest to the lowest is a member of the *Stand*. In this manner the ideal and the hope of advanc-

[111] "Die politischen Grundlagen der Wirtschaft," address delivered at Graz April 13, 1925, reprinted in *Seipels Reden in Österreich und anderwärts. Eine Auswahl zu seinem 50. Geburtstag*, Josef Gessl, editor (Vienna: Heros-Verlag, 1926), p. 204.

[112] "Die Tübinger Kritik der Demokratie," *Der Kampf um die österreichische Verfassung* (Vienna: Wilhelm Braumüller, 1930), p. 183.

[113] "Was sind 'Stände,'" *Reichspost*, October 20, 1929, reprinted in *Der Kampf um die österreichische Verfassung*, p. 203.

ing in life, held by all members, can be realized without having to leave the *Stand*. In the latter all those similarly situated in life form a class from which those who wish to improve their position must move into another class."[114] A *Stand*, therefore, would be a vertical organization in which individuals could rise to the top without leaving the shelter of the *Stand* organization, while the class was a horizontal group of those occupying a similar economic level of society. Seipel insisted that he could not accept any reform which simply replaced parties with economic pressure groups disguised as *Stände*. Seipel, as well as Cardinal Piffl, died before the creation of the corporative state. Like Piffl, Seipel had predicted with considerable precision what would happen in a sham corporative system. Just the same, one wonders whether Seipel, had he been alive, would not have presided over the kind of corporative state he condemned during 1928-1929, and whether the Cardinal would have spoken up for the workers after 1934 in the same manner as he had in 1931.

Seipel welcomed *Quadragesimo anno* because it enabled him to plead for the abolition of parties, parliament, and trade unions, in short, for the destruction of institutions of the Austrian Republic he had been attacking increasingly since 1927.[115] Like the members of the hierarchy, Seipel stressed the pro-capitalist elements in the encyclical and noted that the social reforms demanded by Pius XI did not touch the capitalist mode of production at all and did not require any reconstruction of economic organization. At the same time, he stressed the fact that the encyclical had called for the elimination of the existing economic classes, based on membership in one of the *Arbeitsmarktparteien*, in favor of occupational groups. Again, he attacked the Solidarists who had maintained that *Stand* organization need not be the only valid Catholic social organization.[116]

Three points emerge clearly from Seipel's discussion of *Quadragesimo anno*: classes, trade unions, and political parties would have no place in the new order. Seipel's position on classes has been outlined above. Concerning trade unions, he noted that the Pope had given his approval to such organizations, but that

---

[114] *Ibid.*, p. 204.
[115] Seipel, "Die neue Gesellschaftsordnung nach der Enzyklika 'Quadragesimo Anno,'" *Die soziale Botschaft*, pp. 81-90.
[116] *Ibid.*, pp. 84-85.

their position was a "delicate" one and that they would have to take their place in the corporative order.[117] This was obviously a warning that the future corporative state would have no room for trade unions, even Catholic ones. Seipel seemed to be very pleased that political parties had not been mentioned in *Quadragesimo anno*. He drew the conclusion that parties had been omitted because they were not corporative organs, but merely territorial organizations which, though appropriate for the atomistic society, would be out of place in a corporative order. Parties were artificial constructs, he concluded, which were doomed to extinction.[118]

One might ask why such distortions and misinterpretations of the encyclical went unchallenged in Austria. The answer has been provided by Rudolf Hausleithner, a priest, who wrote in 1937: "*Quadragesimo anno* has had a curious fate in Austria. So far only a single small excerpt has been widely publicized, and that only in mutilated, slogan-like form, i.e., the passage dealing with occupational groups. If one takes this section out of context . . . one can easily get the erroneous impression that the whole problem of social reconstruction was merely an organizational problem. All that was needed to replace the free, individualistic, with the controlled, corporativist society and economy was this minor institutional change."[119] This brief comment raises a fundamental issue concerning the Austrian corporative regime, namely, its failure to implement the "State of *Quadragesimo anno*," so fervently proclaimed on May 1, 1934. By 1937, the only part of the encyclical that had received wide circulation in Austria was the one dealing with corporative organization. This was the only part of the social reconstruction that the rulers of Austria were prepared to carry out. Seipel's eagerness to eliminate parties and trade unions, and his reluctance to consider economic and social reforms, were shared by a large number of Austrian Catholics.[120] In his commentary

[117] *Ibid.*, p. 88.   [118] *Ibid.*, p. 89.

[119] Hausleithner, *Der Geist der neuen Ordnung*, op.cit., p. 99.

[120] Hausleithner complained that the preoccupation with *Sozialpolitik* had led Catholics to accept liberalism and capitalism: "We have become so enamored of *Sozialpolitik*, the child of our age, the product of our labor, that we considered as permanent what was at best a transitory arrangement." *Ibid.*, p. 21.

on *Quadragesimo anno,* his last effort before his death, Seipel proved again to be a perfect representative as well as a successful leader of Austrian Catholics.

(b) Engelbert Dollfuss. For his speeches and articles Engelbert Dollfuss drew on the three principal sources of Austrian Catholic social thought: Romantic social theory, the Austrian tradition of vocational organization (especially in agriculture), and the social encyclicals. From these three sources, Dollfuss fashioned his criticism of the existing social and economic order, as well as his proposals for corporative organization. But in spite of his sponsorship of the Corporative Constitution of 1934, Dollfuss remained close to the pro-capitalist position of the Austrian hierarchy. This is not surprising, because Dollfuss was not an original social theorist at all, and his references to corporative and general Catholic social principles were motivated by practical political considerations. As a result, his use of ideas from Romantic and Catholic social thought serves to highlight the role Catholic and Romantic social doctrines played in the destruction of the Austrian Republic. Catholic politicians simply picked out whatever seemed the most effective anti-republican and anti-democratic argument and were little concerned with questions of compatibility of the Romantic and Catholic ideas they used in this indiscriminate fashion.

Dollfuss' early pronouncements, while he was an official of the Lower Austrian Peasant Chamber, reflected his personal experiences with occupational organization. He saw the *Bauernstand* as a moral and ethical as well as an economic organization, because, in addition to caring for its members in many ways, such as administering social insurance and social services, it was also an instrument for the practice of social charity.[121] There is no doubt that this was, at least in part, an idealized picture of the Austrian *Bauernschaft,* which comprised a less socially and economically homogeneous group than one would suspect from his description. There was often considerable friction between large and small landholders, and strong social tensions between

---

[121] Engelbert Dollfuss, address before the *Niederösterreichische Landwirtschaftskammer,* November 1927, reprinted in Edmund Weber (ed.), *Dollfuss an Österreich. Eines Mannes Wort und Ziel* (Vienna: Reinhold Verlag, 1935), p. 180. This collection will be cited as *Dollfuss an Österreich.*

the landed peasant and the agricultural laborers, the *Knechte und Mägde*.[122]

The most comprehensive critique of the existing social and economic system was contained in Dollfuss' *Trabrennplatz* address of September 1933, when he sounded the keynote for the establishment of the corporative state.[123] His description of the decay of the existing order reflected both Romantic and Catholic social thought. He first drew a picture of the organic order which supposedly had existed before the French Revolution, an order based on the association of all those pursuing the same *Beruf*. This arrangement was destroyed in 1789, chiefly because the old *Stände* and guilds had become rigid and claimed unjust privileges. Money became the dominant economic instrument, and the weak were suppressed by the strong. Rationalism and empiricism strengthened the drift toward materialism, and faith and religion were belittled if not condemned outright. But the liberal order which resulted from these influences was, in turn, replaced by an even more brutal form of materialism, namely, Marxism. Finally, in the nineteenth century technical developments leading to industrialization intensified this crass materialism.

Having reviewed these evil developments, Dollfuss called for the reconstruction of the political and social order: "The day of the capitalist system, the era of the capitalist-liberal economic order is past. . . . We demand a social, Christian, German Austria, on a corporative basis and under strong authoritarian leadership."[124] No other statement epitomizes so well the hodge-podge of contradictory Romantic and Catholic social doctrines which had become the stock-in-trade of Catholic anti-democrats in Austria. Dollfuss seemed to demand sweeping reforms of both attitudes and institutions, especially capitalism, but obviously was not really prepared to tackle the problem of replacing these existing attitudes and institutions. He also failed to distinguish, as did most of his Austrian co-religionists, between *Stände*, as autonomous social organs and *Stände* as organs of public law, executing state functions under strict state supervision.[125] Like Ignaz

---

[122] See the reference to social and economic tensions within the peasantry in Seipel, *Der Kampf um die österreichische Verfassung*, p. 203.
[123] Reprinted in *Dollfuss an Österreich*, pp. 19-45.
[124] *Ibid.*, pp. 30-31.   [125] *Ibid.*, pp. 31-33.

Seipel, he insisted that the task of representing the workers be taken out of politics, because he did not want to replace political parties with political *Stände*. At the same time, he proposed that the people organized in these *Stände* should participate in and influence legislation. Austria's workers soon discovered what was meant by taking the task of representing their interest "out of politics." It meant destruction of all worker organizations after the February rising of 1934, and the appointment of an extreme reactionary *Heimwehr* leader to the post of minister for social welfare.[126] On the other hand, both Dollfuss and Schuschnigg made several attempts to reach a *modus vivendi* with the industrial proletariat after February 1934, most notably the *Aktion Winter*. Ernst Karl Winter was appointed vice-mayor of Vienna with the task of establishing liaison with the workers.

As late as December 1933, Dollfuss ridiculed those who were devising theoretical constitutions based on outmoded forms.[127] But a few months later he appeared as architect and chief sponsor of a corporative constitution based, apparently, on these same outdated models.

(c) The "Realistic" Theorists: Messner, Dobretsberger, and Zehentbauer. Johannes Messner, Josef Dobretsberger, and Franz Zehentbauer represented a group of academic theorists who best understood the weaknesses of the Catholic social reform program. They tried to eliminate the utopian elements of that program and develop an economically and sociologically "realistic" set of proposals.[128]

---

[126] See Fritz Klenner, *Die österreichischen Gewerkschaften. Vergangenheit und Gegenwartsprobleme* (Vienna: Verlag des österreichischen Gewerkschaftsbundes), II, 1101-1183.

[127] *Reichspost*, December 24, 1933, reprinted in *Dollfuss an Österreich*, pp. 51-52.

[128] The writings of this group before 1934, and their subsequent activities in the corporative state, illustrate what Dobretsberger, writing after the end of the Second World War, called the great conflict between Catholic social theory and Catholic social action, namely, the uncompromising opposition to liberalism and capitalism in theory and the readiness for compromise in practice: "There developed thus a discrepancy . . . between theory and practice. One always did in practice what theory strictly forbade." Dobretsberger, *Katholische Sozialpolitik am Scheideweg*, p. 24. In their writings these men had shown a willingness to abandon the utopian formulas of the Romantics and to develop a reform program free of slogans and high-sounding phrases. Just the same, they served the corporative state, which cloaked its unwillingness to carry out economic and social reforms with the very Romantic slogans they had severely criticized.

Johannes Messner attempted to fashion a social theory within the Catholic social tradition, but free from the extreme Romanticism of the Vogelsang school.[129] He claimed that his system of social criticism, *Sozialkritik*, was based on a clear understanding of actual conditions, and on a grasp of the objective social order, the *Kulturnormen*. Romantic social theory, Messner argued, had selected some past situation, made it objectively valid for all times, and used it as a yardstick for all subsequent situations. His own procedure for social inquiry, *Sozialkritik*, on the other hand, called for freedom from bias, and an ability to feel oneself into a situation, while at the same time keeping a distance so that one could discern significant interrelationships.[130]

Messner rejected not only the Romantic method of social inquiry, but also the Romantic reform proposals because they lacked what he called Christian realism. He contended that the reformer must always establish a connection with the existing situation as a starting point for an evolutionary reform program. Messner prescribed two fundamental rules for a realistic reform program. The first was that neither natural law nor revealed truth could provide concrete directives for social reorganization. According to the second, an economic ethics, *Wirtschaftsethik*, could not be developed simply on the basis of general moral norms, but must take into account actual economic conditions and economic theory.[131] Most important, Messner argued, the social reformer should be able to relate economic theory to actual economic conditions, and recognize that social ethics and economic theory will not contradict each other, if he clearly understands their respective scope. For example, the social reformer could not disregard the operation of the market, because a "just wage" could never be established by an act of faith, but only by translating the ethical principle of the "just wage" into economic terms, such as measures for the regulation of supply and demand. He also denied that a reduction of the interest

---

[129] Johannes Messner, "Katholizismus und Sozialwissenschaft," *Das Neue Reich*, x (1928), pp. 634-636.
[130] "Sozialkritik," *Staatslexikon*, IV, 1696-1699.
[131] "Sozialordnung," *Staatslexikon*, IV, 1673-1680.

rate by fiat would prove workable, unless steps were taken simultaneously to foster savings.[132]

Josef Dobretsberger's social and economic "realism" strongly resembled that of Messner: "[We] reject the theory of straightline evolution of the economy towards an ideal form . . . as well as the notion that absolute economic and social value can be assigned either to the free or the controlled economy. Consequently we also deny that the social ethic requires us to espouse either a system of freedom or of control. . . . There is no ideal economic organization valid for all time which would guarantee prosperity if obeyed and would cause crises if disregarded. . . . The tasks of organization, of social politics, and of economic ethics are all tasks of an immediate present, and not of an aprioristic, transcendent will."[133]

As a result, Dobretsberger repudiated the entire set of Romantic social doctrines which centered around an ideal economic order, based on medieval social institutions.

The swing of the pendulum between free and controlled economic systems, according to Dobretsberger, was reflected in a number of economic changes. As the pendulum swung from the free to the controlled economy, there was a shift of emphasis from the private to the public economy,[134] from insecurity of income to security of income,[135] and from free competition to monopoly.[136] He denied that "booms and busts" were caused by adherence to certain forms of economic organization; on the contrary, the ups and downs of the business cycle determined the organization of the economy. During times of expansion a free economy would be appropriate, and in times of depression and contraction a controlled system.[137] Consequently, Dobretsberger rejected both the utopian *Ständestaat* of the Romanticists and the limited state of the pro-capitalist Catholics. He noted that both of these groups claimed the sup-

[132] *Sozialökonomie und Sozialethik; Studien zur Grundlegung einer systematischen Wirtschaftsethik* (Paderborn: Ferdinand Schöningh, 1931), pp. 72-73.

[133] Josef Dobretsberger, *Freie oder gebundene Wirtschaft. Zusammenhänge zwischen Konjunkturverlauf und Wirtschaftsform* (Munich: Duncker & Humblot, 1932), pp. 165.

[134] *Ibid.*, pp. 105-123.

[135] *Ibid.*, pp. 123-130.

[136] *Ibid.*, pp. 95-105.

[137] *Ibid.*, p. 163.

port of Christian ethics and theology for their favorite economic schemes.

In a series of special studies about the time of *Quadragesimo anno*, this group of theorists developed important elements of a Catholic social and economic theory, such as social justice, interest, and property. They tried to show that Catholic social theory was based on a realistic understanding of social institutions, and that Catholics could use that theory to achieve tangible reforms within the existing social and economic system.

Shortly before the publication of *Quadragesimo anno* Messner attempted to define the concept "social justice."[138] He stressed the social and economic aspects of that concept, and tried to make it operative not only within the sphere of the state, enforced by the state's legal power, but in society as a whole. In his desire to avoid the pitfalls of Romantic *étatisme*, Messner tended to play down the role of the state and the need for state action in social reforms. He probably recognized that Austrian Catholics could be brought to deal realistically with social problems only if they were freed once and for all from the influence of Romantic doctrines.

Messner criticized his co-religionists for forgetting to distinguish between state and society, and for relying too much on state action for social and economic reform: "Perhaps Catholic social science has lost sight in recent years of this differentiation of state and society. For a long time it has been under the influence of a theory of state absolutism . . . which seemed to have given rise to the hope that the state . . . would be able to solve the social question."[139] He admitted that the state possessed legal controls over economic activity, but denied that it had either the duty or the capacity to organize the national economy.[140]

The modern economic system, Messner argued, differed radically from the one familiar to Scholastic theorists. The complexity and high degree of interdependence which characterized the modern economy made it extremely difficult to determine the just share of the various participants in the economic proc-

---

[138] Messner, "Zum Begriff der sozialen Gerechtigkeit," *Die soziale Frage*, pp. 416-435.

[139] *Ibid.*, p. 423.

[140] *Ibid.*

ess. Therefore, in establishing standards of social justice, the entire society and its economic system would have to be taken into consideration. This made setting the just wage immeasurably more difficult than in the simple economic system of the Middle Ages.

Finally, Messner insisted that the claims of social justice were societal claims, not claims against the state; they were claims of various social and economic groups against each other: "It is not the state which distributes shares of social welfare in order to insure private welfare. Rather, for the sake of the common good the social groups parcel out among each other whatever they are entitled to on the basis of their contribution to the social welfare. . . . Social justice remains, therefore, justice within society, that is to say, the rightful claims on which it is based are not claims against the state, but those which various social groups have against each other. . . ."[141] Messner concluded that there were five elements in his definition of social justice: (1) The obligations of social justice were obligations established by natural law. (2) These obligations were to be met within economic society to the extent that economic activity constituted a recognized part of the total social purpose. (3) Its *objectum formale* was the common good of society. (4) Its *objectum materiale* was the claim of social groups to a share of the social product; the regulation of these claims, if that was not already provided for by the rules of legal, distributive, and commutative justice, was part of the *gemeinsame Unterhaltungsfürsorge*. (5) The organized social groups (*Stände* and classes) were the organs entitled to advance the claims of their members.[142]

A comparison of Messner's treatment of social justice, written shortly before the publication of *Quadragesimo anno*, with the manner in which Pius XI handled that concept shows that the Pope was inclined to assign the state a much greater share of responsibility for social justice than Messner was prepared to concede. Nevertheless, Messner's attempt to define the concept of social justice remains a significant contribution to the "realistic" social theory developed by this group of young Catholic theorists.

[141] *Ibid.*, pp. 432-433.
[142] *Ibid.*, p. 433.

In a study on interest, Franz Zehentbauer defended the official stand of the church, as expressed in c. 1543 of the revised *Codex Iuris Canonici,* against the radical theories of the Romanticists.[143] The principal error of Romantic theorists according to Zehentbauer had been their unwillingness to admit that money played an entirely different role in the modern industrial economy than it had in the Middle Ages. In the modern economy, Zehentbauer asserted, money was being used generally to express values, not only of consumption goods, but of capital goods as well. Money, in short, had become a value-creating device for the rational distribution of the products of the industrial economy. In medieval times, on the other hand, the state of the economy did not permit the productive investment of money.[144] Zehentbauer therefore defended the position of the *Codex,* which permitted the taking of interest at the legally established rate, by arguing that the position of the church on the question of interest was not defined by dogma. It could, therefore, be modified in the light of changing conditions. Just as the church was not committed to a specific form of government, it was not committed to a specific form of economic organization.[145]

Following the publication of *Quadragesimo anno,* Austrian Catholics held a number of conferences to study and interpret the encyclical. Messner's study of property, presented at such a conference, was an attempt to interpret *Quadragesimo anno* as a pro-capitalist and anti-Romantic document.[146]

Messner defended the moderate theorists and the encyclicals against the accusation of the social Romanticists that Catholics had succumbed to the capitalist spirit. At the same time, he tried to prevent the Romanticists from claiming *Quadragesimo anno* as supporting their anti-capitalist doctrines. Consequently, he attempted to show that private property had a prominent place

[143] Franz Zehentbauer, "Das Zinsproblem," *Die soziale Frage,* pp. 189-200.

[144] *Ibid.,* pp. 195-196; see Messner, *Sozialökonomie und Sozialethik,* p. 71.

[145] Zehentbauer, *op.cit.,* pp. 189-190. Zehentbauer argued that just as the taking of interest on money loans was forbidden by the church during the Middle Ages because that was appropriate for the economic system of that period, so the statement of the church in the 1917 revision of the *Codex* permits the taking of interest because this fits into the economic system of capitalism, *ibid.,* p. 200.

[146] Johannes Messner, "Das Eigentumsrecht nach 'Quadragesimo Anno,'" *Die soziale Botschaft,* pp. 18-34.

in the encyclical, and that both Leo XIII and Pius XI had desired to increase private property, because they considered the acquisition of property the best method for improving the condition of the worker.[147]

There were fundamentally three wrong approaches to the definition of property, Messner argued: *laissez-faire*, socialism, and Romantic doctrine.[148] *Laissez-faire* taught that the owner of property could do with it whatever was not expressly forbidden. Messner considered such a definition incompatible with Catholic social teachings. Socialism went to the other extreme, and denied that man had any absolute right to property at all. It considered man only an administrator of property in the interest of the community who would forfeit any title to the property if he misused it. The Romantic doctrine on property actually differed little from that of socialists, Messner believed. The Romanticists claimed that the state could take private property in the interest of the common good because property never belonged to a single individual, but belonged to all men. They also maintained that an individual had a legal duty to relinquish any surplus beyond his needs of a *standesgemässer Unterhalt* (maintenance according to one's station).[149] If he did not do so voluntarily, the state had the right to confiscate that surplus and redistribute it among the members of society.

It had been the main purpose of *Quadragesimo anno*, according to Messner, to reject these wrong definitions of property and put a correct one in their place. In doing so, Pius XI had declared that the church recognized the need for modifying its teaching on property relationships to meet changing conditions, but that it could never change its teaching on the concept of property itself, because it considered the right of the individual to private property anchored in natural law. However, the individual was entitled to private property not simply to satisfy his individual selfish demands, but for the sake of his position in the social order; that is to say, property always fulfilled a social *Ordnungsfunktion*.[150] This dual character of property, social and individual, would have to be recognized at all times, even though details of property relationships could change with changing conditions.

[147] *Ibid.*, p. 18.   [148] *Ibid.*, pp. 19-20.   [149] *Ibid.*   [150] *Ibid.*, p. 22.

Messner placed special emphasis on those passages of the encyclical which rejected the Romantic contention that misuse of property justified expropriation, and that surpluses should be redistributed. He reiterated the papal warning that ". . . the rights of property and the use of property ought to be restricted only to the extent called for by the general welfare. Therefore, it is entirely wrong to treat as theft all private property which seems to be surplus."[151] One could grant the state the right to regulate property, Messner claimed, without having to argue that such a grant destroyed all individual titles to property. He denied Romantic and socialist contentions that state regulation or state ownership were the only alternatives to monopoly. He thought that the state could control monopoly by laws on banking, cartels, bankruptcy, etc., without having to resort to outright ownership. He concluded that the encyclical, contrary to Romantic interpretations, had visualized only occasional state intervention, not collectivist experiments and total planning.[152]

(d) Hans Schmitz. Hans Schmitz showed less social "realism" than Messner and Dobretsberger, but his interpretation of *Quadragesimo anno* generally followed that of the hierarchy. Schmitz realized that the restrictions on production, as well as other restrictive practices, considered by many Catholics an integral part of Catholic social theory, would not solve the social question. He urged, therefore, increased productivity so that workers could increase their share of the social product. At the same time, he condemned large-scale enterprises as encouraging production merely for profit and discouraging a proper regard for the moral aspects of human development. He urged the creation of a small-scale artisan type economy, strictly in the Vogelsang tradition of the closed state.[153]

In spite of these pro-Romantic tendencies, Schmitz defended the concept of the just wage as defined in *Quadragesimo anno.*[154] He denied that the encyclical had omitted productivity (*Leistung*) as a factor in the determination of the just wage. Like Messner, he argued that the complexity of the modern industrial

[151] *Ibid.,* p. 25.
[152] *Ibid.,* p. 30.
[153] Anton Orel, *Wahre Ständeordnung; ihr Geist, Wesen, Wirken; Grundsätzlich-praktische Klarstellungen* (Graz: Ulrich Moser, 1934), pp. 52-53.
[154] Hans Schmitz, "Lohnfrage und Entproletarisierung," *Die soziale Botschaft,* pp. 35-44.

economy had made it almost impossible to determine the exact value of a worker's effort in a given product.[155] In *Quadragesimo anno* the Pontiff had concentrated on the principle of need as the basis for social justice, but had retained "continued existence of the enterprise" as a factor in determining the just wage: "It seems as if *Quadragesimo anno* had centered its attention only on the principle of 'need.' But it would be wrong to conclude from the encyclical's failure to refer to the productivity principle that the latter was of no significance."[156] Schmitz, like the Solidarists, felt it necessary to prove that the demands of social ethics were not in conflict with economic reality. He opposed the replacement of the *Lohnvertrag* with a *Gesellschaftsvertrag*, but insisted that it was economically feasible to modify the former by granting the worker a share in profits or a voice in management.

(e) *Österreichische Aktion: Bridge to Sozialreform.* Though all parts of the program of the *Österreichische Aktion* were strongly influenced by Romantic social theory, the economic and social thought of the *Aktion* remained fundamentally pro-capitalist.[157] The writers of the *Aktion* tried to appeal to the industrial workers by condemning capitalism and industrialism. But their preoccupation with the restoration of the Hapsburgs prevented them from developing a program of social and economic reforms which went beyond the established capitalist system.

The *Aktion* held economic and political liberalism responsible for the present deplorable condition of the lower classes in Austria. It contrasted this with the past when the Austrian emperor had always been concerned with the fate of these lower classes. In support of this contention *Österreichische Aktion* cited the policy of the Metternich regime, which had attempted to protect the artisans by preventing industrialization. Subsequently, the enlightened bourgeoisie and the bureaucracy had undermined these imperial directives by fostering *laissez-faire* policies. In the end, liberalism had destroyed *Kaisertum*, the

---

[155] *Ibid.*, p. 40.   [156] *Ibid.*, pp. 42-43.

[157] The two essays in the *Österreichische Aktion* which deal with the social question were written by August M. Knoll: "Kaisertum und Proletariat oder die soziale Monarchie," pp. 186-215; and "Entproletarisierung," pp. 216-243. August M. Knoll (ed.), *Die österreichische Aktion. Programmatische Studien* (Vienna: Im Selbstverlag der Verfasser, 1927).

only political organization under which public policy could have been developed in the interest of the general welfare and the common good: "Because of the heredity principle which causes it to endure forever, true monarchy can pursue the kind of far-sighted policies necessary for deproletarization. The elected party politician lacks the resources for this task, both psychologically and physiologically."[158] Only the monarch, the image of the priest and the *paterfamilias*, could be a true head of state and father of his people. Parties and party politicians, on the other hand, could act only for the short run and for the selfish ends of the groups they represented.

While political individualism had thus destroyed the true political rule, economic liberalism had destroyed the organic corporative order. It had freed economic activity from the responsibilies which the corporative system had imposed on all sectors of life. It had separated labor and capital and destroyed the organic relations between the two. Finally, it had made possible the formation of huge production units which destroyed the mass of individual producers.

The *Aktion* analyzed the condition of the industrial proletariat and found it to be the exact opposite of ideal *Kaisertum*; that is to say, the industrial worker lacked the characteristics of that *Kaisertum*, independence, tradition, a true *Heim und Haus*, and a true *Stand und Beruf*.[159]

The worker had lost his personality because of the impersonal nature of political and economic organization. The anonymity of the modern corporation and of the democratic representative process gave rise to irresponsibility, and ultimately led to ill-treatment and exploitation of the worker. The excesses of such exploitation, the *Aktion* argued, would have been impossible under an absolute monarch or a single entrepreneur: "The question is whether the capitalist factory owner and the absolute monarch are not to be preferred to the anonymity of the business corporation and of mass democracy. One might be tempted to answer this question in the affirmative. A personal conscience will prevent the tyrant and the capitalist exploiter from going to extremes. Can one say that a group of stockholders or popular representatives have a personal conscience?"[160] The *Aktion* predicted that in his revolt against such irresponsibility the worker would turn to a dictator who would assume the responsibility the democratic politician and the director of a modern corporation had refused to take. Only social monarchy could provide an alternative for such a dictator, or prevent the growth of dictatorship in the future.

The separation of labor and capital had robbed the worker of his independence and placed him completely at the mercy of the capitalist who could hire and fire at will and dictate the level of wages workers could earn. The *Aktion* condemned as trickery the way in which political individualism had given the worker the vote, while at the same time economic individualism had made him a slave of the capitalist. The *Aktion* particularly condemned the actions of the so-called benevolent capitalists who provided their workers with homes and even cars: "From the point of view of economic independence he [the worker] is worse off today. The proletarians living in company towns are tied more securely to the factory than ever before. They have now sunk below the level of the medieval serf."[161] The level of wages prevailing in a liberal, industrial economy had deprived workers of a true *Heim und Haus*. The fundamental reason for that was the separation of work and residence, when the worker entered the factory and no longer pursued his occupation in his home. Furthermore, when the liberal economic system depressed the wages workers received in these factories, all members of the family were forced to go to work. The conditions of family life in urban slums destroyed the last vestiges of family unity. This breakup of the home only served to drive the worker further into feverish activity outside the home. As a result of these conditions, the worker had ceased to consider himself the head of a family and could not grasp, therefore, the role of the monarch as *Landesvater*: "The individual proletarian who cannot attain the royal attributes of fatherhood, family, and home on his own level will only hate the monarch for possessing in full measure what he lacks. . . . The young proletarian, too, will be unable to grasp the role

[160] *Ibid.*, p. 199. [161] *Ibid.*, p. 200.

of the prince as father of the country, simply because he has never seen his own father perform as sire and king in his proper domain."[162]

The methods of industrial production had deprived the worker of a *Beruf* and of his standing in society as the member of a *Stand*. The worker no longer had a chance to learn a skill, and with it a set of values and attitudes. As a result, he considered his occupation merely a means for earning an income, but not a *Beruf*, a true vocation. Furthermore, the destruction of the organic order by economic individualism had made the worker the member of a class, based on money and income. Consequently, he had ceased to be a member of a *Stand* which had been a grouping of those pursuing a common *Beruf*.

Having lost personality, independence, *Heim und Haus*, and *Stand und Beruf* the worker had lost the sources of all his traditions and had become completely rootless in modern society. The *Aktion* considered three possible methods for remedying this rootlessness and for uplifting the proletariat (*Entproletarisierung*): socialism, the "cold" solution; *Sozialpolitik*, the "lukewarm" solution; and conservatism, the "hot" solution.[163] Socialism, the *Aktion* claimed, proposed to eliminate the separation of labor and capital by the socialization of capital. It assumed that the class condition of the proletariat was a normal situation and proposed to concentrate all power in the hands of the proletariat. Therefore, it rejected all reform proposals which left the existing system untouched. The *Aktion* conceded that the grandiose scheme of socialism constituted at least a "moral act": "The positive accomplishment of socialism was its ambitious attempt to reunite property and labor which capitalism had separated. Thus socialism rejected the *status quo* . . . and sought to reshape the world. . . . This was a genuine cultural program (*Kulturprogramm*) . . . a genuine moral act."[164] However, it denied the possibility of realizing the socialist scheme except through a dictatorship which it considered unacceptable.

The *Aktion* also rejected the *Sozialpolitik* solution because it was limited to eliminating the worst hardships facing the proletariat: "Modern *Sozialpolitik* does not really attempt to lift the proletariat out of the morass, but merely protects it

162 *Ibid.*, p. 202.   163 *Ibid.*, pp. 207-209.   164 *Ibid.*, p. 207.

from the worst forms of pauperization. By producing some slight increase in the amount of material goods, it hopes to make the proletariat content with its condition of slavery."[165] Though many political parties had pursued *Sozialpolitik*, the writers of the *Aktion* reserved their sharpest criticism for their fellow Catholics who had accepted a social program which the *Aktion* claimed, did not really help the worker at all.

Only conservatism, social monarchy, offered two genuine measures of *Entproletarisierung: Kaisertum* and a controlled decentralized economy. The remnants of the old trader and artisan groups still in existence would have to be rescued, and a new middle class created into which the industrial proletariat would be absorbed. A compulsory industrial service would be created to provide workers for those large-scale industrial enterprises which were considered indispensable.[166] The program of the *Österreichische Aktion*, like most other Catholic social programs, devoted considerable effort to a critique of liberalism and industrialism, but had little to show in the way of a comprehensive program of reform. In spite of the elaborate critique of the conditions of the industrial proletariat and the repeated demands for *Entproletarisierung*, the proposals of the *Österreichische Aktion* remained fundamentally middle class and pro-capitalist. For this reason *Österreichische Aktion* has been considered part of the lay theorists who followed the leadership of the hierarchy in social questions. But the writers of the *Aktion* were less amenable to church leadership in social doctrine than any of the others discussed in the present chapter. They were close to the Romantic theorists whose *Sozialreform* doctrines will be analyzed in the next chapter. In this sense *Österreichische Aktion* provides the bridge between *Sozialpolitik* and *Sozialreform*.

[165] *Ibid.*, p. 208.
[166] *Ibid.*, p. 234.

CHAPTER VI

THE CRITICISM OF CAPITALISM:
RELIGIOUS SOCIALISM
AND THE ROMANTIC TRADITION

THE neo-Romanticists and a small group of Religious Socialists were the severest critics of capitalism and industrialism during the period 1918-1934. They maintained an uncompromising hostility to the modern state and the modern economy throughout this period, and continued to demand radical reforms which would do away with existing political and social institutions. Because they had little patience with those of their co-religionists who were satisfied with gradual changes, they often directed their most violent outbursts against anti-Romantic Catholics, instead of liberals or socialists. No one attacked Austrian political and social institutions with such violence as did Anton Orel, who accused priests and bishops of being the principal supporters of a Godless republic and an exploiting economy.

1. The Unity of the *Sozialreform* Critique

There was a multiplicity of schools and tendencies in the Romantic camp. Often there were as many views as there were theorists, but all drew on the Müller-Vogelsang tradition of Romantic social thought. Much of this Romantic literature was pedestrian, petty, and uninspired, and added little to the development of Romantic ideas. The only writer in the Romantic tradition who achieved a measure of originality was Ernst Karl Winter. However, his social theory, in which he attempted a synthesis of Romantic, Kantian, and Marxian ideas, failed to receive any support in the Catholic *Lager*. But in spite of a seeming diversity of social doctrines there was general agreement on a fundamental hostility to capitalism and industrialism, and a desire to ameliorate the conditions of those social groups most severely affected by the evils of the modern economy. As a result, all the Romantic theories developed after 1918 seemed to be concerned with the fate of the industrial proletariat. There were many proposals for the uplifting of the proletariat (*Ent-proletarisierung*), for reabsorbing the worker into the social body, the metaphor of the "proletariat as a social precipitate" which the neo-Romanticists had borrowed from Vogelsang,[1] and for assuring the worker his proper share in the product of his labor. Most of these theorists, however, talked about these reform measures merely in general terms. When it came to implementing them, the detailed proposals they made were essentially pre-industrialist, and petty bourgeois. In short, they proposed to solve the problems of the modern industrial economy by turning every worker into a petty bourgeois *Handwerker,* and by creating a static economy in which people would prefer high-quality hand-produced goods over mass-produced goods at low prices. In spite of the elaborate structure of social theory and social criticism developed by the neo-Romanticists, most of their reform proposals during the First Republic can be reduced to such a petty-bourgeois, pre-industrialist formula.

The essential unity of anti-capitalist doctrines was not limited to the Romantic camp; there were striking similarities, as well, between the anti-capitalist ideas of the Romanticists and the Religious Socialists. The latter drew on Marxian, as well as non-Marxian, socialist ideas, but tried to maintain their position as members of the Catholic faith, while the Romanticists, who derived their fundamental ideas from Catholic social teachings and medieval social institutions, were also influenced by some of the same socialist ideas which inspired the Religious Socialists.

Some of the Romanticists, like *Österreichische Aktion* and Ernst Karl Winter, stressed the socialist elements of their program, hoping thereby to draw the workers away from Marxian socialism. At the same time, the Religious Socialists attempted to eliminate from their doctrines those parts which tended to create a conflict between socialism and Catholic social and religious teaching. They did this by playing down socialism as a *Weltanschauung,* and by stressing non-Marxian elements in their doctrines. In this manner the social theories of these two groups began to appear quite similar. This similarity was further increased because both concentrated their attention on the

---

[1] Vogelsang, *Lehren,* p. 318.

same features of capitalism and had a tendency to devote more of their effort to the criticism of existing institutions than to proposals for reform. For example, both Romanticists and Religious Socialists charged that capitalism had been responsible for freeing private property from all social obligations. Both pointed to the growth of monopoly capitalism and charged that the misery of the workers and the lower classes in general had been the result of evil monopolist practices. Both groups also failed to account for the changes in the capitalist economy since the days of Marx, Müller, and Vogelsang. As a result, their capitalist criticisms were equally outdated, as were their reform plans, which, though quite dissimilar in many ways, were based on identical, outdated assumptions.

2. The Religious Socialists

Because the existing Catholic social program had been unable to stem the mass desertion of the industrial workers from the church and from the Catholic faith, the Religious Socialists attempted to develop a program which would win the workers back from the organized Socialist movement. They hoped to accomplish this by meeting the economic and social demands of the industrial workers and by dissociating the church from any support of the existing capitalist system or of any authoritarian political regime. Unlike the Catholic trade unions whose *Linzer Programm* was strongly in the Romantic tradition, the Religious Socialists adopted much of the social and economic criticism of Marx and other socialist writers while disregarding socialism as a *Weltanschauung*.

(a) The Development of Religious Socialism. Modern Catholic religious socialism or Christian socialism dates from the period following the publication of *Rerum novarum*. The enthusiasm for social reform among some groups of Catholics had been so great that within ten years after *Rerum novarum*, Leo XIII was forced to deal with these Catholic radicals.[2] In the encyclical, *Graves de communi*, published in 1901,[3] Leo XIII

---

[2] See above Ch. 1, section 2.

[3] The encyclical is reprinted in *The Church Speaks to the Modern World; The Social Teachings of Leo XIII*, Etienne Gilson, editor (New York: Doubleday & Company, Inc., 1954), pp. 315-328.

warned against two dangers threatening the new Catholic social movement. Catholic radicals, by taking sides with the workers against the established economic order, were resisting constituted authority. "Let there be no question," Leo warned, "of fostering . . . any intention of diminishing the spirit of obedience, or of withdrawing people from their lawful rulers."[4] They also tended to view the social question purely as an economic question and, according to the Pope, forgot that it was ". . . above all, a moral and religious matter, and for that reason must be settled by the principles of morality and according to the dictates of religion."[5] In spite of this warning, Catholic radicals continued their reform activities, and many of them were attracted to Marxian socialist parties and identified themselves with the historic socialist movements. In Austria, Religious Socialists became active soon after the end of the First World War, at the same time that similar movements arose in Germany.[6]

(b) Otto Bauer and the Religious Socialists. The most prominent group of Austrian Religious Socialists was the one led by Otto Bauer, a metal worker.[7] They believed that their efforts to win industrial workers would succeed only if they maintained their position within the organized Socialist movement and accepted the historic Socialist program. They obviously realized that the Austrian industrial workers were so firmly tied to the Socialist *Lager* that no individual or group identified politically and socially with the Christian-social conservative *Lager* would ever be able to gain the support of the workers.

The Religious Socialists in their 1930 Berndorf program[8] defined socialism as a new method of organizing economy and society according to democratic-cooperative principles.[9] They believed that the cooperative organization of economic activity would eliminate the separation of labor and capital. In this man-

---

[4] *Graves de communi*, 9, p. 319.

[5] *Ibid.*, 11, p. 321.

[6] See Richard Schmitz, "Sozialismus und Kirche," *Die soziale Botschaft*, pp. 52-73; Benedikt Beham, "Katholischer Sozialismus," *Die soziale Frage*, pp. 468-477; and Gustav Gundlach, S.J., "Religiöser Sozialismus," *Staatslexikon*, IV, 834-845.

[7] The leader of the Religious Socialists was not the same Otto Bauer who was the principal Marxist theorist and leader of the Social Democratic party.

[8] *Ziele und Wege der religiösen Sozialisten Österreichs* (Vienna: Im Selbstverlag, 1930).

[9] *Ibid.*, p. 1.

ner outright state ownership and operation would be kept at a minimum, while artisans and peasants would be permitted to continue their individual enterprises. The Religious Socialists hoped thereby to satisfy Catholic social theory, which demanded the maintenance of private property and of a variety of forms of ownership.[10]

At the same time, the Religious Socialists tried to reach an understanding with socialism on matters of *Weltanschauung*: "The Social Democratic cultural and educational program [*Kulturprogramm*] derives its principal concepts from a definite ideology. Our own cultural and educational demands are formulated in such a way as to preserve the ideological neutrality of the [Social Democratic] party. This will enable both freethinkers and practicing Catholics to follow, without any conflict, their consciences in cultural and educational matters."[11]

Pius XI tried to stop the activities of groups like the Austrian Religious Socialists led by Otto Bauer, who insisted that the Marxian program of the Austrian Social Democratic party was purely an economic program which faithful Catholics could support. In *Quadragesimo anno* he declared that "Catholic" and "Socialist" were contradictory terms.[12] The Pontiff insisted that socialism was fundamentally a materialist *Weltanschauung* which contradicted the fundamental tenets of the Catholic faith. He also attacked as cultural socialism the attempts of Socialist movements to spread their *Weltanschauung* through education and by gaining control of all aspects of the individual's life.[13] But in spite of the strong criticism of religious socialism in *Quadragesimo anno* the group led by Otto Bauer maintained its loyalty to the Social Democratic party and the Socialist trade unions.[14]

[10] *Ibid.*, p. 3.
[11] *Ibid.*, p. 11.
[12] *Quadragesimo anno*, 120, p. 158; see above, Ch. v, n. 46, for the edition of the encyclical used for this analysis.
[13] *Ibid.*, 121, p. 158.
[14] Schmitz, *op.cit.*, pp. 68-69 quoted Otto Bauer as having made the choice between church and socialism after the publication of *Quadragesimo anno*. Bauer expressed grave scruples about breaking with the Social Democratic party and finally decided that the correct course was to remain with the party because "the capitalist system can be overcome only [if we are] in organic unity with it, not [if we are] apart from it, and certainly not [if we are] in opposition to it."

(c) Other Religious Socialist Groups. Other scattered groups of Religious Socialists also supported the Marxian social and economic criticism, but did not favor as close an alliance with the Social Democrats as the group under Otto Bauer. A small group, led by Richard Redler, insisted that socialism as an economic and social system was compatible with Catholicism, but not as a *Weltanschauung,* or as a sociological system: "It is imperative that we do not deny the existence of dynamic forces in the Marxist ideology, simply because they do not conform to certain traditional categories. The Marxist dynamism must be seen for what it is: an immanentist religion and a genuine religious struggle. . . ."[15] At the same time, Michael Pfliegler, a member of this group, praised the reform program contained in *Quadragesimo anno,* in spite of the Pope's attacks on Religious Socialism.[16]

Aurel Kolnai, another Religious Socialist, attempted to disprove the view, held by many Catholics, that socialism was an extension and a logical consequence of liberal-individualistic ideas.[17] He defended socialism as a system which was based on the consciousness of individuals perceiving common ends: "Socialism is a program for the construction of a free society based on a social consciousness and on the mutual recognition and affirmation [by all members] of a set of social goals."[18] He thought that such a definition of socialism was contrary to an individualism based on the principle of "unlimited profit."[19] He found it to be in accord, however, with a "deep and consequent individualism" which recognized the existence of complex and far-reaching ties. Kolnai considered this ideal of "personality" specifically Christian, and therefore urged Catholics to recognize that the industrial worker had found "personality" outside the Christian *Ideenkreis,* in the socialist movement, the

[15] *Wiener Politische Blätter,* I (April 16, 1933), p. 52.

[16] Michael Pfliegler, *Die Kirche und der Sozialismus im Lichte der "Quadragesimo anno"* (Vienna: Gsur & Co., 1933), p. 16. See also Oskar Katann, *Aufbau: Bausteine zur sozialen Verständigung* (Vienna: Reinhold Verlag, 1932).

[17] Aurel Kolnai, "Sozialismus und Ganzheit," *Wiener Politische Blätter* I (May 20, 1934), 37-48; see also "Gegenrevolution," *Kölner Vierteljahrshefte für Soziologie,* X (1931-1932), pp. 170-199, 295-319, and "Die Machtideen der Klassen," *Archiv für Sozialwissenschaft und Sozialpolitik,* LXII (1929), pp. 67-110.

[18] "Sozialismus und Ganzheit," p. 45.

[19] *Ibid.,* p. 44.

trade union, and party organization.[20] Kolnai argued that this had been possible because Marxian doctrine did not limit itself to satisfying purely economic and material needs, but called for full emancipation of the worker, for the satisfaction of his cultural, spiritual, and other needs.[21] Socialism and Catholicism were one in the search for such a personalism, Kolnai argued. Finally, Kolnai's religious socialism was fundamentally democratic. He considered the democratic state which secured freedom of opinion and recognized the rights of the opposition more nearly an integral (*ganzheitlich*) system than any authoritarian state. Kolnai's writings demonstrated the similarity of the anticapitalist criticism of the Religious Socialists and the Romanticists, as well as the fundamental differences between the reform program of the two groups. Kolnai was convinced that the individual would be able to lead a better life in a state based on a moderate socialist program, than in a Romantic, authoritarian state which supposedly pursued a social program based on Catholic teachings.

The destruction of the trade unions and of the Social Democratic party following the February 1934 disturbances, and the establishment of a Corporative State on May 1, 1934, reduced still further the number and significance of the various Religious Socialist groups.

3. The *Linzer Programm*

The social and economic criticism of the Catholic trade unions' *Linzer Programm* was strongly influenced by Romantic social doctrines.[22] But concern for the immediate welfare of the industrial worker prevented the trade union leaders from leaving their Romanticism in a Cloud-Cuckooland of vague aspira-

[20] The democratic system of trade unions and cooperative societies within the workers' movement were the instruments for the achievement of this "personalism." *Ibid.*, p. 45. Kolnai, like many of the Religious Socialists, tried sincerely to understand the position of the worker and to recognize the achievements of the Socialist movement on behalf of the worker.

[21] *Ibid.*, pp. 46-47.

[22] Karl Lugmayer (ed.), *Das Linzer Programm der christlichen Arbeiter Österreichs* (Vienna: Verlag der Typographischen Anstalt, 1924). This contains both the text of the *Programm* and Lugmayer's commentary. Roman numerals refer to section of the *Programm* itself. See also, Franz Arnold, "Wiener Richtungen," *Staatslexikon*, v, 1295-1305, and Johanna Gierse, "Sozialromantische Richtungen im Katholizismus der Gegenwart," *Soziale Revue* xxxii (1932), pp. 143-152.

tions and compelled them to include concrete reform proposals in their program. It was this more earthy empiricism which clearly distinguished the *Linzer Programm* from the productions of the other Romanticists.

(a) The Romantic Basis of the Programm. The anti-capitalist criticism of the *Linzer Programm* was entirely in the Romantic tradition: "Society is hurtling toward dissolution. The lust for power and profit plunges the people into ever deeper misery. We need a new order whose principles and ultimate salvation must come from Christian teachings."[23] Here, then, were the principal elements of traditional Romantic social doctrine: society was moving rapidly toward disintegration because of a struggle for power and profit which dominated life. As a result of this drive for profit, the worker had failed to receive protection and had been denied his full share of the economic product. There was, therefore, need for a "new order" based on Christian principles, for under the old order the failure of state and society to control the use of property in the interest of the common good had resulted in anarchy. This condition of anarchy had weakened the position of the workers: "The workers must again be recognized as full members of human society. This will be impossible as long as their families are in danger, and they lack a secure and sufficient income, property, and permanent residence. In *Rerum novarum* Leo XIII has shown us how we might remedy these conditions."[24]

The solutions for these problems, according to the *Linzer Programm*, must be sought in Christian social doctrines which regulate directly basic social institutions, and teach that Christ had given man moral laws which ought to control interpersonal relations in society: "Christ has taught us the moral laws which govern our relations to God and to one another. The Church which is the guardian of this message must have sovereign power for this task. Christian teaching protects labor and regulates the use of property. It assigns to labor the full value of its products, puts property in the service of the community, and condemns our present blood-sucking economy."[25] The *Programm* con-

23 *Ibid.*, I, p. 7; see also commentary, pp. 15-21.
24 *Ibid.*, v, p. 8; see also commentary, pp. 73-93.
25 *Ibid.*, II-III, p. 7; see also commentary, pp. 22-47.

cluded that the existing exploiting economy violated all these Catholic doctrines. This tendency to elevate Catholic social teaching to the level of dogma and revelation was shared by most of the Romanticists, but was condemned not only by anti-Romantic groups like the Solidarists, but also by the church itself. Both Leo XIII and Pius XI had declared repeatedly that the social teachings of the church were based on reason and natural law and should not be taken to endorse for all times a specific set of social institutions.

(b) The Linzer Reforms. The *Linzer Programm* considered *Familie* (family), *Beruf* (vocation), and *Siedlung* (internal colonization) to be the foundations of society.[26] Of these three, the family was the principal social institution. Its sanctity was protected by Christian marriage laws, while property and labor provided it with material goods. The writers of the *Programm*, like most Romanticists, emphasized the crucial role of the family in social organization. However, they did not follow all the way the lead of the *Österreichische Aktion*, which, under the influence of the Platonic-Augustinian tradition, considered all social organizations, including the state, to be based on the family and shaped exclusively in the image of the family.

Labor and property were closely related in the *Linzer Programm* and, because of their intimate connection with the family concept, were central to the social doctrines of that program: "Labor and nature are the original sources [*Urquellen*] of economic value, but the well-being of society rests entirely on labor. Property is the foundation of the family and has its fullest justification in that task."[27] Even in a complex industrial economy based on intricate production processes, labor remained the sole creator of value, the authors of the *Programm* argued. The introduction of machinery had not reduced the contributions of labor to the economic process but had actually increased it. Capital, on the other hand, was not a separate factor in production at all, but simply a mixture of labor and nature. Therefore, the final result of all labor belonged to labor and nature: nature provided the raw materials and labor pro-

[26] *Ibid.*, IV, p. 7; see also commentary, pp. 48-69.
[27] *Ibid.*, III, p. 7.

duced the *Mehrwert*.[28] The owner of capital, under such a system of distribution, would be entitled only to a payment for the use of the means of production. No other contract between the worker and the capitalist would be permitted according to the *Linzer Programm*, except one which like the *Gesellschaftsvertrag*, condemned by Pius XI in *Quadragesimo anno*, recognized these claims of labor.[29] Finally, because labor's was the only valid claim to a share in the economic product, any wealth or other value created in society which could not be assigned to an identifiable person or group of persons as producers belonged to the society as a whole, and was to be used for communal purposes.

The *Linzer Programm* contradicted the social doctrines of the encyclicals on several important points. The *Programm* rejected the separation of labor and capital, while the encyclicals taught that this separation was not bad in itself, but had certain evil consequences which should be remedied.[30] Because he opposed such limitations on the right of capital to share in the economic product as contained in the *Programm*, Pius XI rejected the labor theory of value, but there is no evidence that the *Linzer Programm*, written in 1923, was modified significantly after the publication of *Quadragesimo anno*. The Pontiff expressly denied the applicability of the Pauline judgment, that only those willing to work should eat, to the problem of dis-

[28] The labor theory of value formulation in the *Linzer Programm* differed slightly from that of Anton Orel. While Orel recognized only labor as a value-producing factor, the *Programm* admitted that "nature" as well as "labor" were entitled to a share: "Therefore the final results of all produced value belong only to labor and nature . . ."; p. 55; see also Arnold, *op.cit.*, p. 1300, and Ch. v, n. 63, above.

[29] The entrepreneur is entitled to a share according to the amount of labor (manual or mental) he contributes; he is also entitled to payment for the use of means of production—but no more; *Linzer Programm*, pp. 60-69.

[30] In spite of Lugmayer's assertion that the *Programm* was based on the encyclicals of Leo XIII, the *Programm* does not admit the equal share of labor and capital in the creation of economic value. Though Leo XIII was eager to assert the just claims of labor to a share in the economic product, he never denied the claims of capital. The Pope's statement that "only by the labor of workingmen . . . States grow rich" cannot be taken in isolation, but must be viewed against his discussion of the just wage in which he claimed for the worker a wage ". . . sufficient to enable him comfortably to support himself, his wife, and his children . . . ," *Rerum novarum*, 34, 46. Pius XI reiterated the Leonine teaching on the just wage and specifically rejected the labor theory of value. See above, Ch. v, section 3 c.

tributing shares of value between labor and capital.[31] Nevertheless, this statement of St. Paul's remained a stock argument in Romantic attacks on unearned income.

The *Programm's* concept of private property not only clashed with the social teachings of the church; it also proved internally inconsistent. The authors of the *Programm* had assigned private property a subordinate role in their proposed social system, because they believed that it had only one function, namely, to strengthen the family by enabling its head to care for its members and to provide for their future. Such a subordination of private property contrasted sharply with the importance assigned it in the social encyclicals. Furthermore, the *Programm* was internally inconsistent in its treatment of private property. On the one hand, it recognized property only to the extent that it strengthened the family.[32] On the other hand, it seemed to envisage the continuation of much private property, for it demanded an end to the class struggle, and peace between workers and employers on the basis of justice and mutual help.[33] But if private property were abolished, or at least severely restricted, an inference one can legitimately draw from the *Programm's* deprecation of private property, would there still be workers and employers? The authors of the *Programm* never answered that question or resolved that conflict.

The organization of society in units larger than the family was to be governed by the principles of *Beruf* and *Siedlung*.[34] Those engaged in the same *Beruf* would form *Standesgruppen* and these, in turn, would unite into *Berufsstände*. *Beruf* was defined in the *Programm* in the manner of the Romanticists as well as the encyclicals, namely, a grouping of those pursuing the same vocation, irrespective of their social and economic standing.[35] The *Beruf* organizations were to consist of employee organizations (trade unions) and employer groups, and would have a wide field of autonomous action, including arbitration of internal affairs, administration of social security, welfare, housing, etc. The *Beruf* organization would also influence the actions of the state on such matters as taxation and labor legislation. Finally, the *Berufsstände* would have the power to reconstruct

---

[31] Arnold, *op.cit.*, p. 1301.   [32] *Linzer Programm*, III, p. 7.
[33] *Ibid.*, IV, p. 8.   [34] *Ibid.*, IV, pp. 7-8.   [35] *Ibid.*, pp. 78-85.

the market on the principle of *Bedarf*. This notion of production limited to the "right" needs of the consumer was part of much of the Romantic literature. The Romanticists attacked capitalist economic practices, which, they claimed, aimed at increasing profits by stimulating consumer demand for whatever goods capitalists considered profitable. Furthermore, through the *Bedarfsdeckungsprinzip* the Romantic philosophers hoped to direct the lives of the people in accordance with correct social principles. The Romantic theorists whose views about the industrial economy had been shaped by conditions during the late nineteenth and early twentieth centuries continued to equate mass production with shoddiness and handicraft with high quality. They never stopped to inquire whether the changes in industrial techniques had not led to mass production of inexpensive but well-made consumption goods. In this way, they built an elaborate social theory on empirical data whose validity they never bothered to recheck. In practice, these strictures against mass production were received favorably by artisans and shopkeepers who had suffered from the competition of the department store selling mass-produced goods at low prices.

Through *Siedlung*, families and occupational groups were organized on a territorial basis. Apparently, the theorists of the *Linzer Programm* did not propose to eliminate all territorial political organizations in favor of corporative ones, as some Romanticists had suggested.[36] However, the *Linzer Programm* gave few details about the future form of *Siedlung*.

The social theory expounded in the *Programm* showed strong Romantic influences and pointed toward a drastic reconstruction of the social order. But the specific reforms advocated in the *Programm* seemed to envisage the continuation of a capitalist economy and went little beyond the *Sozialpolitik* method of making adjustments in the existing economic order. The most radical of these specific reform proposals was the one establishing the family wage (*standesgemässe Lebensführung*) which would insure the worker and those entrusted to his care a proper standard of living. But at the same time the *Programm* demanded that the wage stand in a just relationship to the result of the

[36] The *Programm* envisaged both a popular assembly and a corporative chamber which would divide powers and functions. *Ibid.*, pp. 68-69.

labor.[37] The authors of the *Programm* did not see the contradiction between these two wage criteria (family wage and productivity) and their claim on behalf of labor for the full share of its industry. They apparently did not consider these two possibilities: the full share of the product to which labor was entitled might be less than the family wage, or it might be more than the share to which the worker was entitled on the basis of achievement or productivity. Furthermore, they never bothered to resolve any of the conflicts that might arise between the claims of the family wage and those of productivity. Most of the other demands of the *Programm*, such as the eight-hour day, limitations on the labor of women and children, social insurance, paid vacations, etc., were no longer considered radical demands in Austria even in 1923 when the *Programm* was drafted.[38]

Despite a preference for corporative organization, which the *Programm* shared with other Romantic social theories, it did not exhibit their leanings toward political authoritarianism as was shown in the analysis of the *Programm's* political section in Chapter IV.[39] Without a stand in favor of political democracy the *Programm* would have lost all attraction for the industrial worker. Actually, the *Programm* was influenced too strongly by Romantic ideas to appeal to the industrial workers who were firmly rooted in the Socialist *Lager*. At the same time, the Catholic trade unions, in spite of their impeccable record as faithful followers of the hierarchy, were considered dangerous radicals by the *Heimwehr* and the industrialists who influenced Christian Social policies.

4. Vogelsang, Kant, and Marx: The Synthesis of Ernst Karl Winter

The most original contribution to the *Sozialreform* program in Austria between 1918 and 1934 came from the pen of Ernst Karl Winter. In his writings he attacked not only capitalism and the Solidarist defense of capitalism, but also many of the

[37] *Ibid.*, VI, pp. 8-9, 93-112. The *Programm* stated: "Wage must stand in a just relation to productivity. It must secure for the worker an appropriate [*standesgemässer*] standard of living (family wage)."

[38] *Ibid.*; see also the commentary, pp. 112-132.

[39] See above, Ch. IV, section 4.

social Romantic doctrines of the Vogelsang school. He shared a genuine concern for the industrial worker with the Religious Socialists and the proponents of the *Linzer Programm*, but he quarreled with all these groups over questions of social theory as well as social institutions. However, his reform proposals ultimately differed little from those of the other anti-capitalist critics.

(a) *Winter's Career.* Winter had participated in the work of the *Österreichische Aktion* in 1927.[40] Subsequently, under the influence of Kantian and Marxian ideas, he moved away from the organized monarchist movement and became profoundly interested in the conditions of the industrial working class. Throughout 1933, he pleaded with the Christian Socials to restore Parliament and govern constitutionally.[41] He became known as the one person in the Christian-social conservative camp most sympathetic to labor's cause. After the uprising of February 1934, Dollfuss appointed him third vice mayor of Vienna and charged him with establishing liaison with the industrial workers and winning them to the corporative regime. When Schuschnigg became chancellor after the assassination of Dollfuss the *Aktion Winter* ceased to receive the support of the leading figures in the authoritarian regime. Winter and his *Aktion* came under increasingly heavy attack from the *Heimwehr* and other reactionary elements in the *Vaterländische Front*. Finally in 1936, he was ordered to suspend all his organizational and literary activities. Undoubtedly the rulers of the corporative state had given up any hope of winning the workers. Having just made their peace with Hitler, they embarked on a pronounced nationalist and bourgeois course. Though Dollfuss had exhibited some leanings toward a radical social program, Schuschnigg maintained an uncompromising hostility to labor until the very end and even refused the help of labor groups in organizing a last-minute resistance against the Anschluss in 1938. Winter's writings and his organizational activity on behalf of the workers were one of the most significant epi-

---

[40] See above, Ch. IV, n. 84.

[41] During that year he began the publication of *Wiener Politische Blätter*, which appeared regularly until 1936, when he was ordered to suspend all political activities.

sodes in the generally authoritarian and anti-labor record of the Austrian *Sozialreform* proponents during the First Republic.

(b) The Three Sources of Winter's Social Criticism. Winter's social criticism contained elements of neo-Kantianism, Romantic doctrines, and socialism.[42]

Under the influence of the Marburg neo-Kantians (Cohen, Natorp, Kelsen),[43] Winter tried to develop a precise distinction between theology and sociology.[44] He claimed that the Scholastics had failed to make this distinction and had, thereby, subverted empirical studies in the interest of theology. They had developed a "pastoral sociology" which was not based on indigenous sociological principles, but was merely an extension of theology into the social sciences. Winter traced to Aristotelian sources the Scholastics' inability to separate clearly sociology and theology.[45] He contended that under the guise of conducting empirical investigations Aristotle had subordinated all fields of empirical research to the rules and methodology of metaphysics. Ultimately, by establishing a purely spurious distinction between "is" and "ought" Aristotelianism had made possible the control of the "is" by the "ought." Using this curiously perverted Aristotelian analysis as a basis, Winter concluded that

[42] The principal sources for the analysis of Winter's thought were *Die Sozialmetaphysik der Scholastik* (Leipzig: Franz Deuticke, 1929); and *Platon. Das Soziologische in der Ideenlehre* (Vienna: Gsur & Co., 1930); as well as the *Wiener Politische Blätter* which he edited and for which he wrote a large number of articles, book reviews, etc. He also contributed to *Hochland, Schönere Zukunft*, and some of the other Catholic journals. Of special interest are three articles in *Zeitschrift für öffentliches Recht*: "Kirche und Staat. Kritische Bemerkungen zu Jacques Maritains Lehre von der *Potestas indirecta*," IX (1929), pp. 44-65; "Der paternale Staat," X (1930), pp. 213-257; and "Der wahre Staat in der Soziologie des Rechtes. Ein Beitrag zur kritischen Abgrenzung der Transzendentalsoziologie von reiner Rechtslehre, scholastischer Metaphysik und Ganzheitssoziologie," XI (1931), pp. 161-205.

[43] Arnold, *op.cit.*, p. 1304.

[44] Winter developed this distinction for the first time in *Sozialmetaphysik der Scholastik* in 1929. See above, n. 42.

[45] *Ibid.*, p. 3. Winter's writings must be understood as part of the age-old controversy between the Jesuit and Dominican orders, between the Platonic-Augustinian and the Aristotelian-Thomist traditions in Catholic thought. Furthermore, he also was a partisan in the Romantic-anti-Romantic controversies among Central European Catholics. Finally, he attempted to introduce Kantian ideas into those intra-Catholic disputes. The result was indeed "unusual" but, as Franz Arnold has pointed out, Winter's system failed (1) because it abandoned the Scholastic theory of knowledge, and (2) because it misunderstood Scholasticism altogether; *op.cit.*, p. 1304. See also Winter, *Platon*, pp. 13-18.

the Scholastics, relying on Aristotelian methods, had conquered one field of empirical investigation after another, had subjected them to the rule of dogma, and had subordinated them to the pastoral requirements of the church: "Scholastic methodology rests on the rigid axioms of a religious faith. This means that, consciously or not, it will always return to its dogmatic home base no matter how many subject matter areas it has managed to conquer. . . . It is not religion, religious thinking, or a religious way of life which interferes with science; rather a naïve fusion of the two prevents maturation and progress in both religion and science."[46]

In modern times the papal encyclicals, and in Central Europe the Jesuits, had continued the traditions of this spurious separation of faith and science. One result of this false separation, according to Winter, was the tendency of these neo-Scholastics to support the claims of the whole over the parts in social organization: "The basic concepts of this Scholastic political science are . . . the necessary 'natural' character of state and state power, the formal priority of the 'whole' over the 'parts,' and of the general welfare over the private good."[47] Furthermore, this false duality of faith and science enabled the neo-Scholastics to give their sanction to whatever happened to exist. Dictatorship, Winter insisted, could be called a child of the Scholastics, as well as of Hegel. For the aim of the Scholastics, arguing the case of the church, was to establish the rule of the church. A dictatorship, a unitary political system, was probably better adapted to this purpose than a democracy.[48]

Winter contrasted this Aristotelian-Thomist tradition which culminated in Hegel with the Platonic-Augustinian tradition

[46] *Sozialmetaphysik*, p. 49. Winter has given a penetrating analysis of the Scholastic method and the relations of Thomist thought to the "pastoral" necessities of the church. The outsider finds it difficult to see, however, in what way Winter's introduction of Romantic doctrines into political and economic science differed from the methods of the Thomists whom he attacked.

[47] *Ibid.*, p. 139; see also "Der paternale Staat," 249.

[48] *Sozialmetaphysik*, pp. 140-141. There is considerable merit in Winter's analysis of the totalitarian tendencies of modern democracy. It would also be difficult to disagree with Winter's characterization of the Jesuit order as masters of the art of finding an accommodation with whatever "powers that be." But it simply will not do to take these arguments and twist them into a condemnation of Peter Tischleder and Heinrich Rommen as defenders of dictatorship.

which found expression in a true duality of science and theology based on Kant's duality of *Sein* and *Sollen*, of *Begriff* and *Idee*.[49] He claimed to have established a true dualism of sociology and theology based on this Kantian duality and influenced by Kelsen's pure theory of law, which recognized a social order transcending the legal order but which simultaneously insured the freedom of legal norms from interference by criteria from another order. A division like Kelsen's between law and sociology, between fact and norm, would be more conducive to a respect for the claims of the society, Winter argued:

"In Hans Kelsen's pure theory of law the tension between fact and norm is the foundation of the legal order. The application of the basic norm to concrete cases is the very completion and fulfillment of the creative process in this legal order. These individual applications of the basic norm reflect a balance between social reality and legal norms. . . . The basic norm determines the extent to which considerations of social reality, humanitarianism, personalism, in short, considerations of fair play [*Billigkeit*], should balance the demands imposed by the strict application of legal norms. This dualism of, this tension between, fair play and legal justice represents a positive recognition that there exists a social order which transcends the legal order. . . . Such a legal order manages to take into account social reality far more effectively than a natural law metaphysics which feigns the existence of a dual legal order, and thus fails to give positive law social roots, but rather adorns it with religious trappings."[50]

Winter proposed to apply the duality of fact and norm to theology and sociology in the same manner as Kelsen had applied it to sociology and law. He argued, with Kant, that synthesis preceded analysis, that facts never spoke for themselves.[51]

---

[49] *Ibid.*, pp. 34-35. S. Körner, *Kant* in *The Pelican Philosophy Series*, A. J. Ayer, editor (Hammondsworth: Penguin Books, 1955), Ch. 3: "The System of *A Priori* Concepts," pp. 43-70.

[50] *Sozialmetaphysik*, pp. 88-89.

[51] *Ibid.*, pp. 43-44; Körner, *op.cit.*, pp. 18-20, and Ch. IV: "The System of Synthetic *A Priori* Principles," pp. 70-104. It seems that Winter has simplified Kant to the point of perverting the fundamental notions of Kant's system. But, as Körner has pointed out: "The organized wealth of original and profound conceptions and subtle analyses which is the *Critique of Pure Reason* contains, of course, the seeds of many modern philosophies. Concentration on the positive

Therefore he rejected the neo-Thomist methods in the social sciences because they naïvely advocated empirical investigations of facts which they claimed would then speak for themselves. Such a neo-Thomist study of facts, Winter argued, only gave rise to a judgment of the facts on the basis of criteria introduced clandestinely from another sphere, usually theology. He concluded that the only correct method for a Catholic social science was his own *Methodendualismus*[52] which recognized that theology and sociology each were governed by autonomous principles. He pictured the relation of the two spheres in terms much like Kelsen's, that is to say, the *Grundnorm* of the social order was fashioned according to the principles of the theological order, but from then on the social order was governed by principles all its own.[53]

Though Romantic doctrines influenced Winter's social criticism, he disagreed with the Romantic social theory of the Vogelsang school. His chief quarrel with the Romanticists was over their tendency to assign permanent and transcendent values to the social institutions of the Middle Ages. He also condemned them for tying their defense of the monarchical principle to outmoded social and political institutions, namely, nobility and absolute monarchy: "It was the tragedy of the Baroque-Romantic sociology down to Vogelsang that it sought political identification with concrete regimes and that it saw in the rul-

---

doctrine of the Dialectic to the exclusion of most other theses of the Kantian system leads, as we have seen, to pragmatism. . . . Even phenomenology and existentialism contain many recognizable Kantian elements. They certainly at least abound in Kantian terms." *Op.cit.*, pp. 125-126.

[52] *Sozialmetaphysik*, pp. 164ff.

[53] "The quest for the reason of validity of a norm is not—like the quest for the cause of an effect—a *regressus ad infinitum*; it is terminated by a highest norm which is the last reason of validity within the normative system. . . ." Kelsen, *General Theory of Law and State*, Andres Wedberg, transl. (Cambridge: Harvard University Press, 1945), p. 111. Kelsen notes in the foreword that this work reformulated ideas expressed in his earlier writings, including *Reine Rechtslehre* and *Allgemeine Staatslehre*, which served Winter as a basis for his analysis of Kelsen. See, for instance, *Allgemeine Staatslehre* (Berlin: Julius Springer, 1925), p. 14; and "Sittengesetz und Rechtsnorm," *Hauptprobleme der Staatsrechtslehre. Entwickelt aus der Lehre vom Rechtssatz* (Tübingen: J. C. B. Mohr [Paul Siebeck], 1923), pp. 33-57. Erich Voegelin suggested that Kelsen's "pure theory of law" was typically Austrian; that is to say, it was a natural product of Austrian legal experience with a supra-national state without a popular basis, *Der autoritäre Staat* (Vienna: Julius Springer, 1936), pp. 128-130.

ing princes the realization of its teachings. By rendering political services to the princes it [Romantic sociology] associated significant sociological principles with political forms which were often useless and had become empty shells. . . . Conservative sociology could have spoken to modern man more effectively if it had been able to abandon these political and religious identifications. . . ."[54] Instead, Winter advanced his own version of Romantic social thought which stressed the familial basis of social organization: "The family 'produces' the state, it is the idea underlying the state. . . . Society is organized on a familial basis, it is a hierarchical structure consisting of families, fathers, and personalities."[55] This concept of the familial basis of social organization was identical with that of the *Österreichische Aktion* to which Winter had contributed several essays. In spite of his disagreement with the Romantic tradition, Winter sided with the Romanticists in their controversy with the German Jesuits over the nature of sovereignty and the modern economy.[56] He supported the Romantic defense of monarchy against the claims of popular sovereignty advanced by political Solidarists like Tischleder. Winter also agreed with the Romanticists that the *mariage de convenance* which had been consummated in the social encyclicals between Romanticism and *Sozialpolitik* had robbed the Romantic tradition of its truly social element.[57]

Winter had become a socialist because of strong humanitarian feelings for the industrial proletariat, and because he accepted the validity of the socialist critique of capitalist social and economic institutions.[58] He discerned three elements in twentieth-century socialism: (1) a commitment to state control and total planning of the economy; (2) spontaneous organization of the proletarian masses; and (3) primacy of the urban

[54] *Sozialmetaphysik*, p. 157.
[55] "Der paternale Staat," pp. 233-234.
[56] "Die beiden Schulen des mitteleuropäischen Katholizismus" (Karl von Vogelsang and P. Heinrich Pesch S.J.), *Neue Ordnung*, III (1927), pp. 121-126.
[57] *Sozialmetaphysik*, pp. 112-115.
[58] The Marxian element in Winter's thought does not appear openly until 1933, when he began publication of *Wiener Politische Blätter*. See especially "Was Wir Wollen," I (April 16, 1933), pp. 1-10; "Österreich und Nationalsozialismus," I (December 3, 1933), pp. 193-234; as well as two articles which did not appear until after 1934: "Platonismus, Thomismus und Marxismus," III (June 23, 1935), pp. 101-106; and "Christentum oder Sozialismus," IV (January 19, 1936), pp. 1-11.

over the rural complex of life.[59] However, Winter considered socialism not simply a matter of economic planning. Rather, he believed that it was a synthesis of a planned economy and of the ethical concepts of individual freedom and universal participation in decision-making. It had been the historic achievement of Marxism, he said, to have made the industrial workers conscious of their class character and to have aided them in their struggle for liberation.[60]

Winter saw only one solution for the social question: "Critical thinking can give only one answer to the question: 'Christianity or Socialism?' The inescapable political decision today must be: neither Christianity nor Socialism, but Christianity and Socialism."[61] The ideas of Marx and Vogelsang complemented each other. Both the "expropriation of the expropriators" and the "deproletarization of the proletariat" were required for effective social reform, because both were only partial answers. Marx had failed to see that socializing the means of production would not solve any economic problems. On the other hand, Vogelsang's deproletarization of the proletariat was doomed to failure because of the pre-industrialist methods Vogelsang proposed to employ.

In spite of this elaborately developed philosophical framework, neither Winter's criticism of capitalism, nor his reform proposals, differed significantly from those of other Romantic theorists. His criticisms of capitalism were those traditionally advanced by Romantic social critics. Winter deplored the degradation of the industrial worker under conditions of modern industrial production. He joined other Romanticists in their attack on the pro-capitalist theories of Heinrich Pesch and his school. He repeatedly stressed the gulf which divided the two Catholic social schools of Pesch and Vogelsang on such questions as interest, the economic organization of agriculture, and the wage problem.

(c) Winter's Corporative System. Winter's corporative reform proposals also were in the Romantic tradition. Though he demanded the complete corporative reorganization of society, and

[59] *Wiener Politische Blätter,* I, 223.
[60] *Ibid.,* pp. 224-225.
[61] *Ibid.,* IV, 11.

especially of economic activity, he disagreed with the Romanticists over political organization of the corporative state and over the form of labor representation. Like the Solidarists he denied that a corporative system must necessarily be governed dictatorially. But he also recognized what most Romanticists failed to see, that without firm control by the state corporativism would disintegrate into anarchy. He did not share the naïve belief of the Romanticists that the state would wither away once the corporative system was established: "There is no historical evidence to support the assertion that an authoritarian state would use its power to dissolve itself and yield to anarchical producers organizations each of which would be more vicious and selfish than all the old parties taken together."[62] He urged the continuation of strong trade unions in the corporative system and suspected that many who advocated corporativism did so merely to destroy organized labor.

Winter's reform proposals are best summarized by the slogan first developed for *Österreichische Aktion,* namely "To stand with the right and to think with the left." By this he meant the combination of a radical social reform program with political conservatism—in short, "social monarchy." In Winter's proposed economic organization, the workers would maintain strong trade unions, but would be organized with employers into *Stände* which would administer their own affairs. The corporative organization would be supplemented by a multitude of cooperatives, in agriculture as well as industry. To these producer cooperatives would be added a network of consumer cooperatives. Like many other Romantic theorists, Winter placed great hopes in an "internal colonization" scheme, a project for resettling "unneeded" industrial workers on the land. Ultimately, all these corporations, cooperatives, land settlement schemes would be part of an over-all economic plan enforced by the state.[63] This reform plan places Winter midway between the Religious Socialists and the Vogelsang school. Like the Religious Socialists he was very skeptical about the essentially petty bourgeois, pre-industrialist schemes of the Romanticists, and as-

[62] *Arbeiterschaft und Staat* (Vienna: Reinhold Verlag, 1934), pp. 68-69.
[63] *Wiener Politische Blätter,* I, 1-10, and "Dokumente der Aktion Winter," II (December 23, 1934), pp. 136-137.

signed the state without hesitation a large role in his reform program. This honesty contrasted sharply with the hypocrisy of the Vogelsang reformers and Spann, who envisaged the ultimate disappearance of the state, but who really had no intention of doing away with strong state controls in their proposed corporative system.

There were two fundamental weaknesses in Winter's ideas. The first was that neither his elaborate philosophical framework nor his slogan "Rechts stehen, links denken" led to a reform program which differed significantly from that of the Romanticists. The second was his failure to demonstrate how the Platonic-Kantian *Methodendualismus* produced unique results in social theory, or a sociology significantly "purer" than that of the neo-Thomists. His disagreement with Solidarist political and economic theory over sovereignty and interest can be traced to the conventional Romantic elements in his thought, while his disagreement with the Romanticists stemmed largely from his theoretical Marxism. His preference for Romantic ideas led him to justify social monarchy with the aid of Catholic social theory in much the same manner in which Tischleder, and later Rommen, sought to prove that their preference for democracy and popular sovereignty was grounded in church doctrine. Like Spann, whom he condemned, Winter developed a social science methodology with which he proceeded to prove what he had set out to prove, namely, that social monarchy was the only correct form for organizing the modern state and the modern economy.

5. Othmar Spann: The Apogee of the Neo-Romantic Tradition

The criticism of capitalism and the corporative reform proposals of Othmar Spann were based on his universalist philosophy. Though he attempted to prove with the aid of what he called social science methodology that universalism was simply a correct form of social research as well as the only correct theory of society, there was little doubt that Spann's universalism had no scientific basis but was an elaborate ideological scheme with which he explained his preferences for Romantic doctrines.[64]

[64] "With this work I want to bring to a close my fight against individualism, atomism, psychologism, Marxism, and other dead sciences." Foreword to *Tote*

Many Catholics had serious doubts about the compatibility of Spann's universalism with Catholic social thought, but they nevertheless welcomed his attacks on political and economic individualism and his prescription for the corporative reorganization of society, state, and economy.[65]

(a) *The Nature of Universalism.* According to Spann, universalism, part of the Romantic *Ideenkreis,* assigned original reality (*ursprüngliche Realität*) to society (*Ganzheit*) and not to the individual. It rejected individualism and materialism in favor of an organic, spiritual *Weltanschauung.*[66] Before considering universalism in some detail it might be well to summarize the Romantic *Ideenkreis* as Spann conceived it, for it is within this Romantic setting that Spann developed his entire social and economic scheme.

Spann summarized the Romantic *Ideenkreis* in this manner: "Objective instead of subjective;

"Aprioristic instead of relativistic (the totality is governed by its own inner laws);

"Intuitive instead of empirical (inner instead of outer experience) inward being instead of Enlightenment;

"Knowledge which defines organizations and purpose rather than causal knowledge;

"Interlaced with irrationality instead of the rule of pure rationality;

"Metaphysical rather than non-metaphysical, spirit is concerned only with itself, the economy is to be reduced in importance and controlled;

"Pure instead of utilitarian morality;

"Corporative-organic rather than capitalistic."[67]

Spann considered several universalistic interpretations of society, but rejected them all in favor of "kinetic universalism,"[68] because it alone avoided the dangers of a static interpretation

---

oder lebendige Wissenschaft. Abhandlungen zur Auseinandersetzung mit Individualismus und Marxismus (Jena: Gustav Fischer, 1925), p. xiv.

65 See above, Ch. IV.

66 *Kategorienlehre* (Jena: Gustav Fischer, 1924), pp. 99ff.

67 *Der wahre Staat. Vorlesungen über Abbruch und Neubau der Gesellschaft* (second rev. ed.; Leipzig; Quelle & Meyer, 1923), pp. 97-98.

68 *Ibid.,* pp. 31-34.

of society, he claimed. It might seem surprising that a Romantic thinker like Spann was concerned with dynamism in society. Actually, Spann, who disagreed with other Romantic theorists over their preference for a closed, static system, was convinced that only the presence of dynamic elements could prevent the decline and ultimate collapse of any corporative system.

Spann rejected the "theory of environment" because it considered man simply a reflection of the totality of the material world around him. Next, he rejected the theory of the "social drives of the individual" because it explained society as a result of the sex and other social drives of the individual. A society based merely on such drives would be a limited form of "togetherness." Spann then admitted that Platonic idealism provided an acceptable explanation of the origin of the *Ganzheit*, but could offer only a static explanation, "resistance of matter to idea," for the origin and development of individuality. This was a satisfactory explanation for the origin of one form of individuality at one given point in time, but did not explain how a multitude of different individualities developed over a period of time. Only kinetic universalism, based on the dynamic principle of *Gezweiung*, placed reality in the whole without destroying the individuality of the parts. This was possible because the relationship between the two component parts of a *Gezweiung* was a moral relationship.

Spann's principle of *Gezweiung*[69] was based on the contention that an intellect could flourish only when it interacted with another intellect in the manner of the teacher-pupil, mother-child, artist-audience relationship. Individuality developed only through an intellectual and moral interaction between the two partners. Spann then took this relationship as a model for the relationship between a *Ganzheit*, a totality, and its parts; that is to say, he considered the individual never the primary object but merely potential. Whatever an individual could become, he could become only as a part (*Glied*) of a *Ganzheit*, and spiritual and material development of the individual was possible only within society. But this dependence on the whole did not destroy the part, for the former, by definition, consisted of a *variety* of different component members. Therefore, the

[69] *Ibid.*, p. 35.

organism was interested in fostering the growth of such a variety and not in destroying it.[70]

Spann insisted that in his system of kinetic universalism the relationship between the individual and the whole was a moral not a contractual one.[71] "I live with my neighbors because it is to my advantage" was an erroneous statement about that relationship. The morality of these relationships rested on the primacy of the *Gesamtgeistiges* (total spirituality), which was the source of individual spirituality.[72] Because the interests of the individual and the totality had the same source, the "total spirituality," whatever threatened the individual threatened him only as a member of a totality. Therefore, Spann concluded, the totality could never damage the individual and claim that this was done in the interest of the totality, for such an action would damage the totality as well. It is difficult to see how Spann or some of his Catholic defenders could claim that in his universalist system "reality can rest in the totality without this being a threat to the uniqueness of the individual."[73] Obviously, with the aid of the entire arsenal of organic theory the individual was strictly subordinated to the collectivity.

It was this universalist hodgepodge of Romantic doctrine and Hegel which served as the basis for Spann's critique of existing institutions and for his proposals for corporative reorganization. He insisted that economic activity was relegated to a secondary position in the universalist edifice, because only religious, artistic, or moral activity occupied a primary position while material actions (*Handeln*) existed only for the purpose of serving the spiritual.[74]

(b) *Spann's Critique of Capitalism.* Spann condemned capitalism because it was part of the individualistic *Ideenkreis*, and defined the economic crisis of his day as part of the crisis of individualism.[75]

Capitalism, which Spann considered to be the manifestation of individualism in the material sphere, had given rise to three

[70] *Ibid.*, p. 51; *Gesellschaftslehre* (second rev. ed.; Leipzig: Quelle & Meyer, 1923), pp. 123-131.

[71] *Der wahre Staat*, p. 48: "The relationships between individuals and between individuals and the community are essentially moral relationships."

[72] *Ibid.*, p. 46; see also Arnold, *op.cit.*, pp. 1295-1296.

[73] *Der wahre Staat*, pp. 74-76.   [74] *Ibid.*, pp. 84-85.   [75] *Ibid.*, pp. 123-124.

evils: materialism, economic freedom, and economic equality. Materialism resulted when individuals were permitted to follow their desires and to place principal emphasis on outward material achievements and successes. The demand for goods of many kinds stimulated technical developments which enabled men to produce the goods for which individualism had created a demand. Ultimately this drive for material achievement caused all phases of life to become subject to judgment by material standards. Next, economic freedom, the principal symbol of capitalism, had freed private property from the mercantilist or corporative controls of earlier periods. Finally, economic equality and equality of economic opportunity, unlike economic freedom, which had become an effective element of capitalism, had remained largely "formal" and had never been realized. What had happened was that unlimited competition had intensified the inequalities of economic means (*Wirtschaftsmittel*) that had existed from the beginning. As a result, the capitalist system favored the strong (the capitalists) at the expense of the weak (the workers), the monopolist producer at the expense of the retailer and customer. Because of these inequalities, Spann considered capitalism not really economic liberalism but economic Machiavellianism, the victory of the weak over the strong: "Individualism is the essence of capitalism. But it is not a natural law individualism which rejects competition, the war of all against all, and which nullifies the triumph of the strong over the weak with its original contract. Rather it is a Machiavellian individualism which awards the palm of victory to the strong. To grasp this is indispensable for an understanding of capitalism; but neither Marx nor the founders of economic liberalism, Quesnay, Smith, and Ricardo managed to do so."[76] This failure of capitalism to establish genuine equality led to continuous attacks on the system by those who had suffered from its operations.

Having analyzed the evils of capitalism, Spann then attempted to answer the question: "What are the causes of the crisis of capitalism?" He found that the ultimate failure of capitalism could not be traced to economic shortcomings but to spiritual and social ones.

[76] *Ibid.*, p. 125.

The immediate cause of the capitalist crisis was the destruction of the healthy organic order which had once existed. Fortunately, complete capitalism had never been realized, for various restrictions on economic freedom—such as monopolies, cartels, tariffs, trade unions, etc.—had remained from the precapitalist period or had been reestablished after the rise of modern capitalism. But the atomization and insecurity created by capitalism, even in this modified form, had brought forth efforts to reform it, including *Sozialpolitik*, the cooperative movement, and socialism. All these were actually efforts toward a *ständische Bindung*: "All these measures are not merely negative restrictions on economic freedom, they are constructive efforts, uncoordinated, planless, and insufficient, to be sure, but nevertheless significant because they attempt to replace the medieval corporative order with a new form of corporative organization of society."[77] *Sozialpolitik* attempted to protect the economically helpless through legislation. At first the legislator intervened directly, but later on bodies for economic self-government took over this task. Next, the cooperative movement tried to protect the small producers who had survived into the capitalist era as well as the consumer. Finally, socialism had been the most comprehensive effort to eliminate the economic evils of capitalism.

Spann traced the ultimate failure of capitalism to its spiritual and social weaknesses. Capitalism's material achievement had never been seriously questioned. It had created great material wealth which had been distributed fairly well in spite of some glaring instances of maldistribution, especially during the early capitalist phase. The real crisis of capitalism was the atomization and "externalization" of life: "Mankind can take poverty in its stride, because poverty will always be with us. But insecurity, rootlessness, and insignificance are conditions nobody is prepared to suffer quietly."[78] Capitalism had made the worker *standlos*; it had declassed him, uprooted him, and deprived him of his proper place in society. This social insecurity was intensified by economic insecurity and affected even the wealthy in the capitalist system, who suffered the same spiritual ills as the poor.

[77] *Ibid.*, pp. 128-129.
[78] *Ibid.*, p. 127.

(c) The Corporative System. Spann proposed corporative *(ständische)* reorganization as a remedy for the evils of individualism in state and society. Like the Romanticists, Spann created an elaborate system of corporative organizations, and, as in all the Romantic theories, the entire system was controlled by a strong, autocratically ruled state and lacked any real corporative autonomy.[79]

Social reconstruction would be based on three fundamental laws which governed the universalist society.[80] (1) The component parts of society would be organically unequal, because their contributions to society, though equally indispensable, were of many kinds. (2) Some *Glieder* (members) of society would be more valuable than others. (3) The basic components of the new society would not be isolated individuals but *Gemeinschaften* which would be hierarchically arranged but not centrally controlled. They would form an organic order, not a mass of mechanically arranged atoms.

From these laws Spann deduced the organization into hierarchically organized *Gemeinschaften* called *Stände*.[81] These would be composed of individuals not entirely identical, but with many things in common, and would be small in size. The place of the unit in the hierarchy would be determined by its function.

These *Stände* could be organized on a variety of principles. Spann suggested four of these:

1. *Vor-Stand*: a latent community, a division of spiritual and intellectual activity into certain major categories

2. *Voll-Stand*: a grouping of people according to their material or intellectual activities, but not formally organized

3. *zünftiger Stand*: a formal organization based on common activity; it could be subdivided vertically, or several of them could be grouped together horizontally

4. *politischer Stand*: the organization of rulers in their ruling capacity.

[79] *Ibid.*, "Dritter Aufbauender Teil," pp. 195-315.

[80] *Ibid.*, pp. 196-197. See also *Gesellschaftslehre*, p. 123.

[81] This presentation of the corporative system is of course highly simplified. Spann's was probably the most elaborate corporative proposal in the Austrian Romantic tradition since 1918.

The organization of human society, according to Spann, would require first the identification of the spiritual basis of human activity (division into *Vor-Stände*) and then the division of that activity into several *Voll-Stände*. He proposed, therefore, three spiritual communities (*Vor-Stände*): (1) the community of those engaged in material activity; (2) the section of the higher spiritual community whose members participated in spiritual activity but made no original contributions, like teachers and performing artists; (3) the section of the higher spiritual community whose members both participated in spiritual activity and made original contributions. Spann then proposed the establishment of five *Voll-Stände*: (1) manual workers; (2) higher workers; (3) creators of economic organization; (4) creators of public organization (leaders of state, administration, armies, etc.); and (5) the creative group (the wise men of the community). Finally, Spann also suggested that *Stände* could be organized on the basis of the economic tools and the methods they employed, such as (1) agricultural *Stand*, the producers of raw materials; (2) *Gewerbe*, the processors and finishers of raw materials; and (3) trade and commerce, including banking.

Spann devoted most of his attention to the fully organized *Stand*, the *zünftige Stand*, and proposed that it have the following characteristics. First, he defined it as comprising a group of people engaged in common, though not necessarily identical, tasks. Even within a single *Stand* individuals would pursue a variety of occupations. Therefore the *Stand* should be loosely organized to permit such varied pursuits. The degree of economic interdependence between the various *Stände*, as well as within a single *Stand*, would vary considerably and would make impossible comprehensive planning on a large scale. Next, though the *Stand* would be characterized by internal "equality among equals," the *Stand* as a whole would take its proper place in a well-defined hierarchical order. Third, the individual within the *Stand* would deal most often with the governing organs of his *Stand* and only rarely with the central government and its organs. This would end the depersonalization of public affairs, characteristic of the liberal state. Spann, like most Romanticists, wanted to reduce the powers of the state by turning over its functions to corporative organs and thereby purify it of the corrupting influences of economic and other controversies. Finally, Spann believed that though some forms of competition would continue, within the *Stand* as well as between *Stände*, the individual would be assured of *Aufgehobenheit* (security) within his *Stand*: ". . . in the corporative order even the contemplative individual will have a chance for full development. Peace, introspection, composure will be the hallmarks of the corporative order. . . . Only in that order will we find both action as well as introspection, together with fealty, strength, and honor. Tradition and steadfastness will give the corporative order its distinctive style of life. . . ."[82] The all-pervasive spirit of competition, characteristic of the individualistic order, would disappear; instead, the basic attitudes would be introspection and spirituality. Thus the individual would be able to develop his special talents and skills within the corporative order, but never in violation of the fundamental spirituality of that order.

Moving from the characteristics of the individual *Stand* to the nature of the entire corporative system, Spann suggested that the system of *Stände* be highly decentralized. He rejected the centralization characteristic of both absolute monarchy and of the liberal state, in favor of a high degree of decentralization which would give the corporative groups a large degree of autonomy. However, the superior *Stand* would always give binding orders to the inferior one. In addition, within each *Stand* the orders of the corporative leader would command obedience and respect, for this new type of corporative leader would be far superior to the democratic politician and capitalist entrepreneur. He would be an all-around leader, a *Lebensführer*, in the sense of the medieval lord or squire: "The knight of the Middle Ages not only administered the manor, he was also judge, chief of local government, and commander of the armed forces in war and peace. This was true also of the leaders of guilds and municipal corporations who were political leaders as well as military commanders. Unfortunately this is a concept totally removed from our formalized, specialized, and bureaucratized age."[83]

Perhaps better than any other *Sozialreform* theorist Spann captured the flavor of the ideal order all Romanticists were search-

---

[82] *Ibid.*, pp. 244-245.   [83] *Ibid.*, p. 236.

ing for. This idyll of a decentralized, yet strictly controlled, hierarchy in which everyone lived in peace and security led by a group of wise men, pictured so vividly by Spann, was the epitome of all the Romantic utopias. Ernst Karl Winter was correct when he said: "The idea of a corporative state is a metaphysical goal performing the same heuristic functions as the eschatology of the classless society. Playing the role of transcendent goals, both are legitimate bases for a concrete set of social policies. . . . It is quite clear that every political ideology needs a set of more or less similar goals for the spiritual basis of its action program."[84] The corporative state was the eschatology of the Romantic movement which was accepted by the entire Christian-social conservative *Lager* in 1934. Many of those who made use of this ideological tool had no more intention of translating this ideal state into practice than did many of those who fervently proclaimed the coming of the classless society.

When Spann tried to apply these general principles to specific reform proposals, he proved to be considerably more flexible and realistic than many of the Catholic Romanticists. He considered the need for reform greatest in the area of the future economic *Stände* because the economy had suffered most severely from the evils of individualism. He warned against two dangers in economic reconstruction. Any efforts in such reconstruction should be tied organically to existing institutions in order to avoid radical and unrealistic proposals. He also warned against making the new system rigidly hierarchical; there should be full social mobility within, as well as between, *Stände*.

The two most important problems of corporative reorganization, according to Spann, were: the nature of property and the economic organization of the *Stände*. Spann demanded that existing forms of property be modified considerably and subjected to increased controls. He proposed three forms of property: private property, *Lehen*, and public ownership.[85] Though private property would continue to exist in the corporative system, it would be subject to strict controls by the state and by corporative organs. Most of the property, however, would not be owned

[84] "Die Stunde des Konservativismus," *Wiener Politische Blätter*, I (June 18, 1933), p. 71.
[85] *Der wahre Staat*, p. 267.

privately, but would be held in the form of *Lehen*; that is to say, the individual would have the use of the property but would be expected to render services to the community in exchange for the benefits he might derive from its use. Like all other Romantic theorists, Spann really had no notion how the medieval feudal system could be effectively applied in the twentieth century. However, this did not prevent him from advocating these medieval institutions. Finally, there would also be outright ownership and operation of many properties by municipalities, corporative organs, and the state.

Internal economic relations within the *Stand*, as well as relations between *Stände*, would be based on a *Gesamtarbeitsvertrag*.[86] Spann predicted that such a *Vertrag* would have far-reaching effects on the corporative system. The *Vertrag* would cover wages, hours, working conditions, worker representation, etc., over a wide segment of the economy; it would cover at least one and probably several *Stände*. Eventually it would be broadened to regulate the prices of goods produced under its terms. Furthermore, such a *Vertrag* would strengthen the *Zunft*-type of organization, Spann argued, and would encourage other forms of cooperation among employers and employees, such as cooperative buying, apprentice training, etc. Finally, its comprehensive terms would help to soften the impact of economic crises.

Spann suggested several measures to produce a minimum degree of dynamism in his corporative system.[87] He suggested that the *zünftige Stand* should not have legal powers to control access to its activity, for if "latent" competition were permitted to continue, ossification could be prevented. Certain small and family-sized enterprises should be left outside the *Stand* organization altogether, as should be trade, finance, and banking. The retention of a "free-moving" capitalist element in the national economy would provide the flexibility necessary for a dynamic system. However, it is difficult to see, for example, how economic corporative organs could carry out their various objectives if the country's fiscal and trade policies were left in the hands of capitalist merchants and bankers. Spann, unfortunately, provided

[86] *Ibid.*, pp. 269-273; August M. Knoll, "Die Frage nach der 'besten' Wirtschaftsform bei Othmar Spann," *Soziale Revue*, xxviii (1926), pp. 152-164.
[87] *Der wahre Staat*, pp. 290-294.

no answer to this and many other contradictory features of his corporative utopia.

Spann handled the relations between the state and the corporative system in conventional Romantic fashion;[88] he even went further than some Romanticists in his theoretical efforts to eliminate the state and the territorial assembly. He proposed that the corporative organs absorb all economic functions of the state, and thereby free the state from the evil influences of materialism. In addition, the *Stände* would also take over many legal and administrative tasks formerly carried out by the state. The *Stand* system and the state would be united at the apex in a corporative chamber, and there would be no political legislature based on political parties and territorial constituencies. The true nature of this corporative system now stands clearly revealed. Obviously the only group in such a system which could speak for the entire nation were the political leaders, the *politische Stand*.[89] As a group, they were the leading corporative organ. It followed that in spite of the elaborate provisos for decentralization and dynamism an autocratic regime would have absolute control. Thus, the *Wahre Staat* of Othmar Spann turned out to be simply another Romantic autocracy.[90]

6. The Vogelsang School

The writers of the Vogelsang school during the period 1918-1934 elaborated the social criticism of the nineteenth-century Romanticists. They took little notice of changing economic conditions, and continued to prescribe the authoritarian, pre-industrialist, and petty-bourgeois solutions of Müller and Vogelsang. They hailed the publication of *Quadragesimo anno* as a vindica-

---

[88] *Ibid.*, pp. 284-290.

[89] "It is the state, the all-encompassing social organization which establishes the value system on the basis of the prevailing norms . . ." *Gesellschaftslehre*, p. 252.

[90] Paul Jostock came to the conclusion that in spite of scattered references to sociological concepts acceptable to Catholics, Spann's Romantic corporative system was imbued chiefly with a "pagan-authoritarian spirit." *Der deutsche Katholizismus und die Überwindung des Kapitalismus. Eine ideengeschichtliche Skizze* (Regensburg: Friedrich Pustet, 1932), p. 204. But Jostock, who was chiefly concerned with writing a pro-Solidarist history of Catholic social ideals, failed to point out that in spite of fundamental incompatibilities between Spann's thought and Catholic social doctrine, Austrian Catholics continued to consider him a valuable ally in their fight against "individualism."

tion of their social Romantic ideas, but did not propose to modify their own *Reform* ideas. As a result, they continued their controversy with the Solidarists and with the Austrian hierarchy over economic and social doctrines.

(a) Josef Eberle and the Critique of Solidarism. Josef Eberle represented a moderate tendency within the Romantic group. His periodical, *Schönere Zukunft*, was open to Catholic writers of many different "schools."[91] Though Eberle was not identified with any one *Richtung*, he consistently opposed Solidarism and the Solidarist defense of capitalism. After the publication of *Quadragesimo anno*, he attempted to bring the various Romantic schools into harmony with the social theory of the encyclicals. However, this could have been done successfully only by doing violence both to Romantic social theories and to the encyclicals, especially on such questions as the nature of property and the labor theory of value.[92]

The essay on Solidarism, by Eberle's coeditor, Eugen Kogon, illustrates best the social doctrines of the circle around Eberle and *Schönere Zukunft*.[93] Kogon stated his fundamental disagreement with the Solidarists when he rejected their proposition that the various economic systems were "equally sociologically correct": "Considered sociologically not all economic systems are equally valid. This applies particularly to capitalism which can never be a correct economic system. Only what meets specific cultural and educational needs is sociologically correct. Whatever is not part of society's basic nature is invalid and will remain so as long as there exists a human will."[94] He therefore condemned capitalism because it was not in harmony with the true nature of society. In his definition we meet all the familiar Romantic shibboleths: capitalism is a system which is based on the market and on usury and which rejects production for *Bedarf*; there is also the usual list of capitalist evils, such as atomization, separation of labor and capital, unrestricted competition, anonymity of capital, etc.[95] It is not surprising that Kogon cas-

[91] Arnold, *op.cit.*, pp. 1301-1302, Gierse, *op.cit.*, pp. 152-167.
[92] Arnold, *op.cit.*, p. 1302.
[93] "Der Ständestaat des Solidarismus," *Hochland*, xv, pt. 2 (1928), pp. 1-21, 178-200, 291-300.
[94] *Ibid.*, p. 178.
[95] *Ibid.*, p. 4.

tigated the Solidarists for trying to reach an accommodation with the capitalist system. He condemned in especially caustic tones what he called the Solidarists' admiration for the dynamic qualities of capitalism, and added that one might as well praise the devil for being a dynamic and energetic fellow.[96]

Kogon, like the *Österreichische Aktion,* suggested three possible solutions for the social question: socialism, *Sozialpolitik,* and *Sozialreform.* He rejected socialism because he considered it unacceptable to Catholics for social, economic, and religious reasons. He also rejected *Sozialpolitik* because it rested on the pro-capitalist assumptions of Solidarism. Kogon's hostility to Solidarism can be traced to two causes. The Solidarist attempts to make capitalism acceptable to Catholics had exposed the latter to the capitalist poison and had prevented them from assuming an anti-capitalist position. Because Solidarism had thus placed the official blessing of the church on capitalism, Catholics could never hope to regain the support of the masses. Kogon also criticized Solidarism because it defended capitalism by dismissing its fundamental evils as "excesses" and by preaching "love and charity" to those who demanded radical social action against the capitalist system: "It is no longer sufficient to demand justice and love, or even to live by these principles. One can imagine a slave who is just and loves his master, but this will not cause slavery to be abolished. Yet we must break the capitalist [slavery]. . . . It is shocking to find that Catholics are all too easily inclined to treat every new Satanic manifestation of capitalism as an excess, and to excuse it as a kind of childish prank, or as a symptom of growing pains."[97]

Kogon attacked Heinrich Pesch for accepting the "free, private economy" as the only correct form of economic organization. He also suggested that Pesch was primarily a moral theologian who exhorted the people to do "right" and who saw no need for any social organization, if only the people would practice love and charity. Finally, he criticized Pesch for wanting to heal the excesses of capitalism without having a clear notion

[96] "Let us not argue that the capitalist spirit always pursues its goals with intensity, accuracy, animation, and perseverance. These qualities are meaningless by themselves. . . . The Devil, too, will be intense, accurate, animated, and persevering if it should be appropriate, but that does not make him good." *Loc.cit.*

[97] *Ibid.,* pp. 8-9.

of "health" in a social organism. Because of this, Pesch had failed to understand the need for the corporative reconstruction of society and was satisfied with the *status quo* in the modern state. Though Kogon found many useful details in Pesch, he considered his writings merely a manual for *Sozialpolitik*, but of little use to anyone interested in a comprehensive social reform program.

Sozialreform was the only workable solution for the social question, Kogon concluded. He defended the Romanticists against the charge that they were dreaming about the Middle Ages and that their reform proposals were impractical, but admitted that the tendency of the Romanticists to tie their reform proposals to outdated institutions had been responsible for the weakness of the *Sozialreform* tradition. Kogon's subsequent reform proposals need not be discussed in detail because they followed Spann's corporative doctrines analyzed in the preceding pages. Kogon's definition of society, and of *Stand*, as well as his concept of the relations between the state and the corporative order, were all copied from Spann. Like many other Catholics Kogon seemed to notice no contradiction between the Hegelian *Ganzheit* which dominated Spann's system and the personalist basis of the Catholic faith and Catholic social teachings.[98]

(b) Richard Schmitz. Richard Schmitz's *Der Weg der berufsständischen Ordnung in Österreich* is important chiefly because of its treatment of the history of corporativism in Austria.[99] Schmitz simply suppressed the liberal-democratic tendencies in Austrian Catholic thought and presented the development of that thought as a succession of corporative triumphs. These triumphs had been the work of a broad anti-liberal front which included four major elements: federalistically inclined agrarian elements which still remembered the provincial parliaments (*Landtage*) based on the old estates; German nationalist particularists; the church, which was engaged in a fight against Free-

[98] They failed to see that a deep gulf *should* divide them from the Hegelian system of Spann. Actually, the Catholic Romanticists found Spann congenial because they themselves had no clear notion of society and social organization apart from the state. Kogon, for instance, came to the following conclusion: "Thus there is no fundamental distinction between public and private law; the public law of the corporation becomes the law governing its members . . . "; *ibid.*, p. 189.

[99] Vienna: Manzsche Verlags- und Universitätsbuchhandlung, 1934.

masonry and radicalism; and finally the peasant-artisan coalition which opposed economic liberalism.[100]

Schmitz's analysis of Catholic social theory suffered from an ambivalence concerning the proper scope and method of social reconstruction common to many Catholic theorists. On the one hand, he considered corporative reforms "social" in nature and insisted that state and society be recognized as distinct entities in the task of social reconstruction, in order to avoid the mistakes of Italian Fascism criticized in *Quadragesimo anno*.[101] On the other hand, he urged the state to enforce social reconstruction measures, if necessary: "There ought to be no question that the leadership of the state acts in the spirit of the Encyclical if it initiates, fosters, protects, and, if necessary enforces, reforms in society. . . . We cannot possibly do without the assistance of the state. It alone has the power to overcome instinctive and tendentious resistance. . . . At the same time the state leadership must resist the temptation to influence social reforms in a one-sided political manner and to regard the occupational corporations mere tools of power politics and subjects of the state."[102] It was unfortunate that Richard Schmitz, when he became an official of the corporative state, did not heed some of the warnings in this essay. He certainly influenced social reforms in a "one-sided-political" manner, and helped make the corporative organs "instruments of power politics" dependent on the state.

Like all other Romantic theorists, Richard Schmitz expressed great concern for the industrial worker and considered the uplifting of the proletariat the most important task of social reform. But the corporative organization he hoped to create, namely producers' cooperatives, would have benefited peasants and artisans, but not the workers.[103]

(c) Romanticists and Quadragesimo anno: Das katholisch-soziale Manifest. The *Katholisch-soziales Manifest*, published in 1932, was the result of cooperation among a number of Catholic Romantic theorists.[104] It attempted to harmonize Romantic social doctrines with the social encyclicals.

---

[100] *Ibid.*, p. 9.   [101] *Ibid.*, p. 26.   [102] *Ibid.*, pp. 29-30.   [103] *Ibid.*, pp. 35-51.
[104] Studienrunde katholischer Soziologen, *Katholisch-soziales Manifest* (Mainz: Mathias Grünewald, 1932); see also Arnold, *op.cit.*, 1303, and Justus Beyer, *Die Ständeideologien der Systemzeit und ihre Überwindung* (Darmstadt: L. C. Wittich, 1941), pp. 158-166.

The *Manifest* opened with a condemnation of the capitalist economy, its system of distribution, and the results of its production processes. Capitalism divided people into classes based on wealth. The workers who actually produced all the wealth did not receive proper compensation for their labor and also lacked social status. Furthermore, the goods produced under the capitalist system lacked cultural-educational value because the capitalist producer was interested only in maximum profit without regard for either the economic claims of the workers or for the cultural-educational value of the goods produced.

The reform of society according to the *Manifest* required proper social organization and the establishment of correct principles of social action. The corporative order which would result from this reorganization would have both socio-economic and moral-religious aspects. However, these two aspects were really inseparable because they were two manifestations of the central idea of the corporative order, the concept of *Beruf* (vocation). Man's human personality as well as the material basis of his existence all turned around this vocational principle.[105] The material basis of the corporative order was the principle of *Lehen* (fief), which recognized that God as creator was the possessor of all worldly goods. Man was entitled to the use of these material goods, provided he pursued proper social goals. Property rights had, therefore, a dual aspect: social as well as individual. This meant that individuals would retain title to property, but only under strict safeguards.[106]

Based on property and organized on the principle of *Lehen*, economic activity would be governed by the principles of *Stand* and *Beruf*: "*Stand*, a community of those engaged in the same vocation, has the following functions: regulating cultural-educational affairs with proper safeguards for the needs of society; protecting the economic and social existence of its members; and insuring that the vocational achievement of its members serve social needs. *Beruf* is the individual's life work to which he is led by his inclination, his capacity, or the external conditions of his life. It enables him to achieve a full development of his personality and his values. . . ."[107] *Stand*, in brief, was a

---

[105] *Katholisch-soziales Manifest*, sec. II, par. 6, p. 21.
[106] *Ibid.*, sec. II, par. 11, p. 21. [107] *Ibid.*, sec. I, pars. 10, 11, p. 16.

community of those exercising a like *Beruf* in society. By pursuing a *Beruf* under the control of a *Stand*, the individual would be assured a *standesgemässer Unterhalt*. It would enable him to care for himself and those entrusted to his care, as well as to pursue his cultural goals, namely, family maintenance, education of the young, security for old age, etc.[108] To this wage all would be entitled, but no one would be entitled to more: "In the money economy equal exchange of output and payment is the only correct formula. It is measured by the amount of socially useful labor. Maintenance according to one's station [*standesgemässer Unterhalt*] is the qualitative yardstick for the exchange value of labor, while its quantitative measure is the socially necessary average expenditure in work and costs."[109]

This complex, self-contradictory, and thoroughly muddled definition of the just wage in the *Manifest* is evidence of the difficulties encountered in drafting a statement which would satisfy those of the Romantic theorists who sincerely tried to find a *modus vivendi* with *Quadragesimo anno*, and those, like Orel, who insisted on the purity and correctness of their own ideas, including the labor theory of value. The moderates carried the day, and as a result the *Manifest* contained two important modifications of Romantic theory. It recognized the claims of private property to a greater degree than in traditional Romantic theory, and it rejected the labor theory of value in favor of the family wage (*standesgemässer Unterhalt*). However, as the definition of the just wage analyzed above indicates, the attempt to satisfy two contradictory wage theories produced a hardly intelligible result which pleased no one.[110]

(d) Die neue Gesellschaft. In *Die neue Gesellschaft*, a group of Carinthian Catholics developed a social theory in the Romantic tradition of Vogelsang and Spann.[111] According to this group, corporative organization would be a reflection of the deity; that is to say, human society would be in the image of the supernatural *Gemeinschaft*.[112] They took their basic organiz-

---

108 *Ibid.*, sec. I, par. 12, pp. 16-17.

109 *Ibid.*, sec. I, par. 24, p. 19.

110 Arnold, *op.cit.*, p. 1303.

111 (Klagenfurt: Klagenfurter Soziologenrunde, 1932); see also Beyer, *op.cit.*, pp. 153-157.

112 *Die neue Gesellschaft*, pp. 59-61.

ing principle from Spann, namely *Ausgliederung*, the articulation of society in a hierarchical chain which descended from the creator: "This articulation of eternal life at the hands of God has become the prototype for the articulation of countless human societies."[113] Corporative society, therefore, would be indirect, federal, non-atomistic, and decentralized.

For the broad outline of their corporative organization the writers of *Die neue Gesellschaft* adopted the three traditional German estates: *Lehrstand* (teachers), *Wehrstand* (soldiers), and *Nährstand* (agriculturists).[114] They considered the church the prototype of the perfect corporative organization, a fully developed *zünftiger Stand*. The state was defined in the Romantic tradition of Müller, as the "totality of all human affairs."[115] However, the *Staatstand* (the estate of those controlling the state) was considered merely one of several subgroups of the *Lehrstand*. Like most Romanticists, the writers of *Die neue Gesellschaft* had no clear conception either of the distinction between state and society, which supposedly was the foundation of their corporative arguments, or the totalitarian implications of Müller's definition of the state.

They included all economic activities in the *Nährstand*, which they divided into three chambers (agriculture and forestry, industry and the trades, and commerce and communications), but gave few details concerning the methods of corporative reorganization.

(e) Anton Orel. Anton Orel was the most extreme anti-capitalist of the Romantic critics. His violent attacks on capitalism and on those Catholics who accepted the social teachings of the encyclicals were definitely in the tradition of Karl von Vogelsang.

Orel condemned capitalism, which he defined as a system of absolute property and interest slavery,[116] as a heresy as equally repugnant to faithful Catholics as communism: "The organizing

---

[113] *Ibid.*, p. 23; see Spann, *Der wahre Staat*, pp. 205-206, and *Gesellschaftslehre*, pp. 241-242.

[114] *Die neue Gesellschaft*, p. 84.

[115] *Ibid.*, p. 121.

[116] *Das Verfassungsmachwerk der "Republik Österreich" von der Warte der immerwährenden Philosophie aus und im Lichte von der Idee, Natur und Geschichte Österreichs geprüft und verworfen* (2nd ed.; Vienna: Vogelsang Verlag G.m.b.H., 1921), p. 5.

principle is no longer the naturally healthy, morally correct social need, but the individualistic profit motive to which everything has become subject. The individualized goal of those engaged in economic activities is acquisition and wealth, not simply maintenance according to one's station. They no longer pursue vocations in common, but try to overpower, nay devour, each other in free competition."[117]

The foundation of this capitalist system, according to Orel, was the individualistic property concept of Roman law. It had made possible the victory of a money economy over *Naturalwirtschaft* (barter). It had also insured the triumph of the capitalist interest system over a Christian economy based on labor: "The owner is responsible to no one for the use he makes of his property. The essence of property rights is now to dispose of one's property irresponsibly and at will."[118] This triumph had been the cause of the "social question," for it was the individualistic property concept which had made possible the creation of "capital"—the source of all forms of unearned income.

The first step in Orel's reform program was the creation of a natural law-Christian-Germanic system of property and labor: "The causal relationship of labor and property lies in this: all economic exchange value derives from labor and not from property. Neither land, nor tools and machinery are productive capital, they are only instruments of capitalist exploitation. Capital has only fictitious value, but has no true productive capacity. Because labor alone creates value, it alone is *entitled to the full proceeds* from property and from exchange value."[119] Only labor, never mere possession, could create exchange value. Neither land, nor money, nor capital goods were capable of producing income, only labor. Therefore, labor was entitled to the *voller Ertrag* of the exchange value of goods produced. If this system were adopted, Orel claimed, all unearned income would disappear and with it capitalism as an economic system.

Orel urged the church to assume the leadership of the workers by championing their claim to the full share of their industry: ". . . the Marxist system is not entirely false. The most important,

117 *Wahre Ständeordnung. Ihr Geist, Wesen, Wirken. Grundsätzlich-praktische Klarstellungen* (Graz: Ulrich Moser, 1934), pp. 32-33.
118 *Ibid.*, p. 77.
119 Quoted in Arnold, *op.cit.*, p. 1298.

the central concept of Marxian economics, the labor theory of value, is really an old Catholic inheritance, even though not in its present Marxian form. . . . Little used till now, the labor theory of value might well become a mighty bridge between the Catholic Church and the proletarian movement."[120] Orel's hopes to win the industrial proletariat with the help of the labor theory of value were never realized. By 1931, the social, political, and ideological chasm between the industrial proletariat and the church, and the social groups who defended it, had become so great that the workers questioned the *bona fides* of anyone purporting to defend their interest who was not clearly identified with the Socialist *Lager*. Furthermore, by 1931 Austria's industrial workers, under the influence of a fundamentally gradualist and revisionist leadership, had become more interested in collective bargaining and welfare benefits than in abstract Marxian principles.

The fundamental ideas of Orel's economic doctrines were rejected by the church in *Quadragesimo anno*. Of the many discrepancies between the social theory of Pius XI and that of extreme Romanticists like Orel there are three which testify to the fundamental disagreement between the Romanticists and the hierarchy. Pius XI strongly insisted that Leo XIII's theory of property was not the private opinion of a man who happened to have been head of the church, as Orel had suggested, but was the accepted theory of the church.[121] The Pontiff in 1931 also defended the productive capacity of land and capital, and reiterated the stand of the church on the permissibility of income from rent and interest.[122] Finally, Pius XI, by establishing three

---

[120] *Kirche-Kapitalismus-Proletariat* (Vienna: Vogelsang Verlag G.m.b.H., 1928), pp. 52-53.

[121] "Nevertheless there are some who attach little importance to this Encyclical. . . . In the course of these years, however, doubts have arisen concerning the correct interpretation of certain passages of the Encyclical or their inferences, and these doubts have led to controversies among Catholics, not always of a peaceful character." *Quadragesimo anno*, 39, 40, p. 135. See also above, Ch. v, section 2 b for the controversies between Orel and the Austrian hierarchy.

[122] Pius XI condemned those who ". . . attack and seek to abolish all forms of ownership and all profits not obtained by labor, whatever be their nature or significance in human society, for the sole reason that they are not acquired by toil." The Pope then went on to deny the applicability of St. Paul's judgment, that those who were not willing to work should not eat, to the question of value distribution in the modern economy. Therefore, "each class, then, must receive its due share, and the distribution of created goods must be brought into con-

definite criteria for the "just wage," had clearly rejected the labor theory of value—a central concept in Orel's thought.[123]

Little need be said about the details of Orel's plans for corporative reconstruction because most of them were contained in the *Katholisch-soziales Manifest*. But Orel, who had helped to write that document, did not accept the compromises with the encyclicals on which the moderates had insisted. Like the *Manifest*, Orel placed the concept of *Lehen* at the base of his corporative system. However, he refused to grant any individual title to property at all; property was for use only.[124] He identified two principal tasks in social reconstruction. First, each family should be provided with *Land und Haus*; those families who expressed such a desire and were considered capable would receive land and a home. This scheme was part of a project of "inner colonization" which Romanticists considered an essential part of their reform program. Second, every morally and technically competent man should be assured economic independence. Orel proposed that factory production be eliminated in favor of small independent producers, because the people did not derive any "real" benefits from large-scale factory production. These measures, he concluded, would produce a genuine socialism: "They will restore the worker to full citizenship and reconstruct the family by giving it land and home, and by assuring the economic independence of qualified heads of families; they will also bring about the reestablishment of occupational corporations. Thus, the corporative order will be true socialism."[125]

7. The Critique of Capitalism: An Evaluation

This evaluation of Austrian social Catholicism during the period 1918-1934 will be concerned chiefly with the Catholic critique of existing institutions and will touch only briefly on some of the fundamental problems raised by the various proposals for social reconstruction analyzed in the preceding chapters. These proposals will be considered in the following chap-

formity with the demands of the common good and social justice. . . ." *Quadragesimo anno*, 57, 58, pp. 141-142.

[123] *Ibid.*, 55, p. 141.

[124] *Wahre Ständeordnung*, pp. 26-28.   [125] *Ibid.*, p. 97.

ter, which will be devoted to an analysis of the Corporative Constitution of 1934, viewed as the culmination of Catholic criticism of democracy and capitalism during the period of the First Austrian Republic.

Catholic criticisms of modern capitalism fall into two broad categories: those which deal primarily with economic institutions, and those which address themselves to the social effects of the modern economy. Whereas there was fundamental disagreement about the nature of economic institutions between the proponents of *Sozialpolitik* and *Sozialreform*, the two schools were in general accord concerning the deplorable results of capitalism and industrialism.

The advocates of *Sozialpolitik* were committed to the maintenance of existing social institutions and of the capitalist economy. Though they were forced to modify this position somewhat by the encyclical *Quadragesimo anno* they never abandoned their pro-capitalist stand. They claimed that forms of economic organization were theologically indifferent, much as Leo XIII in his encyclicals on the modern state had declared that Catholics could live under any form of government which met certain specified conditions. Therefore, they accepted capitalism in principle, as Leo XIII had done in *Rerum novarum*, but criticized certain excesses, in the manner of the Austrian hierarchy, which condemned "mammonistic" capitalism. The theorists of *Sozialreform*, on the other hand, continued the nineteenth-century Romantic tradition of uncompromising opposition to capitalism. They condemned the institution of private property as based on a pagan system of law, the division of labor and capital, because it had deprived the worker of the just share of the product of his industry and created great discrepancies of wealth, the modern financial system; because it had violated the ban on interest and usury, and large-scale production; because it had destroyed the established pattern of handicraft methods. Catholics should overthrow capitalism, Romanticists urged, because it violated principles of Catholic theology and natural law, and they should put in its place the correct social order based on the institutions of the Christian Middle Ages.

Though *Sozialpolitik* and *Sozialreform* analysts differed over forms and principles of economic organization (it often seemed that Catholic theorists reserved their sharpest barbs for their co-religionists), they found common ground in condemning the social consequences of economic individualism. They blamed capitalism, which they considered the manifestation of individualism in the economic sphere, for the disintegration of the organic society and the destruction of social groups in which men had lived in harmony. Instead, men were now divided into antagonistic economic classes which were engaged in a ruthless struggle for survival. As a result, private property was freed from all social obligations and men used it to exploit those who were economically defenseless. Removal of all restrictions on the use of property had also led to unlimited economic competition, which again placed the weak, the workers, at the mercy of the strong, the capitalists. Inevitably, because every one was drawn into this ruthless fight, materialism had become the dominant attitude in society, and standards of material achievement the only valid standards. In short, the treatment of the social question during 1918-1934 followed the broad outlines of Catholic social criticism developed during the nineteenth century. It also continued to be influenced by Marxian anti-capitalist doctrines. In the social thought of Religious Socialists and of some Romanticists the Marxian elements were often more conspicuous than the Catholic ones. These thinkers acknowledged the influence of Marx, as well as of some of the other socialist schools, such as Lassalle and the *Kathedersozialisten*, and considered the labor theory of value their principal weapon for attacking unearned income. Though the *Sozialpolitik* theorists rejected the extreme anti-capitalist strictures of the Romanticists, there was agreement among members of both groups on the evil consequences of expanding capitalism and industrialism in modern society.

The writers of the *Sozialpolitik* tradition, following the lead of the hierarchy, attacked the excesses of "mammonistic" capitalism, and deplored the effectiveness of cultural socialism in undermining the loyalty of many Austrians to the church and the Catholic faith. But they were prevented from carrying their anti-capitalist strictures as far as they might have wanted, because they had become the victims of a tension which had arisen in the Christian-social conservative *Lager*, between the pro-big business policies of Christian Social governments and Catholic social doctrines which favored the peasants and the urban petty bourgeoisie. Nevertheless, these champions of *Sozialpolitik* persisted in their anti-capitalist critique, not only because they wanted to satisfy the mass of faithful Catholics, but also because they thought that with it they could woo the workers from the Social Democrats. In short, these anti-capitalist slogans became political weapons in the perpetual battle between the three *Lager*. The man who used them most skillfully for this purpose was Ignaz Seipel. He freely admitted his skepticism about the feasibility of corporative institutions, and at the same time hailed the corporative proposals of *Quadragesimo anno* as heralding the coming of a new state and a new society in which there would be no room for democracy, political parties, and trade unions. This ambivalence, as well as Seipel's support of what Ernst Karl Winter has called the new "authoritarian-militaristic" element, leads one to wonder whether Seipel's ideal society amounted to more than a military dictatorship in which the church and the capitalists would enjoy unlimited power.

The only serious *Sozialpolitik* effort to remove utopian and theological blinders from Catholic thinking on the social question was made by "realistic" theorists like Messner and Dobretsberger. However, they failed in this effort, and when civil war came they loyally supported the Catholic camp and served the corporative state. They had no taste either for military dictatorship or big business leadership, and would probably have felt more at home in the welfare state of the New Deal or of the British Fabians. Unfortunately, they had no choice, for there was no room for a *tertium quid* in the civil war.

The sources of *Sozialreform* can be easily identified: the Romantic tradition of Müller and Vogelsang. But for a full understanding of the Romantic ideology it is necessary to recall some of the conclusions about the nature of Austrian Catholic thought stated at the end of Chapter II. It was proposed there that Austrian Catholic thinkers failed signally to grasp the distinction between the state as the area of compulsory and society as the area of voluntary action. As a result, they claimed to subscribe to a pluralistic theory, when they actually supported what J. D. Mabbott, in his classification of relations between the state and other associations, has called "concrete monism"—a system which admits the value of functional units but regards them simply as parts of the state. Though such a view of society was diametrically opposed to official church doctrine which the Romantic thinkers, as faithful Catholics, professed to accept, it was, in fact, the only one it is possible to deduce from their social theories and specific reform proposals. There is still another factor which contributes to the understanding of *Sozialreform* ideas. It is what one might call the nature of the clientele for which Romanticists constructed their ideologies: a lower middle class whose position was threatened by economic collapse and by the rise of competing social groups.

The principal weaknesses of *Sozialreform* were its divorce from empirical research and its pro-petty bourgeois bias. The Romantic attacks on capitalism and industrialism were based on the works of Müller, Marx, and Vogelsang, as well as on the theories of *laissez-faire* capitalism, as understood by the Romanticists, and were tailored exactly to meet the needs of the Romantic clientele. When the Romanticists cried out against the disintegration of the medieval organic society, they simply transposed into a different key the complaints of master tailors who were threatened by the new clothing stores selling ready-to-wear clothes. When they deplored the evils of the class struggle, did they not want to destroy trade unions which, they claimed, had made the workers arrogant? Even if one grants the sincere anti-capitalism of men like Anton Orel, it is difficult to find an answer to the question: what sort of state and society did these Romanticists propose to put in the place of existing institutions? Winter once observed that "corporative state" or "corporative reconstruction of society" became the utopias, the eschatologies, first of the Romantic tradition, and, after *Quadragesimo anno*, of all Austrian Catholics. This was the device which, Catholics hoped, would solve all the problems thrown up by the Austrian Republic. The atomistic society would disappear and in its stead would develop the rich group life described in the encyclicals. But when it came time to translate these proposals into action, Catholics only created an authoritarian regime which became the very antithesis of all their social reform proposals. This was not really surprising because

Austrian Catholics had consistently failed to understand the need for a division of spheres between state and society, especially in economic matters; they therefore created the kind of monistic system alluded to earlier. They also failed to see that the destruction of democratic institutions placed the corporative system at the mercy of the authoritarian leadership. Finally, they were extremely naïve about the chances of social harmony in the complex industrial society of the twentieth century. They believed that the establishment of the occupational groups called for in the encyclicals would quickly produce social harmony. They overlooked the fact that if they failed to bring about such harmony, the only alternative to corporative anarchy would be domination by authoritarian leaders.

The corporative experiment initiated in 1934 can be studied in a number of ways. One way, for example, would be to review the record of the years 1934-1938 to determine what efforts had been made to establish occupational corporations and what functions they actually performed in society. Another would be to examine the corporative constitution, the first step in this experiment, to ascertain to what extent it reflected the long tradition of Catholic social thought. This latter is the method selected for this study. The examination of the Corporative Constitution of 1934 should prove especially worthwhile because that document foreshadowed the failure of corporative reconstruction during the four years which followed, and foretold the ultimate collapse of the corporative experiment.

CHAPTER VII

THE CULMINATION
OF CRITICISM: THE CORPORATIVE
CONSTITUTION OF 1934

LONG-STANDING CATHOLIC dissatisfaction with the modern state and the modern economy converged with internal Austrian developments as well as with certain external events, such as the coming to power of the Nazis in Germany, to produce a powerful movement for the overthrow of the Austrian Republic and its replacement by an authoritarian corporative regime. Catholics who had only reluctantly accepted the extreme "democratic" features of the 1920 constitutional settlement began to intensify their demands for constitutional reform as the tide of postwar radicalism receded. Dissatisfaction with the constitutional changes of 1925 and 1929, and the influence of the *Heimwehr's* Fascist ideology and the corporative proposals of *Quadragesimo anno,* caused Catholic revisionist demands to rise to a crescendo after 1929.

The rise of the Nazi movement after 1930 threatened the continuation of the anti-Socialist alliance which had existed between the Christian-social conservative and the Nationalist *Lager* since 1922. In the meantime, the Socialists, concerned over growing anti-democratic tendencies in the Catholic camp, had become convinced that it would be their duty to defend the Republic with force of arms against possible Fascist and Nazi attacks. As a result, there was a tragic crumbling of the inter-group coalition which had produced the Constitution of 1920, so that the Catholics, who refused to join the Socialists in an anti-Nazi coalition, were forced into a two-front war. Their minority position in such a three-cornered fight inclined them to seek a new constitutional framework which would strengthen the position of the executive and would recognize those social and economic interests friendly to the Catholic camp. They found the necessary constitutional formulas in the fund of

Romantic authoritarian and Catholic pluralistic doctrines which had dominated modern Austrian Catholic thought for over a century. The Corporative Constitution of May 1, 1934, which was the result of these efforts, reflected accurately the balance of ideas which had influenced Catholics in the past; that is to say, it was a *mélange* of Romantic, Catholic, and specifically Austrian ideas. As had happened in the past, the *étatiste* and authoritarian ideology of the Romantic tradition won the upper hand in the regime of the Corporative Constitution, and the demands for social and economic reforms inspired by Catholic social doctrines never received a hearing by the groups who gained control of the corporative state.

1. Constitutional Reform and the Failure of Consensus, 1918-1934

(a) The 1920 Settlement. Though all three *Lager* cooperated in writing the Constitution of 1920, Catholics were dissatisfied with the constitutional settlement because it reflected the balance of political power during the first postwar years, namely, the predominant position of the Socialist *Lager*.[1] Catholics had defended the monarchy and the Hapsburg Dynasty until the last possible moment, and had accepted only reluctantly what they considered an excessively "democratic" document. Under the leadership of Ignaz Seipel they were able to push through the Constituent Assembly their own proposal for a federal distribution of powers, but had to give way to Socialist demands for an omnicompetent assembly and a list system of proportional representation. They also scored a victory when they managed to prevent consideration of a new bill of rights and secured, instead, an inter-party agreement to readopt the civil rights legislation of the 1860's. In the end, impelled by the radical *Zeitgeist* of the postwar period, Catholics accepted the 1920 Constitution. But the settlement was a precarious one and they never ceased to agitate for a presidential government like that of the Weimar Constitution, and for some changes in the electoral system to secure the representation of economic and cultural interests. This latter demand was based on corporative ideas which had

[1] See above, Ch. III, section 3b.

played a prominent role in Catholic social thought long before the publication of *Quadragesimo anno*.

(b) The Three Lager and Constitutional Reform, 1922-1929. From 1922 on, when Seipel became federal chancellor, the country was governed by a coalition consisting of the Christian Socials and one or more of the minor Nationalist parties. Though the partners to this coalition did not see eye to eye on cultural policy and on the issue of clericalism, their anti-Socialist and pro-capitalist sympathies overrode these other differences.[2] As a result of this coalition, anti-Socialist forces gained control of the executive branch of the federal government, as well as most *Land* governments, and began to eliminate Socialist influences in the civil service, the police, and the armed forces. The Socialists continued to maintain a strong position in the federal legislature and polled between thirty-five to forty-five percent of the total vote in national elections, but their influence on government policy and on the general outlook of the country diminished as the tide of postwar radicalism receded. Consequently, the 1920 Constitution ceased to reflect correctly the earlier balance of political power, and Catholic demands for revision of the basic law became more insistent.

In 1925, a number of changes were made in the 1920 Constitution.[3] These dealt chiefly with details of provincial and local administration, and with intergovernmental relations in the field of education; in short, they were technical changes to repair shortcomings which had developed during the first years of operation under the 1920 framework. Because these reforms did not touch on the points of the Constitution which had displeased them all along, Catholics continued their demands for adjustments in the basic law.

The years 1925 to 1927 marked the zenith of postwar economic recovery and political peace.[4] By 1925, Austria's currency

[2] See above, Ch. IV, section 1.

[3] Hans Kelsen, "Die Verfassung Österreichs," *Jahrbuch des öffentlichen Rechts*, XV (1927), pp. 51-148; see also Mary Macdonald, *The Republic of Austria 1918-1934. A Study in the Failure of Democratic Government* (London: Oxford University Press, 1946), pp. 46-48.

[4] Rudolf Schlesinger, *Central European Democracy and Its Background. Economic and Political Group Organization* (London: Routledge & Kegan Paul Ltd., 1953), p. 312: "the interlude between the establishment of some degree of political equilibrium after the stabilization crisis and its shattering by a new

and economy had been stabilized with foreign assistance, administered chiefly through the League of Nations. At the same time, the three *Lager* had reached a *modus vivendi*, and the anti-Socialist coalition came to be dominated by the so-called provincial Christian Socials, who, as has been pointed out above, were often the less militantly-anti-Socialist element in the Catholic camp.[5] This period of political peace was shattered by the 1927 riots, which culminated in the burning of the Ministry of Justice building in Vienna. The Socialists had been greatly disturbed by the tendency of provincial juries and courts to free *Heimwehr* and other right-wing defendants accused of assault or murder growing out of political demonstrations. But the riots which started spontaneously, and which the Socialist leadership failed to control, demonstrated the firm control the anti-Socialist coalition had gained over the executive branch. Social Democrats now were forced to give ground to the growing Catholic demands for constitutional reform, backed up by *Heimwehr* threats of a *coup d'état*.

(c) *The Reforms of 1929.* Late in 1929, agreement was reached in Parliament among the three *Lager* on these major changes: the position of the executive, intergovernmental relations, and the composition of the upper chamber of the federal legislature.[6] The extreme form of assembly rule which had been incorporated into the 1920 document as one of the many "democratic" demands of the Socialists was modified by providing for the direct election of the federal president, and by giving him power to select chancellor and cabinet and to dissolve the legislature.[7] Next, the powers of the federation were strengthened at the expense of the *Länder*.[8] Debate on this issue revealed a complete reversal of Christian Social and Socialist positions since 1920. The former's unbroken control of the federal executive since 1922 had inclined them to support strong powers for the

---

right-wing offensive did not last longer than two years . . . during which period the Government of the Provincial Christian Socials . . . was in office."

[5] See above, Ch. III, section 4b.

[6] Hans Kelsen, "Die Verfassung Österreichs," *Jahrbuch des öffentlichen Rechts,* XVIII (1930), pp. 130-185; see also Macdonald, *op.cit.,* pp. 49-62, and Brita Skottsberg, *Der österreichische Parlamentarismus* (Göteborg: Elanders Boktryckeri Aktiebolaget, 1940), Ch. IX, "Die Verfassungsreform von 1929," pp. 351-404.

[7] Kelsen, "Die Verfassung Österreichs" (1930), pp. 141-142.

[8] *Ibid.,* p. 132.

federation, while the latter, once champions of a unitary state, had become defenders of "states' rights" in their concern for the autonomy of Vienna.[9] Finally, the Christian Socials repeated their proposal, first advanced in the constitutional drafts of 1918-1920, for a corporative upper chamber, or at least for a modification of the existing one, to permit the representation in it of *Stände* as well as *Länder*.[10] However, the Socialists were unalterably opposed to any corporative proposal because they suspected that social groups friendly to the Catholic camp, peasants and industrialists, would gain the upper hand in such a corporative assembly and would then proceed to destroy the political and economic advantages gained by the Austrian proletariat since 1918. These Socialist fears, as will be seen below, were well grounded. As a result, Catholics had to be satisfied with a statement of intentions that a future constitutional law would transform the existing *Bundesrat* into a *Länder- und Ständerat*.

Because all constitutional changes required a two-thirds vote in the *Nationalrat*, the Socialists could block all attempts at reform unpalatable to them. Therefore, the result of the 1929 changes, wrung from the reluctant Socialists to the accompaniment of *Putsch* gestures by the *Heimwehr*, failed to satisfy many members of the anti-Socialist coalition. The clamor for radical political changes continued without interruption, especially from the *Heimwehr* and other right-wing groups in the Catholic camp.

(d) The Collapse of Consensus 1929-1934. This Catholic insistence on the need for constitutional reform, especially for strengthening the executive, and for changing the system of representation, together with the rapid rise of the Nazi movement, and increased Socialist restlessness, finally destroyed the precarious balance between the three *Lager*. Within the Catholic camp, inspiration for reform of the basic law after 1929 came chiefly from two sources: the Fascist ideology of the *Heimwehr*, and the corporative proposals of *Quadragesimo anno*. Encouraged by important Catholic elements under Seipel's leadership, the *Heimwehr* threatened a *coup d'état* against the

[9] Skottsberg, *op.cit.*, p. 390.
[10] *Ibid.*, pp. 375-376.

Republic and loudly proclaimed its Fascist ideology. The blatantly anti-democratic Korneuburg Oath was meekly accepted by the Christian Social leadership as compatible with the principles and program of their party. Only Leopold Kunschak and the Catholic trade union group had the courage to declare that faithful support of the Republic as well as of Catholic doctrines could not be reconciled with the totalitarian elements of the *Heimwehr* program.[11] These totalitarian predilections showed most clearly in the constitutional *Patent* which was made public during the abortive *Heimwehr Putsch* in 1931.[12] It was influenced chiefly by Fascist ideology and Fascist institutions: there was an omnicompetent chief executive assisted by a *Führerrat* and a *Staatsrat*. The former was the body of chief political leaders, while the latter consisted of the principal government, police, and militia officials.

The publication of *Quadragesimo anno* in 1931 further strengthened the hand of those in the Catholic camp who had agitated all along for the overthrow of the Republic and who now proposed to replace it with an authoritarian regime based on the type of corporative organization proposed in the encyclical. Seipel's eagerness to quote *Quadragesimo anno* as authority for the destruction of political parties, democracy, and trade unions was only one of many such statements from the Catholic camp.[13]

These two groups joined forces, with the result that in the last years of the Republic there remained little or no support within the Catholic *Lager* for the principles embodied in the 1920 settlement.[14]

During the early years of the Republic, the Nationalist *Lager* had been represented by two small bourgeois parties, *Grossdeutsche Volkspartei* and *Landbund*, which were basically committed to democratic institutions. With the simultaneous rise

[11] Leopold Kunschak, *Österreich 1918-1934* (Vienna: Typographische Anstalt, 1934), pp. 118-119. The Catholic trade unions passed the following resolution: "We reject the 'Korneuburger Programm' because its essential points conflict with the socio-cultural and political principles of the Christian workers and employees movement." Reprinted in *ibid.*

[12] *Neue Freie Presse*, September 14, 1931. For another *Heimwehr* "constitution" see Skottsberg, *op.cit.*, p. 404, n. 1.

[13] See above, Ch. v, section 5ᵃ.

[14] See the chart in Ch. iv, p. 105.

of the Nazis in Germany and Austria, they rapidly lost their followers to the new Nationalist movement, though the leaders of these parties remained in the cabinet until 1934. The arrogance and aggressiveness of the Austrian branch of the NSDAP was a far cry from the moderate and democratic views of old Nationalist leaders like Schober. Hitler's coming to power in Germany finally destroyed all chances for a coalition between Catholics and Nationalists. Catholics could not cooperate with the new forces in the Nationalist *Lager* which intended to make Austria simply another *Gau* in Hitler's *Grossdeutschland*.

At the same time, the anti-democratic posture of the Catholic *Lager* had increased the restlessness of the Socialists and made them doubt the wisdom of their faithful adherence to a policy of change by constitutional means. The left wing of the party agitated for the use of force to counter what it considered insolent anti-democratic threats of the *Heimwehr*, as well as the Nazis. But the entire movement, including moderates like Renner, felt the frustration of having been close to gaining a majority for over a decade. Socialists began to realize, especially after 1927, that while they were condemned to a permanent minority position with a dwindling influence over the state and its policies their opponents had been able to consolidate their hold over the civil executive, the army, and the police. Finally, the Socialist *Lager* also suffered from the ambivalence of its leaders, who preached a revolutionary Marxism but were fundamentally committed to peaceful change. Disillusionment and indecision set in because the call for taking over the state never came and the chances for success in this undertaking dwindled rapidly. When the Socialist leaders finally issued the call to arms, not for an offensive but actually a defensive action, the movement failed to respond, and poor leadership did the rest in frustrating Socialist success in civil war.

As a result of these developments in the Nationalist and Socialist camps, the Catholics, who had decided against an anti-Nazi alliance with the Socialists, were forced into a two-front war against the other two *Lager*. Because this would place them in a permanent minority position in a freely elected assembly, they became further inclined toward an authoritarian course. When on March 4, 1933 the resignation of the three presiding officers over a procedural dispute left the *Nationalrat* without any one in authority to call it into session, Dollfuss used the occasion to suspend the Constitution and govern with the aid of World War I emergency powers. The elimination of Parliament destroyed the next to last constitutional stronghold of the Socialists, the last being the municipal government of Vienna, from which they were dislodged in February 1934, and did away with the need for new elections, which would probably have brought a substantial number of Nazi deputies into the *Nationalrat*.

Plans were now made for the establishment of an authoritarian state with a single political movement, the *Vaterländische Front*, and on September 11, 1933 at the first mass rally of the *Front*, Dollfuss announced the Catholic intention to create a "social, Christian, German Austria, on a corporative basis and under strong authoritarian leadership."[15] The *Trabrennplatz* speech, which has been discussed in some detail in a preceding chapter, clearly established the Romantic and Catholic parentage of the prospective state of *Quadragesimo anno*.[16] The Socialist uprising in February 1934 hastened the process of constitution-making, and the new Corporative Constitution was proclaimed on May 1, 1934. This event was preceded on April 30, 1934 by a comic-opera rump session of the *Nationalrat* which had been purged of its Socialist membership. In a session which lasted only a few hours, the *Nationalrat* ratified hundreds of emergency decrees enacted since March of the previous year, and ratified the new Constitution. There was also an elaborate effort on the part of the Dollfuss government to "prove" that the new basic law was a rightful successor of the 1920 instrument. But, as Erich Voegelin has pointed out: "This perfectly straightforward constitutional situation [the coming into effect of a new constitution which had no ties with past institutions] was complicated by the desire of the federal government to establish 'legal continuity' between the new constitution and the document of 1920/ 1929. It had two reasons for trying to do that: (1) the widely held popular opinion that only a legitimate process of transition

---

[15] Reprinted in *Dollfuss an Österreich. Eines Mannes Wort und Ziel*, ed. Edmund Weber (Vienna: Reinhold Verlag, 1935), pp. 30-31.

[16] See above, Ch. v, section 5b.

could validate the institutions of the new constitution, especially the new federal government; and (2) the obvious sympathy of at least some members of the federal government with this point of view."[17] Though the Constitution of May 1, 1934 contained significant elements from past Austrian constitutional and political traditions, there was, legally as well as politically, a clear break between it and the document ratified by an all-party coalition in 1920.

The new Constitution was not put into effect immediately. A transitional constitutional law, subsequently issued on June 19, 1934 fixed the dates on which various parts of the Constitution should go into effect. When Hitler's *Wehrmacht* crossed the Austrian border during the night of March 11-12, 1938 large parts of the corporative experiment were still waiting for implementation.

2. The Structure of the Corporative Constitution

The Corporative Constitution of 1934 was a detailed document which consisted of a preamble and 183 articles grouped into thirteen *Hauptstücke* (sections).[18] The most important of these, for the purposes of this study, were Sections 1 through 5, which dealt with general provisions, civil rights, intergovernmental relations, the federal legislature, and the federal executive. The remaining eight sections covered *Land* and local administration, emergency powers, the Court of Accounts, and the Federal Court (*Bundesgerichtshof*).

(a) The Preamble. Though the preamble had no legal binding force, it is important for an understanding of the Constitution, its general political ideology, and its fundamental organizing principles: "In the name of God the Almighty, who is the source of justice and law, the Austrian people receive this constitution for a Christian, German, federal state on a corporative basis." The preamble thus contained four of the five organizing principles of the Constitution (*Baugesetze*) analyzed below:

[17] Erich Voegelin, *Der autoritäre Staat. Ein Versuch über das österreichische Staatsproblem* (Vienna: Julius Springer, 1936), p. 172.

[18] The text of the Constitution is reprinted in Otto Ender (ed.), *Die Verfassung 1934. Mit den Übergangsbestimmungen, dem Text des Konkordates und dem Gesetz über die Vaterländische Front* (Vienna: Österreichischer Bundesverlag für Unterricht, Wissenschaft und Kunst, 1935).

Christian, German, federal, corporative, and authoritarian. But since Dollfuss' *Trabrennplatz* speech there had never been any doubt that the new state would be under "strong authoritarian leadership." Therefore the authoritarian principle which ran like a thread through the entire constitutional framework must be included in any list of organizing principles of the 1934 basic law.

(b) General Provisions. The first section fixed some of the fundamental characteristics of the corporative state. Austria was declared to be a federal state "organized in a corporative manner" (Art. 1).[19] This served to expand and give legal force to the phrase "corporative basis" contained in the preamble. German was recognized as the national language, but the language rights of minorities, forced on Austria by the Treaty of St. Germain, were not to be touched by this provision (Art. 7). Section 1 then provided that Austria's character as a *Rechtsstaat* was to be preserved: "The administration of state power can be exercised only pursuant to law" (Art. 9). But at the same time the highest organs of the federation were charged with the *Leitung* (direction) and *Aufsicht* (supervision) of all state activities. The corporative organs were excepted from the provisions of this article but, as will be seen below, did not escape sweeping state control (Art. 11).

(c) Civil Rights. Section 2 (Arts. 15-33) fixed *allgemeine Rechte der Staatsbürger* and incorporated into the new Constitution the text of the Concordat concluded with the Holy See in 1933 (Art. 30,4). Under the influence of Catholic doctrine, the Corporative Constitution abandoned the concept of individual rights which had been introduced in Austria during the liberal period of the 1860's and had been absorbed into the 1920 document: a constitution inspired by Catholic doctrine could not possibly affirm the principles of the Revolutionary tradition.

Having thus discarded the concept of an area of individual freedom immune from state intervention, the framers of the Constitution permitted state interference in matters of individual freedom and conscience. In effect, the 1934 document

[19] All references to the various articles and sections of the 1934 Constitution will be given in the text. If the reference is only to one paragraph of a given article, it will be given thus: Art. 2,1.

merely legalized the practices and policies of the Dollfuss government since March 1933. For example, the right to hold either elective or appointive office was now reserved to loyal and patriotic citizens (Art. 16,3). The equal rights of women, granted in the Constitution of 1920, could now be abridged by simple legislation (Art. 16,2). Catholics had condemned this grant all along because it was based on the abstract rights of 1789 and contradicted the natural position of women in the family. Men and women performed different social functions and should, therefore, not be granted equal privileges. Finally, pre-publication censorship of the press, theatres, radio, motion pictures which the Dollfuss regime had instituted by decree was now fixed in the Constitution (Art. 26,2).

The Concordat concluded with the Vatican was incorporated in the Constitution and the legal position of so-called recognized religious communities was strengthened. At the same time, the state abandoned its religious neutrality and took responsibility for insuring the "religious-moral" character of public education (Art. 31,6) and for enforcing attendance at religious ceremonies by school children as well as civil servants (Art. 27,3).

Article 32 protected the free choice of occupation, but tied this *laissez-faire* principle to two paragraphs which formed one of the principal parts of the Constitution's corporative structure: "Legislation will fix the area of autonomous administration, under state supervision, of vocational affairs by occupational corporations [*Berufsstände*]. Vocational education and the exercise of a vocation are subject to legislation and rules, adopted pursuant to law, by the occupational bodies (Art. 32,2-3)." Nowhere is the weakness of the Constitution's corporative element better illustrated than in Article 32. Though the leaders of the Catholic camp had no intention of abandoning the capitalist system, they felt it necessary to satisfy the demands of their petty bourgeois followers for the introduction of "corporative restrictions" on economic activity. The result was a constitutional provision which, while leaving the individual free to choose his occupation, gave the corporative groups the right to administer their own affairs, to regulate professional training, and to fix the conditions under which the various occupations were to be carried on.

(d) Intergovernmental Relations. Section 3 (Arts. 34-43) regulated the distribution of powers between the federation and the *Länder* in a manner favorable to the former. The powers of the federation were expanded considerably from those assigned in the 1920 document and the autonomy of the geographic subdivisions, the *Länder*, districts, etc., as well as of all types of autonomous organs, including occupational groups, was severely restricted.

(e) The Federal Legislature. Section 4 (Arts. 44-72), which dealt with the federal legislative branch, contained the heart of the Constitution's corporative system. Federal legislative power was vested in the *Bundestag*, which voted the laws (Art. 44). The federal executive was required to submit bills dealing with certain subjects, and could submit all other bills to one or several of the four consultative chambers: *Staatsrat, Bundeskulturrat, Bundeswirtschaftsrat,* and *Länderrat.* This system of assemblies provided further proof of the limitations placed on the corporative principle: only two of the four consultative assemblies were corporative chambers, and the *Bundestag*, though it contained some corporative elements, was not a corporative assembly at all. Thus, the occupational and cultural corporations played only a subordinate role in the formulation of state policy.

The *Bundeskulturrat* (Art. 47) consisted of thirty to forty representatives of the legally recognized churches and religious communities, and of education, the sciences, and the arts. The *Bundeswirtschaftsrat* (Art. 48) consisted of seventy to eighty representatives of the seven *berufsständische Hauptgruppen*: agriculture and forestry, industry and mining, *Gewerbe*, commerce and transportation, money, credit, and insurance, free professions, and public service. These seven were to be represented in the *Bundeswirtschaftsrat* according to the size of their membership. However, no corporation could have less than three representatives.

The other two consultative assemblies represented the authoritarian and the federal principle, respectively, in the legislative process. The *Staatsrat* (Art. 46) consisted of forty to fifty members chosen for ten-year terms by the federal president.

They were to be selected on the basis of their knowledge of and understanding for the needs of the state. In short, they were a group of notables who had the full personal confidence of the authoritarian Executive. The *Länderrat* (Art. 49), the organ of the constituent geographic units of the federation, consisted of the governor and the principal fiscal officer of each *Land*, as well as of the mayor and principal fiscal officer of the federal city of Vienna.

The *Bundestag* (Arts. 50-51), the only truly legislative federal assembly, was composed of representatives from the four consultative chambers. The members from the two corporative chambers (ten from the *Bundeskulturrat* and twenty from the *Bundeswirtschaftsrat*) barely outnumbered those from the noncorporative bodies (twenty from the *Staatsrat* and nine from the *Länderrat*). Finally, the *Bundesversammlung* (Arts. 52-54) was the joint meeting of the four consultative assemblies. Its principal duty was to prepare a slate of three candidates for submission to the electoral college choosing the Federal President. It also voted on declarations of war submitted by the Executive.

Though this elaborate machinery was meant to create the illusion of a parliamentary system, it had, in fact, little in common with institutions bearing similar names in France, Great Britain, or the United States: "The relations between legislature and executive in the 1934 Constitution were arranged in such a manner that the latter could never be the source of political will in the state. The only methods for articulating such a will in an assembly, parties, clubs, parliamentary groups, will have been carefully eliminated. . . . To define 'parliament' loosely enough to include even an authoritarian chamber seems to be stretching the definition beyond its reasonable meaning which ought to be centered around the concept of 'carrier of political will.' If the assembly no longer has any political power potential, one can no longer call it a parliament even though the place it has been given in the constitutional structure and its manner of participating in the legislative process make it look like a parliament."[20] In short, Voegelin concluded that an assembly which did not represent the independent political will of a

[20] Voegelin, *op.cit.*, pp. 238-239.

people did not deserve the name "parliament" even if the constitutional architecture gave that assembly a parliamentary appearance. The subjection of the legislative branch to the authoritarian executive left little room for the expression of opinion on public policy not sanctioned by that executive.

The machinery of the legislative assemblies was controlled by the Executive in a number of ways. The Federal President appointed the presiding officer of the *Staatsrat* (Art. 56,1) and had to confirm the presiding officers elected by the other assemblies (Art. 56,2). He also could dissolve both *Bundeswirtschaftsraat* and *Bundeskulturrat* before the expiration of their six-year terms (Art. 55,2). Furthermore, the assemblies were denied the right to select their own staffs and had to accept civil servants detailed for this purpose by the Federal Chancellor (Art. 58,1). They were not even permitted to draw up their own standing orders but had to rely on rules embodied in a federal law drawn up by the Executive (Art. 57).

The legislative process of these assemblies likewise was tightly controlled by the Executive (Art. 61-67). Government draft bills submitted to any of the four consultative chambers had to be reported out within a period fixed by the government. Failure of the assembly to act within the time specified freed the Executive from further obligations to that consultative assembly (Art. 61,2). The *Staatsrat*, the truly authoritarian chamber, was permitted to give advice on all types of bills, while the other three advisory bodies were limited to reviewing bills dealing either with cultural, economic, or federal problems (Art. 61,6). The federal budget, proposals for federal borrowing, and ratification of treaties could not be submitted to any of the consultative chambers, but had to be sent directly to the *Bundestag* (Art. 51).

Though the *Bundestag* was the decision-making organ of the legislative branch, its power was limited to accepting or rejecting without change the bills submitted by the Executive (Art. 62,3). A government reporter explained the bill, after which one opposing report could be submitted. Then the *Bundestag* voted to accept or reject the measure without debate. Any bills that might happen to have been rejected by the *Bundestag* could be submitted to a popular referendum (Art. 65).

(f) *The Federal Executive.* Section 5, entitled "Federal Executive," maintained the democratic fiction that the President and the Chancellor were only executing public policy determined by the legislative branch, when, in effect, the Corporative Constitution made them the supreme power in the state (Arts. 73-97). The Federal President, the formal executive, was elected for a seven-year term by an electoral college consisting of all the Austrian mayors—a device designed to give the Catholic-controlled villages permanent control over that office (Art. 73). However, all actions of the President, except for the decree dismissing the chancellor and the appointment of a new one, required the counter-signature of the Federal Chancellor (Art. 80). In the years 1934-1938 the Federal President, Wilhelm Miklas, was a figurehead while political control rested entirely in the hands of Dollfuss, and later Schuschnigg, the federal chancellors.

The day-to-day operation of state affairs was in the hands of the federal government (Arts. 81-94), consisting of the chancellor and the cabinet. The former was not simply *primus inter pares* but was charged with determining the basic lines of policy (Art. 93).

(g) *Land and Local Government.* In spite of the declaration in Art. 2 that Austria was a federal state, *Land* and local governments were subject to close control from the center (Sections 6-9). The head of the *Land* government could be removed at will by the *Bundesregierung*. (Art. 114,4) and the Federal Chancellor had an absolute veto over all *Land* legislation (Art. 111,2). This type of central control not only weakened the independent position of the *Länder*; it also weakened the influence of the corporative elements in the *Land* assemblies which were to contain members selected by the same groups represented in the *Bundeswirtschaftsrat* and *Bundeskulturrat* (Art. 108,2). Local units of government were under strict control of *Land* as well as federal officials, and had practically no independent sphere of action (Arts. 123-135).

(h) *Emergency Powers.* Section 10 of the Constitution provided the federal government a set of far-reaching emergency powers. It is indeed curious that the architects of the Corporative Constitution thought it necessary to add emergency powers to the vast arsenal of control instruments already at the disposal of the federal government. They evidently wanted to create the impression that the government under this basic law was committed to constitutional methods and would, therefore, need some means for dealing with emergencies. The framers further elaborated the fiction of constitutional government by providing for the *Bundestag* and the Federal Court *(Bundesgerichtshof)* to control the exercise of these emergency powers (Arts. 147,5 and 148,2).

(*i*) *Other Provisions*. In the remaining sections, the Corporative Constitution set up a Court of Accounts and a Federal Court. The Court of Accounts supervised administrative performance on all levels of government and thereby served as an instrument of centralization (Arts. 149-162). The Federal Court combined the work of two courts which had existed under the Republic, the Administrative Court and the Constitutional Court (Arts. 163-180). It was charged with insuring the constitutionality of all laws, and the legality of all administrative orders. It was, therefore, one of the strongest *Rechtsstaat* elements in the authoritarian basic law of 1934.

3. The Principles of the Constitution

The 1934 Constitution was based on a general ideology as well as a set of organizing principles *(Baugesetze)* drawn from Romanticism, Catholic doctrine, and Austrian institutions.[21] But it also contained elements which conflicted with its avowed ideology and *Baugesetze*.

(*a*) *The Constitutional Ideology*. The Constitution rested on Catholic universalism, expressed most prominently in the preamble, which recognized "God as the constituent authority." This implied a rejection of the social contract or of popular sovereignty as fundamental principles of political organization, and reflected the long-standing opposition of Catholics to the modern state. This universalism was not applied consistently throughout the Constitution, but was contradicted repeatedly by individualistic elements, clearly at odds with fundamental Catho-

21 Adolf Merkl, *Die ständisch-autoritäre Verfassung Österreichs. Ein kritisch-systematischer Grundriss* (Vienna: Julius Springer, 1935), p. 144. The notion of the "Baugesetze" has been adapted from Merkl.

lic assumptions about the nature of the correct social order. One might argue that these discordant features were simply meant to conceal in a cynical fashion the similarity between Austria's authoritarianism and that of Germany and Italy. However, it is possible to interpret the inclusion of institutions bearing the stamp of political and economic individualism, ranging from the *Rechtsstaat* principle to the ban on the imperative mandate, as a testimony to the strength of Austria's liberal tradition.

(b) The Five Baugesetze of the Constitution. The specific *Baugesetze*—Christian, German, federal, corporative, and authoritarian—were a hodge-podge of Romantic, Catholic, and specifically Austrian ideas.

The *Christian principle*, one should rather say Catholic, for that is the correct translation of the term *"christlich,"* found expression in the preamble, in the inclusion of the Concordat as an integral part of the Constitution, in the provision for occupational group representation along the lines of *Quadragesimo anno*, and in the treatment of individual rights. In this manner the framers of the basic law attempted to restore the church and the Catholic spirit to the position of primacy they had enjoyed under the monarchy: "We want to extend the scope of Catholicism in Austria beyond its influence over the individual. Catholicism should not merely be a part of our public and political life but should have a formative influence on the character of our political system."[22] Though the church had relied in the past, and continued to do so after 1934, on the social and political influence of Catholic governments and ruling groups for the protection of Catholic principles, it welcomed the constitutional settlement of 1934 because it gave legal sanction to what the church considered its rightful role and position in Austrian life.[23]

[22] From an address by Dollfuss quoted in Johannes Messner, *Dollfuss* (Innsbruck: Verlagsanstalt Tyrolia, 1935), p. 131.

[23] Max Stoffel observed correctly that the influence on the Constitution of Catholic ideas in general, and of *Quadragesimo anno* in particular, "was more profound than was, or could be made, apparent. To grasp the full significance [of the influence] of this body of ideas one must study the past as well as the present constellation of affairs in Austria." *Die österreichische Ständeordnung. Ihre ideellen und verfassungsmässigen Grundlagen und die Anfänge ihrer konkreten Verwirklichung* (doctoral dissertation; University of Zurich, 1938), p. 138, n. 26. For this reason the 1934 Constitution becomes comprehensible only if one

The *German principle* appeared in the provision which established German as the official language of state, school, and public life (Art. 7). Though there were small national minorities in rump-Austria after 1918, the Republic which emerged from the postwar settlement had been relieved of one of the most difficult problems of the old Empire, the disruptive national struggles which had divided Germans in the western half of the Empire before 1918.

The *federal principle* can be found in many places in the Constitution, beginning with the preamble, but especially in the section which outlined the division of powers between the *Bund* and the *Länder*. By 1934 the latter had become fully established units of government, most of them controlled by Christian Social officials and party groups. As a result, these foci of power had to be preserved in some form, even if the authoritarian regime at the center would have preferred a unitary state.

The inclusion of the *corporative principle* met a long-standing Catholic demand for a system of representation which would recognize interests not represented in the territorial legislature: "Vocation and common endeavors bind people together more effectively than even the best party platform. In the corporative state the individual must first prove himself in his vocation as well-qualified and trustworthy. The vocational groups will then send their best men to help shape our public life."[24] Austrian concepts of occupational organization, Romantic ideology, and Catholic social doctrines had combined to produce the preference for corporative organization in Austrian Catholic thought: ". . . better than any other country Austria was able to keep alive until today a fund of truly cooperative organizational principles. No other people have clung as steadfastly as have the Austrians to corporative ideas as the tools for overcoming the effect of liberal-Marxian disintegration. There is a direct line from Vogelsang to Schindler and ultimately to Dr. Seipel who, two years before *Quadragesimo anno*, advocated corporative

views it against the perspective of Catholic thought in Austria during the nineteenth and twentieth centuries. If that is done, the document emerges as the culmination of these persistent traditions.

24 Messner, *Dollfuss*, p. 114.

reconstruction of the Austrian community shattered by 'formal' democracy."[25]

The basic corporative provisions of the Constitution were not systematically developed but were scattered throughout the document. The corporative nature of the Constitution was established in the preamble, and given legal sanction in Article 2. The establishment of the corporations as public law bodies was included in the section on civil rights (Art. 32), while the corporative elements of the federal, *Land*, and municipal assemblies were treated in the sections dealing with these assemblies. The Constitution, following the lead of Romantic theorists like Spann, recognized economic as well as cultural corporations as the basis for the two federal corporative chambers, *Bundeskulturrat* and *Bundeswirtschaftsrat*.

The corporative principle of the Constitution had both organizational and functional aspects.[26] The organization of the corporative element took the form of two corporative advisory bodies on the federal level, and the inclusion of members chosen by a corporative system of representation in other assemblies on the federal, *Land*, and municipal levels. Because the framers of the 1934 document were not prepared to abandon all forms of territorial representation, they followed the Catholic recommendation of 1929, for the establishment of mixed assemblies, containing both territorial and occupational representatives. The functions of the cultural and economic corporative groups were defined in sweeping terms as their "proper occupational affairs" (Art. 32). But at the same time, the Constitution provided, that this autonomy be strictly defined by law, and placed the activities of these corporative units under the *Aufsicht* of specified state officials at the federal, *Land*, and local levels (Arts. 34,1 and 36,1).

In spite of a strong Austrian tradition of Catholic social thought, the corporative principle was overshadowed, as were all the other *Baugesetze*, by the *authoritarian principle* of the document. Though not expressly provided for in the preamble, the authoritarian nature of the Corporative State was clearly established by Dollfuss in his *Trabrennplatz* speech of 1933.

25 *Ibid.*, p. 103.
26 Merkl, *op.cit.*, pp. 147-148.

The Constitution vested authoritarian control in the Federal Executive, which was, in effect, the highest authority in the state, and not a mere executor of the laws. It was charged with "direction and supervision" over the executive branch, as well as over the *Selbstverwaltungskörper*, including the corporative organs, on all levels of government (Art. 11,1). Its authority was never challenged, either by the principle of separation of powers, or by the federal system. The *Staatsrat*, an authoritarian assembly, provided one-third of the *Bundestag* membership, to which must be added the *Länderrat* representatives in that body, who also were amenable to the desires of the Executive, which could remove them at will. In addition, the Constitution denied the *Bundestag* the right to substitute its own proposals for those of the Executive, and limited it to accepting or rejecting, unchanged and without debate, the bills submitted to it by the Executive. The Federal Executive also exercised strict authoritarian control over all subordinate territorial and occupational groups. The Federal Chancellor could veto all *Land* and local laws and ordinances, and could remove at will all officials on these levels. In addition, the Federal Executive was charged with supervision over all *Berufsstände* organizations, their national as well as their regional units. Finally, the federal president was chosen by an electoral college whose members, the mayors, held office only with the consent of that same Executive.

During the period 1934 to 1938 this constitutionally sanctioned authoritarianism was reinforced by the political power concentrated in chancellors like Dollfuss and Schuschnigg, who were the leaders of the only legally recognized political movement, the *Vaterländische Front*.[27]

(c) Inconsistencies and Contradictions. This survey of the principal *Baugesetze* revealed striking inconsistencies, resulting chiefly from the inclusion of the authoritarian principle, which nullified, in effect, the federal as well as much of the corporative nature of the constitutional settlement. The strict application of hierarchical political controls from the center, in addition to the constitutional checks on the *Länder* and local governments, outlined above, made impossible the kind of local self-rule

---

[27] *Bundesgesetz vom 1. Mai 1934, betreffend die "Vaterländische Front,"* reprinted in Ender, *op.cit.*, pp. 131-133.

which is the foundation of federal government.[28] The application of these same controls to the occupational groups destroyed the autonomy of the corporative structure.

The authoritarian principle also violated the proclaimed pluralistic doctrines of Catholic social thought (the Christian principle of the Constitution) which supposedly provided the foundation of the Corporative Constitution. It not only denied the dichotomy of state and society; it also infringed on the principle of subsidiarity according to which no superior unit should interfere with subordinate units in matters falling legitimately within the latters' proper sphere. As Pius XI had emphatically stated in *Quadragesimo anno*: ". . . it is an injustice, a grave evil and a disturbance of the right order for a larger and higher organization to arrogate to itself functions which can be performed efficiently by smaller and lower bodies. This is a fundamental principle of social philosophy, unshaken and unchangeable and it retains its full truth today."[29]

These five *Baugesetze* not only contradicted one another; they also clashed with the principles drawn from the individualistic ideology. As a result, unitary, liberal, democratic, and parliamentary influences repeatedly came into conflict with Catholic universalism and the Christian, German, federal, corporative, and authoritarian principles of the Constitution.

Unitary elements in the Constitution weakened still further the federal principle, already threatened by the authoritarian influences analyzed earlier. As a result, the power of the *Länder*, which had been weakened by the 1929 constitutional reforms, was reduced even further in 1934. The *Land* assemblies, which had enjoyed full legislative powers under the 1920 document, shared the fate of the national parliament and were reduced to rubber stamps like the *Bundestag*. The weakening of the *Land* assemblies, together with the removal and veto powers of the federal chancellor over *Land* officials and *Land* legislation, made

[28] K. C. Wheare, *Federal Government* (3rd ed.; London: Oxford University Press, 1953) put it this way: The test I apply for federal government is then simply this. Does a system of government embody predominantly a division of powers between general and regional authorities, each of which is co-ordinate with the others and independent of them. If so, that government is federal," pp. 32-33.

[29] *Quadragesimo anno*, 79, p. 147. See above Ch. v, n. 46, for the edition of the encyclical used for this analysis.

a mockery out of the very first article of the 1934 constitution which made Austria a federal state. These unitary features also contributed to the attenuation of corporative autonomy, by giving the central government power to supervise closely the territorial subdivisions of the seven major corporative groups.

The liberal-democratic features of the basic law testified to the persistent vigor of the individualistic ideology in Austria, and to the strength of the country's constitutional tradition, reaching back to the middle of the nineteenth century. The inclusion of a section on individual rights and of the *Rechtsstaat* principle were the most prominent inheritance from Austria's liberal past. The Constitution also retained the principle of majority decision in all assemblies and provided for electing the leaders of the major corporative organs, and of the corporative representatives in the various legislative assemblies.[30] Next, the Constitution upheld, at least in principle, the independence of the judiciary, and set up two courts which would have far-reaching powers over the action of state officials at all levels. The Court of Accounts would control the accountability of all state officials on behalf of the *Bundestag* (Art. 149,2) and the Federal Court would be empowered to test the constitutionality and legality of laws and administrative acts. Finally, by including a section on emergency powers (*Notrecht*), the framers of the 1934 Constitution attempted to clothe the federal executive with a semblance of constitutional respectability; that is to say, they wanted to give the impression that these powers of this government were so strictly defined that in cases of emergency it would need additional powers not subject to the usual constitutional checks. At the same time, the Constitution provided that the use of these emergency powers would be subject to *ex post facto* review by the Federal Court and the *Bundestag*. The inclusion of this section on emergency powers could easily be dismissed as a piece of utter cynicism, as another of the little tricks by which the dictators of Austria attempted to give their authoritarian enterprise a respectable front. It would be a mistake to do this, because it leads one to underestimate the vitality of Austria's liberal-democratic herit-

[30] Merkl, *op.cit.*, pp. 148-149.

age which forced the builders of this corporative façade to pay their respects to a tradition shared by a large number of Austrians, including some members of the Catholic camp.

Finally, the basic law also attempted to preserve some elements of parliamentary government. Erich Voegelin was forced to admit that "the formative influence of parliamentary constitutional ideas was so strong and vital that they were able to force a compromise: in spite of the peculiar non-parliamentary nature of the Austrian authoritarian chambers the relations between federal executive and federal legislature [prescribed in the Constitution] were a mixture of old parliamentary and the new authoritarian formulas."[31] The Constitution tried to preserve the fiction that the *Bundesregierung* merely executed the laws enacted by the *Bundestag*, that it was a government exercising only strictly defined powers. It is noteworthy that the Constitution should choose to underline this subservience of the Executive to the *Bundestag* by providing the right of unlimited debate on the budget, as well as on the reports of the Courts of Accounts, a right denied in the case of all other forms of legislative proposals submitted to the chamber (Art. 63). The Constitution further strengthened the parliamentary character of the *Bundestag* by making it the only assembly empowered to enact the laws and by reducing the corporative bodies to a consultative status. In the *Bundestag* itself, the corporative element had only a majority of one vote over the representatives from the other assemblies. But the government would obviously always be in a good position to block the maneuvers of the corporative representatives, if they should ever decide to agitate for proposals not favored by the authoritarian executive.

This part of the Corporative Constitution bore most clearly the mark of Ignaz Seipel's influence, rather than that of doctrinaire Romantic theorists. Seipel had warned all along that it would be disastrous to hand the state over to the representatives of purely economic interest groups. He had also cautioned against creating a multicameral corporative assembly because he thought that the difficulties of parliamentary government, as he saw them, could not be solved by creating several parlia-

[31] Voegelin, *op.cit.*, p. 238.

ments where there had been only one before.[32] In constitutional theory at least, the 1934 basic law avoided that mistake, but committed an equally serious one instead. By making the state paramount over the representatives of the cultural and economic interests, the Constitution handed control of Austria to those who had managed to assume that political leadership. The constitution makers of 1934 in seeking to avoid the Scylla, "corporative anarchy," had fallen into the Charybdis, "omnicompetent state."

There were several other ways in which the architects of the Constitution stressed the parliamentary nature of the various legislative assemblies. For instance, they provided six-year terms for the two corporative chambers and gave the Federal President power to dissolve them at any time before the expiration of that term. They even continued the ban on the imperative mandate from the previous Constitution, an entirely incongruous feature in a corporative assembly whose members sat only as spokesmen for specific economic, cultural, or other social groups.

4. The Constitution in Relation to the Traditions of Austrian Catholic Thought

What were the dominant features in this seemingly capricious jumble of corporative, authoritarian, Catholic, Romantic, liberal, and parliamentary elements? Without doubt, the essential nature of the Corporative Constitution was determined far more by Austrian constitutional and social developments, as well as by Romantic ideology, than by *Quadragesimo anno* and Catholic pluralistic doctrine. In this the document reflected accurately the balance of the very influences which had shaped Austrian Catholic social thought in the past, and thus emerged as a constituent part of Austria's tradition, as the culmination of Catholic criticism of the modern state and the modern economy.

(a) The Romantic Tradition. Romantic authoritarian ideas played a prominent role in fixing the character of the 1934 document. The omnicompetent state of Müller and Spann was a suitable instrument for Catholics who opposed the Austrian

---

[32] *Der Kampf um die österreichische Verfassung* (Vienna: Wilhelm Braumüller, 1930), pp. 183-184.

Republic and the modern state in general. Though Spann ridiculed the 1934 Constitution and scorned it as a perversion of his corporative ideas, the inspiration provided by his "true state" was clearly visible in the corporative system of 1934. The minority position in which the Catholic camp found itself in the last years of the Republic made this Romantic ideology more attractive than ever before. Even Johannes Messner, whose realistic *Sozialpolitik* doctrines distinguished him sharply from the utopian Romantic dreamers in the Catholic camp, now termed monarchy the only form of political organization consonant with Catholic dogma and natural law: "A constitution which meets the requirements of natural law must necessarily be monarchical. Only by thus concentrating the powers of the state will it be possible to realize the common good under any and all conditions. . . . Christian-natural law political theory has always taught that state power along with all other forms of authority originated from God . . . and that it is a grave error to restrict the power of the state by appealing to the so-called rights of the people. . . . The Catholic constitutional ideal therefore calls for the establishment of an authoritarian state."[33] Austrian Catholics abandoned the Republic they had helped to create in 1920 and easily found their way back to the social monarchy of Vogelsang and to the 1918 pastoral letter of the Austrian hierarchy in which the bishops had condemned false ideas like "self-determination of nations" and "popular sovereignty" as undermining the foundations of the Catholic social order and had concluded that Divine Providence had placed the Hapsburgs on the Austrian throne.

(b) Austrian Influences. The specifically Austrian influences on the Constitution were twofold. There was first the influ-

[33] "Der katholische Staatsgedanke," *Schweizerische Rundschau,* xxxiv (1934), pp. 286-287. By 1934 the struggle between the three *Lager* and the *Weltanschauungen* they represented had destroyed any basis for discussion. Members of the Catholic camp had become convinced that the Republic was the work of Godless forces. But now the time had come to correct these evils, to replace the Godless democracy with a "true democracy." Even Otto Ender, the spokesman of the Vorarlberg Catholics, who had been considered a moderate, and a democrat of sorts—had not Vorarlberg voted to join Switzerland?—concluded his introduction to the official edition of the 1934 Constitution with this hymn of praise for corporativism: "The corporative organs have been assigned important tasks. With the help of these new organs there will develop the noblest form of democratic self-government," *op.cit.,* p. 32.

ence of Austria's liberal tradition. Though many of the liberal-democratic provisions of the Constitution were never put into effect between 1934 and 1938, the traditions of the *Rechtsstaat,* and of an executive controlled at least in some manner by an assembly proved stronger than many of the Catholic authoritarians were willing to admit. Voegelin, who would have preferred the 1934 document to be a purely authoritarian instrument, found it disturbing that it contained devices intended to check the leadership of the state.[34]

Specifically Austrian influences can also be seen in the manner in which the Constitution reflected the pattern of relationships between *Sozialpolitik* and *Sozialreform* tendencies, characteristic of Austrian Catholic thought. Austrian Catholics, though united by 1934 in their opposition to the Republic, were divided on the question of capitalism. Catholic social theorists who had maintained an almost unbroken anti-capitalist *Sozialreform* tradition, reaching back to Adam Heinrich Müller, had been denied, since the days of Lueger, any part in shaping Catholic social policy. In other words, by 1934 the majority of Austrian Catholics had reached a satisfactory accommodation with capitalism and was not prepared at all to apply either the extreme anti-capitalist prescriptions of the Romanticists, or even the more moderate reform proposals of the encyclicals.

(c) The Constitution and the Encyclicals. In the face of these strong Romantic and Austrian influences, did Catholic social doctrine, then, play any role at all in the creation of the corporative basic law? It is usually argued that Catholic *social* theory can provide little guidance in writing the constitution of a *state.* However, Austrian Catholics who were prepared to impose Catholic social doctrines on their country had a splendid opportunity in 1934 to give effect to these doctrines to the fullest extent. They failed to do this, and as a result the corporative and Catholic pluralistic elements of the Constitution were overshadowed, in true Romantic fashion, by an authoritarian ideology.

In *Quadragesimo anno,* Pius XI, though concerned primarily with social reconstruction, acknowledged the important role the state and its leaders would play in this task. However, he

---

[34] Voegelin, *op.cit.,* pp. 285-286.

offered no prescription for fitting the correct social organization into the constitutional framework of the state because he believed that men should be free to work out the forms of political and economic organizations in a voluntary fashion.[35] The architects of the Constitution would, therefore, have been justified in omitting, from that document, all references to occupational groups. However, the corporative provisions they finally included hopelessly prejudiced social reconstruction along the lines of *Quadragesimo anno* as long as the 1934 basic law remained in effect.

Quadragesimo anno posed three political and constitutional problems concerning the nature and establishment of occupational groups, and indicated in some instances how these problems might be solved.[36] There was first the question whether corporations should grow voluntarily or whether they should be established by state fiat. The encyclical stressed the importance of voluntary action, but admitted that only the state could grant the corporations legal personality. Next, the encyclical tried to define the scope of the corporations' sphere of autonomous action, and the permissible limits of state control over them. Though it recognized that full corporative self-government would only lead to anarchy, it noted the evil effects of excessive state controls. Adolf Merkl, an Austrian commentator concluded: "Corporative autonomy does not mean that the occupational groups are free to adopt whatever rules they choose. Rather, the requirements of corporative autonomy will have been satisfied if the constitution formulated by the state authority enables these groups to carry out freely the vocational functions assigned them by the Encyclical."[37] Finally, the encyclical

[35] "When We speak of the reform of the social order it is principally the State We have in Mind." *Quadragesimo anno*, 77, p. 147. He concluded the discussion of social reconstruction with this warning: "It is hardly necessary to note that what Leo XIII taught concerning the form of political government, can, in due measure, be applied also to vocational groups. Here, too, men may choose whatever form they please, provided that both justice and the common good be taken into account." *Ibid.*, 86, p. 149.

[36] Adolf Merkl, "Der staatrechtliche Gehalt der Enzyklika Quadragesimo Anno," *Zeitschrift für öffentliches Recht*, XIV (1934), pp. 208-239. This is an extremely interesting treatment of the political problems of social reconstruction. Merkl, a professor of law, examined the encyclical sympathetically but did not hesitate to point out the difficulties raised by Pius XI's proposals—difficulties the Romantic dreamers usually refused to face.

[37] *Ibid.*, p. 124.

raised some questions concerning the internal organization of the corporative organs. Should the group have legal personality; that is to say, should it be a *Körperschaft* under Austrian law, or merely a *Kollegium*, a collection of individuals which did not enjoy the advantages of legal group personality? The encyclical probably would have preferred the former, because it made possible the assigning of definite functions of self-government to these groups. Pius XI also had definite views about the organization of employers and employees within the corporation. He opposed separate organizations for these two groups because his principal aim in social reconstruction had been to eliminate groupings based on the status of individuals in the "labor market." Therefore, a corporative organization which continued to separate these two groups violated a fundamental principle of social reconstruction.

The framers of the Constitution made some effort to solve these problems in the manner of *Quadragesimo anno*, but the bulk of their corporative devices violated both letter and spirit of the encyclical.

The Constitution violated papal instruction on the first point discussed above by fixing the number of *berufsständische Hauptgruppen* in the Constitution at seven and thereby stunting severely the growth of voluntary organization in any part of society. Once these seven *Hauptgruppen* had achieved status as public law corporations, no further voluntary development was possible. On the second point, as well, the Constitution came into a fundamental conflict with church doctrine. It provided that the corporations could administer their "own affairs" only according to regulations established by law, and under the supervision *(Aufsicht)* of appropriate state officials: "When all is said and done, the occupational corporations' scope of independent action demanded by the Encyclical has been reduced to a bare minimum while state influence which should have been subordinate actually predominates. The corporative organs can best be characterized . . . as units of the decentralized state administration. The extent of decentralization will depend on whether the federal and the *Länder* governments will be satisfied with exercising the supervisory control provided for in articles 32/2, 34/1, and 36/1, or whether federation and *Länder* will decide to use their powers of direction contained in article 11. If the latter happens then the corporations will lose their character as self-governing entities and one will have to raise against them the same objections the Encyclical raised against the Italian corporative state."[38]

As a result, it is impossible to consider these corporations autonomous and their activity an exercise of self-government: the outline of their organization was fixed in the Constitution; detailed regulations would come from a state authority which also had to approve any changes in the *modus operandi* of these corporations. As was pointed out above, such an arrangement violated the fundamental dichotomy of state and society, as well as the principle of subsidiarity: the state, instead of respecting the area of society and instead of leaving to subordinate units those tasks they were equipped to carry out, attempted to control all segments of life and to prescribe in detail what all subordinate units should do.[39] Finally, though the Constitution was silent on the internal organization of the corporative *Hauptgruppen*, the manner in which these were subsequently organized clearly violated the injunction in *Quadragesimo anno* against separate organizations for employers and employees. The projected corporative organization of industry was to be accomplished in three stages. In the first stage workers and employees would be organized into a unified trade union federation. Next, employers would be organized. Finally, the two organizations would be united into a single corporative unit. The first two stages were partially completed by 1938, but no efforts had been made to move on to the last one, so that for the life of the corporative experiment the existing occupational organizations violated one of the fundamental principles of social reconstruction proclaimed by Pius XI.[40]

Given the nature of Austrian Catholic social thought and of the political and social bases of this body of ideas, it was not surprising that events under the corporative regime took the

[38] Stoffel, *op.cit.*, p. 145.

[39] Stoffel pointed out that the Constitution itself recognized the principle of subsidiarity, but that "the laws implementing [the Constitution] went off in another direction and thereby extended the scope of the state beyond what was envisaged [in the Constitution]." *Op.cit.*, p. 240.

[40] *Ibid.*, p. 147.

turn predicted by Gundlach and condemned by the church in the *Osservatore Romano* article.[41] From the beginning, the *étatiste* bias of these Austrian ideas had favored whoever could get control of the state. Austrian theorists always granted all power of the state to the ruler, but never established any institutional safeguards to insure that such authority should be exercised in the interest of those individuals and groups on whose behalf the very grant had primarily been made. The framers of the 1934 Constitution continued in that tradition. Having first silenced the opposition by force of arms, they then destroyed the system of democratic controls and handed the state over to the very capitalists whom the Vatican had castigated for cloaking their selfish ends with Catholic doctrines. In addition, the sham corporative system erected in 1934 enabled these same industrialists to tighten their control over the economy still further.[42] As a result, they now could rule both state and economy without interference.

[41] See above, Ch. v, pp. 183-186, and Ch. v, n. 84.
[42] Erich Hula, "The Corporative Experiment in Austria," *Social Research*, VI (1939), pp. 40-57.

EPILOGUE

THE failure to distinguish between the state as the area of compulsory action and society as the area of voluntary action has emerged as the outstanding feature of Austrian Catholic social thought. This tendency to conceive of human life in unitary or monistic terms can be traced to a view of society as an organic whole, actuated by a single belief system. In the manner of St. Thomas, Austrian Catholics thought of society as an "apt arrangement of a plurality of objects" in which the various groups and organs fitted harmoniously into a higher order. But modern society, with its bewildering multitude of groups pursuing different and often conflicting aims, does not always achieve the harmony which St. Thomas so confidently expected would result from the interplay of social groups. Nevertheless, Austrian Catholics accepted the Thomist view of society as motivated by a single purpose and saw no reason why the realization of that social purpose should not be entrusted to a single agent, the state. The 1934 Constitution, which was an attempt at monism, disguised with pluralistic trappings, aptly illustrated the dangers of such a monistic scheme. Those who succeed in getting control of the state can then subvert both state and society for their selfish purposes, without fear of meeting organized resistance.

Another characteristic of Austrian Catholic thought suggested earlier was confirmed by the trend of events after 1918, and especially by the 1934 document. Though the encyclicals had clearly envisaged a limited state, one which would recognize the legitimate spheres of economic, social, and cultural groups, their Romantic tendencies inclined Austrian Catholics toward a total state. The manner in which the Federal Executive, under the 1934 instrument, exercised authoritarian control over all aspects of life, made the corporative experiment the very antithesis of the social pluralism ostensibly advocated by the encyclicals. Finally, the failure to distinguish between state and society led Austrian Catholics to deprecate democracy and the political institutions of the democratic state, free elections, and political parties. This contempt for democracy which had been a dominant theme of Catholic political thought all along reached its apogee in the authoritarianism of the corporative regime. Catholics in 1934 reasserted their contention that an authoritarian state was the one form of political organization which corresponded most nearly with the Catholic constitutional ideal.

One is forced to conclude, therefore, that the social doctrines of a group of people, even if they profess to adhere strictly to the church and its teaching on social questions, are the result of a variety of influences, of which Catholic social ideals need not be the most powerful. On the other hand, it has been suggested that the monistic and authoritarian ideas and institutions favored by Austrian Catholics do not really violate church doctrine but can be traced to causes deeply embedded in Catholicism itself. Is not the pluralism which is the avowed foundation of Catholic social thought based on the implied assumption that the various groups which make up this pluralistic system are fundamentally homogeneous and subscribe to a single belief system? If this is so, it helps to explain the confidence with which so many Catholic theorists approach the task of solving society's conflicts. They conceive of society as an organic whole motivated by a single purpose, and feel certain that the process of adjustment will be concerned only with secondary details. As a result, Catholic theorists tend to go to one of two extremes: either they see little need for autonomy in a society agreed on fundamentals, or they are prepared to grant wide powers of self-government to a variety of occupational and cultural groups, convinced that no irreconcilable conflicts can arise between groups motivated by a single aim. Fundamentally, then, the inadequacy of Catholic social thought in general, as well as Austrian Catholic thought in particular, lies in its inability to devise a set of concepts applicable to the modern, complex, multigroup society.

With minor exceptions, such as the "realistic" theorists Messner, Dobretsberger, and others, Austrian Catholic social theorizing during the early part of the twentieth century was based on assumptions which had become invalid, on empirical data about capitalism and society of the previous century and on the assumption that the principal problem facing modern society was an economics of scarcity. Therefore, the proper remedies were to be the closed state, the hierarchical society, and an economic system which would insure that what little there was of the social product would be parceled out carefully. Catholic social theorists were convinced that this type of reform program was the only one appropriate for the period 1918-1933, and especially for the years following the 1929 crash and depression. However, they never bothered to check whether the assumptions on which their social theorizing was built were still valid. Just as the proponents of *Sozialreform* insisted that medieval social institutions which had developed in response to a specific set of conditions were correct for all times, so the *Sozialpolitik* thinkers assigned permanent value to the forms of capitalism of the late nineteenth and early twentieth centuries.

It is possible now to return to the starting point of this study, where I suggested that the Catholic critique of the modern state and the social question would help us to understand the process of transition from a traditional to a modern society such as that now taking place in Asia and Africa.

There is no doubt that the Catholic social movement is at its best when it examines critically the consequences of rapid and seemingly unplanned social change. Certain persistent themes clearly emerge from this critique: (1) the destruction of the traditional family unit and the atomization of the individual in the mass society; (2) the shattering of social groups other than the family in which men had lived in harmony; (3) the separation of work from residence and the deplorable consequences of this separation for basic social institutions; (4) the alienation of man from his traditional religion; (5) the anonymity and emptiness of the urban way of life; (6) the freeing of economic activity from traditional social and ethical restrictions which had led to a ruthless, competitive struggle through which all segments of life became subject to crass materialistic considerations; (7) the commercialization of the media of communication and entertainment which had resulted in lowering the moral standards of the people, and in alienating them from their traditional values and mores; (8) the ascendancy to leadership of an elite completely opposed to traditional values; and (9) the centralization in the hands of the "state" of matters formerly left to intermediate groups and private social organizations.

If one were to substitute the term "natives" for "people" and "'detribalized intelligentsia" for "elite completely opposed to traditional values" these characteristics, and perhaps a dozen more, could be incorporated without difficulty into such analytic schemes as Margaret Mead's *Cultural Patterns and Social Change*[1] and Lucian Pye's "The Non-Western Political Process."[2] This seems to me to offer additional proof for the proposition advanced earlier that the Catholic social movement is most effective when it subjects the process of transition to an avowedly hostile critique and measures the products of this transition against its ideal-type traditional society.

But our respect for the perspicacity of the Catholic social critics must not blind us to their almost complete inability to prescribe successfully for the ills of transition and to propose workable alternative institutions and ideals. Their devotion to remedies appropriate for a simple and static society and their commitment to a turning back of the clock to an agrarian, pre-capitalist, pre-democratic age seem to invalidate even that part of their analysis which otherwise would deserve attention.

However, even that, the weakest part of their writings, merits consideration. In calling attention to the Catholic literature on the modern state and the social question I am not suggesting that we can find in it specific prescriptions for the problems of Asian and African societies in transition. In the preceding passages I have tried to demonstrate the relevance of the Catholic critique to the transition process itself; and there is still another way in which this literature can prove useful. The singular failure of Catholic critics to propose workable alternatives and their fondness for certain sets of institutions and ideas should serve to remind us that we ought to proceed carefully in proposing Western democratic and capitalistic instrumentalities of modernization. Because we have failed to be impressed by the melancholy fate of the Catholic corporativists who continued to dream of converting the industrial worker into an

[1] New York: The New American Library, 1955.
[2] Lucian W. Pye, "The Non-Western Political Process," *The Journal of Politics*, xx (August 1958), pp. 468-486.

artisan and settling him on a little plot of land in the country, we have to be reminded forcibly by men like Prime Minister Bandanaraike of Ceylon that they consider parliamentary government on the Westminster or Washington model unworkable in Asia and that democracy can survive only if it finds new forms appropriate for the societies of Asia and Africa.

We can help in this process of transition only if we have a full and sympathetic understanding of the problems posed by it, and if we can make proposals for new institutions that are not based on models inappropriate for those who are to operate them. For both of these tasks the Catholic literature on the modern state and the social question should prove a valuable guide.

BIBLIOGRAPHY

o◄❉► BIBLIOGRAPHY ◄❉►o

As ADAM WANDRUSZKA indicated in the bibliographical essay to his "Österreichs politische Struktur" (part II of *Geschichte der Republik Österreich*, ed. Heinrich Benedikt): "So far we do not have a scientific history of Austrian political movements. . . ." Without quarreling over the use of the term "scientific," the present writer would tend to agree with this judgment. Like Wandruszka he hopes that his own work will help to fill this gap in the history of political movements and their ideas.

At the present time the student of Austrian political ideas, movements, and institutions is confronted with a twofold difficulty: (1) the unsatisfactory condition of the general and political history of modern Austria, especially since 1850; and (2) the absence of a comprehensive study of the Austrian Catholic social movement, or even of monographs dealing with the principal leaders and theorists and with the major ideas.

The status of the literature on Austria, both before and after 1918, is not very satisfactory. Much of the writing is highly polemical, especially the studies dealing with the national and social struggles of the Empire and the First Republic. There are very few studies, dealing with the internal history and politics of the period, which deserve to be listed as fundamentally "disinterested." Obviously all historical writing is biased and it would help to improve the quality of such writing if more historians, and political scientists as well, would cease to misunderstand Leopold von Ranke's dictum about history "wie es eigentlich gewesen ist." However, much of the literature on Austria is not only biased; it is also intensely "interested" and partisan. The authors take sides in the national, social, and religious struggle of Empire and Republic, using "history" to take a pro-clerical, or pro-nationalist, or anti-Semitic, or anti-labor stand in the struggles which hastened the downfall of the Empire and the First Republic. Sometimes a foreign scholar is taken in tow by one of the contending groups and then produces another tract, this time in English or French instead of German. Perhaps the best example of this is Charles A. Gulick, *Austria from Habsburg to Hitler*, which is an unrestrained paean of praise of the Social Democratic party and all its works. A more balanced though incomplete view of the accomplishments of the Social Democrats can be found in C. A. Macartney, *The Social Revolution in Austria*.

Some of the best surveys of historical and political developments during the monarchy are autobiographies and biographies, such as

Josef Redlich, *Emperor Francis Joseph of Austria*, or Rudolf Sieghart, *Die letzten Jahrzehnte einer Grossmacht*. A very good one-volume study in English is Oszkar Jaszi, *The Dissolution of the Hapsburg Monarchy*. Good examples of the Pan-German nationalist view of Austrian history are Viktor Bibl, *Der Zerfall Österreichs* and the work of Heinrich Ritter von Srbik and his school; such as Josef Nadler & Heinrich von Srbik (eds.), *Österreich: Erbe und Sendung im deutschen Raum*. A very fine survey of the national ideas and views on the "national question" in the Empire is Robert Kann, *The Multinational Empire; Nationalism and National Reform in the Habsburg Monarchy, 1848-1918*.

Until 1938 Austrian historical scholarship, including the academic writers on political movements and ideas, was dominated by the Pan-German nationalists led by Srbik. After 1945 the outspoken Nazi sympathies of this school tended to discredit its members, and control over academic scholarship in history and politics passed to a group essentially friendly to the existence of an independent Austria and to the Catholic character of such an independent state. But as a reaction against the blatant Pan-German sentiments of their predecessors this group has produced a revisionist literature which centers, at present, around Hugo Hantsch's two-volume *Die Geschichte Österreichs* and the symposium volume *Spectrum Austriae*, edited by Otto Schulmeister, with contributions by Hantsch, Kann, Wandruszka, and many others. Some, like Adam Wandruszka, who also wrote the section on political movements in the volume edited by Benedikt, *Geschichte der Republik Österreich*, have maintained a balance between a desire to revise and the demands of disinterested scholarship. Others have yielded to the temptation to rewrite the history of the Empire and the First Republic in the terms of an ideological analysis which the present study has examined in detail. In their attempt to build up the image of an independent Catholic Austria, liberals, socialists, and German nationalists are all condemned in sweeping terms. While Hantsch in the second volume of his *Geschichte Österreichs* treats the Christian Social program quite uncritically (pp. 442-447), he has this to say about the Social Democrats' Hainfeld program of 1891: ". . . even the last and most secure bond of human solidarity, religion, shall be eliminated from public life which will now become the battlefield of class interests. The worker shall be trained as a fighter in the class war . . . social life which undoubtedly needs thorough reforms, is made an object of a violent power struggle" (p. 449). Willy Lorenz, writing the chapter "Der Katholizismus: Geschichte-Gestalt-Probleme" in *Spectrum Austriae*, characterizes the 1934 civil war and the imposition of the Corporative Constitution in this manner: "Under the pressure from many quarters, both external and internal, the government, overwhelmingly controlled by active Catholics, sought new forms of political organization with which to replace the 'formal democracy' [*Formaldemokratie*] which had become unworkable. Thus the corporate state was established" (p. 103). Here indeed is Ignaz Seipel's "true, correctly conceived democracy" in the guise of objective scholarship.

The second difficulty facing the student of Austrian political and social movements is the absence of both a comprehensive study and major monographs about the Austrian Catholic social movement. Books by and about men prominent in the Catholic social movement such as Friedrich Funder and Leopold Kunschak are now making their appearance. Edgar Alexander's long essay on German and Austrian Catholics in *Church and Society; Catholic Political and Social Thought and Movements 1789-1950*, edited by Joseph Moody, is perhaps the best summary statement in the English language, but it is only a beginning. Basically unfriendly commentaries on the *Sozialreform-Sozialpolitik* controversy can be found in Gulick's monumental two-volume study and in Justus Beyer, *Die Ständeideologien der Systemzeit und ihre Überwindung*. More sympathetic treatments are Richard Schmitz, *Der Weg zur berufsständischen Ordnung in Österreich*, Paul Jostock, *Der deutsche Katholizismus und die Überwindung des Kapitalismus. Eine ideengeschichtliche Skizze*, and especially Alois Hudal (ed.), *Der Katholizismus in Österreich. Sein Wirken, Kämpfen und Hoffen*.

With this warning, advice, and explanation should go the customary disclaimer that the listing which follows does not pretend to be exhaustive, but contains those items found useful for the present study. These materials have been arranged in the following manner:

I. The Writings of Austrian Catholics: (A) The Austrian Hierarchy. (B) Books. (C) Collections of Essays. (D) Articles. (E) Encyclopedias.

II. General Bibliography: (A) Papal Encyclicals. (B) Books. (C) Articles. (D) Unpublished Materials. (E) Official Publications of the Austrian Government. (F) Magazines and Newspapers.

Because Catholics were engaged in a continuous battle with the proponents of political and social institutions that they condemned, much of their writing on social and political questions was polemical. Their polemics can be found only in pamphlets and magazines, newspaper articles, and the proceedings of Catholic conferences. Some of the important Catholic newspapers and magazines are listed and identified in II (F).

I. THE WRITINGS OF AUSTRIAN CATHOLICS

A. THE AUSTRIAN HIERARCHY

Knoll, August Maria (ed.). *Kardinal Piffl und der österreichische Episkopat zu sozialen und kulturellen Fragen 1913-1932.* Vienna: Reinhold Verlag, 1932.

Hirtenbriefe des deutschen und österreichischen Episkopats. Paderborn: Junfermannsche Buchhandlung, various dates. 1926-1936.

B. BOOKS

Allmayer-Beck, Johann. *Vogelsang. Vom Feudalismus zur Volksbewegung.* Vienna: Herold, 1952.

Baxa, Jakob (ed.). *Adam Müller. Ausgewählte Abhandlungen.* Second enlarged & revised edition. Jena: Gustav Fischer, 1931.

Bugelnig, Philip. *Der Ständestaat. Ein Organisationsplan.* Klagenfurt: Carinthia Verlag, 1932.

Dobretsberger, Josef. *Freie oder gebundene Wirtschaft. Zusammenhänge zwischen Konjunkturverlauf und Wirtschaftsform.* Munich: Duncker & Humblot, 1932.

————. *Katholische Sozialpolitik am Scheideweg.* Graz: Ulrich Moser, 1947.

————. *Die wirtschaftspolitischen Aufgaben des neuen Staates.* Vienna: Österreichischer Verlag für Kunst und Wissenschaft, 1937.

Eberle, Josef. *Grossmacht Presse. Enthüllungen für Zeitungsgläubige. Forderungen für Männer.* Vienna: Verlag der Buchhandlung Herold, 1920.

————. *Der Weg ins Freie. Christi Segensgüter für Kultur, Staat und Wirtschaft.* Stuttgart: Schwabenverlag AG, n.d.

Ender, Otto (ed.). *Die Verfassung 1934. Mit den Übergangsbestimmungen, dem Text des Konkordates und dem Gesetz über die Vaterländische Front.* Vienna: Österreichischer Bundesverlag für Unterricht, Wissenschaft und Kunst, 1935.

Frodl, Ferdinand. *Gesellschaftslehre.* Vienna: Thomas Verlag Jakob Hegner, 1936.

Funder, Friedrich. *Aufbruch zur Sozialreform.* Vienna: Herold Verlag, 1953.

————. *Vom Gestern ins Heute.* Vienna: Herold Verlag, 1950.

Günther, Raimund. *Diktatur oder Untergang. Neue Wege für Staat und Gesellschaft.* Vienna: Carl Konegen, 1930.

Häring, Johann (ed.). *Kommentar zum neuen österreichischen Konkordat. Text des Vertrages mit Erläuterungen.* Innsbruck: Tyrolia Verlag, 1934.

Hantsch, Hugo. *Die Geschichte Österreichs.* 2 vols. Graz-Vienna: Styria Steirische Verlagsanstalt, 1947-1950.

Hausleithner, Rudolf. *Der Geist der neuen Ordnung. Einblicke in das päpstliche Gesellschaftsschreiben "Quadragesimo Anno."* Vienna: Typographische Anstalt, 1937.

Heinl, Eduard. *Über ein halbes Jahrhundert. Zeit und Wirtschaft.* Vienna: Wilhelm Braumüller, Universitäts-Verlagsbuchhandlung Ges. m.b.H., 1948.

Hildebrand, Dietrich von. *Engelbert Dollfuss. Ein katholischer Staatsmann.* Salzburg: A. Pustet, 1934.

Höslinger, Robert. *Rechtsgeschichte des katholischen Volksschulwesens in Österreich.* Vienna: Bundesverlag für Unterricht, Wissenschaft und Kunst, 1937.

Kasamas, Alfred. *Programm Österreich. Die Grundsätze und Ziele der österreichischen Volkspartei.* Vienna: Österreichischer Verlag, 1949.

Katann, Oskar. *Aufbau: Bausteine zur sozialen Verständigung.* Vienna: Reinhold-Verlag, 1932.

Klagenfurter Soziologenrunde. *Die neue Gesellschaft.* Klagenfurt: Im Selbstverlag, 1932.

Klopp, Wiard von. *Leben und Wirken des Sozialpolitikers K. Fr. v. Vogelsang.* Vienna: Typographische Anstalt, 1930.

——— (ed.). *Die sozialen Lehren des Freiherrn Karl von Vogelsang. Grundzüge einer katholischen Gesellschafts- und Volkswirtschaftslehre nach Vogelsangs Schriften.* Second revised edition. Vienna: Reinhold-Verlag, 1938.

Knoll, August Maria. *Das Ringen um die berufsständische Ordnung in Österreich.* Vienna: Manz, 1933.

——— (ed.). *Von der Romantik bis Rerum Novarum.* Vol. I of *Der soziale Gedanke im modernen Katholizismus.* Vienna: Reinhold Verlag, 1932.

Kralik, Richard. *Karl Lueger und der christliche Sozialismus.* Vienna: Vogelsang-Verlag Ges.m.b.H., 1923.

———. *Die neue Staatenordnung im organischen Aufbau.* Innsbruck: Tyrolia Verlagsanstalt, 1918.

Kunschak, Leopold. *Österreich. 1918-1934.* Vienna: Typographische Anstalt, 1934.

Kuppe, Rudolf. *Dr. Karl Lueger. Persönlichkeit und Wirken.* Vienna: Brüder Hollinek, 1947.

Lugmayer, Karl (ed.). *Das Linzer Programm der christlichen Arbeiter Österreichs.* Vienna: Typographische Anstalt, 1924.

Merkl, Adolf. *Die ständisch-autoritäre Verfassung Österreichs. Ein kritisch-systematischer Grundriss.* Vienna: Julius Springer, 1935.

Messner, Johannes. *Dollfuss.* Innsbruck: Verlagsanstalt Tyrolia, 1935.

Messner, Johannes. *Um die katholisch-soziale Einheitslinie.* Vienna: Verlagsanstalt Tyrolia, 1930.

―――. *Das Naturrecht. Handbuch der Gesellschaftsethik, Staatsethik und Wirtschaftsethik.* Innsbruck: Tyrolia Verlag, 1950.

―――. *Die soziale Frage in der Gegenwart.* Innsbruck: Verlagsanstalt Tyrolia, 1934.

―――. *Sozialökonomie und Sozialkritik. Studien zur Grundlegung einer systematischen Wirtschaftsethik.* Veröffentlichungen der Sektion für Sozial- und Wirtschaftswissenschaft der Görres-Gesellschaft, v. l. Paderborn: Ferdinand Schöningh, 1931.

Miklas, Wilhelm. *Der Bundespräsident Spricht . . . Von Österreichs Wesensart und Sendung.* Edited by Nikolas Hovorka. Vienna: Reinhold Verlag, 1934.

Müller, Adam Heinrich. *Elemente der Staatskunst.* 3 vols. Ed. Jakob Baxa. Jena: Gustav Fischer, 1922.

―――. *Von der Notwendigkeit einer theologischen Grundlage der gesamten Staatswissenschaften.* New edition. Vienna: Österreichische Leogesellschaft, 1897.

Neustädter-Stürmer, Odo. *Die berufsständische Gesetzgebung in Österreich.* Vienna: Österreichischer Bundesverlag für Unterricht, Wissenschaft und Kunst, 1936.

Orel, Anton. *Kirche-Kapitalismus-Proletariat.* Vienna: Vogelsang Verlag, 1928-1929.

―――. *Das Verfassungsmachwerk der "Republik Österreich" von der Warte der immerwährenden Philosophie aus und im Lichte von der Idee, Natur und Geschichte Österreichs geprüft und verworfen.* Second edition. Vienna: Vogelsang Verlag G.m.b.H., 1921.

―――. *Vogelsangs Leben und Lehren.* Vienna: Vogelsang Verlag, 1922.

―――. *Wahre Ständeordnung. ihr Geist, Wesen, Wirken. Grundsätzlich-praktische Klarstellung.* Graz: Ulrich Moser, 1934.

Pfliegler, Michael. *Die Kirche und der Sozialismus im Lichte der "Quadragesimo Anno."* Vienna: Gsur & Co., 1933.

Schmitz, Hans. *Die Sozialpolitik im autoritären Staat.* Österreichischer Heimatsdienst, Schriften zur berufsständischen Ordnung, No. 2. Vienna: Manzsche Verlags- und Universitätsbuchhandlung, 1935.

Schmitz, Richard. *Der Weg zur berufsständischen Ordnung in Österreich.* Vienna: Manzsche Verlagsbuchhandlung, 1934.

Schulmeister, Otto (ed.) with the collaboration of Johann Christoph Allmayer-Beck und Adam Wandruszka. *Spectrum Austriae.* Vienna: Verlag Herder, 1957.

Schuschnigg, Kurt. *Dreimal Österreich.* Vienna: Thomas Verlag Jakob Hegner, 1937.

————. *Ein Requiem in Rot-Weiss-Rot. "Aufzeichnungen des Häftlings Dr. Auster."* Zurich: Amstutz, Herdeg & Co., 1946.

Seipel, Ignaz. *Der christliche Staatsmann.* Augsburg: Haas und Grabherr, 1930.

————. *Der Kampf um die österreichische Verfassung.* Vienna: Wilhelm Braumüller, 1930.

————. *Nation und Staat.* Vienna: W. Braumüller, 1916.

————. *Seipels Reden in Österreich und anderwärts. Eine Auswahl zu seinem 50. Geburtstag.* Ed. Josef Gessl. Vienna: Heros Verlag, 1926.

————. *Wesen und Aufgaben der Politik.* Vienna: Tyrolia Verlag, 1930.

Spann, Othmar. *Gesellschaftslehre.* Second revised edition. Leipzig: Quelle und Meyer, 1923.

————. *Tote und lebendige Wissenschaft. Abhandlungen zur Auseinandersetzung mit Individualismus und Marxismus.* Second revised and enlarged edition. Jena: Gustav Fischer, 1925.

————. *Types of Economic Theory.* Transl. Eden & Cedar Paul. London: George Allen & Unwin, Ltd., 1930.

————. *Der wahre Staat. Vorlesungen über Abbruch und Neubau der Gesellschaft.* Second revised edition. Leipzig: Quelle & Meyer, 1923.

Starhemberg, Ernst Rüdiger Prince. *Between Hitler and Mussolini.* New York: Harper & Brothers, 1942.

Streeruwitz, Ernst Ritter von. *Springflut über Österreich. Erinnerungen, Erlebnisse und Gedanken aus bewegter Zeit.* Vienna: Bernina Verlag, 1937.

Studienrunde katholischer Soziologen. *Katholisch-soziales Manifest.* Mainz: Mathias Grünewald, 1932.

Thurnher, Eugen. *Katholischer Geist in Österreich. Das österreichische Schrifttum im zwanzigsten Jahrhundert.* Bregenz: Verlag Eugen Russ, 1953.

Ude, Johann. *Soziologie; Leitfaden der naturvernünftigen Gesellschafts- und Wirtschaftslehre im Sinne der Lehre des hl. Thomas von Aquin.* Wienacht (Switzerland): Siegfried Verlag, 1931.

————. *Das Wirtschaftsideal des Volks- und Staatshaushaltes.* Graz: Verlagsbuchhandlung "Styria," 1924.

Waitz, Sigismund. *Der christliche Staat.* Innsbruck: Tyrolia Verlag, 1921.

Weber, Edmund (ed.). *Dollfuss an Österreich. Eines Mannes Wort und Ziel.* Vienna: Reinhold Verlag, 1935.

Winter, Ernst Karl. *Arbeiterschaft und Staat.* Vienna: Reinhold Verlag, 1934.

————. *Monarchie und Arbeiterschaft.* Beihefte zu den *Wiener Politischen Blättern,* No. 1. Vienna: Gsur & Co., 1936.

Winter, Ernst Karl. *Platon. Das Soziologische in der Ideenlehre.* Vienna: Gsur & Co., 1930.

———. *Die Sozialmetaphysik der Scholastik.* Wiener Staats- und Rechtswissenschaftliche Studien, edited by Hans Kelsen, v. XVI. Vienna: Franz Deuticke, 1929.

Zernatto, Guido. *Die Wahrheit über Österreich.* New York-Toronto: Longmans, Green and Co., 1938.

Ziele und Wege der religiösen Sozialisten Österreichs. Vienna: Im Selbstverlag, 1930.

C. COLLECTION OF ESSAYS

Hudal, Alois (ed.). *Der Katholizismus in Österreich. Sein Wirken, Kämpfen und Hoffen.* Innsbruck: Verlagsanstalt Tyrolia, 1931.

Die katholisch-soziale Tagung in Wien, 1929. Vienna: Volksbund Verlag, 1929.

Die soziale Botschaft. Vorträge über Quadragesimo Anno. Vienna: Volksbundverlag, 1931.

Strieder, Jakob and Johannes Messner (eds.). *Die soziale Frage und der Katholizismus. Festschrift zum 40jährigen Jubiläum der Enzyklika "Rerum Novarum."* Veröffentlichungen der Sektion für Sozial- und Wirtschaftswissenschaft der Görres-Gesellschaft, v.2. Paderborn: Ferdinand Schöningh, 1931.

D. ARTICLES

Biederlack, Josef. "Das Recht der Arbeiter auf den vollen Arbeitsertrag (Zur Frage der rechten Auslegung der Arbeiterenzyklika Leos XIII)," *Das Neue Reich*, VI (1923), pp. 767-769.

———. "Die sogenannte 'neue Wiener Richtung' in der Sozialpolitik," *Theologisch-praktische Quartalsschrift*, LXXX (1927), pp. 715-726.

Brzobohaty, Josef. "Sebastian Brunner," *Die Kultur*, IX (1908), pp. 293-301.

Eberle, Josef. "Die dermalige Ausschaltung Habsburgs aus der Weltpolitik," *Das Neue Reich*, IV (1921-1922), pp. 129-135.

———. "Kaiser Karls zweite Ungarnfahrt," *Das Neue Reich*, IV (1921-1922), pp. 69-71.

Hugelmann, Karl Gottfried. "Parlamentarismus oder organische Demokratie," *Hochland*, XV, pt. 1 (1917-1918), pp. 178-187.

Knoll, August M. "Die Frage nach der 'besten' Wirtschaftsform bei Othmar Spann," *Soziale Revue*, XXVIII (1926), pp. 152-164.

———. "Die ideengeschichtlichen Grundlagen der Sozialphilosophie Ignaz Seipels," *Neue Freie Presse*, November 14, 1934.

Kogon, Eugen. "Der Ständestaat des Solidarismus," *Hochland*, XXV, pt. 2 (1928), pp. 1-21, 178-200, 291-300.

Kolnai, Aurel. "Gegenrevolution," *Kölner Vierteljahrshefte für Soziologie*, x (1931-1932), pp. 170-199, 295-319.

———. "Die Machtideen der Klassen," *Archiv für Sozialwissenschaft und Sozialpolitik*, LXII (1929), pp. 67-110.

———. "Sozialismus und Ganzheit," *Wiener Politische Blätter*, I (1933), pp. 37-48.

Lagler, Ernst. "Der berufsständische Aufbau der österreichischen Landwirtschaft," *Ständisches Leben*, III (1933), pp. 147-151.

Lux, Josef August. "Demokratie—Demagogie," *Das Neue Reich*, IV (1921-1922), pp. 735-737.

Merkl, Adolf. "Der staatsrechtliche Gehalt der Enzyklika Quadragesimo Anno," *Zeitschrift für öffentliches Recht*, XIV (1934), pp. 208-239.

Messner, Johannes. "Der katholische Staatsgedanke," *Schweizerische Rundschau*, XXXIV (July 1934), pp. 281-289.

———. "Katholizismus und Sozialwissenschaft," *Das Neue Reich*, x (1928), pp. 634-636.

Oehl, Wilhelm. "Richard Kralik," *Die Kultur*, XIII (1912), pp. 385-410.

Schmitz, Hans. "Katholische Kirche und Industriearbeiterschaft," *Volkswohl*, XVI (1925), pp. 81-89.

Seipel, Ignaz. "Die Organisation der Menschheit," *Die Kultur*, XVI (1915), pp. 3-21.

———. "Das Problem der Revolution," *Hochland*, XV, pt. 1 (1917-1918), pp. 543-553.

Spann, Othmar. "In eigener Sache," *Ständisches Leben*, II (1932), pp. 330-333.

———. "Gesellschaftsphilosophie," *Staat und Geschichte*. Edited by Julius Stenzel and others. Vol. IV of *Handbuch der Philosophie*. Munich: R. Oldenbourg, 1934. Pp. 5-167.

Steiner, Alfred. "Der ständische Aufbau in Österreich. Demokratischer Zentralismus," *Ständisches Leben*, III (1933), pp. 555-556.

Vogelsang, Maria Freiin von. "Aus dem Leben des Sozialpolitikers Karl von Vogelsang," *Das Neue Reich*, VII (1924), pp. 43-46, 64-66.

Waitz, Sigismund. "Das moderne Staatsrecht—ein Verhängnis für die Völker," *Das Neue Reich*, IV (1921-1922), pp. 789-792, 816-818.

———. "Quadragesimo Anno und Solidarismus," *Das Neue Reich*, XIV (1932), pp. 650-655.

———. "Papst Leo XIII. und die französische Republik," *Das Neue Reich* IV (1920), pp. 27-31, 39-41, 59-61, 71-74.

Winter, Ernst Karl. "Die beiden Schulen des mitteleuropäischen Katholizismus (Karl von Vogelsang und P. Heinrich Pesch S.J.), *Neue Ordnung*, III (1927), pp. 121-126.

Winter, Ernst Karl. "Kirche und Staat. Kritische Bemerkungen zu Jacques Maritains Lehre von der *Potestas indirecta*," *Zeitschrift für öffentliches Recht*, IX (1929), pp. 44-65.

―――. "Der paternale Staat," *Zeitschrift für öffentliches Recht*, X (1930), pp. 213-257.

―――. "Heinrich Pesch S.J. (1854-1926) im Rahmen der Katholischen Soziologie," *Schönere Zukunft*, I (1926), pp. 831-876.

―――. "Der wahre Staat in der Soziologie des Rechtes. Ein Beitrag zur kritischen Abgrenzung der Transzendentalsoziologie von reiner Rechtslehre, scholastischer Metaphysik und Ganzheitssoziologie," *Zeitschrift für öffentliches Recht*, XI (1931), pp. 161-205.

―――. "Wiener Wohnbaupolitik," *Hochland*, XXVIII, pt. 2 (1931), pp. 117-136.

E. ENCYCLOPEDIAS

Staatslexikon im Auftrag der Görresgesellschaft. Herausgegeben unter Mitwirkung zahlreicher Fachleute von Hermann Sacher. Fifth edition. 5 vols. Freiburg i.B.: Herder & Co. G.m.b.H., 1926-1931.

II. GENERAL BIBLIOGRAPHY

A. PAPAL ENCYCLICALS

Five Great Encyclicals. Labor-Education-Marriage-Reconstructing the Social Order-Atheistic Communism. New York: The Paulist Press, 1939.

Gilson, Etienne (ed.). *The Church Speaks to the Modern World. The Social Teachings of Leo XIII*. New York: Doubleday & Company, Inc., 1954.

B. BOOKS

Adamovich, Ludwig. *Grundriss des österreichischen Staatsrechtes*. Second edition. Vienna: Julius Springer Verlag, 1932.

Aris, Reinhold. *History of Political Thought in Germany from 1789 to 1815*. London: George Allen & Unwin, Ltd., 1936.

Barker, Ernest. *Essays on Government*. Second edition. London: Oxford University Press, 1951.

―――. *Principles of Social and Political Theory*. London: Oxford University Press, 1951.

Bauer, Otto. *Die Nationalitätenfrage und die Sozialdemokratie*. Vienna: Wiener Volksbuchhandlung, 1907.

―――. *Die österreichische Revolution*. Vienna: Wiener Volksbuchhandlung, 1923.

―――. *Sozialdemokratie, Religion und Kirche*. Vienna: Verlag der Wiener Volksbuchhandlung, 1927.

Baxa, Jakob. *Einführung in die romantische Staatswissenschaft.* Second edition. Jena: Gustav Fischer, 1931.

———. *Die Geschichte der Produktivitätstheorie.* Jena: Gustav Fischer, 1926.

Benedikt, Heinrich (ed.). *Geschichte der Republik Österreich.* Vienna: Verlag für Geschichte und Politik, 1954.

Bergsträsser, Ludwig (ed.). *Der politische Katholizismus in Deutschland. Dokumente seiner Entwicklung.* Vol. II: *1871-1914.* Munich: Drei Masken Verlag, 1923.

Bernatzik, Edmund (ed.). *Die österreichischen Verfassungsgesetze mit Erläuterungen.* Vienna: Manz, 1911.

Beyer, Hans. *Die Strukturwandlungen der österreichischen Volkswirtschaft nach dem Kriege.* Leipzig: F. Deuticke, 1929.

Beyer, Justus. *Die Ständeideologien der Systemzeit und ihre Überwindung. Forschungen zum Staats- und Verwaltungsrecht,* ed. Reinhard Höhn. Reihe A: *Abhandlungen,* v. VIII. Darmstadt: L. C. Wittich, 1941.

Bibl, Viktor. *Der Zerfall Österreichs.* 2 vols. Vienna: Rikola Verlag, 1922-1924.

Birk, Bernhard. *Dr. Ignaz Seipel. Ein österreichisches und europäisches Schicksal.* Regensburg: Verlagsanstalt vorm. G. J. Manz A.G., 1932.

Blüml, Rudolf. *Prälat Dr. Ignaz Seipel. Ein grosses Leben in kleinen Bildern.* Klagenfurt: Im Verlag der St. Josefs-Bücherbrüderschaft, 1933.

Böhme, Kurt. *Solidarismus und Liberalismus. Eine Kritik des Solidarismus von Heinrich Pesch S.J. vom liberalen Standpunkt.* Doctoral dissertation, University of Frankfurt a.M., 1929.

Borkenau, Franz. *Austria and After.* London: Faber and Faber, 1938.

Brügel, Ludwig. *Soziale Gesetzgebung in Österreich von 1848 bis 1918. Eine geschichtliche Darstellung.* Vienna: F. Deuticke, 1919.

———. *Geschichte der österreichischen Sozialdemokratie.* 5 vols. Vienna: Wiener Volksbuchhandlung, 1922-1925.

Bullock, Malcolm. *Austria 1918-1938. A Study in Failure.* London: Macmillan & Co., 1939.

Bunzel, Julius (ed.). *Geldentwertung und Stabilisierung in ihren Einflüssen auf die soziale Entwicklung Österreichs.* Vol. 169 (1925) of *Schriften des Vereins für Sozialpolitik.* Munich: Duncker und Humblot, 1925.

Buttinger, Joseph. *In the Twilight of Socialism. A History of the Revolutionary Socialists in Austria.* New York: Frederick A. Praeger, 1953.

Charmatz, Richard. *Österreichs innere Geschichte. 1848 bis 1907.* Second edition. 2 vols. Leipzig: B. G. Teubner, 1911-1912.

Drage, Geoffrey. *Austria-Hungary.* London: John Murray, 1909.

Driesch, Hans. *Philosophie des Organischen.* Leipzig: Quelle und Meyer, 1928.

Elbow, Matthew. *French Corporative Theory 1789-1948. A Chapter in the History of Ideas.* New York: Columbia University Press, 1953.

Frisch, Hans von. *Die Gewaltherrschaft in Österreich 1933 bis 1938. Eine staatsrechtliche Untersuchung.* Leipzig: Johannes Gunther Verlag, 1938.

Gentz, Friedrich. *The French and American Revolutions Compared.* Transl. John Quincy Adams. Chicago: Henry Regnery-Gateway Editions, 1955.

Gregory, J. D. *Dollfuss and His Times.* London: Hutchinson & Co., Ltd., 1935.

Gulick, Charles A. *Austria. From Habsburg to Hitler.* 2 vols. Berkeley and Los Angeles: University of California Press, 1948.

Gundlach, Gustav. *Zur Soziologie der katholischen Ideenwelt und des Jesuitenordens.* Doctoral dissertation, Friedrich-Wilhelms Universität at Berlin, 1927.

Hancock, W. K. *Australia.* Volume in *The Modern World. A Survey of Historical Forces.* Edited by H. A. L. Fisher. London: Ernest Benn, 1930.

Hantsch, Hugo. *Die Geschichte Österreichs.* 2 vols. Graz: Styria Verlag, 1947-1953.

Heinrich, Walter. *Die soziale Frage; ihre Entstehung in der individualistischen und ihre Lösung in der ständischen Ordnung.* Jena: G. Fischer, 1934.

Herberg, Heinz. *Eine wirtschafts-soziologische Ideengeschichte der neueren katholischen Soziallehren in Deutschland.* Doctoral dissertation, University of Bern, 1933.

Herrfahrt, Heinrich. *Das Problem der berufsständischen Vertretung von der französischen Revolution bis zur Gegenwart.* Stuttgart: Deutsche Verlagsanstalt, 1921.

Huemmer, Karl. *Der ständische Gedanke in der katholisch-sozialen Literatur des 19. Jahrhunderts.* Doctoral dissertation, University of Würzburg, 1927.

Januschka, Emil. *The Social Stratification of the Austrian Population.* United States Works Progress Administration Foreign Social Science Monographs, No. 21. New York: Columbia University, 1939.

Jarlot, Georges. *Le Régime Corporatif et les Catholiques Sociaux. Histoire d'une doctrine.* Paris: Flammarion, 1938.

Jaszi, Oszkar. *The Dissolution of the Hapsburg Monarchy.* Chicago: Chicago University Press, 1929.

Jöhr, Walter Adolf. *Die ständische Ordnung. Geschichte, Idee und Neuaufbau.* Leipzig: Felix Meiner, 1937.

Jostock, Paul. *Der Ausgang des Kapitalismus. Ideengeschichte seiner Überwindung.* Munich: Duncker & Humblot, 1928.

————. *Der deutsche Katholizismus und die Überwindung des Kapitalismus. Eine ideengeschichtliche Skizze.* Regensburg: Friedrich Pustet, 1932.

Kann, Robert. *The Multinational Empire. Nationalism and National Reform in the Habsburg Monarchy 1848-1918.* 2 vols. New York: Columbia University Press, 1950.

Kelsen, Hans. *Allgemeine Staatslehre.* Berlin: Julius Springer, 1925.

————. *General Theory of Law and State.* Transl. Andreas Wedberg. Cambridge: Harvard University Press, 1945.

————. *Hauptprobleme der Staatsrechtslehre. Entwickelt aus der Lehre vom Rechtssatz.* Second enlarged edition. Tübingen: Verlag von J. C. B. Mohr (Paul Siebeck), 1923.

————. *Österreichisches Staatsrecht.* Tübingen: J. C. B. Mohr (Paul Siebeck), 1923.

Klenner, Fritz. *Die österreichischen Gewerkschaften. Vergangenheit und Gegenwartsprobleme.* 2 vols. Vienna: Verlag des österreichischen Gewerkschaftsbunds, 1953.

Kluckhohn, Paul. *Persönlichkeit und Gemeinschaft. Studien zur Staatsauffassung der deutschen Romantik.* Halle: Max Niemeyer, 1925.

Körner, S. *Kant. Pelican Philosophy Series.* Edited by A. J. Ayer. Hammondsworth: Penguin Books, Ltd., 1955.

Kothen, Robert. *La Pensée et l'Action Social des Catholiques, 1789-1944.* Louvain: Em. Warny, 1945.

Krehbiel, Fritz. *Der Ständestaatsgedanke in der letzten österreichischen Verfassung.* Doctor of Laws dissertation, Albert-Ludwigs Universität at Freiburg i.B., 1938.

Lux, P. T. *Österreich 1918-1938. Eine Demokratie?* Graz: Leykam Verlag G.m.b.H., 1946.

Mabbott, J. D. *The State and the Citizen. An Introduction to Political Philosophy.* London: Hutchinson's University Library, 1947.

Macartney, C. A. *The Social Revolution in Austria.* Cambridge: At the University Press, 1926.

Macdonald, Mary. *The Republic of Austria, 1918-1934. A Study in the Failure of Democratic Government.* London: Oxford University Press, 1946.

MacIver, Robert M. *The Web of Government.* New York: The Macmillan Company, 1947.

Meinecke, Friedrich. *Weltbürgertum und Nationalstaat. Studien zur Genesis des Deutschen Nationalstaates.* Sixth revised edition. Munich: R. Oldenbourg, 1922.

Menger, Anton. *Das Recht auf den vollen Arbeitsertrag in geschichtlicher Darstellung.* Stuttgart: J. G. Cotta, 1886.

Mises, Ludwig von. *Socialism. An Economic and Sociological Analysis*. Transl. J. Kahane. New York: The Macmillan Company, 1932.

Mitrofanov, Paul von. *Josef II. Seine politische und kulturelle Tätigkeit*. 2 vols. Vienna: C. W. Stern, 1910.

Moody, Joseph N. (ed.). *Church and Society. Catholic Social and Political Thought and Movements 1789-1950*. New York: Arts, Inc., 1953.

Moon, Parker T. *The Labor Problem and the Social Catholic Movement in France*. New York: The Macmillan Company, 1921.

Müller, Anton. *Gesellschaft und Wirtschaft in der katholischen deutschen Literatur der Nachkriegszeit*. Doctoral dissertation, University of Freiburg i.B., 1929.

Mueller, Franz. *Heinrich Pesch and his Theory of Christian Solidarism*. Vol. 7 of *Aquin Papers*. St. Paul: The College of St. Thomas, 1941.

Mulcahy, Richard. *The Economics of Heinrich Pesch*. New York: Henry Holt & Co., 1952.

Muret, Charlotte, *French Royalist Doctrines since the Revolution*. New York: Columbia University Press, 1933.

Nadler, Josef and Heinrich von Srbik (eds.). *Österreich. Erbe und Sendung im deutschen Raum*. Salzburg: Anton Pustet, 1937.

Nell-Breuning, Oswald v. *Die soziale Enzyklika. Erläuterungen zum Weltrundschreiben Papst Pius' XI. über die gesellschaftliche Ordnung*. Cologne: Katholische Tat-Verlag, 1932.

Nielsen, Frederick. *The History of the Papacy in the XIX Century*. New York: E. P. Dutton, 1906.

Österreich. Die soziale und wirtschaftliche Struktur. Arbeitswissenschaftliches Amt der Deutschen Arbeitsfront. Berlin, 1938.

Pesch, Heinrich. *Lehrbuch der Nationalökonomie*. 3 vols. Freiburg i.B.: Herdersche Verlagsbuchhandlung, 1905-1913.

Pirou, Gaetan. *Essais sur le Corporatisme*. Paris: Librairie du Recueil Sirey, 1936.

Redlich, Josef. *Emperor Francis Joseph of Austria. A Biography*. New York: The Macmillan Company, 1929.

————. *Das österreichische Staats- und Reichsproblem. Geschichtliche Darstellung der inneren Politik der Habsburgischen Monarchie von 1848 bis zum Untergang des Reiches*. 3 vols. Leipzig: P. Reinhold, 1920-1926.

Rintelen, Anton. *Erinnerungen an Österreichs Weg. Versailles-Berchtesgaden-Grossdeutschland*. Second edition. Munich: F. Bruckmann, 1941.

Rohden, Peter Richard, *Demokratie und Partei*. Vienna: L. W. Seidel & Sohn, 1932.

Rommen, Heinrich. *The State in Catholic Thought. A Treatise in Political Philosophy*. St. Louis: B. Herder Book Co., 1950.

Rothschild, K. W. *Austria's Economic Development Between the Two Wars.* London: Frederick Muller, Ltd., 1947.

Sauzain, Louis. *Adam Heinrich Müller (1779-1829). Sa Vie et son Oeuvre.* Paris: Librairie Nizet et Bastard, 1927.

Schilling, Otto. *Die christlichen Soziallehren.* Cologne: Oratoriums-Verlag, 1926.

————. *Die Staats- und Soziallehre des hl. Thomas von Aquino.* Paderborn: F. Schöningh, 1923.

Schlesinger, Rudolf. *Central European Democracy and its Background. Economic and Political Group Organization.* London: Routledge & Kegan Paul, Ltd., 1953.

Schmitt, Carl. *Die politische Romantik.* Second edition. Munich: Duncker & Humblot, 1925.

Schneider, Friedrich (ed.). *Bildungskräfte im Katholizismus der Welt seit dem Ende des Krieges.* Freiburg i.B.: Herder & Co. G.m.b.H., 1936.

Schwalber, Josef. *Vogelsang und die moderne christlich-soziale Politik.* Munich: Leohaus, Hauptstelle katholisch-sozialer Verein, 1927.

Schwer, Wilhelm. *Catholic Social Theory.* Transl. Bartholomew Landheer. St. Louis: B. Herder Book Co., 1940.

Sieghart, Rudolf. *Die letzten Jahrzehnte einer Grossmacht. Menschen, Völker, Probleme des Habsburger-Reichs.* Berlin: Ullstein Verlag, 1932.

Skottsberg, Brita. *Der österreichische Parlamentarismus.* Goteborg: Elanders Boktryckeri Aktiebolaget, 1940.

Soderini, Eduardo. *The Pontificate of Leo XIII.* Transl. Barbara Barclay Carter. London: Burns Oates & Washbourne, Ltd., 1934.

Soecknick, Gerda. *Religiöser Sozialismus der neueren Zeit, unter besonderer Berücksichtigung Deutschlands.* Jena: Gustav Fischer, 1926.

Somerville, Henry. *Studies in the Catholic Social Movement.* London: Burns Oates & Washbourne Ltd., 1933.

Stoffel, Max. *Die österreichische Ständeordnung. Ihre ideellen und verfassungsmässigen Grundlagen und die Anfänge ihre konkreten Verwirklichung.* Doctoral dissertation, University of Zurich, 1938.

Stolper, Gustav. *Deutsch Österreich als Sozial- und Wirtschaftsproblem.* Munich: Drei Masken Verlag, 1921.

Tatarin-Tarnheyden, Edgar. *Die Berufsstände. Ihre Stellung im Staatsrecht und die deutsche Wirtschaftsverfassung.* Berlin: C. Heymann, 1922.

Tawney, R. H. *Religion and the Rise of Capitalism. A Historical Study.* London: J. Murray, 1926.

Thomson, David. *Democracy in France. The Third Republic.* London: Oxford University Press, 1946.

Thormann, Werner. *Ignaz Seipel. Der europäische Staatsmann.* Frankfurt a.M.: Carolus Druckerei, 1932.

Tischleder, Peter. *Die Staatslehre Leo XIII.* M.-Gladbach: Volksvereinsverlag, 1925.

———. *Ursprung und Träger der Staatsgewalt nach der Lehre des hl. Thomas und seiner Schule.* M.-Gladbach: Volksvereinsverlag, 1925.

Troeltsch, Ernst. *The Social Teachings of the Christian Churches.* 2 vols. Transl. Olive Wyon. London: George Allen & Unwin, Ltd., 1950.

Tuszewski, Johannes. *Die Stellung der Arbeit in der Volkswirtschaft nach katholischer Auffassung.* Doctoral dissertation, University of Munich, 1925.

van der Velden, Josef. *Die berufsständische Ordnung. Idee und praktische Möglichkeiten.* Cologne: Katholische-Tat Verlag, 1932.

Vercesi, Ernesto. *Pio IX.* Milan: Edizione Corbaccio, 1930.

Vigener, Fritz. *Ketteler: Ein Bischofsleben aus dem 19. Jahrhundert.* Munich: R. Oldenbourg, 1924.

Voegelin, Erich. *Der autoritäre Staat. Ein Versuch über das österreichische Staatsproblem.* Vienna: Julius Springer, 1936.

Waentig, Heinrich. *Gewerbliche Mittelstandspolitik. Eine rechtshistorisch-wirtschaftspolitische Studie auf Grund österreichischer Quellen.* Leipzig: Duncker & Humblot, 1898.

Werner, Ruth. *Die Wiener Wochenschrift "Das Neue Reich" (1918-1925); ein Beitrag zur Geschichte des politischen Katholizismus.* Breslauer historische Forschungen, Nr. 9. Breslau: Priebatsch, 1938.

Williams, Philip. *Politics in Post-War France. Parties and the Constitution in the Fourth Republic.* London: Longmans, Green, & Co. Ltd., 1954.

Young, Sir George. *The Pendulum of Progress. An Essay in Political Science and Scientific Politics.* New Haven: Yale University Press, 1931.

C. ARTICLES

Bergsträsser, Arnold. "Neue Literatur zum Gedanken des berufsständischen Staates," *Schmollers Jahrbuch für Gesetzgebung, Verwaltung und Volkswirtschaftslehre,* XLVII (1923), pp. 283-299.

Brauer, Theodor. "Die Bedeutung des Lehrbuch Heinrich Pesch," *Volkswohl,* XVII (1926), pp. 168-173.

———. "Der deutsche Kapitalismus und die soziale Entwicklung des kapitalistischen Zeitalters," *Archiv für Rechts- und Wirtschaftsphilosophie,* XXIX (1930-1931), pp. 209-254.

Briefs, Goetz. "Das gewerbliche Proletariat," *Die gesellschaftliche Schichtung des Kapitalismus*. Vol. ix, part ii of *Grundriss der Sozialökonomik*. Tübingen: J. C. B. Mohr, 1926. Pp. 142-240.

Cathrein, Victor. "Der 'Volksstaat' im Sinne des hl. Thomas Aquin," *Archiv für Rechts- und Wirtschaftsphilosophie*, xii (1918-1919), pp. 104-107.

Eckardt, Johannes. "Clemens Maria Hofbauer und die Wiener Romantikerkreise am Beginne des 19. Jahrhunderts," *Hochland*, viii, pt. 1 (1910-1911), pp. 17-27, 182-192, 341-350.

Engel-Janosi, Friedrich. "Die Theorie vom Staat im deutschen Österreich, 1815-1848," *Zeitschrift für öffentliches Recht*, ii (1921), pp. 360-394.

Getzeny, Heinrich. "Um die Grundlegung der Soziologie. Zu E. K. Winters Schriften," *Hochland*, xxviii, pt. 2 (1931), pp. 357-362.

Gierse, Johanna. "Sozialromantische Richtungen im Katholizismus der Gegenwart," *Soziale Revue*, xxxii (1932), pp. 129-176, 193-233.

Gundlach, Gustav. "Christlich-soziale Tragik," *Stimmen der Zeit*, cxvi (1929), pp. 176-184.

———. "Fragen um die berufsständische Ordnung," *Stimmen der Zeit*, cxxv (1933), pp. 217-222.

———. "Konservativismus und die antiliberale Konjunktur," *Stimmen der Zeit*, cxi (1923), pp. 289-299.

———. "Stand und Klasse," *Stimmen der Zeit*, cxvii (1929), pp. 284-293.

Heinrich, Walter. "Die Unzulänglichkeit der Begriffe 'Horizontal' und 'Vertikal' zur Erklärung des wirtschaftlichen Verbändewesens. Ein Beitrag zur Organisationslehre der ständischen Wirtschaft," *Ständisches Leben*, i (1931), pp. 27-49, 168-187.

Hula, Erich. "The Corporative Experiment in Austria," *Social Research*, vi (1939), pp. 40-57.

Kelsen, Hans. "Der Drang zur Verfassungsreform—Eine Folge der politische Machtverschiebung," *Neue Freie Presse*, October 6, 1929.

———. "Die Verfassung Österreichs," *Jahrbuch des öffentlichen Rechts*, xi (1922), pp. 232-274.

———. "Die Verfassung Österreichs," *Jahrbuch des öffentlichen Rechts*, xii (1923-1924), pp. 126-161.

———. "Die Verfassung Österreichs," *Jahrbuch des öffentlichen Rechts*, xv (1927), pp. 51-148.

———. "Die Verfassung Österreichs," *Jahrbuch des öffentlichen Rechts*, xviii (1930), pp. 130-185.

Mannheim, Karl. "Das konservative Denken. Soziologische Beiträge zum Werden des politisch-historischen Denkens in Deutschland," *Archiv für Sozialwissenschaft und Sozialpolitik*, lvii (1927), pp. 68-142, 470-495.

Müller, Franz. "Um den Solidarismus Heinrich Pesch," *Soziale Revue*, XXVII (1927), pp. 385-396.

Nell-Breuning, Oswald von. "Um den berufsständischen Gedanken. Zur Enzyklika 'Quadragesimo Anno' vom 15. Mai 1931," *Stimmen der Zeit*, CXXII (1931), pp. 36-52.

Noppel, Constantin. "Rerum Novarum und Quadragesimo Anno," *Stimmen der Zeit*, CXXII (1931), pp. 156-169.

Renner, Karl. "Die christlich-soziale Partei und ihr veränderter Charakter," *Der Kampf*, XVI (September-October 1923), pp. 293-303.

———. "Die Christlichsozialen in Österreich und das Zentrum im Reich," *Die Gesellschaft*, VI (1929), pp. 137-148.

Sander, Fritz. "Othmar Spanns 'Überwindung' der individualistischen Gesellschaftsauffassung," *Archiv für Sozialwissenschaft und Sozialpolitik*, LIII (1924), pp. 11-80.

Schmitt, Carl. "Der Begriff des Politischen," *Archiv für Sozialwissenschaft und Sozialpolitik*, LVIII (1927), pp. 1-33.

Schweizer, M. Baptista. "Kirchliche Romantik—Die Einwirkung des hl. Clemens Maria Hofbauer auf das Geisteslebens Wiens," *Historisches Jahrbuch* 48 (1928), pp. 389-460.

D. UNPUBLISHED MATERIALS

Alexich, Georg Maria von. *A Study of Political Parties in Austria, 1918-1938*. Unpublished Ph.D. dissertation, Georgetown University, Washington, D.C., 1948.

E. OFFICIAL PUBLICATIONS OF THE AUSTRIAN GOVERNMENT

Bundesamt für Statistik. *Statistisches Handbuch für die Republik Österreich*. 1918-1934.

Bundesgesetzblatt. 1918-1934.

Nationalversammlung. *Stenographische Protokolle über die Sitzungen der provisorischen Nationalversammlung Deutschösterreichs*. 1918-1919.

Nationalversammlung. *Stenographische Protokolle über die Sitzungen der konstituierenden Nationalversammlung der Republik Österreich*. 1919-1920.

F. MAGAZINES AND NEWSPAPERS

(a) MAGAZINES

Der christliche Ständestaat (Catholic), 1933-1934.

Hochland. Monatsschrift für alle Gebiete des Wissens, der Literatur u. Kunst (Catholic), 1918-1934.

Neue Ordnung. Monatsschrift für katholische Sozial-, Wirtschafts- und Kulturpolitik (Catholic), 1925-1934.

Das Neue Reich. Wochenschrift für Kultur, Politik und Volkswirtschaft (Catholic), 1918-1932.

Schönere Zukunft. Katholische Wochenschrift für Religion, Kultur, Soziologie und Volkswirtschaft (Catholic), 1925-1934.

Ständisches Leben. Blätter für organische Gesellschafts- und Wirtschaftslehre, 1931-1934.

Stimmen der Zeit. Monatsschrift für das Geistesleben der Gegenwart (Catholic), 1918-1934.

Wiener Politische Blätter (Catholic), 1933-1936.

(b) NEWSPAPERS

Neue Freie Presse (liberal-bourgeois), 1918-1934.

Reichspost (Catholic), 1918-1934.

absolute monarchy, 8

Action Française, 13, 18, 125

Advent Pastoral Letter, 167-69. *See also* Austrian hierarchy

Aktion Winter, 221. *See also* Ernst Karl Winter

anarchism, 134

ancien régime, 7, 18

anti-Semitism, 39; in Catholic social thought, 39-40; in *Linzer Programm,* 122; in Orel's political thought, 144

Aquinas, Thomas, 82, 118. *See also* Scholastic social theory

Aristotelianism, Winter's critique of, 222

Arnold, Franz, 139

assembly rule, 84, 85

Ausgleich, 40

Australian Court of Conciliation and Arbitration, 15n

Austria, Catholic character of, 31, 116

Austrian Catholic political movements, causes of diversity, 49; controversies between, 47-48; Vogelsang's influence on, 47

Austrian Catholic social thought, basic characteristics, 30, 101; chart, 105; contempt for democracy in, 286-87; development of, 154; monism, 286; 19th century feature, 65; pluralism, 286; relation of theory and practice, 195n; scope of state activity in, 285; sources of, 193; state and society in, 149, 151, 286; two tendencies, 156-57; validity of assumptions of, 287-88

Austrian Catholics, 29; abandon democracy, 104; abandon republic, 261; accept neutral state, 71; accused of subverting democracy, 111; conflict with German Catholics, 184; fear of republic, 83; form anti-Socialist alliance, 83, 256; and Hapsburg Dynasty, 80; identified with "right" position in Austrian politics, 103; loyalty to Hapsburg Dynasty, 155; and the modern state, 101; and monarchy, 82; and non-German nationalities, 72; and postwar democracy, 70; and postwar reforms, 71, 72; public policy of, 154; and *Quadragesimo anno,* 170;

reasons for opposing republic, 97; reconsider social theories, 156; reject "left" position in politics, 103; relations with Nationalist *Lager,* 83; and republic, 71; and republican form of government, 11; and Socialist *Lager,* 149-50; Vogelsang's influence on, 46; and Wilsonian program, 72. *See also* Christian Social party, Christian-social conservative *Lager*

Austrian Constitution of 1920, 83-87; basic principles, 84; bibliography, 83; electoral system under, 257; reflects position of three *Lager,* 84, 84n, 257; rejected by Orel, 143

Austrian Constitution of 1934, *see* Corporative Constitution of 1934

Austrian corporativism, sources, 106

Austrian economy after 1918, 87-91, 88n, 91n, 258-59; effect of postwar collapse on social classes, 72; postwar collapse, 72

Austrian hierarchy, 105, 251, 280; abuses of democracy condemned, 118; admonishes industrial workers, 168; accepts republic, 117; and Christian Social governments, 167; and church-state separation, 120; condemns Romantic tradition, 187-89; condemns Social Democrats, 117, 120; and conflict between *Lager,* 120; defends monarchy, 116-17; excess of capitalism condemned by, 168, 168n; and forms of government, 117; urges vote for parties loyal to church, 118-19; liberalism condemned by, 119; marriage regulations condemned, 119, 119n; and moral reform, 187; and *Quadragesimo anno,* 186-89; problems of social reforms avoided by, 169; self-government defined, 118; and social conflict in Austria, 169n; and social question, 167-70, 186-89; and worker organization, 186

Austrian Romanticists, 10n, 22. *See also* Romantic movement, Romantic social theory, Romantic tradition, *Sozialreform,* Karl von Vogelsang

Austro-Marxismus, 75, 75n

authoritarianism, and Catholic social thought, 280
authoritarian principle, dominates Corporative Constitution of 1934, 275-76
authoritarian state, plans for, 263

Baader, Franz von, 9, 20, 167
Bandanaraike, S. W. R., 290
Barker, Ernest, 67, 151; defines democratic government, 97
Basic Laws of 1867-1869, 40, 86
Bauer, Otto, 79, 90; influence of writings on research in Austrian politics, 94n; on relations between peasants and urban elements in Christian-social conservative *Lager*, 93-94
Bauer, Otto (Religious Socialist), 211-12, 212n
Bedarfsdeckungsprinzip, 219
Berndorf program of Religious Socialists, 211-12
Beruf, in *Linzer Programm*, 218-19
Berufsstände, in Corporative Constitution of 1934, 266
Beyer, Justus, 138
Biederlack, Josef, 63
Bonald, Louis, 167
Borodajkewycz, Taras von, 31
Brunner, Sebastian, 39
Bundeskulturrat, 267, 268
Bundesrat, reform in 1929, 260
Bundestag, 267, 268
Bundesversammlung, 268
Bundeswirtschaftsrat, 267, 268
Burke, Edmund, 35
Buss, Franz Josef Ritter von, 9
Buttinger, Joseph, 74n

capitalism, 5, 14, 136; attempts at reforms of, 234; Austrian Catholic critique of, 251; Austrian hierarchy on, 167-70; Catholics condemn social consequences of, 252; condemned in *Katholisch-soziales* Manifest, 245; condemned by Orel, 247; crises of, explored by Spann, 233-34; critique of in *Linzer Programm*, 215; divergent Catholic views on, 251; evils of, in *Quadragesimo anno*, 179-81, 179n; excesses of, 252; Kogon's critique of, 241; mammonistic, 168; remedies for evils of, in *Quadragesimo anno*, 180; Romantic attacks on, 208-09; social consequences of, 168; Spann's critique, 232-34; spiritual crisis of, 234.

See also labor and capital, labor theory of value, social question
Catholic, definition of term, 26
Catholic church, and social order, 164n, 173n; and social question, Pius XI examines relation of, 172. *See also* Austrian hierarchy, Christian-social conservative *Lager*, social question, Solidarism
Catholic church in Austria, and Hapsburg Dynasty, 100; position of, 41; social position, 31. *See also* Austrian hierarchy, Christian-social conservative *Lager*, church-state relations, church-state separation, social question, Solidarism, *Sozialpolitik*, *Sozialreform*
Catholic Conservatives, and Vogelsang, 47
Catholic criticism of democracy, sources of, 72
Catholic critique of new regimes, 4
Catholic fraternities, 86, 86n
Catholic opposition to capitalism, 103, 104
Catholic organization, and social classes, 186-87
Catholic popular literature, 39
Catholic social thought, 18, 26; and authoritarianism, 280; bases of, 216; diversity in, 13; in France, 21; in Germany, 21; inability to cope with social change, 289; pluralism, 287; relation to theology, 26; social change considered in, 288-89
Catholic *sociologia perennis*, defined by *Österreichische Aktion*, 129n
Catholic trade unions, 30, 124, 154n, 172, 210, 261; and Christian-social conservative *Lager*, 220; conflict with *Heimwehr*, 155, 220, 261n; and corporative state, 123-24; general social thought, 121; origins in Austria, 121; size of, 122; support monarchy, 81. *See also* Leopold Kunschak, *Linzer Programm*, Karl Lugmayer
Catholicism, and socialism compatibility, 212, 214; and socialism, compatibility examined in *Quadragesimo anno*, 181, 181n; and Spann, compatibility of, 230; and Vogelsang, compatibility of concepts, 46
Charles I, 80, 107; and Christian Social Party, 81

Christian Democracy, in France, 13; in Italy, 13

Christian-social conservative *Lager*, 77-78; accepts republic, 91; and Catholic church organizations, 77; condemned by *Österreichische Aktion*, 129; demand for constitutional reform in, 256-57; determination to destroy First Republic, 157; diversity of social groups in, 96, 154, 252-53; effects of postwar conditions on, 91-96; forms anti-socialist coalition, 154; position of industrialists in, 92, 154; position of peasants in, 93; relations between peasants and urban elements, 78, 78n, 92-94; rise of authoritarian elements in, 115, 260-61; social base of, 77; struggle against Socialists, 77; and Spann, 240n, 243n; two-front war, 262

Christian Social governments, and Catholic church, 86. *See also* church-state relations, church-state separation

Christian Social party, 80; control over *Länder*, 273; and *Landbund*, 76; origins, 48; supports Empire, 81; and Vogelsang, 47. *See also* Catholics in Austria, Christian-social conservative *Lager*

church-state relations, 6, 8, 17; in Austria, 116; in Vogelsang, 46. *See also* church-state separation, Concordat, throne and altar in Austria

church-state separation, in Austria, 31, 41; views of Austrian hierarchy, 120. *See also* church-state relations, Concordat, throne and altar in Austria

civil rights, 41, 85-86, 265. *See also* Corporative Constitution of 1934, individual rights

civil war, in Austria, 83, 263; causes of, 96

Center party, 10n; condemned by Eberle, 145

civil authority, divine origin of, 10, 11

Clam-Martinitz, Count, 81

clergy in politics, in Austria, 117

communism, in *Quadragesimo anno*, 180

Concordat of 1855, 38-39, 41

Concordat of 1934, 86, 266

consensus, 4; failure of, 78-80, 256, 260, 280n

conservative, definition of term, 102

conservative Catholic, definition of term, 102

conservatism, 101, 104; defined in *Österreichische Aktion* program, 125; and uplifting of workers, 207

Constituent Assembly, 85, 91

constitutional reform, demands for, 96; Kelsen's view, 86; views of *Lager* on, 87, 258; of 1925, 258; of 1929, 259-60

consumer needs, defined in *Linzer Programm*, 219

corporative autonomy, in Corporative Constitution of 1934, 283-84

corporative chambers, 137

Corporative Constitution of 1934, 86, 106, 157; Austrian influences on, 280-81; authoritarian features of, 274, 275, 276; *Berufsstände* in, 266; Catholic social doctrine as foundation of, 266, 271-72; "Christian" organizing principles of, 272; and Concordat of 1934, 266; consultative chambers in, 267-68, 283; constitutional ideology, 264-65, 271-72; continuity with 1920 constitution, 263-64; corporative character of, 273, 274; dominance of central government in, 276; emergency powers in, 270-71, 277; failure of corporative reconstruction under, 159n; failure of pluralism in, 276; federal executive in, 269, 270, 275; "federal" organizing principle in, 267, 273; five organizing principles of, 264-65, 272-75; "German" organizing principle, 273; inconsistencies in, 275-79; independence of judiciary in, 277; *Land* and local government, 270; legislative-executive relations in, 275, 278; legislature in, 267-69; and liberal tradition, 276-79, 277, 281; Messner's relation to, 280; organization of corporative organs in, 266, 274; parliamentary elements in, 278-79; pro-capitalist tendencies under, 159, 285; and *Quadragesimo anno*, 179, 192-93, 272n, 283-84; Romantic tradition in, 279-80; rule of law in, 265; Seipel's influence over, 278-79; and social encyclicals, 281-85; sources of, 257; Spann's relation to, 280; state and society in, 279, 284; workers' organization under, 284

corporative institutions, in Austria, 29, 30, 154

corporative monarchy, 35
corporative organization, influences on, 273
corporative organs, legal character of, 283
corporative principles of *Quadragesimo anno*, violated by Corporative Constitution of 1934, 283-84
corporative reconstruction, 29, 171, 209, 243; authoritarian nature of, 255; defined by Seipel, 190-92; demands for, by Austrian Catholics, 150; difficulties analyzed, 282-85; in Dollfuss' thought, 194-95; eschatological nature of concept, 238, 254; in *Katholisch-soziales Manifest*, 245; lack of pluralism in, 254; in *Linzer Programm*, 215, 218-19, 219n; Orel's proposals for, 250; in *Quadragesimo anno*, 176-79, 282; role of Catholic theology in, 215; in Spann, 235-40; Vogelsang's proposals, 58; in Winter's thought, 227-29. *See also* Austrian hierarchy, Corporative Constitution of 1934, *Quadragesimo anno*, *Sozialreform*
corporativism, in Corporative Constitution of 1934, 265, 266; Gundlach cautious against, 183; in Nell-Breuning, 185-86
Cortes, Donoso, 82, 167
counter-reformation in Austria, 32
Court of Accounts, 271, 277
Czechs and Hapsburg Dynasty, 100

democracy, in Austrian Constitution of 1920, 84; Catholic critique of, 108, 148, 286-87; critique by Austrian hierarchy, 118; critique by Eberle, 146; critique by *Heimwehr*, 130; critique by *Österreichische Aktion*, 124, 127; critique by Orel, 142; critique by Seipel, 106-16, 191; critique by Spann, 132-40; defined by Spann, 135-36; endorsed by *Linzer Programm*, 122; Religious Socialist position on, 214; Seipel's definition, 108-11
Democrazia Cristiana, 104
depersonalization in politics and economics, in *Österreichische Aktion*, 204-05
Diuturnum illud, 10, 12
Dobretsberger, Hans, 189, 195, 253, 287; economic systems analyzed, 197-98; social question in, 197-98

dogmatic theology, 26
Dollfuss, Engelbert, 189, 274, 275; corporative reconstruction demanded, 194; and industrial workers, 195; suspends parliament, 263; social thought of, 193-95; traces decay of organic order, 194; use of Romantic doctrines, 193
Dreyfus affair, 13

Eberle, Josef, 145; position in Romantic tradition, 145; and *Quadragesimo anno*, 241. *See also Das neue Reich*, *Schönere Zukunft*, Vogelsang school
economic liberalism, 14
economic theory, relation to moral order, 172
Eisner, Kurt, 110
Ender, Otto, 280n
Enlightenment, 32, 100, 118
Entproletarisierung, 126, 206, 209. *See also* industrial workers, Romantic tradition, social question, Vogelsang school
Erzberger, Matthias, 64

family, destruction of, 14
Fascist ideology, in *Heimwehr* program, 131. *See also Korneuburg* program, Benito Mussolini, Ernst Rüdiger Prince Starhemberg
Febronianism, 8
Federal Court, 271, 277
federal government, defined by Wheare, 276n
federalism, in Austrian Constitution of 1920, 84; in Corporative Constitution of 1934, 267; modified in 1929, 259-60; supported by Christian-social conservative *Lager*, 257
feudalism, in Orel's political thought, 143. *See also Lehen*, Romantic movement, Romantic social theory, Romantic tradition, *Sozialreform*, Karl von Vogelsang, Vogelsang school
Fichte, Johann Gottlieb, 35
Fink, Jodok, 92
First World War, 70
Förster, Friedrich Wilhelm, relation of ideas to Austrian Catholic conservatism, 127
France, Third Republic, 82, 103
Francis Joseph I, 71. *See also* Hapsburg Dynasty, Hapsburg Empire
free trade unions, in Austria, 30, 74.

See also Social Democratic party, Socialist *Lager*
French Revolution, 3, 5, 8, 19, 136
Frühromantik, 35

Gallicanism, 8, 27
Gentz, Friedrich von, 35n
German Catholics, and the modern state, 12n
German Jesuits, 10n. *See also* Gustav Gundlach, Oswald von Nell-Breuning, Heinrich Pesch, Solidarism, *Sozialpolitik*
Germans in Hapsburg Empire, decline of influence, 40; and Hapsburg Dynasty, 100
Gesellschaftsvertrag, 175-76, 217, 239; rejected by Hans Schmitz, 203
Gewerbe, 29, 154
Girondists, 7
Giskra, 54
Görres, Josef von, 167
Gralbund, 127
Graves de communi, 13, 210-11. *See also* Leo XIII, Religious Socialists
Gregory XV, 8
Grossdeutche Volkspartei, 76, 261. *See also* Nationalist *Lager*
Guild Socialists, 137
Gundlach, Gustav, 16, 165, 285; concept of class examined, 166; concept of *Stand* examined, 166; and corporativism, 183; and *Quadragesimo anno*, 182-83; validity of corporative concept examined, 166-67. *See also* Austrian hierarchy, social question, Solidarism

Haider Thesen, 60. *See also* Karl von Vogelsang
Haller, Karl Ludwig von, 167
handicrafts, destruction of, 14
Hapsburg Dynasty, 30, 31, 70, 99, 280; causes of fall, 99; defended by *Österreichische Aktion*, 129. *See also* Austrian hierarchy, Hapsburg Empire, Hapsburg restoration, monarchist movement, throne and altar in Austria, Vogelsang school
Hapsburg Empire, 129; internal struggles in, 32
Hapsburg restoration, 105, 203. *See also* monarchist movement
Hauptverband für Industrie, 92

Hausbesitzer, economic position after 1918, 89
Hausleithner, Rudolf, 124n, 192
Heimwehr, 91, 93, 105, 124, 195, 256, 259; and Catholic trade unions, 95, 155; clash with Kunschak, 123; clerical wing, 94; nationalist wing, 94; origins, 94; political ideas, 130-31; relations with Christian-social conservative *Lager*, 95-96, 131, 260-61
Hertling, Georg von, 22, 64
Hitze, Franz, 64
Hofbauer, Karl Maria, 38; and the Romantic movement, 33
Hohenzollern dynasty, 17
Holy Roman Empire, 40
Hussarek von Heinlein, Max, 81

individual rights, 6, 7; in 1920 Constitution, 85; in 1920 Constitution, Kelsen's views of, 85. *See also* civil rights
individualism, 18, 185n; crisis of, 134; elements of, in Corporative Constitution of 1934, 272, 276-79; examined by Spann, 132ff, 137, 231, 232-33; rejected by Pesch, 165. *See also* liberalism
Industrial Revolution, 3, 5, 14, 16
industrial workers, in Austria, 30; conditions of, examined in *Quadragesimo anno*, 204-06; needs of examined, 168. *See also* Social Democratic party, social question, Socialist *Lager*, working class
inflation, effect on social groups, 89, 155
Immortale dei, 10, 117
Instructio pro clero in re sociale, 169
interest, 14; as defined by Zehentbauer, 200; role in modern economy, 200
Iron Ring, 41
Italian Fascist corporativism, examined in *Quadragesimo anno*, 178-79

Jacobins, 7, 19
Jesuits, 155; criticized by Winter, 223, 223n. *See also* German Jesuits, Solidarism
Jews, role in Socialist *Lager*, 75n. *See also* anti-Semitism
Joseph II, 32. *See also* Enlightenment, Josephinist reforms
Josephinist reforms, 8, 32, 79, 100; abandoned, 33; consequences of, 32
just price, 14

just wage, 14; in Messner, 196-97; in *Katholisch-soziales Manifest*, 246; in *Quadragesimo anno*, 175-76; defended by Schmitz (Hans), 202

Kant, Immanuel, influence on Winter, 222-25, 224n
Kathedersozialisten, 163, 252
Katholisch-soziales Manifest, attempts compromise on just wage, 246; and *Quadragesimo anno*, 246; and social question, 244-46
Kelsen, Hans, 113, 225; influence of pure theory of law, 224-25; influence on Winter, 222
Ketteler, Wilhelm Emmanuel von, 9, 17, 21, 54, 82, 166n; and Lassalle, 22; influence on Vogelsang, 42; and Thomist revival, 22
Klopp, Wiard von, 62, 175
Kogon, and social question, 241-43; and Spann, 243. *See also* Josef Eberle, Vogelsang school
Kolnai, Aurel, 213-14, 214n
Kolping, Adolf, 21
Korneuburg program, 123, 130, 261. *See also Heimwehr*
Kralik, Richard, 126
Kulturkampf, 27
Kun, Bela, 110
Kunschak, Leopold, 78, 95, 124, 261; biographical sketch, 122-23; clash with *Heimwehr*, 123. *See also* Catholic trade unions, *Linzer Programm*

labor and capital, 162; claims to economic product in *Quadragesimo anno*, 174-75; in *Linzer Programm*, 216-17; in *Österreichische Aktion*, 204-06; in Religious Socialist thought, 211-12
labor theory of value, 175n; in *Katholisch-soziales Manifest*, 246; in *Linzer Programm*, 215, 216; Orel's advocacy of, 248, 249; in *Quadragesimo anno*, 174-75; in Vogelsang's thought, 61
Länderrat, 268
Lager, 73; collapse of balance of power between, 96; and consensus, 78-80; origins of, 73; role of Austrian hierarchy in conflict between, 120; totalitarian character of, 79
laissez faire, 14, 15, 203, 254; property concept in, 201
Lammasch, Heinrich, 81

Lammenais, Robert de, 9
Landbund, 76, 186, 261
Lassalle, Ferdinand, 166, 166n, 252; and Ketteler, 22
"left" position in Austrian political spectrum, 102
left-right dichotomy in Austrian politics, 102
legitimate authority, familial basis of, 128; in *Österreichische Aktion* program, 128; in Orel, 144
Lehen, 54, 59, 239, 245. *See also* feudalism, property, Romantic tradition, state and society
Lehrl, Josef, 116
Leo XIII, 6, 9, 17, 23, 34, 48, 116, 117, 129, 155, 159, 171, 201, 210, 249, 251; and church-state relations, 13; and forms of government, 11, 18n; and individual rights, 11-12; and Ketteler, 24; and modern state, 10; and scope of state activity, 12; and social question, 23-25; warns Religious Socialists, 211. *See also Immortale dei*, *Libertas praestantissimum*, *Rerum novarum*
Leogesellschaft, 125
Lerner, Daniel, 3
liberal, definition of term, 102
liberal Catholic, definition of term, 102
liberal Catholicism, in France, 8; in Low Countries, 9; origins in Austria, 49-51. *See also* social Catholicism, social question, Solidarism, *Sozialpolitik*
liberal-democratic features in Corporative Constitution of 1934, 277, 281
liberalism, 14; in Austria, 29, 38, 41, 102; condemned by Austrian hierarchy, 119; defined by Austrian Catholics, 51; defined by Spann, 135; examined by *Österreichische Aktion*, 203-06; rejected by Dobretsberger, 197
Libertas praestantissimum, 10, 12, 13
"liberties of 1789," 11
Lichtenstein, Prince Alois von, 62-63
Linz program of Social Democratic party, 75, 102n
Linzer Programm, 210; conflicts with social encyclicals, 217-18, 217n; contrast with *Österreichische Aktion*, 216; foundation of society in, 216; impact of, 122; inconsistencies in economic doctrine, 219-20; political

ideas of, 122; relation to Romantic tradition, 215-16, 219-20; social question in, 214-20. *See also* Catholic trade unions, Romantic tradition, Socialist *Lager*

Loi le Chapelier, 7, 60

Los von Rom movement, 80

Lueger, Karl, 47, 76, 141, 281; aversion to doctrinaire formulas, 141n; on economic reconstruction, 157-58. *See also* Christian Social party, Karl von Vogelsang

Lugmayer, Karl, 121

Lux, P. T., 79

Mabbott, John D., 69n, 253-54

Macartney, C. A., 79, 120

Machiavellianism, 134

De Maistre, Joseph, 167

majority rule, attacked by Seipel, 112; in Spann's political thought, 135-36

market economy, 5, 14. *See also* capitalism, social question

Marx, Karl, 4, 15, 166, 210, 227, 252, 254; and Winter, 226-27, 226n. *See also* labor and capital, labor theory of value, social question, socialism

Maurras, Charles, 13. *See also Action Française*

Mead, Margaret, 289

Meinecke, Friedrich, 35

mercantilism, 14

Merkl, Adolf, difficulties of corporative reconstruction analyzed by, 282-85

Mermillod, Cardinal, 23

Messner, Johannes, 189, 195, 253, 287; and Corporative Constitution of 1934, 280; emphasizes right to private property, 202; just wage in, 196-97; role of society in social reform, 199; social justice in, 198-99; social question in, 196-97, 198-99, 200-02

Methodendualismus, 225, 229

Metternich regime, 8, 16, 20, 203; and social question, 54. *See also* Romantic movement, Romantic tradition, Carl Schmitt

Middle Ages, 14, 136; as defined by Romanticists, 19

middle class, economic position after 1918, 89; economic theories espoused by, 90; position in Empire, 154. *See also* Christian-social conservative *Lager*, Nationalist *Lager*

Middle East, 3

Mirari vos, 8-9, 12

Mises, Ludwig, 90, 164

modern state, 6, 70; defined by *Österreichische Aktion*, 127; rejected by *Österreichische Aktion*, 127. *See also* church-state separation, democracy, liberalism, neutral state

monarchist movement, 82, 105, 124. *See also* Hapsburg restoration

monarchy, in Eberle's political thought, 147; in *Österreichische Aktion*, 204. *See also* Hapsburg Dynasty, Hapsburg Empire, Hapsburg restoration, monarchist movement

Monatsschrift für Sozialreform, 42

monism, in Austrian Catholic social thought, 286

MRP, 104

Müller, Adam Heinrich von, 19, 33, 136, 140, 167, 247, 253, 254, 281; and Catholicism, compatibility of concepts, 36-38; and corporativism, basic concepts, 52; dialectics, 52; influence on Vogelsang, 42; and modern state, 35-38; organic society defined by, 52; political thought, sources of, 35; productivity theory, 53; property defined, 53; Smith's views rejected, 53; and the social question, 52-54. *See also* Romantic tradition

de Mun, Albert, 21

Münchener Kritik, 113n

München-Gladbach, 64. *See also* workers organization

Mussolini, Benito, 95, 124

Nachwächterstaat, 7

Napoleon, 8

Nationalist *Lager*, 76-77; developments in, 261-62; and Nazi movement, 77; relations with Christian-social conservative *Lager*, 76-77; social base of, 76

natural law, 18, 22

natural reason, 26

Nazi movement, 256; relations with Nationalist *Lager*, 96, 262

Nell-Breuning, Oswald von, 16, 165; and *Quadragesimo anno*, 183-86; *Quadragesimo anno* claimed as procapitalist, 185

Die neue Gesellschaft, and social question, 246-47; influence of Romantic tradition on, 247; influence of Spann on, 247

Neue Reich, Das, 145
neutral state, 5, 5n, 8. *See also* church-state separation, modern state

Österreichische Aktion, 189, 209; criticism of democracy, 124; disagreement with other Romantic schools, 126; condition of industrial workers examined, 204-06; members of, 125; opposition to Thomism, 130; relation to Platonic-Augustinian tradition, 128; and social question, 203-07; and Winter, 226, 228
Österreichische Volkspartei, 104
Orel, Anton, 126, 175, 208, 217n, 246, 254; and Christian Social party, 142; conflict with Austrian hierarchy, 169-70; criticism of democracy, 142; and Marxist doctrines, 248-49; forms of government reviewed, 143, 144; and 1920 Constitution, 143; proposes corporative reconstruction, 250; and *Quadragesimo anno,* 249, 249n; and social question, 247-50; and Vogelsang, 142
organic order, destruction of, 15

papal infallibility, 13, 41
parliamentary elements in Corporative Constitution of 1934, 278-79
Parsifal, 126
pastoral considerations, 17
peasants in Austria, 30; economic position after 1918, 90; social conditions of, 193-94. *See also* Christian-social conservative *Lager,* Jodok Fink, Anton Rintelen
Pesch, Heinrich von, 16, 139, 156, 159, 227; individual-society relations defined, 161; influence of *Kathedersozialisten* on, 163; Kogon's critique of, 242-43; nature of society defined, 161; organization of economy outlined, 162-63, 163n, 165; position of individual in system, 160; private property concept defined, 162, 162n; role of corporative organs defined, 163; Romantic tradition rejected by, 161; social question in, 160-65; Solidarism defined by, 161-62
Pfliegler, Michael, 213
Piffl, Friedrich Gustav Cardinal, 117, 191; warns against corporative reconstruction, 188
Pius IX, 6, 9, 14, 141

Pius XI, 13, 156, 201, 249, 276, 281; and corporative organization, 283; social doctrines of, 172-79. *See also Quadragesimo anno,* Solidarism, *Sozialpolitik, Sozialreform*
Platonic-Augustinian tradition, 128, 222n. *See also* Jesuits, social science methodology, Ernst Karl Winter
pluralism in Catholic social thought, 286, 287
pluralistic social theory, 12
Poles, and Hapsburg Dynasty, 99
political Catholicism, definition of term, 5. *See also* modern state, neutral state, state and society
political obligation, 6, 7
political parties, and armed formations, 131n; condemned by Seipel, 192; ideological character of, 80, 97, 149-50; views of Austrian hierarchy on, 118-19
political party controls in legislature, criticized by Seipel, 111-12
Popolari, 103
postwar democracy, 70
postwar profiteers, 90
postwar reforms, sponsored by Socialist *Lager,* 155
president, mode of election changed, 259
professional class, economic position after 1918, 89. *See also* middle class
profit, workers share in, 176
property, 252; dual character of, 173, 201; inconsistencies in *Linzer Programm* examined, 218; in *Katholisch-soziales Manifest,* 245; in *Linzer Programm,* 216; in Nell-Breuning, 184-85; in Pesch's system, 162, 162n; Messner's definition, 201-2; Müller's definition, 53; Orel's treatment of, 248; place in *Quadragesimo anno,* 173-74; in *Quadragesimo anno,* Messner's analysis, 201; Spann's treatment, 238-39; and state action in Messner, 201; three definitions analyzed by Messner, 201
proportional representation, 84, 85

Quadragesimo anno, 106, 156, 157, 251, 253, 256, 272, 276; analyzed, 170-82; and Austrian hierarchy, 186-89; and corporative reconstruction, 176-79, 260, 261, 282; examines Italian Fascist corporativism, 178-79; and forms of economic organization, 281-82; impact of *Rerum novarum* reviewed, 171, 173; impact on Austrian corporative state, 192-93, 272n; interpreted by Messner, 200; just wage, 175-76; and labor theory of value, 174-75; Nell-Breuning's commentary on, 183-86; Orel's doctrines rejected by, 249, 249n; position of church on social reform stated, 172; property in, 173-74; rejects Romantic doctrines, 176; Religious Socialists condemned, 212; role of state in economy in, 174; and Romantic tradition, 173ff; settles dispute over worker organization, 171; state and corporative reconstruction in, 282n; used by Seipel to justify abolishing democracy, 191; vocational groups in, 177-78. *See also* Pius XI

Quanta cura, 9, 12

Raab, Julius, 93, 131
Radical Socialists, 103. *See also* France, Third Republic
rationalism, 12
Redler, Richard, 213
Reichsrat, 80
Reichswirtschaftsrat, 137
Religious Socialists, 104, 169-70, 181, 208, 210, 228; in Austria, 211-14; position on democracy, 214; relations with Socialist *Lager*, 211; and Romantic tradition compared, 209-10; and socialist ideology, 212-14; sources of social thought, 209
religious toleration, 7
Renner, Karl, 262
rentiers, economic position after 1918, 89
representation, modification of existing methods urged, 112
republican form of government, 5, 71
Rerum novarum, 17, 51, 141, 153, 155, 159, 170, 210, 251; analysis of, 23; labor and capital, 24; labor theory of value, 24; nature of reform measures, 23-24; private property, 24; reception of, 25; right of workers to organize, 24; state intervention, 25; victory for *Sozialpolitik*, 25
Revolutionary tradition, 7, 8, 18, 19
"right" position in Austrian political spectrum, 102
Rintelen, Anton, 75n, 78, 78n

Roman Catholic Church, 3, 4, 6; in Europe, 3; loss of influence, 4. For all other references to Roman Catholic, *see* Catholic, as in Catholic Church in Austria, Catholic social thought, etc.
Roman law, Orel's critique of, 248; rejected by Vogelsang, 58
Romantic movement, 18, 19, 20; in Austria, 33ff; defined, 33; and French Revolution, 34; revolt against rationalism, 34. *See also* corporative reconstruction, Adam Heinrich Müller, Romantic social theory, Romantic tradition, social monarchy, social question, *Sozialreform*, Karl von Vogelsang
Romantic social theory, 29; in Austria, 16; and Catholicism, compatibility of concepts, 34; faith and reason in, 34; in *Linzer Programm*, elements of, 215-16; in *Österreichische Aktion* program, 125. *See also* corporative reconstruction, Adam Heinrich Müller, Romantic movement, Romantic tradition, social monarchy, social question, *Sozialreform*, Karl von Vogelsang
Romantic tradition, 104, 153, 156, 208; Austrian hierarchy condemns, 187-89; in Corporative Constitution of 1934, 279-80; Dobretsberger's rejection, 197; Gundlach condemns, 183; Kogon's defence of, 243; in *Linzer Programm*, 219-20; Messner's rejection, 196; in *Die neue Gesellschaft*, 246; Nell-Breuning condemns, 184-86, 184n; and *Quadragesimo anno*, 173ff, 176; property in, 201; and Religious socialism compared, 209-10; scope of state activity in, 286; and Solidarism, 164, 165; Spann's definition, 230; and Winter, 225-26, 227. *See also* corporative reconstruction, Adam Heinrich Müller, Romantic movement, Romantic social theory, social monarchy, social question, *Sozialreform*, Karl von Vogelsang
Rommen, Heinrich, 26, 223n
Rousseau, Jean-Jacques, 7
Rudigier, Bishop, 41
rule of law, 277, 281; in Corporative Constitution of 1934, 265, 271

St. Germain, Treaty of, 86, 87

Schindler, Franz M., 63, 70, 107, 189, 273; *Sozialpolitik* defined, 63
Schlegel, Friedrich von, 19, 33, 38
Schlesinger, Rudolf, 88n, 97
Schmitt, Carl, 19, 34
Schmitz, Hans, 189; and *Quadragesimo anno*, defends just wage in encyclical, 202-03; and social question, 202-03; and Solidarists, 203; and Vogelsang school, 202
Schmitz, Richard, and social question, 243-44
Schmoller, Gustav, 163
Schober, Johann, 262
Scholastic social theory, 5, 14, 15, 22, 26. *See also* Aquinas
Schönere Zukunft, 145
Schönerer, Georg von, 76, 80, 100
Schöpfer, Aemilian, 63, 77, 79
Schuschnigg, Kurt von, 275
Science and religion, in Winter's thought, 223, 225
scope of state activity, 6; in Austrian Catholic social thought, 285; in Romantic tradition, 286. *See also* capitalism, corporative reconstruction democracy, *laissez faire*, modern state, Adam Smith, social question, state and society
Seipel, Ignaz, 49, 70, 85n, 86, 92, 96, 150, 189, 253, 273; Austrian political institutions criticized, 114; bibliography, 106n; biographical sketch, 107; class and *Stand*, defined, 190-91; and Corporative Constitution of 1934, 278-79; and corporative reconstruction, 114, 126, 190-92; first government position, 81; forms of government discussed, 116; and Gundlach, 190; and Hapsburg Dynasty, 100, 107n; Heimwehr supported, 91, 112; and the modern state in 1916, 50; and *Quadragesimo anno*, 261; scope of economic activity, 189-90; scope of state activity, 189-90; self-determination of peoples, 109; and social question, 189-92; socialist influences condemned, 114; and Vogelsang, 50
  Seipel and democracy, 105-116; accepts democracy, 91, 107, 108; bases of democracy analyzed, 108-111; criticism of democracy, 106-116; decision-making in democracy, 110, 111; leads Catholic abandonment of democracy,

105; majority rule attacked, 112; methods of choosing rulers in democracy, 109; and party government, 114; position on democracy analyzed, 115-16; reform of democracy urged, 112; rejects democracy as incompatible with Catholic doctrine, 113-114; subservience of leaders to popular opinion attacked, 112
Siedlung, in *Linzer Programm*, 216, 219; in Orel, 250
Sieghart, Rudolf, 30n, 49
Skottsberg, Brita, 85, 87
Smith, Adam, 4, 15
Smithianismus, 14
social Catholicism, 5, 14ff, 20ff. *See also* social question, Solidarism, *Sozialpolitik*
social change, 3, 4, 288; Catholic social thought unable to cope with, 289
social contract, 7, 134-35
Social Democratic party, 30, 74. *See also* consensus, industrial workers, political parties in Austria, social question, Socialist *Lager*
social justice, 171; Messner's five elements of, 198-99; Messner and *Quadragesimo anno*, approaches compared, 199; in *Quadragesimo anno*, 174-75; in *Quadragesimo anno*, defined by Schmitz (Hans), 203
social legislation in Austria, 63
social monarchy, 43, 70, 129, 207, 280; in *Österreichische Aktion* program, 125; Vogelsang's definition, 44; in Winter's thought, 228. *See also* Romantic tradition, *Sozialreform*
social question, 14ff, 32, 52, 157, 158; Austrian hierarchy on, 167-70, 186-89; Dobretsberger's treatment, 197-98; Dollfuss' treatment, 193-95; in *Katholisch-soziales Manifest*, 244-46; Kogon's treatment, 241-43; Leo XIII's treatment, 23-25; *Linzer Programm* treatment of, 214-20; Messner's treatment, 196-97, 198-99, 200-02; Müller's treatment, 52-54; in *Die neue Gesellschaft*, 246-47; *Österreichische Aktion* treatment of, 203; Orel's treatment, 247-50; Pesch's treatment, 160-65; Schindler's treatment, 63; Hans Schmitz's treatment, 202-03; Richard Schmitz's treatment, 243-44; Seipel's treatment, 189-93; Spann's treatment, 229-40; Vogelsang's treat-

ment, 54-63; and Vogelsang school, 240-50; Winter's treatment, 220-29; Zehentbauer's treatment, 200

social science methodology, 225; examined by Winter, 223; in Spann, 133n, 229

socialism, 234; and Catholicism, compatibility of, 212, 214; ethical elements in, 227; evils of, in *Quadragesimo anno*, 179-81; property in, 201; rejected by Kogon, 242; and uplifting of workers, 206; Winter's analysis of, 226-27. *See also Austro-Marxismus*, Socialist *Lager*

Socialist *Lager*, 73-75, 119, 154; commitment to republic, 102n; developments in, 262; power position in state, 97, 258, 262; role of church analyzed, 79; identified with "left" position by Catholics, 102; social base of, 75. *See also* consensus, political parties in Austria, Social Democratic party

Solidarism, 16, 155-56, 159, 160n, 165-67; attacked by Romanticists, 164, 165; condemned by *Österreichische Aktion*, 130; influence on Austria, 156, 160n; Kogon's critique of, 241-43; Mises' critique, 164; Pesch's definition, 161-62; and *Quadragesimo anno*, 182; and Vogelsang school, 241-43; and Winter, 226

sovereignty, in *Österreichische Aktion* program, 127

Sozialkritik, 196

Sozialpolitik, 52, 141, 153, 153n, 155, 170, 192n, 234, 281, 288; defined, 16, 20; in Germany, 22; rejected by Kogon, 242, rise in Austria, 63, and uplifting of workers, 206, upheld by Nell-Breuning, 184

Sozialreform, 18, 51, 153, 153n, 156, 170, 208, 281, 288; Austrian hierarchy turns toward, 188, causes of decline in Austria, 140-41; defined, 16; Kogon's defense of, 243; sources of, 253; views on Corporative Constitution of 1934, 157; weaknesses of, 254

Spann, Othmar, 90, 106, 124, 174, 185n; authoritarian elements in, 240; capitalist critique of, 232-34; and Catholicism, compatibility of, 230; and Christian-social conservative *Lager*, 132, 137-40, 240n, 243n; concept of *Stand*, developed, 235; and Corpora-

tive Constitution of 1934, 280; corporative reconstruction in, 235-40; criticism of democracy, 131-40; dialectic elements in, 231-32; dynamic elements in social theory of, 231, 238, 239; impact on corporative theory, 133, 137; individualism defined, 132-34; influence on Kogon, 243; methodology, 133n; and *Die neue Gesellschaft*, 247; organic elements in, 231-32; property defined by, 238-39; relation to Nazi ideology, 138; relations to Solidarists, 139; social question in, 229-40; universalism defined, 132-33, 230-32; theory of categories, 133n; two principles of social organization, 132-33

Staatsrat, 267-68

Stand, 59; in Dollfuss' thought, 194-95; Gundlach's view, 166; in *Katholischsoziales Manifest*, 245-46; Seipel's definition, 190; in Spann, 235ff. *See also Beruf*, corporative reconstruction, Romantic tradition, social question, *Sozialreform*, Karl von Vogelsang

standesgemässe Lebensführung, 219

standesgemässer Unterhalt, 201, 246

Starhemberg, Ernst Rüdiger Prince, 94, 124, 131

state and society, 8; in Austrian Catholic thought, 66, 149, 151, 254, 286; in Barker's social theory, 67n, 151; in Corporative Constitution of 1934, 279, 284; in corporative reconstruction, 244; in Gundlach, 183; Mabbott defines relations of, 69n; Messner's view about role in social reform, 198-99; *Quadragesimo anno* views roles in corporative reconstruction, 282n; scope of action in relation to property, 202; scope of voluntary action, 12; Seipel discusses roles in economy, 189-90; Spann defines scope, 236-37. *See also* capitalism, corporative reconstruction, democracy, *laissez faire*, modern state, scope of state activity, social question, *Sozialpolitik, Sozialreform*

Streeruwitz, Ernst von, 92, 96

Syllabus of errors, 9

Taaffe government, 40

Thomism, rejected by Winter, 225

Thomist revival, 34. *See also* Thomas Aquinas, Wilhelm Emmanuel von Ket-

teler, Leo XIII, Platonic-Augustinian tradition, *Rerum novarum*
throne and alter in Austria, 27, 29, 99, 154. *See also* Catholic church in Austria, church-state relations, church-state separation, Hapsburg Dynasty, Hapsburg Empire
Tischleder, Peter, 10n, 223n
la Tour de Pin, René de, 21
Trabrennplatz speech, 194-95, 263
trade unions, Seipel demands abolition of, 191
traditional order in Europe, 4
Traditionalist Theocrats, 18
Troeltsch, Ernst, 173n
true democracy, 108, 112, 115
Tübinger Kritik, 113n

unearned income, 14
unemployment, 14
Union de Fribourg, 6, 23
universalism, 132-34, 185n, 229, 230-32, 235
urban petty bourgeoisie, in Austria, 30. *See also* Christian-social conservative *Lager*, Christian Social party, Karl Lueger, middle class

Vaterland, 42
Vaterländische Front, 94
vocational groups, 191; in *Quadragesimo anno*, 177-78; *See also Beruf*, corporative reconstruction, Romantic tradition, social question, *Sozialreform*, vocation, Karl von Vogelsang, Vogelsang school
vocation, in *Linzer Programm*, 216, 218-19; *Katholisch-soziales Manifest*, 245. *See also Beruf*, corporative reconstruction, Romantic tradition, social question, *Sozialreform*, vocational groups, Karl von Vogelsang, Vogelsang school
Voegelin, Eric, 225, 263, 268-69, 278, 281
Vogelsang, Karl von, 22, 70, 104, 140, 141, 151, 165n, 175, 175n, 227, 247, 253-54, 273, 280; and Austrian Catholicism, influence on, 46, 61; and Austrian Catholic political movements, 47; *Berufstände*, 59, 60, 61; biographical sketch, 42; and Christian Social party, 47, 48; church-state relations, 46; corporative reorganization proposed, 58; industrialism and capital-

ism explained, 56; influence of *Kathedersozialisten* on, 56; labor theory of value defended, 61; liberalism condemned, 57-58; and modern state, 41-46; and modern state, source of concepts, 42; Müller's influence on, 46, 55; nature of politics, 43; place of state in, 43, 44, 45; and *Quadragesimo anno*, incompatibility of concepts, 62; Roman law rejected, 58; and Romantic tradition, 141; social monarchy defined, 44; and social question, 54-63; and *Sozialreform*, 42; theories of representation, 45
Vogelsang school, 106, 124, 131, 170, 184, 228; political thought of, 140-48; and *Quadragesimo anno*, 240-41; and social question, 240-50; and Solidarism, 241-43. *See also* Romantic tradition, *Sozialreform*, Karl von Vogelsang
Volksverein, 64
voluntary social action, 7, 67

wages, defined in Australia, 15n
Wagner, Adolf, 163
Wagner, Richard, influence on Austrian Romanticists, 126
Waitz, Sigismund, views on republic, 82
Wandruszka, Adam, 73
Weimar constitution, 86
Wheare, Kenneth C., 276n
Wiener Kirchenzeitung, 39
Wiener Richtungen, 139. *See also* Romantic tradition
Wilsonian program, effect on nationalities in Empire, 100
Winter, Ernst Karl, 114, 195, 208, 209, 238, 253; bibliography 222n; biographical sketch, 221; and Christian-social conservative *Lager*, 221; condemns Seipel, 115; conflict with *Heimwehr*, 221; critique of Scholastic doctrine, 222; corporative reconstruction, 227-29; familial basis of state asserted, 226; influence of Jesuits explored by, 223; and Kant, 222-25, 224n; and Kelsen, 222, 224-25; and Marx, 226-27, 226n; and *Österreichische Aktion*, 125, 226, 228; and Romantic tradition, 220-21, 225-26, 227; and Schuschnigg, 221; and Solidarists, 226; and Platonic-Augustin-

ian tradition, 130, 222n; science and religion examined, 223-25; shortcomings in his system, 229; social monarchy advocated, 228; social question in, 220-29

workers organization, 23, 186; in Corporative Constitution of 1934, 284; in *Quadragesimo anno*, 171. *See also* Catholic trade unions, *Quadragesimo anno, Rerum novarum*, social question

working class, economic position after 1918, 88; and Hapsburg Dynasty, 100. *See also* Social Democratic party, Socialist *Lager*

Zehentbauer, Franz, 195; and social question, 200